The Chinese Particle *Le*

The Chinese particle *le* so far has escaped understanding in traditional grammatical terms. *The Chinese Particle* Le is an original study of the various uses of the particle *le* which breaks through the limitations of sentence linguistics by showing how the particle functions in everyday exchange between Chinese speakers. In order to do so the study formulates an explicit model of language behaviour.

The book gives an overview of the various approaches to the particle, and traces the historic development of the particle from Han times to its modern usage. It shows how the idea of 'completion of a situation' in Han time started to develop into a discourse marker during the Song dynasty and thereafter evolved into the modern usage of the particle *le*. Modern usage is grasped through an analysis of more than five hundred contextualised examples, which illustrate uses of the particle *le* in procedural discourse, in children's stories, and in everyday conversations.

The theoretical model developed in this book stresses the interactive nature of language use, and combines mental model theory developed by Johnson-Laird (Princeton) with new insights in language use formulated by Herbert Clark (Stanford). The authors show how the various uses of the Chinese particle *le* can only be understood as a signal for common ground co-ordination in verbal interaction. The particle *le* is used at moments at which a reset of currently shared common ground is intended. It therefore can be recognised as a device to update common ground in verbal interaction.

The Chinese Particle Le has a wide range of implications which request attention from both Chinese scholars and students of Chinese linguistics as well as students of general linguistics. The book suggests that the study of sentence structure should be replaced with the study of language use, which can be approached through the structure of shared common ground. The constituents of common ground structure also are identified.

Marinus van den Berg is a Research Associate at the Leiden University Centre for Linguistics, the Netherlands. **Guo Wu** is a Senior Lecturer at the University of Western Sydney, Australia.

Routledge studies in Asian linguistics
Editor-in-Chief:
Walter Bisang, Mainz University
Associate Editors:
R. V. Dhongde, Deccan College, Pune and Masayoshi Shibatani, Rice University, Texas

Asia is the world's largest continent, comprising an enormous wealth of languages, both in its present as well as in its eventful past. The series contributes to the understanding of this linguistic variety by publishing books from different theoretical backgrounds and different methodological approaches, dealing with at least one Asian language. By adopting a maximally integrative policy, the editors of the series hope to promote theoretical discussions whose solutions may, in turn, help to overcome the theoretical lean towards West European languages and thus provide a deeper understanding of Asian linguistic structures and of human language in general.

1 **Vietnamese–English Bilingualism**
   Patterns of code-switching
   Ho-Dac Tuc

2 **Linguistic Epidemiology**
   Semantics and grammar of language contact in mainland Southeast Asia
   Nick J. Enfield

3 **A Grammar of Mangghuer**
   A Mongolic language of China's Qinghai-Gansu sprachbund
   Keith W. Slater

4 **Functional Structure(s), Form and Interpretation**
   Perspectives from East Asian languages
   Edited by Yen-hui Audrey Li and Andrew Simpson

5 **Focus and Background Marking in Mandarin Chinese**
   System and theory behind *cai, jiu, dou* and *ye*
   Daniel Hole

6 **Grammaticalization and Language Change in Chinese**
   A formal view
   Xiu-Zhi Zoe Wu

7 The Tamil Auxiliary Verb System
  Sanford B. Steever

8 The Chinese Particle *Le*
  Discourse construction and pragmatic marking in Chinese
  Marinus van den Berg and Guo Wu

The Chinese Particle *Le*
Discourse construction and
pragmatic marking in Chinese

Marinus van den Berg and Guo Wu

LONDON AND NEW YORK

First published 2006
by Routledge
2 Park Square, Milton Park, Abingdon, Oxfordshire OX14 4RN

Simultaneously published in the USA and Canada
by Routledge
711 Third Avenue, New York, NY 10017

Routledge is an imprint of the Taylor and Francis Group, an informa business

First issued in paperback 2015

© 2006 Marinus van den Berg and Guo Wu

Typeset in Garamond by Wearset Ltd, Boldon, Tyne and Wear

All rights reserved. No part of this book may be reprinted or reproduced or utilised in any form or by any electronic, mechanical, or other means, now known or hereafter invented, including photocopying and recording, or in any information storage or retrieval system, without permission in writing from the publishers.

The publisher makes no representation, express or implied, with regard to the accuracy of the information contained in this book and cannot accept any legal responsibility or liability for any errors or omissions that may be made.

British Library Cataloguing in Publication Data
A catalogue record for this book is available from the British Library

Library of Congress Cataloging in Publication Data
A catalog record for this book has been requested

ISBN 978-0-7007-1461-2 (hbk)
ISBN 978-1-138-97056-4 (pbk)

Contents

List of illustrations		viii
Preface		x
Acknowledgements		xi
1	Introduction	1
2	Previous studies	17
3	The particle *le* and the study of language use	60
4	The historical development of the particle *le*	87
5	Action-picture stories	100
6	Children's stories	138
7	Conversations	169
8	Discussion	212
9	Theoretical implications	240
	Notes	264
	References	272
	Index	278

Illustrations

Figure

7.1	Occurrences of the particle *le* in a conversational text	171

Tables

2.1	Two functions of LE	23
2.2	One function of LE at two different levels	48
3.1	Examples of three-part chains	72
3.2	Contrasts between essays/speeches and conversations	80
3.3	Example of an action ladder	81
3.4	Example of a joint action ladder	81
5.1	Discourse acts used in the 66 picture stories	102
5.2	Action stories which contain an institutional setting	107
5.3	Occurrence of LE in the 66 picture stories	108
5.4	Action stories without any occurrence of the particle *le*	111
5.5	Occurrences of verbal *-le* in the 66 picture stories	111
5.6	Occurrences of verbal *-le* and *le* in the 66 picture stories	115
5.7	Particle *le* marking a problem in the opening line(s) of a story	117
5.8	Particle *le* marking an upcoming event in the opening line(s) of a story	119
5.9	Particle *le* indexing an involuntary effect	122
5.10	Particle *le* indexing 'solutionhood'	123
5.11	Uses of the particle *le* in verbal interactions	127
5.12	Particle *le* indexing the 'endpoint' of a procedure	129
5.13	Uses of *xiaoxin* ('be careful')	130
5.14	Particle *le* in goal–reaction pairs	132
5.15	Idioms with *-le* in evaluative expressions	133
5.16	Uses of the particle *le* in story 51, 'A Sunday Drive'	133
5.17	Pragmatic marking of clauses containing a time index	135
6.1	Number of occurrences of verbal *-le* and particle *le* in children's stories	139

6.2	Other verb -*le*/*le* sequences in ten children's stories	166
6.3	Particle *le*: common-ground co-ordination	167
7.1	Occurrences of the forms -*le* and *le*/*la* in Chinese 600	170
7.2	Number of occurrences of *le*/-*le* across conversation text units	170
7.3	The particle *le* according to interaction type in Chinese 600	174
7.4	Politeness expressions in Chinese involving the particle *le*	207
8.1	Comparison of uses of verbal -*le* and the particle *le* in discourse environments	213

Preface

This book is the first major study in the new century devoted to the various uses of one Chinese particle, represented in the literature as either verbal -*le* or the particle *le*. It is unique in the sense that it searches for explanations across discourse types (narrated procedures, narratives, and casual conversations) in an endeavour to test the hypotheses developed in one discourse type. The project was planned in 1996 during one of the Functional Grammar conferences, which both authors attended, and was held that year at Cordoba, Spain. The project started in 1998 at Leiden in the Netherlands, when a plan was formulated, time schedules were matched, and a grant was obtained (see Acknowledgements). The final product is the result of intensive co-operation between the two authors. This observation holds for all chapters. However, some chapters more exclusively bear the mark of one of the authors. Chapters 2 and 4, for instance, were first conceived and written by Guo Wu and were adjusted later after the various theoretical chapters and data chapters were completed. Chapter 3 was first written by Marinus van den Berg, and went through a number of revisions, the result of lengthy discussions, before it reached its final form. The three chapters that make up the body of the data (Chapters 5, 6, and 7 on procedural discourse, narratives, and conversational discourse) were treated in a similar way: after a first draft a considerable number of adjustments were made which either related to the interpretation chosen or to a lack of sufficient spread in the type of data available. The second author had to remind the first repeatedly that the world of the particle *le* is more complicated than the relatively stable materials in the first two data chapters suggested. These discussions finally led to the insights presented in Chapters 8 and 9, making this study a truly cooperative work, which, in line with the main topic of the study, can be termed a constant search for 'shared common ground'. Such a search cannot give immediate results, as the following chapters will demonstrate, since it involves challenging all or most of the existing concepts of traditional sentence analysis, and provides an alternative in pragmatic terms. The main contribution of the study, therefore, must be sought in a rephrasing of linguistic fundamentals and a demonstration of their applicability to one of the least-understood phenomena of Chinese grammar.

Acknowledgements

This study would not have been possible without the support of our respective universities, Leiden University and the University of Western Sydney. Most importantly, however, this study at the Dutch side was assisted by generous grants from the Netherlands organisation for scientific research (NWO). The latter organisation provided financial support in 1998 for a six-month visit by Guo Wu to Leiden University. There, housing was arranged through the kind co-operation of the Leiden International Centre, and Guo Wu was welcomed as affiliated fellow of the International Institute of Asian Studies (IIAS). The latter organisation provided office space, mail support, internet access and various other kinds of support facilities. NWO also supported a six-month return visit by Marinus van den Berg to Australia in 2000, a visit that was further assisted by a grant from the University of Western Sydney, which institution at its Parramatta campus provided ample office space, a mailing address, library access, and other support facilities. We hereby express our thanks to the supporting academic institutions and grant councils. We remember the support received with gratitude.

1 Introduction

This study is a functional analysis of the various uses of the particle *le* in Chinese. With *functional* we want to indicate that we look at language as a function of the human capacity to interact with others. This functional approach allows the distinction of three interaction or communication-related modules: *cognition*, *grammar* and *pronunciation*. Of these three, we see cognition as the dominant module. Without a cognitive base that is developed in interaction with the environment and with others, communication is not possible. This is true both for animals and for humans (Searle 1995; Tomasello 2003). The Chinese particle *le* we see as directly related to the organisation of this cognitive base, which is shared across members of a group and which is called 'common-ground structure' in this study (see Clark 1996). The central question of our study therefore is the relationship between the particle *le* and common ground structure. We will try to answer in a precise way how this relationship must be seen. However, in order to do so we will have to provide more information as to what we consider to be the human cognitive base and its various operations. We will do so in Chapter 3, where it will become manifest that our thinking is strongly influenced by the theory of mental models developed by Johnson-Laird (1983, 1993), as well as by recent developments in the study of language use (Clark 1996).

The goal of this study is to provide a comprehensive description of the various uses of the Chinese particle *le* based on empirically relevant data. Our purpose is to define the core function of the Chinese particle *le* in the context of an original theory of language use, and explain why the particle *le* is used in the way it is in Chinese. Explanation implies the identification of what causes the use of the particle *le* (cf. Craik [1943] 1967). This implies the construction of an explanatory model that involves both cognitive organisation and verbal interaction (cf. Huang 1994; Johnson-Laird 1983; Schiffrin 1987; Wu 1998). Our contribution is in particular directed at the theory of language use (cf. de Saussure [1917] 1967; Clark 1996; Lambrecht 1994; Wu 1998). We intend to demonstrate that the concept of linear processing, as used in 'sentence'- and 'syntax'-oriented grammars, is fundamentally inadequate, and that continuous interaction between background knowledge and linguistic indexing is the normal way of 'using language'. We will further argue that linguistic theory, if it is to be taken seriously, needs to take actual language behaviour as the source of its modelling (cf. Gu 1999). The Chinese data discussed in this book suggest that a three-level model of cognitive organisation and language processing is required (cultural common ground, personal common ground, and distribution of information), and we will hypothesise that such modelling is a language/cognition universal.

In the rest of this chapter we will first further discuss what we consider to be two main issues in the analysis of the particle (1.1). We will follow that (1.2) with a general characterisation of the particle's function (Chao 1968). Thereafter we will discuss some of the factors that complicate the analysis (1.3). In the next section of this chapter we present our method of data collection and data analysis (1.4), and will finish with a discussion of the rationale behind the organisation of the book (1.5).

1.1 Main focus

For the Chinese particle *le*, we can rely on a wide range of observations and analyses (see Chapter 2) and start from a well-ploughed field of study. Our criticism is on two points in particular: the validity of the data used and the limitations of sentence-based theorising. We therefore paid much attention to the empirical validity of our data (see also the section on 'Method', pp. 14–16), and developed a theory of language use incorporating psychological concepts of 'cognitive functioning' and 'joint activities'. Our approach recognises cognitive organisation, social interaction, and communicative intent as crucial elements of understanding the uses of the particle *le* (Clark 1996; Johnson-Laird 1983; Tomasello 2003). We argue that a shared cognitive base is necessary for effective communication. This shared cognitive base takes the form of a mental model that is current and traces real-time situational developments (Craik [1943] 1967; Johnson-Laird 1983, 1993). Embedded models can be called on to understand discourse guided configurations (cf. Pike 1954). It is models like this that form the basis for formulating an explanation for the phenomenon under study, the uses of the Chinese particle *le* in various discourse types.

Given this methodical and theoretical orientation and the many valuable previous studies, the central focus in our approach is to the *why* and *when* of using the particle *le* in Chinese. The 'why' question defines the 'core function' of the particle, its role in verbal interactions. The 'when' question directs the particle's use in various situational and discourse contexts. These questions were left out of most or all previous studies. Our view is that if background knowledge is not recognised as a crucial component in language processing, linguistic theorising is empirically not validated. Explanatory claims outside a cognitive theory of 'language use' are by necessity limited in scope and therefore often misleading, as we will amply illustrate. The data chapters in this study will demonstrate in detail the concepts we feel are necessarily involved in an empirically valid analysis. This view further helps to clarify why so far no compelling analysis of the uses of the particle *le* has been advanced.[1]

In our approach we will also make use of recent insights into the study of language use. Following Clark (1996), we will identify 'shared background knowledge' as 'common ground'. We will discuss this concept in some detail in Chapter 3. In that chapter, too, we will discuss 'action theory' and formulate a hypothesis detailing the nature of indexing with the particle *le*, which is supported by psychological research of human interaction. We follow Clark in recognising speaking as a 'joint activity', which is brought forward via 'participatory acts'. These acts jointly constitute 'joint action'. The Chinese particle *le*, we will argue, signals a co-ordination point, which indicates that co-ordination is needed, or in a feedback move that co-ordination is established now. When a need for co-ordination is signalled that is done under the assumption that the addressee can solve the projected co-ordination issue 'immediately', given the 'information' that is being provided in the utterance (participatory act) marked with the particle *le*.

By identifying the function of the Chinese particle *le* as 'common ground co-ordination', we claim to have answered the 'why' question of its use. The second question to react to is the *when* question. In a piece of discourse, there are several places at which the particle *le* can be used, and the question then is what determines the choice of a speaker to use it at one particular place and not at others. This latter question was central in the study of the form LE in Chinese by Vincent Chang (1986). He was the first to draw attention to uses of *le* in narrative discourse, and that study provides the background for our focus on when to use the form LE in wider contexts. We refer to the next chapter for discussion of his work.

1.2 Y.R. Chao's characterisation

In the first fundamental and comprehensive analysis of Chinese grammar, Y.R. Chao (1968) provided a wide-ranging analysis of the particle *le* (and of the homophonous verbal suffix *-le*). He identified seven different uses for the particle. In his analysis the particle indicates a new situation, a command in response to a new situation, progress in a story, an isolated event in the past, a completed action as of the present, a consequent clause to indicate situation, 'obviousness' (Chao 1968: 798–800). We will discuss each of these distinctions in detail in the next chapter. At this point we like to make three observations:

a   a new situation implies a change from a previous situation,
b   there is wide variety of uses, and
c   it is seemingly impossible to relate the various uses listed in a sensible way.

In almost all studies the particle *le* has been associated with the projection of a 'new situation'. We use the term 'projection' to indicate that the change of situation is projected by the situation participant deciding to act as speaker at that point in the situation or discourse. The change does not have to take place at the time of speaking. When a speaker projects 'it's raining', this can be said when it starts raining. However, it can also be said after the fact in order to bring that piece of information to the attention of the addressee. This can be done to remind him about the changed situation and thereby allow him to prepare for it. Also, a new situation always implies a change from a 'previous situation'. It is therefore that in several studies the idea of 'context' was introduced in order to make clear that the particle *le* can only be used in relation to something else (cf. Li and Thompson 1981). In one relatively recent study (Bisang and Sonaiya 1997) the 'previous situation' is redefined as a 'pre-constructed domain', and the use of the particle *le* is explained through a mechanism of either 'conformation' or 'confrontation' with that domain. We will come back to this in the next chapter. Our position regarding the notion 'new situation' is that 'context' and 'pre-constructed domain' represent the common ground speaker and addressee hold at the time of speaking, and the question then becomes which pieces of information are projected when the particle *le* is used and why the particle is used in such a situation.

In the listing of seven different uses of phrase *le* or particle *le*, 'new situation' is only one of the distinctions. The notion 'new situation' can also be seen as applicable in cases when there is 'excess over some expected norm'. Chao groups these uses together under 'change to something new' and refers to it also as 'inchoative *le*'. This inchoative *le* is perceived as being different from the other uses. The uses 'progress in a story' and 'isolated event in the past' seem to be unrelated to inchoativity. How then can the presence of the particle *le* be explained and why is it used? Progress in a story and isolated event in the past can be formulated without the particle *le*. Is this also a 'change to something new'? If so, it cannot be so as objective fact outside of context, but only as speaker projection.

The diverse uses of the particle *le* seem to deny in the first instance the possibility of a central or core function. However, the search for such a unifying function remains crucial in order to avoid making the language model open to random choices. In the search for a core function, we will use notions from common-ground theory and action theory (Chapter 3) in order to be able to understand the 'why' question of using the particle *le*. What motivates speakers to use the particle *le* in certain situations and at certain points in conversational exchanges? We identified this in section 1.1 as a need for common-ground co-ordination. This identification also must allow us to predict the positions in an exchange or discourse where the particle *le* is needed. Before tackling the task of making these claims pervasive, first we will look at some other problems that complicate the analytic situation.

1.3 Related problems

In addition to the diverse uses which have no clear internal relationship, we encountered four more problems. In certain instances the use of the particle *le* seems necessary. Is this a syntactic constraint? Second, in Chinese we have both a word *-le* and a phrase *le* (Chao 1968: 692). Are these two *le*'s related and if so how? Third, apart from wide variation in use across settings (section 2.1), there is also variation across individuals as to the use or non-use of the particle *le* (Chang 1986). How can this be explained? Fourth, there are serious discrepancies as to the level at which the particle is analysed. Is the particle *le* a sentence marker, an attitude marker, a speech act marker, a discourse marker, or something else? In the following we will address these issues one by one.

1.3.1 Syntactic constraints?

Within grammar studies, a distinction can be made between *semantic* and *syntactic* forces. The second distinction focuses on agreed-upon rules for ordering grammatical sequences. Since in the foregoing discussion we assumed that the Chinese particle *le* is a 'common ground co-ordination device', it follows that it cannot be under the control of a syntactic rule. However, examples (1) and (2) seem to suggest a syntactic motivation for the presence of the particle *le*:

(1) [walking on the street / in the office]
Xia yu le
descend rain *le*
'It's raining (now)'.

(2) [child to father during a car ride]
Wo e le
I hungry *le*
'I am hungry (now)'.

And indeed in these instances the particle *le* must be used. One cannot use these phrases without the particle *le* – or at least it is difficult or almost impossible to do. We therefore either need to accept that in certain instances uses of the particle *le* are controlled by syntax, or we must give an explanation for the presence of the particle *le* in pragmatic terms. We opt for the latter possibility. What we need to demonstrate therefore is that in all instances the particle *le* requests or affirms common ground co-ordination. We will try to demonstrate that all uses of the particle *le* can be formulated within this pragmatic framework, and that no syntactic constraints are necessary. We will come back at this issue in Chapters 8 and 9.

1.3.2 One le *or two* le's

Apart from phrase *le* or particle *le* analysis of uses of the particle *le* is further complicated by the need also to recognise a suffix *-le* or 'word' *-le* (Chao 1968: 692). Given this situation, a number of issues present themselves. We identified three:

a   In historical perspective, do these two *le*'s originate from the same source or are there separate sources?
b   Are the uses of word *-le* and particle *le* interchangeable?
c   Should the analysis start from the particle *le* or rather from a detailed analysis of verbal *-le*?

The presence of two *le*'s forced us to take a closer look at the historical development of both verbal *-le* and the particle *le*. That analysis is presented in Chapter 4. The data suggest that both linguistic forms originate from the same source *liao*, 'to complete' (question a). The historical development further shows that the two forms are motivated by a functional delineation at different levels. They therefore cannot be treated as interchangeable (question b). There is continuity in use but the cognitive settings being indexed by *-le* and *le*, though complementary, are different. A pointer at the particle *le* evokes more complex features than indexing with verbal *-le*.

Since we have one form (*le*) and potentially two functions, there are four positions that can be – and are – defended:

1   Two different morphemes (*-le*, and *le*), many uses of both verbal *-le* and the particle *le*.
2   Two different morphemes (*-le*, and *le*), two different functions, verbal *-le* and phrase *le*, and claims for a unifying meaning for each of the functions.
3   One morpheme /*le*/, which is represented at different levels in the grammar, proposition and conversation.
4   One morpheme /*le*/ which can be realised as *-le* or *le*.

The first position was supported by Y.R. Chao in his *A Grammar of Spoken Chinese* (1968). Y.R. Chao, as mentioned, observed that in modern Chinese there are two different morphemes, word *-le* and the particle *le*, each having a different function in the language. He also introduced the notion that historically the two morphemes originate from different sources (position 2). He identified word *-le* as originating from *liao* ('complete'), whereas the particle *le*, he claimed, was historically derived from *lai* ('to come'). Only positions 1 and 2 are compatible with this view. Positions 3 and 4 require a one-source hypothesis. Chao's publication therefore also is the source of an ongoing 'origin' debate. As already indicated, our study (Chapter 4) supports the one-source hypothesis.

People taking the second position recognise the existence of two different morphemes in Chinese grammar and two different functions. They group the various uses of the particle *le* under one heading, and group the various uses of word *-le* under an overarching but different heading, but, following Chao (1968), do not see a clear relationship between the two functions of word *-le* and the particle *le* (cf. van den Berg 1989; Li and Thompson 1981). The third position in our list of analytical possibilities represents the option that both the particle *le* and verbal *-le* are looked at from a unifying perspective (cf. Huang 1988; Bisang and Sonaiya 1997). The claim is that verbal *-le* and the particle *le* are the same form but function at different domains, or perform different functions versus a pre-constructed domain. Interestingly, we find ourselves in agreement with this, but will have to modify the claims made considerably both as regards the method for collecting language use data and the nature of linguistic or cognitive theorising. To prove our position therefore is not a simple and straightforward matter and we will need several chapters to make our position clear. The fourth position, finally, goes even one step further and makes the strongest claim. One morpheme is recognised, which can take the form of either verbal *-le* or the particle *le*. They are interchangeable. As indicated we reject such claims.

1.3.3 *Variation across individuals*

The analytic situation is further complicated by variation of use across individuals. Using narratives, Vincent Chang (1986) demonstrated that recognition of context alone is not enough. In a given context, Chinese subjects differ as regards the need or possibility to use the particle *le*. Example (3), for instance, is the sixth line in a piece of prose, each line of which was judged by 26 native speakers of Chinese as to the use or non-use of *le*. They indicated for each line if they considered the use of the particle *le* as necessary or optional. Line six read as follows (Chang 1986: 126):

(3) [piece of discourse]
 Hai you liangtian __
 still have two-day (*le*)
 '*There are two more days (left).*'

The author of the piece under consideration did not use the particle *le* at this point. However, 42 per cent of the participating judges considered it necessary to use the particle *le* at that position, whereas 12 per cent of the judges were not sure and considered the use of *le* optional. This indicates that less than half of the participating judges in this particular instance agreed with the author of the piece in terms of absence of *le*.[2] Clearly, the 'when' question of the use of the particle *le* involves speaker judgement. Not only do we need to determine what unites the various uses of the particle, it also is necessary to indicate why native speakers would disagree among themselves as to where to use *le* in a piece of discourse.

1.3.4 Levels of analysis

The analysis of particles is a complex undertaking and by necessity reflects the position the researcher takes regarding the nature of language. In this section, we will discuss uses of the particle *le* in relation to *sentences, context, verbal interactions, speech acts,* and *discourse*. When the sentence is accepted as a fundamental unit (what most analysts do), the particle *le* is seen as directly related to the sentence in which it occurs (cf. Chao 1968). Relating the sentence with *le* to a context is the next step (Li and Thompson 1981). If 'verbal interaction' is the focus of analysis, one might be willing to look for an explanation in terms of 'speaker attitude'. Researchers adhering to language as a form of action might be willing to look for an explanation in terms of speech-act theory (Austin 1962). An orientation on discourse phenomena in turn might lead to a proposal in a discourse perspective. We will take a closer look at each of these positions below.

Adding le *to a sentence*

Most analysts consider marking with the particle *le* a syntactic phenomenon (Lu 1975; Rohsenow 1978; Teng 1974; Wang 1965). They therefore expect its appearance or absence to be controlled by a syntactic/semantic mechanism, which can be discovered by adding the particle to a given sentence and reflecting on the effect that is thereby created. When the analysis limits itself to the sentence level, however, little progress can be expected. For example, remark (4), when looked at from the sentence perspective, must be seen as a 'change' or 'a change to something new': 'I was not tired before this remark'.

(4) **Wo lei le**
    I tired *le*
    'I am tired (now).'

However, this analysis does not necessarily hold. The person saying *Wo lei le* – 'I am tired (now)' – may have been tired already for quite some time but chose a certain moment to express that condition. For instance, when requested to take up a task ('Do you mind cleaning my room?'), s/he can react to that request by uttering (4), which in this context counts as a 'rejection', and cannot be described as a sentence-oriented description of 'change' or 'inchoativity'. As this example shows, the sentence approach tends to avoid confrontation with language use data, and notions of 'change' and 'inchoativity' therefore have limited applicability. However, these concepts have remained dominant in sentence-oriented analyses of the particle *le*. A relatively recent example of the sentence-based approach is provided by Sybesma (1999: 64), who stated that:

> sentence-*le* is, in a way, 'added' to the sentence as a whole and that it conveys the idea that the state of affairs described in the sentence is new; it wasn't that way just a second earlier.

He illustrated his claim with the following sentence (example 5), which he gave two possible readings:

(5) **Wo mai zheben shu le**
I buy this-CL book LE
'*I bought this book*' or: '*I'll buy this book*'.

The first reading is a past-tense interpretation of the particle, the second a current-time reading, and one begins to wonder in what contexts these different interpretations could have been reached. Sybesma then specified the context of use in the following way:

> when I utter this sentence walking out of a bookstore with a string-wrapped book under my arm, it will certainly mean: 'I bought this book'. However, when I take a book and hand it to the cashier and then utter (5), it means: 'I'll buy this one'.
> (Sybesma 1999: 62)

The first contextual clarification brings in the notion of past tense by presenting the act of buying as having been completed. The second illustration depicts the act of buying as not yet finished, and only intent to buy is expressed. Now buying and selling is a complicated interactional process and we do not want to go into a discussion of the intricacies involved at this point (cf. Clark 1996). However, there is one serious problem with this analysis. No Chinese person would use the expression *Wo mai zheben shu le*, in the situations described. This is a clear case of armchair scholarship, which is not supported by actual language use data. The claim is not empirically validated. We will have more to say about this in the section on Method (see pp. 14–16). We can conclude, however, that approaching the particle *le* from the perspective of adding it to a sentence is not a very promising one, and can easily lead to erroneous analyses.

Le and context

Adding the particle *le* to a sentence and considering the consequences in isolation is not a promising approach. Therefore most analysts refer to a previous situation or to a context in which information of previous actions and events is stored. For example, Li and Thompson (1981) proceeded this way and identified five sentence-context environments, in which the *le*-sentence specifies a certain semantic content. These contents were specified as 'a changed state', 'correcting a wrong assumption', 'reporting progress so far', 'determines what will happen next', and 'is the speaker's total contribution to the conversation at that point' (see Chapter 2 for a full discussion). The first category, 'a changed state', is then relative to the context of that moment. In essence, therefore, the approach is comparative and pragmatic. This approach confirms the idea of a 'prior state' with which the particle *le* establishes a relationship. What is being expressed by the notion of 'context' is that the 'prior state' is 'contextual', which is a pragmatic notion. It also implies the need for a comparative operation: compare the content of the sentence with *le* to a previous state of affairs.

The second category, 'correcting a wrong assumption', goes even further. That distinction assumes the existence of what we will call a 'shared common ground' (for examples see their book or our discussion in Chapter 2). Their notion of 'context', as this illustrates, is far more complex than just a previous state and recognises the existence of 'habitual behaviour' as well as the projection of a current situation, not as an objective fact but as an interpreted cognitive entity. In the third category 'reporting progress so far', the analysis moves to the 'event' level and to the 'discourse' level (see also Chapter 2). In our view, this kind of analysis is much more attractive than a single-sentence approach. However, it is still limited to the categorisation of uses of the particle mainly. The question 'why' the particle *le* is used still remains open and still needs to be answered.

Elevation of sentence grammar to the level of cognitive structure of events was pioneered by Huang (1988) and Huang and Davis (1989). They observed that verbal -*le* and the particle *le* are both *focus* markers in Chinese, which differ as to their domain of application. In essence, we will support this analysis. Verbal -*le* focuses on events/actions, whereas the particle *le* focuses on certain aspects of human experience. We need, however, clarification as to what is meant by 'focus marking' and what we must understand by 'human experience'. This line of research was further advanced more recently by Chang (2001), who, while agreeing with the 'focus' analysis, introduced 'event structure' as a complementary concept. He proposed that verbal -*le* in Chinese focuses on a point before the culmination point of the event, whereas the particle *le* focuses on the post-event state. The notion 'cognitive structure of events' is an enriching concept and further adds to a better understanding of the use of the particle *le*. However, reliance on the idea of *le* as something added to the sentence strongly limits the claims made. *Wo lei le* ('I am tired') – example 4 on p. 8 – as the rejection of a request comes to mind here again. More strongly, in all sentence analyses there remain two questions to be answered, which are the 'when' and the 'why' questions. When does a speaker decide to focus on a pre-culmination point or post event state, and 'why' would he be motivated to do so? We have already indicated the kind of answer we are defending in this study, 'common ground co-ordination' as the marking of an information 'peak'.

Le *as attitudinal marker*

When the role of the speaker in the interaction is recognised, it becomes possible to identify the particle *le* as a 'carrier of attitudinal or emotive meaning' (cf. Li 1999: 13). Most Chinese linguists follow this approach by calling particles *yuqici* ('mood words'). The attitudinal marking of the particle *le* is often indexed as 'more friendly, more involved, more concerned' (Li and Thompson 1981: 274), but it can also express 'annoyance' or 'irritation' (Li and Thompson 1981: 261). The functional categories resulting from such analyses, however, are generally not well defined and it often remains unclear how some of the (incompatible) functions listed can belong to the same marker. We therefore need to find a way to explain how it is possible that the same marker can become associated with both such contrastive concepts as 'annoyance' and 'friendliness'.

A related question is the form in which the particle appears. Both *le* and *la* are commonly used. Our position is that this is only natural since many expressions with *le/la* index a deviation from normal which can sometimes have disastrous consequences, such as *Zhao huo la!* ('Fire!'). Producing this utterance in the form *Zhao huo le!* will generally be rejected by native speakers. We see this as the result of a mismatch between message content and voice setting. An emotional voice setting can be marked in Chinese with the particle *a*. When in an utterance the particle *le* is used as well, the result of this combination is *la* (*le* + *a*) (see Chao 1968). When it is accepted that verbal signalling is multi-channel and includes the voice setting as one of the indexical channels, both *le* and *la* can be accepted as representations of the same grammatical marking. This is the position taken in this study.[3]

Le *as speech-act marker*

Utterance final particles can also be analysed in terms of 'speech acts' and have been described as illocutionary force-indicating devices (cf. Austin 1962; Searle 1969). However, the neat classification of speech acts cannot accommodate the wide range of tasks that utterance final particles are performing in interaction (Li 1999: 16). This argument seems also to hold for the analysis of the particle *le*. The particle *le*, using examples provided by Li and Thompson (1981: 244–88), can be used in *announcements, questions, suggestions, descriptions, comments, requests, contradicting, responding, consoling, protesting, reporting,* and *complaining*. As these examples illustrate, it is not possible to relate the use of the particle *le* to merely one speech-act type ('announcing', for example).[4] That the particle *le* can become associated with announcements is understandable, given the following example:

(6) **Zhonghua Renmin Gongheguo xianzai chengli le!**
China People Republic now establish LE
'*I herewith declare the People's Republic of China established!*'

This declarative utterance was pronounced by Mao Zedong at Tiananmen Square on 1 October 1949. However, the particle *le* does not take up categorical functions as prescribed by speech-act theory. That model therefore has to be rejected as well (cf. Li 1999: 16).

Le as discourse marker

Elements of a discourse perspective have been applied in the various studies by Li and Thompson (1981) and Li, Thompson and Thompson (1982). No discourse model was presented however. Nevertheless, Li and Thompson use an array of cognitive and discourse-oriented terms. We will first list their observations, which can be directly related to interaction and discourse construction. Thereafter, we will introduce their comments that have to do with cognitive semantics and cognitive organisation. To start with discourse-oriented terms, they observe that when a state of affairs is just about to be realised, an appropriate 'response' is expected (Li and Thompson 1981: 280). Here they deviate from their earlier sentence perspective and evoke a conversational response model. Their observation that the particle *le* is used to regulate the flow of conversation between two people also fits such a model (Li and Thompson 1981: 288). Apart from conversations, Li and Thompson also distinguished different discourse genres, such as narratives, and observed that the particle *le* can be used not only to conclude a lengthy discussion but also to wrap up a story (Li and Thompson 1981: 260, 287).

Elsewhere, they also state that the particle *le* can be an explicit request 'to be brought up to date' (Li and Thompson 1981: 261). As we will argue later, 'update semantics' is an alternative for sentence-oriented 'truth semantics'. Li and Thompson (1981) seem to realise that there is something wrong with sentence semantics when they say that 'change' can be a realisation on the part of the speaker, or that the assumptions of the hearer may be involved (Li and Thompson 1981: 259, 263). However, they do not discuss these issues in any depth in the quoted studies.

Now we reach the level of cognitive organisation and it is here that Li and Thompson make various remarkable observations and touch on the essence of the particle *le* as a cognition index. They talk about 'projects' and 'progress so far', which can be related to action theory and event structure (cf. Clark 1996; Chang 2001). 'Progress so far' and 'What will happen next' make clear that they realise that interactants cognitively trace the development of an event; that insight can also be seen as underlying their observation that certain events have consequences for what the hearer should do next (Li and Thompson 1981: 270-1). Interestingly, these various notions can be directly related to Li and Thompson's earlier statement that the particle *le* is used when something *unusual* occurs, which contradicts our *normal* expectations, or when they relate the particle *le* to a changed state, as opposed to a general or *habitual* state (Li and Thompson 1981: 250, 268). These insights, we will argue, are fundamental for an understanding of the function of the particle *le* in Mandarin Chinese. However, neither Charles Li nor Sandra Thompson have as yet provided a framework in which these observations can be integrated. Nevertheless, their contribution, given its relatively early date, remains important.

When we turn to the discourse perspective in the study of utterance final particles, we see that it is the latter distinction, cognitive organisation, that is recognised as crucial to an understanding of the function and meaning of utterance final particles. The effect of a particle cannot be described in terms of its relation with sentence meaning. It needs to be related to the current cognitive organisation and the effect that is created in the discourse at that point. There also is wide acceptance that the analysis needs to be based on natural speech data rather than on hypothetical examples. Less widely recognised is the idea that particles need to have a 'core' function. This is crucial however since otherwise the contextual diversity of a particle is unfounded (cf. Li 1999: 16–25). The main points to attend to in the analysis of the particle *le* as a discourse phenomenon just discussed are:

1   natural speech data
2   core pragmatic meaning
3   cognitive or discourse effect

In the section on 'Method' (1.4), we will detail the data that were used in this study. We aspire to studying 'natural speech data'. We further strongly adhere to the idea of a 'core pragmatic function'. In the data chapters we study the various cognitive and discourse effects, and on that basis look for a generalisation of the various uses of the particle *le* in Chinese.

Summary

In addition to diversity of use and a rejection of syntactic constraints (section 1.3.1), we distinguished three more problems in the study of the particle *le*. The first of these was the presence of two markers with the same form /*le*/, their historical relationship, and their various functions (1.3.2). We then reported attested wide variation in use across individuals (1.3.3). Added to that was the need to recognise analyses that move from the sentence level, to context, and from there to attitude marking, speech-act marking, and function recognition within discourse and cognitive organisation (1.3.4). We concluded that we need interactional data, a core function, and discussion of the effect created in the discourse.

1.4 Method

For the analysis of the various uses of the particle *le*, we selected three sets of 'natural speech data'. These data were analysed along two dimensions: a quantitative approach and a qualitative method. As part of the latter line of attack, the structure of each data set was analysed.

1.4.1 The data

In order to approach 'natural speech data' we selected three existing sets of material for analysis: (1) action-picture stories, (2) children's stories, and (3) a conversation text. The action-picture stories were in essence examples of procedural discourse, examples of how to do things in the usual way (Longacre 1996). The set consists of 66 picture stories, one action story per page (Frauman-Prickel and Takahashi 1985; Romijn and Seely [1979] 1986). For details we refer to Chapter 5. The Chinese version for this action series was produced by a Chinese colleague residing in the Netherlands at the time.[5]

The second source was a set of ten children's stories translated from the English and published by the Mandarin Daily Press in Taipei, Taiwan. This set has pictures too, but to a lesser extent than the action-picture stories. The stories are told in a colloquial style and we judged this material suitable as natural speech data. Since this latter set introduces the art of storytelling, we paid special attention to the nature of storytelling and to story structure. For details see section 1.4.3, as well as Chapter 6.

Our third source was the conversational text Chinese 600, published in Taiwan in 1976. This text contains 40 dialogues in a variety of settings and was chosen because of its natural language use and situational variation. Conversational interactions, however, are complex forms of interactions which rely heavily on shared background knowledge. The structure of a conversation is not fixed; rather, it is opportunistic. We therefore need further detailing of discourse type, and identification of the various participatory acts or 'moves'. For details see Chapter 6.

1.4.2 Analysis

These three sets of data were first of all compared to the number of occurrences of verbal *-le* and the particle *le*. We found this comparison a useful technique for getting insight into the frequency of the two markers, *le* and *-le*, in the same kind of discourse environment. That data forms the quantitative basis for the uses of the form LE in Chinese, revealing differences across discourse types. The focus, however, remained on a qualitative analysis as to the relation between uses of the particle and uses of verbal *-le* with higher-order variables of cognitive organisation. We tried to answer the question of the why of their occurrence. In the qualitative analysis, we further took an interactive perspective. Our assumption is that the particle *le* has a role to play in the linking and co-ordination of mental models. In order to be able to determine that function, we related the various occurrences of the particle *le* to the notional structure of the discourse genre in which LE occurred. We will take a closer look at those distinctions now.

1.4.3 *Discourse structure*

Our data contain extensive examples of 'procedural discourse'. In this discourse type an apprentice is instructed to follow the various steps of a task, the script of which he supposedly is familiar with. Longacre (1996) analysed the schema of procedural discourse as, (1) problem or question, (2) preparation, (3) main procedure, and (4) final procedure. The 'problem' that triggers the procedure can be something that occurs in everyday situations, such as 'it is late already' followed by a 'going to bed' procedure, or 'my hands are dirty' followed by a 'washing your hands' procedure. The preparatory steps of the procedure make the objects that are necessary for a successful execution of the task available. There must be a 'bed' or 'soap' in the two examples mentioned. The main procedure is organised in such a way that the 'main goal' of the project or task can be reached. The final procedure deals with situations and events that remain after the task has been completed.

The second discourse type analysed in this study are children's stories, which fall in the general category of 'narratives' (Bal 1997). Like procedural discourse, a narrative is highly structured. Usually a narrative starts with an exposition, after which a deterioration cycle follows which creates suspense through an inciting incident of some sort. For instance, in a mountain-climbing story the climber slips and falls down. In the children's stories we further analysed a restoration cycle in which the original state of affairs is restored. The stories typically end with a conclusion or coda, in which either the original situation is restored or the positive effects of the actions illustrated in the story are described. The main question we tried to answer is the relationship between these structural cycles and the occurrences of the form LE, both the particle and verbal *-le*. The notional structure is 'conventional', it can neither be considered a fixed structure that must be followed nor a universal schema in the sense that in each culture the practice of storytelling will take this form. The research question focuses on the relation between occurrences of the particle *le* and the notional structure. Since this kind of analysis has never been performed before, the data (Chapter 6) will reveal the role of verbal *-le* and the particle *le* in these narrative contexts.

The general notion of conversation to be defended is that of a 'joint project' in which participants perform 'participatory acts' (Clark 1996). Conversations do not have fixed or conventionalised structures to the same extent as procedural discourse and stories. We will give a detailed description of the structure of conversations in Chapter 7. We take the view that conversations are 'emergent' and 'locally managed'. That they require

16 *Introduction*

'commitment' to develop into 'joint construals', during which personal interactions are managed and a topic is introduced. In that chapter, too, we will present a 'move typology' which is based on the work by Halliday ([1985] 1994) and Eggins and Slade (1997).

1.5 Presentation

The study sets off with an analysis of various proposals for the function of the particle *le* in Chinese by various authors (Chapter 2). In that process, their strong and weak points will be highlighted. In order to make our own orientation more obvious, we decided to detail the notions we think are necessary for an understanding of language use. That task will be undertaken in Chapter 3. There, we will discuss notions such as mental models, joint activities, co-ordination, joint actions, joint construal, and others that are crucial for a correct understanding of the nature of verbal interaction.[6] Chapter 4 sets the scene for the present study by analysing the historical development of the particle *le*. Two issues needed to be determined urgently. Do the two forms *-le* and *le* originate from the same source, as suggested by some, or do they originate from two different historical lexemes, as proposed by others? The second issue regards the functional distribution of *-le* and *le* in the language. The historical digression is followed by the procedural data in Chapter 5. Our understanding of uses of the particle *le* in the highly structured environment of procedural discourse we demonstrate to be related to uses of the particle *le* in children's stories (Chapter 6). The combined insight of these two chapters is then applied to conversational data in Chapter 7. We conclude the book first with a comparative discussion of our findings and the implications these have for an understanding of the idea of co-ordination (Chapter 8). The final chapter relates the structure of common ground to mental model construction, and formulates a theory of language use that can handle the various moments of marking with the Chinese particle *le*.

2 Previous studies

The particle *le* is one of the most frequently used and discussed, but least understood, elements in Chinese grammar. While *le* regularly features in everyday discourse, traditional studies have mainly focused on its role in the sentence without paying adequate attention to the cognitive marking involved or the interactive social context in which it is used. As a result, the questions of *why* and *when* the particle *le* is used in Chinese have so far remained unanswered. What complicates the matter more is the fact that LE in Mandarin Chinese has two homophonous forms: the particle *le*, which normally occurs at the end of a sentence, and the verb suffix *le*, written as *-le*, which follows a verb. The two forms with potentially different functions, as mentioned in Chapter 1, have led to four positions on LE in the literature:

1. Two different morphemes (*-le*, and *le*), many uses of both verbal *-le* and the particle *le*.
2. Two different morphemes (*-le*, and *le*), two different functions, verbal *-le* and phrase *le*, and claims for a unifying meaning for each of the functions.
3. One morpheme /*le*/, which is represented at different levels in the grammar, proposition and conversation.
4. One morpheme /*le*/ which can be realised as *-le* or *le*.

We now examine the positions in the previous studies one by one.

2.1 Two morphemes and multifunction

The first position was taken by Y.R. Chao in his *A Grammar of Spoken Chinese* (1968), a study that has had great influence on later works in Chinese linguistics. In this work Chao maintains that the two forms of LE need to be distinguished since they have their different distributional properties and have different forms in various Chinese dialects. Most Chinese linguists seem to agree with Chao (1968) and accept the presence of two different but homophonous markers in Chinese grammar. As for the functions of the two forms of LE, Chao assigns a single function – marking perfectivity – to the verbal *-le*, but multifunction to the particle *le*. Chao (1968: 798–800) brings his various observations on Chinese particles together in one section, and there he lists seven functions for the particle *le*:

A. Inchoative *le*.
B. Command in response to a new situation.
C. Progress in a story.
D. Isolated event in the past.
E. Completed action as of the present.
F. Consequent clause to indicate situation.
G. 'Obviousness'.

Chao's examples do cover almost all uses of *le* and we therefore will use this seven-point listing as a descriptive benchmark against which all other approaches, including our own, must be compared. The high level of descriptive adequacy however is not matched with the same level of explanatory power. Chao (1968) does not present a unified explanation for the particle's various functions. We will now first detail the benchmark by taking a closer look at the various uses Chao distinguished, and bring out the points that are outstanding and need to be covered by other approaches and by our own analysis.

A: Inchoativity

The notion 'inchoativity' can manifest itself as a 'new situation', as a 'quality attained', or as an 'excessive degree'. Chao's analysis is not strictly syntactic. He implicitly brings in cognitive distinctions in the analysis when he makes implied comparisons with previous situations. This is remarkable since the framework he used to analyse his data was formal (IC or Immediate Constituent analysis; cf. Chao 1968: 4) and rejected the kind of cognitive approaches which have become popular in recent years (cf. Biq 2000). It is the cognitive orientation that we will focus on in our analysis. Here are examples given by Chao to illustrate 'inchoativity':

(2.1) (a new situation)
       Xia yu le.
       Fall rain LE
       'It's raining (now).'

(2.2) (the quality or degree attained)
       Shiya, shiyi dian ban le.
       Goodness eleven o'clock half LE
       'Goodness, it's (as late as) half past eleven.'

(2.3) (an excessive degree)
Tang xian le.
Soup salty LE
'It's too salty.'

According to Chao (1968: 798) the inchoative *le* applies to a situation, which is 'new' or 'new to the speaker'. A 'new situation' can be an observable fact as in *xia yu le* (a 'new realisation'), as in a new perception of the time-frame one is in, as in *shiyi dian ban le*, or a subjective judgement as in *tang xian le*. Chao's observations and comments are accurate and revealing. His observation that the particle *le* is used in situations in which an 'excess' of something is indicated we already touched upon, and, as we will demonstrate, is crucial for an understanding of the various uses of *le*. One issue he does not comment upon, however, is that each of these examples involves a comparison with something that was there before. This issue (the relation between *le* and a pre-construct or context) will recur in various forms in later writings (cf. Bisang and Sonaiya 1997; Li and Thompson 1981; Liu 2001). Also, Chao does not address the issue of a unifying account. He does not identify the cognitive mechanism underlying these various forms of a 'new situation'. It is these two issues that were foremost in our attention throughout this study.

B: Command in response to a new situation

Chao seemed to have realised that certain situations demand the presence of an audience, and uses of *le* involve appeals to that audience to act in a certain way. When a 'new situation' is created by a situation participant, that participant can indicate that there is a 'new situation' and issue a command, as in:

(2.4) [sentence, no context given]
Chi fan le.
eat meal LE
'Let's eat now!'

Chao did not specify the interactive situation, which makes some of his translations difficult to interpret, as in this case. When the person who did the cooking addressed family members, the English glosses 'Time to eat!', 'Come and eat!', or 'Dinner is ready' indicate what is meant by the Chinese expression (projection). The version 'Time to eat!' also covers the situation that one hotel guest addresses another when, inside the hotel, a bell sound is heard around dinner time. The use by Chao of the word 'now' in the translation is interesting, however, since, as we will see in Chapter 3, this is an endeavour to bring into the text the notion of 'immediacy', which we will claim is associated with uses of *le*.

Also, when this utterance is compared with *chi fan!* – that is, the command without *le* – or with a request to participate as in *Yinyueji laile!* ('The music is here!') addressed to a crowd of university students eating lunch by some of their fellow students, it becomes clear that the *le* utterance is not a command *per se* but is a form of 'announcing' a 'new situation'.[1] The notion 'command' is only there when 'obedience' is already present in the situational context, and 'willingness' to participate is given, as is the case in family settings (cf. Clark 1996). We therefore need to reject the association between 'phrase' *le* and a 'command'. Methodologically, the rejection of this claimed relationship has many implications, the most important of which is that a search for a relationship between a certain 'speech-act' type and *le* needs to be rejected, as we already argued in Chapter 1.

Support for this rejection is offered by the following *le* phrase, which can be used to set up a background for a following 'command':

(2.5) [mother addressing a young family member]
Chi fan le, kuai bai zhuozi!
Eat meal LE hurry set table
'*It's time for dinner. Get the table ready!*'

'Command in response to a new situation' can also be seen as another instance of 'inchoativity', the assertion of a 'new situation', which did not exist before the announcement was made. We need, however, to remain cautious here and keep on distinguishing between situations that are 'created' by situation participants, and those that 'occur' or are created by natural forces as 'involuntary effects' and do not necessarily involve social interaction.

C: Progress in a story

In this category, Chao shows that he realises that it is necessary to distinguish the 'discourse genre' in which the particle *le* is used. In stories, different surroundings for uses of the particle *le* are created. In stories, writers report 'new situations' to their readers, who themselves have no way of verifying the happenings being reported. Compare, for instance:

(2.6) **Houlai tian jiu qing le.**
Afterwards it then fine LE
'*And then the weather cleared.*'

The 'updating' in this move is between a writer and his readers, and the 'new situation' being asserted is not in the immediate environment of the reader. It is reported, and the reader will relate it to an embedded mental model (Johnson-Laird 1983). The use of *jiu* relates this category to 'F: consequent clause to indicate situation', which we will introduce now first.

D: Consequent clause to indicate situation

At this point Chao falls back on a syntactic analysis (consequent clause), but also realises that what is being expressed is a 'new situation'. Here are two examples:

(2.7)   Na wo jiu bu zou le.
        In that case I then not go LE
        'In that case, I won't go, then.'

(2.8)   Ni yi en menling, ta jiu lai kai men le.
        You once press door bell s/he then come open door LE
        'As soon as you ring the doorbell, he will come and open the door.'

In both C and D, *jiu* ('then'), indicates a subsequent new situation, and co-occurs with *le*. This has led to the idea that there is somehow a syntactic relationship between *jiu* and *le* (see pp. 24–37 for the discussion by Li and Thompson 1981). However, as these two examples show, such claims can easily be falsified. The particle is not necessary in these examples, and what is still open is the question of what its presence represents. It is the answer to that question we are looking for. It can also be argued that C and F are instances of 'inchoativity', in this case the reporting of a new situation and the assertion of an event sequence. 'Inchoativity', however, has its limits, as category E illustrates.

E: Isolated event in the past

In conversational exchanges 'isolated events in the past' are often brought in and can be marked with *le*. Such assertions tend to open a conversation or to introduce a new 'topic':

(2.9)   Wo zuor dao Zhangjia chi fan le.
        I yesterday go to the Zhang's eat meal LE
        'I went to the Zhang's for dinner yesterday.'

This category of the use of *le* is an important one. It is not easily interpreted as a new situation in the same way as the other uses discussed so far. For instance, the new situations of *xia yu le, tian qing le, kai men le* discussed above all imply a different previous situation of 'not raining', 'not fine' and 'the door being closed'. Utterances in this category, however, do not have such implications. For example (2.9) does not necessarily suggest 'I didn't eat at Zhang's before', though it may imply eating at Zhang's is not the person's daily routine. If (2.9) also represents a new situation, it has to be of a different kind. Since Chao has not defined his use of 'situation' in any detail, it is difficult to see how these uses can be other instances of 'inchoativity', the creation of a 'new situation'.

Also, an isolated event in the past is typically expressed by a -*le* utterance, as illustrated by (2.10), and it becomes necessary to explain what the difference is between these two ways of marking a 'past event':

(2.10) **Wo zuor dao Zhangjia chi-le yi dun fan.**
I yesterday go Zhang's eat -LE one CL meal
'I had a meal at Zhang's yesterday.'

We will argue that (2.10) reports an isolated event in the past, whereas (2.9) adds a past event to the hearer's knowledge to update their common ground for an upcoming interaction (see Chapter 3).

F: Completed action as of the present

In conversational exchanges it is also possible to mark a completed action with *le*. Here are two examples:

(2.11) **Wo jinr zaochen xie-le san feng xin le.**
I today morning write -LE three CL letter LE
'I have written three letters this morning.' [talking before lunch time]

(2.12) **Wo huilai le.**
I come back LE
'I have come back.'

In these examples, the reference time is or includes the speech time, and, as we have seen, in other instances this is the time of a past situation. Chao's two categories – 'Completed action as of the present' and 'Isolated event in the past' – both relate a past situation to the present interaction, and the main difference is the time of the past situation; that is, whether it has just been completed or was completed some time ago. What we need to look for is a mechanism that explains why in both instances the particle *le* is used or can be used. That question is still wide open and we intend to provide an answer at the end of this study.

G: The 'obviousness' le

Chao's final example, 'obviousness', is another crucial case in the study of the various uses of the particle *le*. Here is an example:

(2.13) **Zhege ni dangran dong le.**
This you of course understand LE
'This, you understand, of course!'

To begin with, such responses can only be made in reaction to a previous remark, and the question is does *le* create the effect of 'obviousness', or does that effect originate elsewhere? We take the latter view. The use of *le* in cases like this depends on the presence of *dangran* ('of course'), which expresses the 'obviousness'. Also, *dangran* ('of course') can be used without *le*, which leaves the nature of the marking with *le* open. Obviousness can't be the answer. Rather we need to look for an explanation of the various uses of the particle *le* in a different direction. The function of the particle *le* is to signal a special cognitive moment, which is further specified by the asserted expression. The question then is what this cognitive moment is, and it is that question we will explore in Chapters 5, 6 and 7.

To sum up, Chao's work on *le* has revealed the essence of the particle's semantics, which is linked to 'inchoativity' and 'new situation'. The main problem with his analysis is that it looks for an explanation inward, to the meaning of the sentence being analysed, and as we have seen in Chapter 1, such an orientation masquerades the discovery of the nature of the particle. Also, Chao fails to find a generalisation for the various uses of the particle *le*, leaving his study descriptively almost adequate, but lacking in explanatory power.

2.2 Two morphemes and two general functions

The second position is taken by Li and Thompson (1981), Li *et al.* (1982), Andreasen (1981), Chang (1986), van den Berg (1989) and Liu (2001). Although these researchers may differ in their views on the particle or verbal -*le*, all of them, nevertheless, assign a single function to either *le* or -*le*. Their different views on the two forms of LE are summarised in Table 2.1. Our discussions in this section on those views will, however, focus on the particle *le*.

Table 2.1 Two functions of LE

Researcher	Function of particle le	Function of verbal -le
Li and Thompson (1981)	Currently relevant state	Perfectivity
Li *et al.* (1982)	Perfect	
Andreasen (1981)	Perfect/background	Perfectivity/foreground
Chang (1986)	Discourse segment	Peak event
Van den Berg (1989)	Actuality	Event viewed as a whole without attention to internal phasing
Bisang and Sonaiya (1997)	Reference to a preconstructed domain	Perfectivity
Liu (2001)	Past tense	Realisation

2.2.1 *Li and Thompson (1981), Li* et al. *(1982)*

Li and Thompson (1981) take a functional approach to language and introduce the notion of context as an essential element in understanding the various uses of the particle *le*. They try to spell out the general semantic and pragmatic functions of the particle *le* used in various communicative contexts and propose that the basic function of the particle 'to signal a "Currently Relevant State" (abbreviated as CRS)'. In their words,

> *le* claims that a state of affairs has special current relevance with respect to some particular situation. (1981: 240)

The wording '*le* claims' can either be taken in a non-personal way, or as an expression of speaker intent. There is evidence in the text that Li and Thompson use it in the objective sense, the claim is in the sentence and holds for both the speaker and the hearer (cf. 1981: 242). In our approach *le* always expresses the speaker's communicative intent. The formulation further assigns 'special current relevance' to a 'state of affairs' in relation to some 'particular situation'. The notion 'state of affairs' in its relation to the particle *le*, Li and Thompson commented upon explicitly (see our discussion of 'state', pp. 28–9). The notion 'particular situation', however, is referred to in general terms as the 'context' or the 'speech context', but also as 'what is going on now'. It is the latter notion, 'what is going on now', which we think is crucial for an understanding of the function of the particle *le* in everyday communication. Li and Thompson do not discuss this notion separately as part of their definition. At this point we can observe a fundamental difference between our approach and Li and Thompson's analysis. The notion of 'what is going on now' – or, in the words of Clark (1996), a 'project' – obtained special attention in our approach, since we were looking at the relation between the particle *le* and the structure of the event going on at that moment. The idea of 'special current relevance' holds centre stage in their discussion, and rightly so. What is 'special' about uses of the particle *le* in terms of relevance is listed as five categories (see pp. 28–36 for the details). We will now take a closer look at the way Li and Thompson define 'current relevance'. Thereafter follows their view on the notion 'state'.

Li and Thompson use two formulations in describing the function of the particle *le* 'special current relevance of some state of affairs' and 'Currently Relevant State' (CRS). When discussing 'current' it is not immediately clear if they are focusing on that notion alone or on the idea of 'current relevance'. This makes the first part of their discussion confusing. They begin by observing that,

> The *le* says that some state of affairs is *current* with respect to some particular situation. (1981: 240)

By this they seem to define 'current' as what is going on 'now', but phrase it in terms of 'relevance':

> the statement signalled by the sentence with the *le* is relevant to *now*, that is, to the situation of the speech context in which the speaker and hearer are engaged. (1981: 240)

Note the use of 'relevant' in this phrase, indicating that what they are talking about here is 'current relevance' and not the idea of 'current' alone. They also observe that 'this is by far the most common case'. We tend to agree with that when the discourse type is taken to be everyday verbal interaction, just to use a wide-ranging concept that will allow further specification later. The same problem as to the distinction of what is 'current' and what is 'relevant' reoccurs in the discussion of their first example:

(2.14) [someone calls Ms Liao who is out; the person who answers the phone may say]
Ta chu-qu mai dongxi le.
3sg exit-go buy thing CRS
'She's gone shopping.'

Since no other situation is mentioned, *le* says that her having gone shopping is 'current' with respect to 'the present situation in which the telephone conversation is taking place'. And, 'since no situation is explicitly mentioned, it is assumed that her having gone shopping is relevant to the present' (1981: 240). So we see that in this example 'current' and 'current relevance' are interchangeable concepts, and there is nothing in that we can object to at this point.

The situation in this regard is different, however, when they talk about cases in which 'another situation is explicitly mentioned' as in example (2.15). About such instances they say:

> then the statement signalled by the sentence with *le* is claimed to be relevant to that particular situation. (1981: 240)

Note that again in the discussion of 'current', the formulation is in terms of 'relevance', and that way of thinking is then projected onto the second example, in which to the previous situation the time dimension *nei tian* ('that day') is added:

(2.15) [Two people discussing whether Ms Liao made a telephone call two days ago]
nei tian ta chu-qu mai dongxi le.
that day 3sg exit-go buy thing CRS
'That day she went out shopping.'

Li and Thompson (1981: 240) comment on this example with the words, 'the state of her having gone shopping was relevant to the situation to that day in the past'. No mention of current at all here, and this creates a serious problem since what is 'going on here' is a conversation between persons who know each other well, and 'current' should here be taken as 'current' with the project going on, and not as 'current' with the time-frame expressed. The latter possibility (that is, the one we reject) is explicitly mentioned in the following examples:

(2.16) [A tries to make an appointment, and B has to decline]
Xiage yue wo jiu zai Riben le
next-CL month I then at Japan LE
'Next month I'll be in Japan.'
(Li and Thompson 1981: 241)

Here, Li and Thompson comment, 'the state of your being in Japan will be current in the situation specified by "next month"'. However, in our view the particle *le*, as a co-ordination device in a joint project, has to function while the project is going on. It signals the necessity of common-ground co-ordination at the speech time, though the content of the assertion may be related to a different time. For example, in (2.15), although 'her having gone shopping' was current on 'that day' in the past, *le*, however, requests the addressee to add this past event to the common ground at the speech time. It is this past event that is currently relevant to the present 'joint project': finding out whether the person could make the phone call that day. Similarly, in (2.16) it might very well be that 'being in Japan' is 'current' with the time-frame 'next month'. However, the 'current relevance' of the whole expression 'being in Japan next month' is related to 'what is going on now', the endeavour 'to make an appointment'. It is the impossibility of making an appointment which is being signalled here. To understand this argument better it will be necessary for us to introduce the notion 'co-ordination of action'; it will be discussed in Chapter 3.

The problems we have with 'current relevance' at this point are:

1 absence of an interactive perspective,
2 use of 'current' as related to an expression within the sentence with *le*,
3 absence of the notion 'immediacy',
4 use of 'context' as a non-defined entity.

In the section in which they focus explicitly on 'relevance', Li and Thompson first observe that this is related to the notion 'context' (pp. 242–3). For example, sentence (2.14) shows that the state of affairs of 'Ms Liao having gone shopping' is relevant to the current situation in the sense that it makes clear that she is not available for a conversation. Similarly, sentence (2.15) can be relevant in the sense that at that day she could not have made a particular phone call.

In this section, Li and Thompson also gave a minimal pair to illustrate the difference between a simple statement and the statement plus *le*, indicating that it is relevant to 'something going on now' (1981: 242).

(2.17) [simple statement]
Zheige gua hen tian.
this – CL melon very sweet
'This melon is very sweet.'

(2.18) [information that is relevant to something going on now]
Zheige gua hen tian le.
this – CL melon very sweet CRS
'This melon is very sweet.'

According to Li and Thompson, while (2.17) is a simple statement, (2.18), in addition, also means that the sweetness of the melon is relevant for the current situation. Thus, (2.18) could be used in situations where one had guessed the melon would or wouldn't be sweet, or where 'one wanted to announce a new "discovery", or wanted the hearer to discover its sweetness' (1981: 243). However, they didn't say how the use of the particle in those situations results in relevance.

In fact, among the above-mentioned situations only the first, where the sweetness of the melon is already activated, is appropriate for (2.18) since the focus of the utterance is on the degree of the sweetness as indicated by *hen* (very). The typical context for (2.18), then, is what Li and Thompson call 'Correct a wrong assumption' (see p. 28). To announce a new 'discovery' a version of (2.18) without *hen* is needed: *Zheige gua tian le* (This melon is now sweet), which focuses on the realisation of the sweetness of the melon. Remarkable in these examples is the use of the speech-act verb 'announce' and the introduction of the 'hearer' as having a focus different from that of the speaker. This is noteworthy since Li and Thompson talked about a state of affairs signalled by the 'sentence' as 'relevant' for both the speaker and the hearer, who can 'infer' from the context in just what way it is relevant (1981: 242). The objection to this view is that in an inference model of communication a speaker's 'communicative intent' is matched by the hearer's strategies for 'intent recognition' (Grice 1975). By being involved in successful communicative events hearers develop inference strategies for the recognition of speakers' communicative intent. Speakers 'imply' and hearers 'infer', their roles are complementary (Yule 1996).

An interesting observation also is that 'relevance' is related to 'something going on now'. We agree with this and consider it a crucial distinction, as will become clear shortly when we look at the notion 'state', and as we will demonstrate throughout this book. The idea of an 'activity' of some sort is not further specified by Li and Thompson, however, and thereby the fundamental notion of a 'project' and its cognitive structure did not get the attention we think it should have received. The essence of this is that the particle indexes the development of the 'project', and in particular a special 'change' in the state of affairs of that project.

We come now to the notion 'state'. By 'state' it is meant that *le* always treats an event signalled by the sentence as a 'state of affairs' rather than an action, and claims that that state of affairs is currently relevant. Li and Thompson illustrate this by pointing out that the quoted Ms Liao example – *Ta chu-qu mai dongxi le* ('She's gone shopping') – concerns 'the state of her having gone shopping and its relevance to the current situation', and not 'the action of her going out or buying' (Li and Thompson 1981: 243). This analysis is convincing, and we will support the basic idea. The question that remains, however, is a specification of this 'state' in cognitive terms. How does a 'state of affairs' marked with *le* relate to other 'states of affairs'?

If it does confirm the basic idea that the particle *le* signals something in the 'background' rather than an activity, which should count as something in the 'foreground', how do these differences manifest themselves in the grammar (cf. Andreasen 1981)? We will look at grammar from the perspective of the construction of mental models, which has different operations for different cognitive states, fast and automatic recognition of perception, and calculation for more reflexive cognitive operations, and we will propose a three-level hierarchy moving from the immediate situation down to distinctions in the background (see Chapter 8 for the details).

The 'special current relevance' introduced by Li and Thompson in their definition of the function of the particle *le*, resulted in a specification of five 'relevant state' categories. In each category, they say, the particle can convey CRS if the state of affairs the sentence represents:

A   Is a changed state
B   Corrects a wrong assumption
C   Reports progress so far
D   Determines what will happen next
E   Is the speaker's total contribution to the conversation at that point

(Li and Thompson 1981: 244)

We will discuss them one by one, and provide comments at those points at which we think the analysis fails or creates inexplicable consequences.

A: Change of state

In this category Li and Thompson proposed that the state of affairs concerned represents a change from an earlier state of affairs. In each case the relevance of the new state of affairs hinges on the fact that it didn't hold before, but holds now as a result of 'change'. This 'change' can be either objective (i.e. the 'state of affairs' is new or changed from the way it was before), or subjective (i.e. the state is changed from the way the speaker thought it was before). They illustrate this idea with a large number of examples. In their presentation 'change' is the largest category (Li and Thompson 1981: 244–63). They open the series of illustrations with what they consider to be clear examples of 'change' (Li and Thompson 1981: 245):

(2.19) **Ta zhidao neige xiaoxi.**
  3sg know that -CL news
  'S/He knows about that piece of news.'

(2.20) **Ta zhidao neige xiaoxi le.**
  3sg know that -CL news CRS
  'S/He knows about that piece of news now (s/he didn't before).'

The example is used out of context which limits the sharpness of interpretation and makes it impossible to recognise the project or projects with which it was or could be related. 'S/He knows about that piece of news now' is a 'change' from a previous 'state of affairs' the person talked about (*ta*: 's/he) supposedly was in. This previous 'state of affairs' in this case can be described as the state 'she didn't know it before now'. Despite the lack of a clear context or project, this example can be taken as illustrating 'change' and we do not disagree with Li and Thompson on this. However, there are other readings possible as conversational data illustrate, and therefore the question remains as to how these various readings relate. Also, we will see in a moment that looking for a negative counterpart of an asserted state of affairs cannot be stressed too far. It does not apply, for instance, with negative sentences or *bie* sentences, or in situations that the speaker realises a 'change' of a 'state of affairs' (see p. 30). Li and Thompson did not further subdivide the category 'change' explicitly, but a close reading reveals that their discussion contains the following distinctions:

- a rule
- a common sentence type
- a discussion of time
- the use of *jiu*
- realisation on the part of the speaker
- expressing annoyance

The general rule describes 'changed states of affairs' expressed by adjectives. The rule is a 'general rule' and modified as a 'good' general rule, which obviously limits its applicability. It is no more than a rule of thumb. In their words:

> whenever one wishes to describe a new, changed state, as opposed to a general or habitual state ... *le* should be used to imply that the case is new or newly noticed.
>
> (Li and Thompson 1981: 250)

This formulation is intriguing and we support the basic idea. The distinction between a 'general' or 'habitual state' and a 'changed state' is crucial in our analysis too, but Li and Thompson limit the application to 'adjectives'. The melon example (2.18) without *hen* for announcing a new 'discovery' – *Zhege gua tian le* ('This melon is sweet') – is given as an example. The general state to which it is opposed is that it is not yet ripe, and now it is, it can be eaten. We will argue that the recognition of a 'general' or 'habitual' state is crucial for an understanding of the notion 'change'. 'Change' in our analysis is limited to cases in which a pre-existing 'general' or 'habitual' state of affairs is part of the common ground which at that moment is shared between the interactants. Also, it remains necessary to indicate what the 'special relevance' is of the 'change' indexed by *le*. There are many changes of state of affairs that are not marked with *le*, so why is *le* used in such instances? And also, when there is agreement among native speakers that the particle *le* must be used, what is the force that creates its presence?

The common sentence type indicating that a 'change of state' is involved is that of 'negative sentences'. Li and Thompson give five minimal pairs and seven individual examples. The minimal pairs in the book are listed with no further comments, apart from those comments added in the translation. When studied in cognitive terms, they illustrate the contrast between availability, an activity, ability, habit, and everyday state of affairs, and the discontinuity of that availability, activity, ability, the change of a habit, and the deviation from a normal property. Here is the example illustrating 'availability' (Li and Thompson 1981: 253):

(2.21) [customer asking waiter whether the restaurant has any *guotie* ('pot stickers')]
 a. **Mei you.**
 not exist
 'No.'
 b. **Mei you le.**
 not exist LE
 '*Not anymore (i.e. we've run out).*'

As said, there are no further comments in the book, and the terminology is our own. If we apply the principle of a 'normal' or 'habitual' state of affairs we can see that in the '*Mei you*' example 'availability' is not an issue as *guotie* is not on offer in that restaurant, whereas in the '*Mei you le*' example the waiter acknowledges that they 'normally' have *guotie* ('pot stickers') but that there is a 'change' from that normal situation now. The nature of this 'change' is the issue in the data chapters of our study (Chapters 5, 6 and 7).

The seven individual sentences illustrate 'change' as 'unexpected' progression of time, a change of opinion, a change in attitude towards some state of affairs, a proposal for a change in conversational direction, a deviation in ability, and two sentences with *bie* 'don't'. We will take a look at the five non-*bie* negative sentences listed first and see how they indicate 'change'. Negative sentences presuppose the 'presence' of the 'positive' state of affairs from which it can be seen as a 'change'. Here is one of the examples, but the argument is true for each of them:

(2.22) [conversational context not specified]
  Wo shizai huobuxiaqu le.
  I really live-can't-continue LE
  '*I can't go on living anymore.*'

When this expression is looked at in terms of 'change', it must be accepted that the person speaking was still living at that moment, that the 'normal' situation of speakers being living creatures also holds in this case. The speaker asserts as his opinion that this 'normal' state of affairs is going to 'change'.

'*Bie*' utterances are special in their own right. Neither a 'negative' state of affairs nor a 'positive' state of affairs can be claimed as the pre-existing basis for the 'change' being asserted now. The activity itself is 'abnormal', in the sense of not the normal way of doing things, as already illustrated by the activity verbs involved *mihuo* ('bewitching someone') and *mi lu* ('losing one's way'), respectively. For further examples of expressions with *bie* we refer to the data chapters of the book.

Li and Thompson did not search for an answer as to what unites these various examples. They accepted the linguistic notion 'negative sentences' as guidance, and such a distinction easily leads to wrong predictions and leaves open the question as to the nature of the indexed 'change'. In our analysis we focus on what these various examples share cognitively, and we will demonstrate that the idea of 'deviation' from a 'habitual state' opens the way to a generalised description of the various uses of the particle *le*.

When Li and Thompson (1981: 255–7) discussed 'change' in the context of time, they opposed the 'time of speaking' to 'general time' and 'future time' (three examples each). It is unclear, however, how they interpreted 'general time'. Their examples illustrated the 'information state' (being informed about something) of the speaker, and travel directions, respectively – the latter actually involving 'future time' (what to do when you get there). The third example seems to be a clear case in the use of 'general time':

(2. 23) [sentence, no context or interaction type mentioned]
  guole shangxiaban de shihou huoche jiu kong le
  cross-PFV ascend–descend–work DE time train then empty CRS
  '*Once rush hour is over, the train becomes empty.*'

In instances such as these involving 'general time' the use of the final *le* is 'obligatory', and this had led to the idea that this is caused by the presence of *jiu* ('then'). We will give a cognitive explanation for this occurrence later, but we need to observe that their second example contains the form *jiu keyi le* ('[then can *le*] that will be okay'), which actually illustrates that *le* in this context is not necessary at all. The expression *jiu keyi* ('that will be okay') is perfectly all right in the given context, and the question as to the relationship between *jiu* ('then') and *le* is therefore still open. Also, the idea of 'change' in this example is problematic. It actually has nothing to do with 'change', as we will demonstrate in Chapter 7.

Li and Thompson (1981: 259) also observed that 'change' can sometimes be a 'realisation on the part of the speaker'. They say that this is the case in the following example, for instance (Li and Thompson 1981: 259):

(2.24) [a three-year-old child who has just noticed the parrot in the zoo]
Zhei shi yingwu le.
this be parrot CRS
'*This is a parrot.*'

We do not deny the correctness of the observation. The example is fine and illustrative. However, we need to observe that it is difficult to make 'realisation on the part of the speaker' the basis for 'change'. The speaker also signals to the addressees that this 'change' has happened. And why would he want to do so? Does this imply that the child had never seen a parrot before and only knew the word, or did he want to demonstrate to his parents that he knows the name of this bird and wants to show off? What is still needed is knowledge of the shared common ground against which this is being asserted.

In some cases, Li and Thompson continue (1981: 261), the realisation on the part of the speaker expresses 'annoyance' or 'irritation'. The example they give is the situation of a bus ticket salesperson who shows his annoyance with a customer who is not familiar with the kind of bus tickets in use. To bring examples such as this one under the notion of 'change' as a 'realisation on the part of the speaker' is something we disagree with. There is considerable confusion with the notion of 'change', which needs to be clarified, and for that purpose we propose the notions of 'deviation' and 'restoration', outstanding moments in the 'co-ordination' of 'shared common ground' (cf. Clark 1996).

B: Correcting a wrong assumption

The particle in this category is used to express a 'state of affairs' that is currently relevant for the purpose of 'correcting a wrong assumption' on the part of the hearer. This wrong assumption may be explicitly mentioned in the conversation, may be part of the speaker's background knowledge about the hearer, or may be normally held by people in general. Here are two examples of the 24 presented by (Li and Thompson 1981: 264–9):

(2.25) [to the accusation that the speaker has spent the afternoon sleeping]
Wo kan-le san-ben shu le.
I look-PFV three-CL book CRS
(What do you mean?!) 'I have read three books!'

(2.26) [comic strip figure Glory Bee is contradicting a normal assumption between her and Goofy]
Ni zui hao bu yao lai kan dianshi le, wo de-le zhong shangfeng.
you most good no will come look TV CRS, I get-PFV heavy cold
'(Contrary to our usual practice,) you'd better not come over to watch TV. (this time) – I caught terrible cold.'

According to Li and Thompson, in all the above cases *le* appears with the sentence to correct a wrong assumption.

The main problem with this analysis is that it is the description of a speaker's communicative intent, and is not a characterisation of the function of the particle *le*. Also, the example is interactive, but the analysis is not. We can observe for instance that in the first example an 'accusation' is being 'contradicted', whereas in the second example a 'deviation' from a 'normal' or 'habitual' state of affairs is asserted, and implies the discontinuation of an habitual project. As we will argue in Chapter 7, the interactive analysis in each of these cases is different, making an accusation and 'countering' that is something quite different from establishing an agenda and working out a temporary 'deviation'.

C: Progress so far

The 'state of affairs' in this category is relevant to the current situation because it 'updates' the hearer on the progress made so far in some 'extensive project or venture' of which both the speaker and the hearer know. Here are two of the 21 examples in the text (Li and Thompson 1981: 270–8):

(2.27) [to someone who knows the speaker is studying Tang dynasty poetry]
Tang shi san-bai-shou wo bei-chu-lai-le yi-ban le.
Tang poem three-hundred-CL I memorise-exit-come-PFV one-half CRS
'I've memorised half of the 300 Tang poems now (so far).'

(2.28) [neutral question, such as a bookstore clerk might pose to an unfamiliar student]
a. Ni nian gao-zhong ma?
You study upper-middle Q
'Are you upper middle school?'

[to a student whom one has known for a long time]
b. Ni nian gao-zhong le ma?
You study upper-middle CRS Q
'*Are you upper middle school?*'

It is interesting to observe how Li and Thompson introduce the notion of 'shared common ground' in this section – in their words 'some extensive project or venture of which both the speaker and the hearer know' (1981: 270). In the first example the 'shared common ground' is introduced as 'someone who knows the speaker is studying Tang dynasty poetry', and in the second example the presence and absence of common ground are illustrated. We support these observations and will claim that the presence of shared common ground is a prerequisite for the successful use of the particle *le*.

D: What happens next

Another class of situations proposed by Li and Thompson (15 examples on pp. 278–82) in which a state of affairs is relevant includes those in which that 'state of affairs' *determines* what happens next. For example, (2.29), as well as expressing 'progress so far', can also be 'currently relevant' as a signal to the hearer that something else can happen now (1981: 278):

(2.29) [project known to addressee]
Wo xi-hao-le yifu le.
I wash-finish-PFV clothes CRS
'*I've finished washing the clothes.*'
(So now: we can go to the movies; you can do your yoga in the laundry room; I'm free to play chess with you etc.)

Such a *le* sentence is often used to announce that a new state of affairs is just about to be realised, and the hearer is expected to make an appropriate response. Li and Thompson give the following minimal pair to illustrate the point (1981: 280–1):

(2.30) **Xiao Huang jiu yao lai**
little Huang soon will come
'*Little Huang will be here soon.*'
(a simple neutral comment or an answer to a question)

(2.31) **Xiao Huang jiu yao lai le**
little Huang soon will come CRS
(Hurry!) '*Little Huang is about to arrive.*'
(so: hide the gifts, put your pants on, get ready to holler 'Surprise', etc.)!

And also compare:

(2.32) **Women gai zou le**
we should leave CRS
'We should go now.'
(so: get your coat, get ready to say good-bye, etc.)

The idea that the 'state of affairs' *determines* what will happen next can only be understood when the idea of 'shared common ground' is in mind. 'States of affairs' determine little if the project phasing is not part of the shared common ground. In essence therefore there are two distinctions relevant here: the 'closure' of a procedure, as in the first example, which immediately 'opens' the possibility for another project to be started (cf. Schiffrin 1987). Such a project can be 'announced' as in *Xiao Huang jiu yao lai le!* ('Little Huang is about to arrive'), which requests the addressees to prepare to take up their respective roles in that project. Project uptake can also be indicated when a summons is responded to as in *Lai le, lai le!* ('I'm coming'), which signals that the speaker is willing to take up the project and is coming to the door.[2] The various examples in this category are not all of the same type, and in our analysis we will distinguish between project 'closings', 'openings' and 'project take-ups'.

E: Closing a statement

In this category *le* signals the 'current relevance' of a 'state of affairs' in its function as a mark of 'finality'. The particle is used to tell the hearer that 'the proposition is relevant to the speech situation by being "newsworthy" in and of itself; it brings a statement into the current situation by tagging it as the speaker's total contribution as of that moment'. Li and Thompson observe that a sentence that answers a particular question may not need *le* as its relevance is clear. However, as a piece of volunteered information, the same sentence will need *le* to 'finish' it. The sentence without *le*, in addition to answering a question, can also serve as background information for some further information. The following minimal pair illustrates the point (Li and Thompson 1981: 284–5):

(2.33) [commenting on a mutual friend]
   a **Ta yijing likai Meiguo le**
      3sg already leave America CRS
      S/He's already left America.

   b **Ta yijing likai Meiguo,**
      3sg already leave America

     i **suoyi ta bu-bi jiao shui**
        therefore 3sg not-need hand:over tax

ii xianzai zai Zhongguo jiao shu
    now at China teach book

'S/He has already left America,
i   so s/he doesn't have to pay taxes.
ii and s/he is now teaching in China.'

The examples in this section are small in number (11 examples) and not all convincing. We see 'finality' as a special form of project 'closure', and it is therefore always necessary to explicate what the wider project is in the context the remark is made in.

In the concluding section of their presentation Li and Thompson observe that the various ways in which 'current relevance' is created (five) is:

> a matter for the hearer to decide on the basis of his/her knowledge of the relationship between him/her and the speaker, of the situation in which they are interacting, and of the world at large.

This is a strong statement, with which we fully agree. In all communication, the knowledge of the situation is involved, as is knowledge about 'rights' and 'obligations' that are activated when a 'role' is taken up, and finally the knowledge shared between the interactants as members of a group and as members of a community. The question remains, however, as to what function the particle *le* has to play in this field of interacting forces; 'currently relevant state' only partially answers this. The problems we have with the CRS analysis, as commented upon, are seven in all. We list them here for ease of reference:

1   problems with the notion 'current' as used in the definition
2   complexities involved in the notion 'change' of a 'state of affairs'
3   the use of 'correcting a wrong assumption' as an indication of speaker's communicative intent
4   the need to generalise the notions 'a more extensive project', and
5   'about which both speaker and hearer know'
6   further details needed for project 'closure' and project 'opening'
7   need for project details in the discussion of 'finality'

Among the five categories of situation distinguished by Li and Thompson, the first category, 'change of state of affairs', lists various frequent occurrences but the nature of the change is varied and needs further explanation. Of the remaining four categories 'correcting a wrong assumption' is a description of a speaker's communicative intention, whereas 'progress so far' and 'what happens next' both involve the notions of 'project' and 'shared knowledge'. In 'progress so far' the existence of 'a more extensive project or venture' is explicitly mentioned, yet the notion is not applied during the discussion of 'what will happen next'. And neither is the notion 'extensive project' used in the analysis of 'total contribution to the conversation at that point'.

2.2.2 Andreasen (1981)

Andreasen regards verbal *-le* as a Perfective Aspect marker and sentential *le* as a marker of Perfect Aspect. In this he follows Li and Thompson (1981). However, Andreasen is also inspired by Hopper (1979) on the use of aspect (perfective and imperfective) in distinguishing foregrounded portions from backgrounded portions of a narrative, and claims that in Chinese narrative,

> foregrounding and backgrounding are accomplished almost exclusively through aspectual opposition.
> (Andreasen 1981: 15–16)

Based on his studies of 11 examples of written narrative, Andreasen (1981: 98) identified verbal *-le* as a typical foregrounding device and assigns the particle *le* the function of marking background distinctions. Unfortunately, his data for the latter claim are extremely limited. The example he gave was taken from a modern short story. It reads:

(2.34) [quote from *Yao* 'Medicine' by Lu Xun; written in 1919]
    a. Qiutian de houbanye
    autumn DE after-half-night
    b. yueliang xiaqule
    moon down-go-LE
    c. taiyang hai meiyou chu...
    sun still not have rise
    'A very early autumn morning. The moon had gone down; the sun not yet risen,...'

The identification of LE in this context as the particle *le* is acceptable, but not unproblematic. It should also be argued that this example also involves marking with verbal *-le*. The simultaneous use of both verbal *-le* and the particle *le* is a very common feature in Chinese, as we will see, but this at least urges a modification of background and foreground marking as proposed by Andreasen. So, in essence we agree with Andreasen that aspect marking in Chinese is used to signal 'background' and 'foreground' distinctions. The objections we have is that his proposal was limited to narrative discourse and that we want to generalise the distinction across all types of verbal interaction. What is needed therefore is a clarification of what is meant by 'foreground' and 'background'. We will argue that the opposition between 'background' and 'foreground' is not enough, that a third dimension is involved here – that of the immediate situation – and that these distinctions

38 *Previous studies*

are moments in the building of mental models, which are handled by different operators for different purposes (see Chapter 8).

2.2.3 Chang (1986)

Chang (1986) extends his investigation of the function of the particle *le* (Chang 1982) to the discourse level. He used the technique introduced by Spanos (1979) and collected the responses on uses of the particle *le* in expository and narrative discourse – first from 26 native speakers and followed that up with a survey in which the responses of 80 native speakers were examined. Chang (1986: 144–6) proposes that *le* should be understood as a discourse-final particle rather than simply a marker of 'change of state'. Chang's findings can be summarised as follows:

A *Le* functions as a discourse-final particle in Mandarin Chinese.
B Native speakers of Chinese may vary in their use of *le* as a discourse unit is not an absolute division.
C *Le* can be used as a marker between sub-topical discourse units since such units are relative.
D *Le* is not used in cases where expressions of classical flavour are included.
E *Le* is not used in factual statements, where a 'change of state' reading is undesirable.

These observations are limited to expository and narrative discourse, and the question therefore remains to what extent the distinctions can be applied to conversational and other exchanges. Before considering that question we will first examine Chang's findings one by one.

A: Le *functions as a discourse-final particle in Mandarin Chinese*

Chang (1986: 129) claims that *le* is in general withheld until the end of a discourse block is reached. For example:

(2.35) (In answer to the question why nobody wants to marry a certain lady)
Ta nianji da, ren ye chou, suoyi mei ren yao le.
She age big person also ugly so no man want LE
'She is old; she is also ugly; so no one wants (her) now.'

Chang further observes that this is a tendency, but is not necessary.

B: Native speakers of Chinese may vary in their use of le

Since a discourse unit is not an absolute division, native speakers of Chinese may vary in their use of *le* depending on their organisation of events, and their world knowledge. *Le* may also be used deliberately to further segment a large discourse unit into smaller ones as shown in (2.36), where each clause constitutes an independent discourse unit, equal in weight.

(2.36) **Ta nianji da le, ren ye chou le, suoyi mei ren yao le.**
She age big LE person also ugly LE so no man want LE
'*She is old (now). What is more, she is/has become ugly (now). So no one wants (her) now.*'

Chang (1986: 129) observes that addition of *le* 'puts more emphasis on each individual piece of information'. This view is supported by others (cf. Chang 2001; Huang 1988), and we agree. However what remains to be explained is why this is so and how this relates to the core function of the particle defined as 'discourse final unit'.

C: Le can be used as a marker between sub-topical discourse units

Le can be used as a marker between sub-topical discourse units since such a unit is relative. However, the more closely related the information units are under the same topic, the less likely *le* is to be used. As the following example shows, native speakers avoid using *le* before the discourse internal tie *na* (that, in that case) and between closely knit co-ordinate structures: *zong-heng-qian-li* (proceed-one-thousand-mile) and *wu-wang-bu-li* (succeed-without-difficulty).

(2.37) a. **Yexu, xingyunde zai rensheng de diyi-ge yizhan**
perhaps fortunately at life DE first-M stage
b. **jiu yudao du-ju-hui-yan de Bole** .04/.00³
then meet unique-possess-clever-eye DE Bole
c. **na ni jiu keyi zong-heng-qian-li** .00/.00 **wu-wang-bu-li le**
.73/.15
that you then can proceed-one-thousand-mile succeed-without-difficulty *le*
(Lun Zhiyu)
'*Perhaps, at the first stage of your life, you fortunately meet Bole – i.e. the person who can really appreciate your talents. In that case, you can (then) proceed freely and smoothly (in your career) and succeed without any difficulty.*'

The presence of the connective *na* ('in that case') in clause (c) makes the marking with *le* at the end of clause (b) unnecessary. Only 4 per cent of the respondents chose to add *le* at that position, whereas no one opted for adding the particle in the middle of a longer expression (Chang 1986: 132). The statistics support the idea that this should be taken as a whole, as one 'discourse unit'. However, doubt remains as to the strength of the association.

When there is a clear case of a discourse final unit, the number of respondents choosing that option is still not 100 per cent. Other factors still need to be involved.

D: Le is not used in cases where expressions of classical flavour are included

In Chang's survey only a small number of respondents (27 per cent) considered *le* obligatory in his (3.44i), given below as (2.38i), which is discourse final but contains expressions of classical flavour:

(2.38) i **Zhi-yi wo shi fou canjia, dei kan xuexiao neng fou buzhu erding** .27/.15
as-to I be not attend must see school can not subsidize decide
'*As for myself, my attendance depends on whether the school will subsidize or not.*'

Chang (1986: 138) observes that only a limited number of respondents (27 per cent) opted for the use of the particle *le* at the end of this clause. He suggests that classical expressions such as *shi-fou* ('be or not') and *(dei kan) . . . erding* ('(must) depend on') are responsible for this effect. When these expressions are replaced by colloquial expressions the occurrence of *le* is more natural. Chang therefore concludes that 'style' is a factor in determining the use of non-use of *le*.

Chang claims that *le* is not used in the context of expressions of classical flavour, but does not explain why this is so. He still needs to appeal to the notion that 'classical style' is perceived differently by different people. We will address this issue again in our presentation of the core pragmatic function of the particle *le*.

E.: Not used in cases where factual statements are asserted

In general, *le* is not used in cases where factual statements are asserted, specifically when its presence would result in an undesirable 'change of state' reading. For instance, *le* is neither appropriate in (2.39), nor in (2.40) because adding *le* forces the clause to have a 'change of state' reading (Chang 1986: 141):

(2.39) f. **wo hui ba nei-ge xin ming-dan (baokuo zengjia han buchong de)**
I will take that-M new name-list (including add and mend DE)
yijiao gei xia-jie zhuban de ren.
transfer to next-M responcible DE man
'*I will transfer this new name list (including other added members) to the next organiser.*'

(2.40) A: **Ni shi neiguo ren?**
You be which-country man
'*What's your nationality?*'

B: **Wo shi Zhongguo ren.**
I be China man
'*I'm Chinese.*'

Talking about the particle *le* as something that can be added to a sentence, after which one can study or imagine various readings without simultaneously activating the wider context of interaction, interpersonal relationships and world knowledge, is a simplification of the object of study which can only result in just that – a simplified version of what is actually going on. The opposition between 'factual statements' and 'change', however, has been made elsewhere as well. For instance, Li and Thompson (1981: 291ff.) observed that *le* is not used 'when the speaker is simply asserting a general truth in an ordinary conversation where no change is involved', 'change' then to be taken as 'change of state of affairs'. This observation is valid and supported by various linguists, and we therefore will address this issue in different terms at the end of our study.

Also, the discourse-final function of *le*, as presented by Chang, is entirely separated from its function of indicating a change of state/status. According to Chang (1986: 36) while 'six of the seven meanings Chao has proposed for le can, in fact, be grouped under one category: change of state/status', only one, the 'obviousness' *le*, in which a change of state is hardly detectable, 'is needed for discourse reasons'. To him *le*'s discourse function, specified by him in terms of topical units, and its semantic function of indicating a change of state, belongs to two conflicting systems. And it is the conflict between the two that explains the withholding of the particle in discourse. This separation makes one wonder where the discourse function of *le* comes from. As will be argued in detail later, this function of *le* in wrapping up a segment of discourse, in our view, is the result of the interplay between *le*'s function of common-ground co-ordination and the information content being co-ordinated. All Chang's examples can be seen in this way.

Conclusion. Chang's account of *le* as a discourse-final particle is a step forward from previous sentence-oriented studies of *le*. The discourse perspective now offers explanations for the use of *le*, which were not available on the sentence level before. To a great extent, a discourse account of *le* explains why *le* regularly occurs in certain places, where it can occur, and why *le* is withheld in some other places where it could have been used when studied within the boundaries of a sentence. However, Chang's account of *le*, while strong on discourse grounds, falls short in a number of areas and we have raised the following four points of criticism:

42 *Previous studies*

1 Undue emphasis on topical units as structuring the use and non-use of *le*.
2 No explanation for the influence of the factor 'classical style'.
3 The separation of *le*'s semantic function and discourse function.
4 Lack of interactive element.

Chang's data are from written narratives and expository prose, which limits the application of his findings to more dynamic interactive situations in which *le* functions most actively. The static view of discourse in terms of topical units does not account adequately for the particle's role in social interactions.

2.2.4 *Van den Berg (1989)*

Van den Berg (1989: 157ff.), in his functional analysis of Chinese grammar based on Dik (1989), attributed the notion 'actualiteitswaarde' (*actuality value*), to the particle *le*, and the notion 'event viewed as a whole without attention to internal phasing' – that is, perfectivity marking – to the verbal -*le*. In the following we will focus on his discussion of the particle *le*. In Functional Grammar (FG) a distinction is made between 'actions', 'processes', 'positions', and 'states' (cf. Li 1990; Tai 1984; Vendler 1967). For Chinese, predications with *shi* ('be') and *you* ('have; to be there') were added as predicates involved in 'identifications' and in the description of 'existential situations'. Three claims were made that concern us here, (1) the generalised function of the particle *le* is 'actuality' marking, (2) the particle *le* is not constrained by the predication type, and (3) face-to-face situations need to be distinguished from imaginary or future situations, as in narratives. For the use of *le* in the latter situation type, the term 'verplaatste actualiteit' (*displaced actuality*) was used (van den Berg 1989: 172). The three points of interest to our discussion are:

1 Generalised function is 'actuality' marking.
2 No constraint by predication type.
3 'Current' situations to be distinguished from 'displaced' situations.

The concept 'actuality' was illustrated with examples involving 'states' and 'actions', was discussed in relation to the 'perfective', 'experiential' and 'durative' aspect, to the enumerative *le*, and a variety of other predicates. In all instances the claim for *le* as a form of 'actuality' marking could be held. The notion was further detailed as implying 'that the speaker directs the attention of the hearer to an upcoming change', or, as in 'short replies', 'the speaker acknowledges the actuality value of what has just been said' (van den Berg 1989: 158).

The claim that the particle *le* is not constrained by the predication type that is involved with the assertion of *le* is a hypothesis, which still stands to be rejected. 'Positions' as 'stable situations' tend to reject the use of *le*, but 'change' does occur as in the following example:

(2.41) [identifying the time of an appointment]
Ta fumu bu zai le.
s/he parent not be-her LE
'His parents have died.'

The opposition between 'current' situations and 'displaced' situations is an alternative for the opposition proposed by Li and Thompson (1981: 240) between the 'current situation' and 'some particular situation', which, as we argued, are in essence the same – they are 'current'.

Among the various examples of 'actuality' discussed, three distinctions are of particular interest. These examples illustrate the function of *le*:

1 as 'remarkable'
2 as 'countering' an opinion
3 in short 'replies'

Van den Berg (1989: 158) observed that a phrase can be marked with the particle *le* when the speaker perceives something as communicatively 'remarkable', as a deviation from the 'normal' situation. The same point was made by Li and Thompson (1981: 250). This study will prove that observation to be correct. The second distinction is a conversational one, and indicates that in conversational exchanges the particle *le* can be used in 'countering' an opinion. That too will be corroborated by our data. Finally, the third distinction continues this line of thought and points to the function of the particle *le* in 'short replies', as in *Dui le* ('Indeed').

The concept of 'actuality' is cognitive in orientation and involves the notion of a 'project', of 'what is going on now' (cf. Li and Thompson 1981: 240, 270). The concept, however, was not explicitly related to that notion and not further related to a particular theory. As a result, the concept remained intuitive and did not reach its full explanatory potential. It was also argued, following Dik (1989, 1997), that the particle is added to a fully formed predication, and as many examples show (cf. [*Fangzi le* 'It's a house (now)]' in Li and Thomspon (1981: 248), that claim is too strong. The theory of functional grammar (Dik 1997) therefore cannot handle distinctions like those of the Chinese particle *le* appropriately. What we need therefore is a new theory that addresses the kind of interaction problems that in the Chinese language are marked by the particle *le*.

2.2.5 *Bisang and Sonaiya (1997)*

Bisang and Sonaiya (1997) examine the Chinese particle *le* and Yaruba *ti* in a typological framework for describing Perfect and its interaction with pragmatics cross-linguistically. They are particularly interested in explaining the motivations of the core functions of markers with a very broad and consistent functional range in different languages. They believe that 'starting from the broadest functional range it may be possible to find a whole sequence of delimitations which finally lead to the core functions' (1997: 143). In their proposed framework, Reference to a Preconstructed Domain is the distinction on the top level with the broadest function providing

> the overall functional explanation into which Perfect is embedded. The function of Reference to a Preconstructed Domain can be restricted on a next lower level by the semantics of the verb or the state of affairs based on it. Reference Time further reduces the functional range of Reference to a Preconstructed Domain until we finally get at the core function of Perfect in which Reference to a Preconstructed Domain is restricted to Current Time.
>
> (Bisang and Sonaiya 1997: 157)

According to this framework, since the Chinese particle *le* has a flexible reference time, which may be a time other than the speech time, the particle doesn't mark Perfect in a narrow sense. Its reference time is not limited to current time. The particle may be said to mark Perfect in a broad sense. However, as Bisang and Sonaiya point out (1997: 155), 'reference time is not relevant in all the functions subsumed under the term *Currently Relevant State* by Li and Thompson (1981) and by Li et al. (1982)'. They do not think, for example, reference time is relevant in functions of Closing a Statement and Correcting a Wrong Assumption proposed by Li and Thompson and by Li *et al.* For this reason, Bisang and Sonaiya conclude (1997: 157) that the function of the Chinese particle *le* 'transcends the function of Perfect' and is entirely governed by discourse pragmatics as argued by Ross (1995: 123). Therefore, Bisang and Sonaiya argue against Li and Thompson's claim that the Chinese particle *le* can be seen as an exponent of the Perfect aspect, and propose that the function of Chinese *le* can be subsumed under a more general pragmatic function of Reference to a Preconstructed Domain, of which Perfect is a subcategory:

> Chinese le has to do with the speaker's reaction towards certain presuppositions or even expectations with regard to a given situation. Thus, the presence of le in any utterance always points to some state of affairs that is already in existence or supposed to be in existence. Chinese le is based on the idea of a Preconstructed Domain. By using le, the speaker expresses her/his reaction or attitude with respect to a given Preconstructed domain. This reaction can be characterized in terms of Conformity or Confrontation (Franckel 1989).
>
> (Bisang and Sonaiya 1997: 145)

In terms of conformity and confrontation Bisang and Sonaiya reanalyse the five categories of examples of Li and Thompson (1981) and Li *et al.* (1982); for example, conformity encompasses one part of Closing a Statement as postulated by Li and Thompson (1981: 283–9), whereas the whole function of Correcting a Wrong Assumption suggested by Li and Thompson (1981: 263–70) is an instance of confrontation.

Bisang and Sonaiya's analysis of particles has established a typological framework for describing the grammatical category, with Perfect as its core in different languages, and provided a cross-linguistic context for the Chinese particle *le*'s function. The pragmatic function of Reference to a Preconstructed Domain proposed by Bisang and Sonaiya is an insightful notion in cross-linguistic analysis. With regard to the Chinese particle it reveals, from a different perspective, the essence of its function and the pragmatic context in which it occurs, complementing Chao's 'new situation' interpretation. While Chao's 'new situation' points out the effect of using *le* with its focus on the resulting new state, Reference to a Preconstructed Domain stresses the previous situation which pragmatically determines the possible occurrence of *le*. The unequivocal identification of a Preconstructed Domain as the prerequisite of the use of *le* represents a step forward in our understanding of the use of *le*. Furthermore, the introduction of the speaker's reaction or attitude into the study of *le* paves the way to a more interactive model of interpretation beyond sentence-oriented studies.

However, the notion of Preconstructed Domain as 'some state of affairs that is already in existence, or supposed to be in existence' still needs to be related to interactional behaviour, and is still very much sentence-oriented as it was put forward for the description of the grammatical category of Perfect and beyond. The effect of using *le*, as proposed by Bisang and Sonaiya, either conformity or confrontation, is speaker-focused with the addressee out of the scene. Therefore the notion of Reference to a Preconstructed Domain does not meet the needs for an account for *le*'s functions in interactions. Furthermore, a Reference to a Preconstructed Domain account does not seem to include the use of *le* in Chao's past events. In their terms, it is not clear what preconstruct it could be for the use of *le* in the following example:

(2.42) Wo zuotain qu Zhang jia chi fan le.
I yesterday go the Zhang' eat meal LE
'*I went to the Zhang's for dinner yesterday.*'

This is what Chao called an 'isolated event in the past' and can be used to initiate a conversation with a friend. It simply says 'I went to the Zhang's for dinner yesterday', and 'having dinner at Zhang's' may be either a rare or common practice of the speaker. There doesn't seem to be a preconstructed domain with which the *le* utterance confirms or confronts. To understand this use of *le*, the notion 'common ground' is needed: it urges the addressee to add this piece of information to the shared common ground. As we will argue in Chapter 3, the particle plays a more dynamic role than 'referring'. It appeals to the addressee to co-ordinate common ground on the basis of information provided, which has a series of implications for the ongoing interaction.

In summary, Reference to a Pre-constructed Domain by Bisang and Sonaiya (1997) is a great contribution with regard to the description of Perfect and its interaction with pragmatics cross-linguistically, but the speaker-oriented notion is still not wide enough for dynamic interactions and for a unified account for *le*'s function.

2.2.6 *Liu (2001)*

Liu Xunniang has studied the various uses of the particle *le* for more than 15 years (Liu 1985, 1990, 2001), and in a recent paper offers an interesting overview of various related issues (Liu 2001). Particularly interesting is that in most of his analysis he takes an interactive approach and observes, for instance, that *le* expresses *for the addressee* a 'new state of affairs', a 'new situation', a 'change', or a 'new insight'. He also makes the following observations:

1 *le* does not express 'change'; the 'change' is related to a previous situation
2 *le* expects a 'background situation'
3 *le* forces inferences from general knowledge
4 'new' means 'new' for the addressee
5 expression is often just a reminder
6 generalised function is 'past tense'

Liu observes that the idea of a 'situation change' is the result of a comparison between the 'current situation' and a 'background situation'. This is particularly easy to see, he notes, in the case of negative sentences. When somebody says, *Wo bu qu Huashengdun le* ('I am not going to Washington anymore'), it is clear that he had a plan to go there. More importantly, Liu realises that this remark is made because the speaker changed his plan, and is aware that the addressee cannot know that and therefore informs him about the change. Using *le*, therefore, he concludes, is always a form of speaking with 'intent' (*yongxin*). The 'something before', he further observes, does not have to be expressed, it can be inferred from general knowledge, as is the case when someone states, *Wo bu zai jiehun le* ('I won't marry again'), which implies that he was married before and probably is divorced now. Also, *le* expresses the 'new situation', which implies knowledge of the previous situation; but the details of that previous situation are not in focus, the new situation is in focus. Finally, the new situation can be the result of a change of some sort, but does not have to be. Often the expression with *le* is no more than a reminder, as when it rained for some time and a person reminds the other that it is raining now *Xia yu le* ('It's raining').

In his discussion, Liu uses the concepts of speaker 'intent' and the notion of the 'co-operative principle' (*hezuo yuanze*), thereby showing that he approaches the study of language from a conversational or interactional perspective. His theoretical orientation, however, was not made explicit, and he has to admit that in some cases the meaning of the sentence with and without *le* is the same. We do not follow him here. In our analysis, the addition of the particle always implies a request to the Addressee to do something, even though, admittedly, in a 'displaced' situation, as in a narrative, the effect of that request on the reader can be minimal. Liu, however, does not make such distinctions.

In the final part of his paper, Liu addresses two issues: that of the 'excessive' interpretation of *tai* ('too'), and the relation between the particle *le* and past tense. In examples such as in *tai gui le* ('too expensive!') *le* is associated with 'excessiveness', whereas in an expression such as *tai hao le* ('very good'), the idea of excessiveness is absent. Liu relates this distinction to 'common sense', and we will partly follow him here. We will take this issue up again in Chapter 8. Liu discusses the issue of 'tense' in Chinese on the basis of an example given by Li and Thompson (1981: 242): *Ta chuqu mai dongxi le* ('She's gone shopping'). Liu observes that in this case a past-tense reading is necessary. Removal of *le* results in a future action: 'She will go shopping'. This difference encourages Liu to look for an explanation, and he observes on the basis of a study by Zhao and Shen (1984), who translated 1,364 English sentences into Chinese, that more that 50 per cent of the past-tense cases received a *le* marking in Chinese. On the basis of this evidence Liu concludes that the core function of the particle *le* in Chinese is the marking of 'past tense'. We do not agree with him on this for the simple reason that the argument is based on the comparison of sentences out of context, which in a pragmatic language such as Chinese is not fitting. We will present a different explanation to deal with past-tense readings. Our main argument is the shared common ground between interactants at the moment of interaction. For details we refer the reader to Chapter 8.

2.3 One morpheme functioning at two different levels

Unlike Chao and other scholars who distinguish two morphemes in the same form of LE, researchers in this camp claim there is one single LE in the language and identify one underlying function of LE at two different levels. The different functions or meanings associated with the particle *le* and verbal *-le* are derived from the interplay between the basic function of LE and the situations, scopes, or domains LE interacts with. In Table 2.2 we list six different approaches in this line of thinking, followed by separate discussions of each.

Table 2.2 One function of LE

Researcher	Function of LE	Situation/scope/domain
Thompson (1968)	Event boundaries	Event, the whole series of events
Spanos (1979)	Realisation	One (event) of a series Particular verb or phrase
Huang (1988)	Boundary marking	Entire clause or sentence Proposition
Huang and Davis (1989)		Contribution to conversation
Shi (1990)	Relative anteriority	Bounded situations Unbounded situations
Chang (2001)	Aspect marker with different focus location	Pre-culmination point Post-culmination state
Yang (2003)	Perfectivity viewpoint	Non-stative situations Stative situations

2.3.1 Thompson (1968)

J. Thompson (1968) acknowledges that tense is not a feature of the Chinese verb system and attempts to 'give a unified view of the temporal particles' by formulating a concept of time, which is in contrast with the tense concept of the Indo-European languages. He proposes to think of Chinese time as 'a series of discontinuous units occurring in succession ... like separate beads coming one after the other on a string' (1968: 70). What is unique about those strings as compared with the English concept of a 'chain of events' is that those beads, with definite boarders at each end, do not link into each other, and the 'event' being described may not coincide with either of the time units, but rather may involve the passing from one into the other. For instance, *ta si le* ('He is dead') involves the passing from one time unit of his being alive to another time unit of his being dead (Thompson 1968: 71). Based on this proposed Chinese concept of time, Thompson formulates the function of Chinese temporal particles: the marker *le* as an event boundary marker; *ne* as a marker for an event whose boundary has not occurred; *guo* as a marker for passing through an event and *zhe* as a marker for two events occurring simultaneously. Thompson's recognition of the fundamental difference between tense in European languages and the temporal system in Chinese, and the need for an alternative framework to explain the Chinese system, is insightful and points to the right direction for any endeavour to decode the Chinese temporal system. And his effort for a unified view of the temporal particles is inspiring, though we don't necessarily agree with him on the functions of the particles suggested. In the following we will limit our discussion to Thompson's account for the marker *le*.

Thompson proposes that *le* indicates an event boundary and that this unifies the uses of *le* for completed actions, for change of state and for incipient actions (1968: 73). As for another use of *le*, which attaches to a verb, it is not 'entirely clear' to him, but 'it seems to indicate that the event is in fact one of a series'. However, Thompson states, when the sentence-final *le* is used in addition attention is focused on the final boundary of the whole series; for example, *ta chi-le sanwan fan le* ('he has eaten three bowls of rice') (1968: 74–5). This is a remarkably early observation (1960s) with regard to the function of the particle *le*. Thompson's view on the marker *le* has since been followed or adopted to various degrees by Chinese linguists such as Li and Thompson (1981), Huang (1988), Huang and Davis (1989) and Shi (1990). We agree in general with Thompson's concept of Chinese time and his view on *le* as an event boundary marker, but feel it is not enough to account for *le*'s function in discourse. Specifically we have the following three points of criticism.

1 As an attempt to account for the Chinese temporal system, Thompson's discussion of the particle *le* is sentence-oriented. Since the use of particle *le* is basically a discourse phenomenon, his generalisation can hardly be supported by discourse data. As we will demonstrate in this book, although the occurrences of *le* coincide with event boundaries, their actual use is mainly regulated by discourse and cognitive factors.
2 As an event boundary marker *le* does not take into account the user of the marker (i.e. the speaker's intent and goal in interaction). Thinking of Chinese time units as beads on a string, Thompson says: 'The particular string being considered depends on the event being described and the speaker's attitude toward it.' This is an important observation, but the speaker's attitude and how it affects the use or non-use of *le* is missing in his formulation. As it is, the use of *le* is unmotivated in terms of interaction.
3 Thompson's formulation of *le* attached to a verb as an indicator for an event being one of a series is too narrow, and his account for the use of *le* attached to a verb involving the complement containing a numeral is inadequate. According to him, the reason for the use of *le* in such cases is that 'the complement of the verb is a series or one of a series'; for example, *ta chi-le sanwan fan* ('He ate three bowls of food'). Similarly, Thompson explains the occurrence of *le* in *ta chi-le neiwan fan* by considering *neiwan* as one of the series: *zheiwan, neiwan, disanwan* ('this bowl', 'that bowl', the 'third bowl'). Such an imagined series, however, does not exist in any native speaker's mind when the utterance concerned is said, and the use of *le* in *ta chi-le yiwan fan* ('He ate one bowl of food') for a single event obviously contradicts this claim.

To sum up, Thompson's view on *le* as marking an event boundary, including the boundary of one event of a series and the final boundary of the whole series, has captured the essence of various uses of the marker *le*, and has since influenced the scholars who defend the one morpheme position regarding *le* in the literature. However, the sentence-based interpretation in a temporal system framework does not reveal the underlying motivation of such markings in discourse and related cognitive processes in verbal interaction, which will be the focus of our discussions in the following chapters.

2.3.2 *Spanos (1979)*

Spanos (1979) was the first to propagate a strict pragmatic approach to the analysis of *le* in Chinese. In his approach he followed Stalnaker (1978), and sees pragmatics as the study of linguistic acts in certain contexts. He proposes a one-morpheme LE schema, in which LE structures

> involve a change concerning the realization of some particular action, process, quality, or state of affairs. The change relates either to the internal semantic structure of the particular verb or phrase involved or to the entire clause or sentence to which LE is attached. In the former case, the realization of the change is construed in the sense of the completion of the particular action, process or quality associated with the verb or phrase. In the latter case, the realization is construed in the sense of a shift in the speaker's perception or attitude towards the particular predication and the state of affairs associated with it.
>
> (Spanos 1979: 73–4)

That is to say, when the change concerns the internal semantic structure of the particular verb, LE in the structure is the so-called verbal *-le*; when the change relates to the entire clause or sentence, LE is the so-called particle *le*. In both cases, the function of LE is the same. We will shortly outline his pragmatically oriented analysis, and position our own work in relation to this attempt in the application of pragmatics to the study of Chinese grammar. Before doing so, let's look at his data collection method, which is worth mentioning.

To begin with, Spanos was the first to elicit language from a group of native speakers and compare their answers. He presented faculty and staff of the Chinese University of Hong Kong and Chinese members of the Chinese Langue Teachers' Association (62 respondents: 37 males, 20 females and 5 unspecified; 39 reported Mandarin as the dialect in which they had the greatest proficiency) with 12 sentences and paragraphs (1–7, 8–12) from which all occurrences of LE (*-le/le*) were deleted. As an illustration we reproduce test sentence one (T1), which shows three positions for the insertion of 'word' *le* (suffix *-le*) and 'phrase' *le* (particle *le*). The respondents were requested to indicate if they considered the insertion of LE at each position [___] 'necessary' or 'optional'. By leaving the position 'blank' they indicated that the form LE could not be used at that position.

(T1)   *chi __ fan you zuo __ yihui cai huilai __*

The glossing for this sentence is [eat __ rice also sit __ a-moment only-then return __], and this immediately makes it clear that respondents can have different interpretations of such sentences, since each respondent constructs his own cognitive environment within which his interpretation holds. One can think of 'I eat first, sit for a while and only then go home', or, 'After eating and sitting for a while they went home'. The results of this exercise showed that the variation between respondents was indeed large:

1   Native speakers varied greatly as to the places that were 'necessary' or 'optional'.
2   They agreed more as to the positions in which the form LE should not be used.

Sometimes a relatively large number of respondents chose the same patterns as in test sentence five:

(T5)   *Wo zuotian kan __ dianying le* (22 subjects)

This is a classic example of the use of the particle *le* for what Chao (1968: 798) called an 'Isolated event in the past'. In his analysis, Spanos did not make a sharp distinction between 'word' *le* and 'phrase' *le*. He pointed at certain regularities in the uses of the form LE, but did not come to a conclusion as to the nature of the variation or the reasons for not using LE. The interesting aspect of Spanos's study is the pragmatic orientation and the endeavour to look at the results from the perspective of Grice's (1975) 'Co-operative Principle'. Spanos (1979) therefore was the first to move away from the 'sentence' and 'truth value' perspective and look for an explanation to language as a co-operative enterprise. When Spanos (1979) looked at Grice's five maxims of (M1) Appropriateness; (M2) Quantity, be informative not over-informative; (M3) Quality, speak the truth, what you say must be based on evidence; (M4) Relation: be relevant; (M5) Manner (obscurity, ambiguity, be brief, be orderly), he tried to demonstrate that (M5) Manner was the maxim that triggered the uses of LE in Chinese. The form LE is used to make things clearer, to solve ambiguity, and to communicate in a brief and orderly way. This reasoning is correct as we will demonstrate later, but the maxims model everyday conversation and do not make it possible to detail the function of the form LE in Chinese. However, as we will see shortly, (M4) 'be relevant', is used in the study by Li and Thompson (1981) and they point to the role of the particle *le* by ascribing it the function of creating 'special relevance'. Despite the criticism expressed, Spanos's claim that the form LE in Chinese is a pragmatic phenomenon stands. That position is also supported by more recent studies of Chinese grammar which point at the fundamental pragmatic nature of Chinese grammar (Huang 1996; Wu

1998). Despite its failure in explaining the various uses of LE, we support Spanos's approach and will demonstrate that the form LE is a pragmatic phenomenon (and not a strictly syntactic one) which can only be understood through a study of verbal interaction.

2.3.3 Huang (1988); Huang and Davis (1989)

Lilian Huang identified the marker LE as a form of aspect marking, and proceeded by comparing aspect marking across several languages. She concluded that in aspectual languages an opposition is created between a DIFFUSE and FOCUSED orientation, and that marked forms are 'focused'. She also takes position in the one-morpheme or two-morpheme debate for the form LE and supports the one-morpheme hypothesis. Both forms of LE (the 'word' le and the 'phrase' le) are ASPECT markers, which differ only as far as their DOMAIN is concerned. 'Word' le is a form of event/verb marking whereas 'phrase' le marks units of a higher level, propositions. As to the function of 'phrase' marking Huang concludes that the SUBSTANCE of this is 'boundary' marking. Whenever the particle le is used it is intended to signal a 'boundary'.[4]

The boundaries Huang has in mind were illustrated by the following examples (1988: 199–200):

(2.43) [no indication of context]
   a. Wo shua-le ya jiu shang chuang
      I brush-LE tooth then ascend bed
      'After I brush my teeth, I will go to bed.'

   b. Wo shua-le ya jiu shang chuang le
      I brush-LE tooth then ascend bed LE
      'After I brushed my teeth, I went to bed.'

   c. Wo shua-le ya le. Wo shang chuang le
      I brush-LE tooth then ascend bed LE
      'I've brushed (my) teeth. I went to bed.'

In example (a) the boundary is set at the 'event' level, and what follows there is future time. In the (b) example the boundary is set at the 'event' level and at the 'proposition' level, and therefore a past reading is necessary. The third example, finally, must be seen as a sequence of two 'proposition' boundaries, the first of which also has an internal event-level boundary.

In the discussion Huang (1988: 177–8) observes that the idea of le marking a 'change of state' has its limitations. In the following example the situation was as indicated and remains like that; the situation does not 'change':

(2.44) [group of friends entering a restaurant]
   Tai chao le!

too noisy LE
'It's noisy here!'

The question we would like to see answered is 'what' does the speaker do here, and 'why' does he do so. Huang answers this by claiming that this is a form of 'boundary' marking, but to us there is more involved here and we find her argument not easy to follow. In other words, there are still some questions to be answered other than those of 'boundary' and 'focus'.

The Huang (1988) approach and analysis is continued in Huang and Davis (1989). In the latter source the proposal for one function for both the particle *le* and the verbal *-le* is maintained (that of marking a 'boundary'), which 'unifies *le* in all its occurrences into a single element' (Huang and Davis 1989: 149). In their view,

> le signals the presence of an interruption, which may be, for example, the boundary of an event, the disruption which occurs upon suddenly recognizing a previously unnoticed entity, or any other circumstance appropriate to this semantics.
>
> (Huang and Davis 1989: 143)

Applying the concept of 'boundary' or 'interruption' to Li and Thompson's (1981) examples, Huang and Davis demonstrate that a boundary can be drawn in each case, and that the boundary may extend its relevance beyond the propositional content to the speech situation marking the boundary of the speaker's contribution. This shows that:

> the domain of le, even broadened from event/verb to propositions, remains too narrow. The very experience of the speakers is subject to the organizing force of le, and it is this extension of the relevancy of le beyond the substance of utterance, to the substance of experience, that accounts for the perception encapsulated by Li and Thompson in their phrase 'Currently Relevant State', and by others in the use of the English Perfect as mode of translation.
>
> (Huang and Davis 1989: 146)

Although their discussion is on the aspectual system, Huang and Davis relate the discourse function of the particle to its function of marking an 'interruption' and recognise that *le*'s function goes beyond an utterance and is realised at the level of the speech situation. Huang and Davis point out correctly that the domain of *le*, even broadened from event/verb to propositions, remains too narrow, and needs to be extended beyond the substance of utterance to the substance of experience. This is a significant step away from sentence- or text-oriented studies of the particle. However, limited by their own framework of aspectual system, as well as Li and Thompson's examples and position on *le*, Huang and Davis stop short of providing a satisfactory account for the particle. Nevertheless, their points are well taken and we agree with both the one-morpheme hypothesis and with the proposal of different domains at which the two representations of the form LE function. As to her claim for a generalised function, we agree with that too, but find that 'boundary marking' is merely a different way of representing the notion 'change of state of affairs', and is not supported by any pragmatic arguments. Also, boundaries marked at the event level and at the proposition level are differently motivated. That motivation is missing. Specifically we would like to make the following two points of criticism:

1. Huang and Davis's argument for *le*'s boundary marking is not a strong one due to their limited data set. All the examples analysed are those from Li and Thompson's that can be interpreted as a kind of change of state in general and when the boundary is a natural feature of such situations. Nothing has been mentioned about past events, or what Chao calls 'isolated event in the past'. In cases such as *zuotian wo kan dianying le* ('I went to cinema yesterday'), we wonder where the boundary is to be drawn since there is no specific previous state implied as in a change of state. Neither can this be interpreted as a sudden realisation of something previously unnoticed. An interruption in such cases is difficult to find.
2. To say that the particle marks the presence of a 'boundary' or 'interruption', though semantically meaningful, is unmotivated in terms of interaction. What is the purpose of marking a boundary or interruption in discourse? Can this marking be described in terms more relevant to the use of *le* in verbal interactions? In this book we will develop a framework based on interactions in which various uses of *le* can be accounted for in a uniform way: the function of 'common-ground co-ordination'.

2.3.4 Shi (1990)

Shi (1990) attempts to offer a unified account for both *le* and *-le*, and proposes that 'perfectivity' (the completion of a situation) and 'inchoativity' (the inception of a situation), are not semantic primitives but rather are the result of the interaction between two components of aspect marking: the 'boundedness' of the sentence and the relative temporal status of the situation expressed by the sentence, where 'bounded' implies that 'temporal, spatial, or conceptual limits are placed on it' (Shi 1990: 101). Shi claims that 'Mandarin Chinese is a language that grammaticalises "relative anteriority" rather than "perfectivity" and "inchoativity"', and that the form *le* is used for that purpose (Shi 1990: 103). This idea is interesting, of course, and merits an evaluation, since it offers an alternative to English-based grammar study and draws the attention to techniques of grammaticalisation, which different languages use in different ways.

'Relative anteriority' makes clear that the particle *le* takes up different functions in different environments. When the particle *le* occurs with bounded situations it signals anteriority relative to the terminal boundary, indicating perfectivity, a meaning associated with verbal *le*. In contrast, when it occurs with states, which are unbounded, the anteriority is relative to the initial boundary, generating the meaning of inchoativity or inception associated with 'sentential *le*'. Does this hold across the various usage types reported by Chao (1968)? Shi admits that an apparent exception to this temporal analysis of LE is the usage where *le* expresses a non-temporal sense of 'excessiveness' (Chao 1968). However, he argues that cases such as *Tang (tai) xian le* ('The soup is too salty'), which indicates a 'comparison between the speaker's expectations and deviation to the extreme from such expectations in reality', are derivable from the inchoative use of the particle. He also observes that 'contexts' seem to be able to provide terminal boundaries to otherwise unbounded activities (Shi 1990: 113–14).

With the latter observation, we come to the heart of our objections. Shi looks at the form *le* as a grammatical phenomenon, and seeks an explanation for the presence of *le* in a grammaticalisation process, isolated from any context. For instance, Shi claims that with *le* in different positions in a sentence, synonymy is possible. He lists the following two examples as proof:

(2.45) [sentence, no context]
    a. **Tamen ba wo jiaole qilai**
    they ba I call-LE rise
    b. **Tamen ba wo jiaoqilai le**
    they ba I call-rise LE
    'They woke me up.'

We need to observe, however, that the two sentences are synonymous only in isolation, not in discourse. They would favour different contexts in actual use. A clause describing a subsequent action of *tamen* ('they') such as *jiu chuqu le* ('then went out') would fit (2.45a) perfectly, but not (2.45b). Shi, though, has to admit that 'context' plays a role, but seems to consider this an outlandish concept that is not part of linguistic analysis, and only called upon when other means fail. We look at this in a quite different way. The understanding of context is crucial, and only when we understand that concept can we contribute to understanding the function of the particle *le*. It is also for that reason that we included Shi's discussion in this chapter. We conclude then that Shi's account of *le* may be useful in the study of aspectual systems, but we cannot support it since it is not adequate for the particle's discourse function, as 'anteriority marking' is unmotivated in terms of interaction.

2.3.5 *Chang (2001)*

Chang (2001) approaches grammar via 'event structure'. As part of that study he also analyses aspect in Chinese. In the analysis of events, five phases are distinguished, a 'pre-inception phase' is followed by an 'inception point', which in turn is followed by an 'extension' and a 'culmination point'. The completion of this sequence allows the recognition of a 'post-culmination' point. Chang (2001), like Huang (1988), recognises that aspect is a form of focus marking, and claims that the focus position of 'word' *le* or verbal *-le*, and 'phrase' *le* are complementary. The focus of 'word' *le* is prior to the culmination point; it is a focus marker of the action. The focus of 'phrase' *le* (or post-sentential *le*, as Chang calls it), is on the post-event state, after the culmination point.

Chang (2001) defends the idea of one aspect marker LE in Chinese. The difference between the two *le*'s is a matter of focus location – one location is at the pre-culmination point, whereas the other is at the post-culmination state. In general, we agree with this analysis. It is also in agreement with proposals made by Huang (1988) and Huang and Davis (1989), who differentiated between an event/action focus and proposition/experience focus. The problems we have with this analysis, however, are two. The analysis is sentence-oriented and does not consider contextual features. That means that the questions as to 'when' to focus and 'why' to focus are still open, and those questions need to be answered before a core pragmatic function of the particle *le* can be identified.

2.3.6 Yang (2003)

The latest to defend the one-morpheme stand is Yang (2003), who examines LE's function within a system of temporality containing three independent and interacting components: situational aspect, viewpoint aspect, and temporal location. Following Thompson (1968) and Shi (1990), Yang (2003: 77) argues that 'there is a single particle LE regardless of its syntactic position and its basic function is to encode the perfective viewpoint'. Since verbal *-le* is widely recognised in the literature as a perfectivity marker, Yang's argument focuses on the relationship between perfectivity and meanings related to the use of the particle, such as perfect, CRS, inchoativity and change of state. Quoting Bybee *et al.* (1994), Yang argues that, historically, perfective developed from perfect as a result of meaning generalisation. Perfective is therefore more general than perfect, which is perfective with speech time as the reference time and thus a better candidate for the basic function of LE. On the other hand, as evidenced by languages in the world (Bybee *et al.* 1994), as perfective morphemes became more grammaticalised and their meanings more generalised, they were extended from non-stative situations to stative situations. The availability of perfective viewpoint to stative situations in Chinese, Yang states,

> removes the obstacle to treating sentential LE as encoding perfectivity and paves the way for explaining closely related functions such as CRS in terms of the way perfective viewpoint interacts with stative situ-

ations and if necessary in terms of the working of pragmatic principles.

(Yang 2003: 92)

Unlike Thompson and Shi, Yang does not claim that the meanings associated with the particle *le* in the literature are a direct outcome of the interaction between LE's event boundary or anteriority/perfectivity marking and stative situations, but applies language-use principles – in particular of conversational implicature and of informativeness, to explain the related meanings on the basis of the interaction concerned. It turns out, according to Yang, that meanings such as change of state, CRS and inchoativity normally attributed to the use of particle *le* are not the basic meaning of the particle but derived from language-use principles as conversational implicature.

In general, we agree with Yang in his analysis in terms of temporality, but do not think the perfectivity encoding function proposed for the particle is adequate to account for its discourse functions in interactions. The temporality framework means that the object of Yang's investigation is sentences, isolated from context and interactants. Although language-use principles are used to explain related meanings of the particle, they are only called for 'if necessary' and only for semantic purposes. Overall, encoding perfective viewpoint to a stative situation is still unmotivated in terms of interaction, and thus our research questions as to why and when the particle is used remain unanswered.

2.4 One morpheme and one function

The fourth position, finally, goes one step further and makes the strongest claim. Just one morpheme is recognised, not two, and there is also one underlying function. Such claims are closest to the written Chinese form, which has the same character for both verbal *-le* and the particle *le*. An early claim to this effect was made by Rohsenow (1978), who, in a strictly syntactic analysis, proposed the atomic predicate 'come about', as accounting for both occurrences of verbal *-le* and phrase *le*. More recently this position was defended by Li (1990: 20–1), who claimed that /*le*/ signals 'contrast to previous state'. For him 'the speaker focuses on a new state of the situation that contrasts with a previous state'. He supported his claim with the following example (1990: 20–1):

(2.46) [child playing with blocks]
 a. Qiche zhuangdaole daqiao.
 car hit-down-LE bridge
 b. Qiche zhuangdao daqiao le.
 car hit-down bridge LE
 'The car knocked down the bridge.'

Li Ping (1990: 22) justified this example and the unified translation by claiming that the bridge being 'down', stands in contrast to a previous state in which the bridge was not yet down (e.g. in which the action of 'knocking' was still taking place). His argument rests on the idea that what is expressed in language has a direct relationship with the development of events in reality. Such a position we find untenable. A more acceptable contrast is that between a cognitively recognised situation in which the bridge is still up and a new situation in which the bridge is knocked down. In child's play both the (a) and (b) expressions can be used. The example is well chosen. However, the conclusion that the uses of *-le* and *le* are interchangeable is based on translation equivalence, which interestingly is constructed by the author himself. Translation unfortunately cannot count as proof. We will claim that when using these forms the speaker is making two different assertions: 'goal attainment' and 'situation change'. Common-ground co-ordination is requested in the latter not in the former. The details of that analysis we will provide in the following chapters.

2.5 Summary

In this chapter we have examined previous studies of the particle in works we consider major contributions to the field. We distinguished four different positions with regard to the identity and functions of the particle *le* and verbal *-le*. We started with a discussion of the detailed analysis of the seven uses of the particle *le* made by Chao (1968). Among these, Chao's examples of *le* in expressing 'past events' and 'obviousness' were especially interesting. However, his analysis presents no unified view on the particle. Nevertheless, Chao's analysis has been a rich resource for further research, and there are various adoptions of the analysis in terms of 'change of state' (Ding *et al.* 1961; Lü 1991; Chang 1986; Li, 1990; Sybesma 1999) which features a contrast with a previous state. We then examined Li and Thompson's Currently Relevant State (CRS), an endeavour from a functional perspective, which links the use of *le* with five categories of situations. Li and Thompson have included in their analysis several notions that are essential to the description of *le*'s function, but their CRS as a unified view on the particle is still unsatisfactory. We also scrutinised other authors' contributions to our understanding of the particle, such as Reference to a Preconstructed Domain and the pragmatic implication of Conformity and Confrontation (Bisang and Sonaiya 1997), the marking of discourse units (Chang 1986), actuality-value marking (van den Berg 1989), and the necessity for the domain of *le* to be broadened to include 'Experience' (Huang and Davis 1989). We find, however, that the various accounts either over-specify the situations or leave out some uses of *le* for a unified interpretation of the particle. In general, they do not clarify the absence or occurrence of *le* in discourse segments, and, above all, they do not relate the use of *le* to an ongoing interaction or examine *le*'s function in the dynamics of an interactive context. It will be our task to demonstrate in this book how these various notions discussed in the literature interrelate and how they can be brought under one overarching view by focusing on the function of the particle in everyday interaction and outlining its relationship to the cognitive notion of 'shared common ground'.

3 The particle *le* and the study of language use

In the previous chapter we introduced various views on the use and function of the particle *le* in Mandarin Chinese. The discussion opened with a listing of possible uses by Chao (1986), and was followed by a search by various scholars for a unified and generalised answer to the various functions listed. Proposals were 'Co-operative Principle', 'Background Marking', 'Currently Relevant State', 'Discourse Final Unit', 'Boundary/Interruption Marker', 'Actuality Marker', 'Boundedness' and 'Relative Anteriority', 'Conformity or Confrontation with a Pre-constructed Domain', 'Past-Tense Marker', and 'Focus Marker'. What seems to be shared in these various analyses are the notions 'background', 'change', 'current', 'boundary'/'interruption', 'focus', and 'actuality' or 'now'. We will discuss the particle *le* in this chapter with these concepts in mind. We feel that what is needed, however, is a theory that integrates these various notions. In this chapter, therefore, we will construct a model that is capable of doing just that; that is, integrate 'background', 'current', 'boundary', and others. We will do this in three steps. First, we will introduce a criticism of 'sentence'-based models (Clark 1996). Thereafter, we will introduce the theory of 'mental models' (Craik [1943] 1967; Johnson-Laird 1983), and discuss various concepts of a theory of language use proposed by Herbert Clark (1996). We feel that the distinctions made in the latter two theories are crucial for an understanding of the various uses of the Chinese particle *le*.

3.1 Language as product or action

The study of 'language use' was blocked by de Saussure a century ago ([1917] 1967) when he created the dogma of linguistics as the study of language structure (*linguistique de langue*) at the expense of the study of language use (*linguistique de parole*). He called the latter enterprise 'ridiculous'. However, an approach to the study of language based on 'language use' seems only natural, and in the eyes of laymen even obvious (cf. Gu 1999). Two broad traditions can be recognised. The first is a 'language-as-product' tradition that endeavours to broaden its scope by starting from sounds, words, and sentences – the products of linguistic analysis (cf. Brown and Yule 1983; Schiffrin 1987 for criticism of this approach). The second tradition is known as the 'language-as-action tradition', which stresses language as a form of action (cf. Clark 1996). The latter tradition developed from work by philosophers (e.g. Austin 1962) and sociologists (e.g. Goffman 1974) and focuses on real-time interactions in actual situations. In this study, our orientation is on the second 'language-as-action' tradition. Before going into some more details as to the basic tenets of a theory of language use, we will list some of the more obvious drawbacks of a language-as-product approach to discourse and communication.

3.1.1 'Sentence' grammar

In the 'language-as-product' tradition, phonetic analysis reveals phonetic elements as vowels and consonants, which combine into syllables and are the formal representation of words and word combinations, which in turn combine to form 'sentences'. And 'sentences' supposedly mean something. They represent the world as it is by being 'true' or 'false', and are combined in cohesive stretches of discourse. However, as Clark observes,

> Sentences, words, and phonetic segments are treated as linguistic types abstracted away from speakers, times, places, and circumstances in which they might have been produced.
>
> (Clark 1996: 56)

'Linguistic types' represent 'potential uses'. They need to be realised in specific 'contexts' in order to mean something for somebody. 'Sentences' therefore seldom mean uniquely. 'Ambiguity' is rampant, and 'contexts of use' need to be called upon to clarify matters.[1] However, in sentence grammar the nature of context is never specified in advance. Rather it is a non-systematic determinant in solving cases of ambiguity, and its application almost comes as an afterthought.[2]

Further, sentences are assigned 'truth values' and presented as representing an objective world of some sort, which can be independently constructed by both speaker and addressee (cf. Lakoff 1987 for extensive criticism). In our view that is a fallacy. It, for one, neglects the concept of the world as a mental representation as it was already recognised in medieval times. It is a view that still stands and is corroborated by the theory of language models presented below. Other drawbacks of the sentence approach are:

1. It is impossible to extend theories of language structure to the discourse level. This means that language-structure theories need to develop a different type of theory to handle discourse structures (cf. Clark 1996; van den Berg 1998, 2001; van Dijk 1997).
2. Sentences abstract away from actual circumstances, including speaker and listener identity, time and place, and other features of the current scene (cf. Clark 1996; Hymes 1974; Levinson 1992).

3   Sentences are analysed as static objects and such constructs have no clear relation to a dynamic environment (Gu 1999).
4   Non-verbal behaviour and non-verbal communicative acts such as eye gaze, winks, body posture, smiles, and other manifest actions are considered not relevant for sentence analysis (cf. Argyle 1975; Clark 1996).
5   Sentences are first of all seen as logical formulas, and context is not considered a legitimate part of the language analysis enterprise. As a result there is little information in that tradition as to that variable (Clark 1996: 57; Lakoff 1987).

As this listing of objections to the sentence as a unit of linguistic analysis shows, it does not seem a very good choice to start the analysis of a little-understood phenomenon from such a scarred base. We will need an alternative, and it is such an alternative that we will develop in this chapter.

3.1.2 Language as action

In this study, we follow proposals that see language as 'action' (Biq 2000; Brown and Yule 1983; Levinson 1992; Schiffrin 1987). In contrast to the 'product tradition', the 'action tradition' focuses on what people do with language, and it is recognised that discourse isn't merely linguistic structure (cf. Austin 1962). Speakers, listeners, times, places, and the circumstances of utterance are taken into account. Attention is also paid to action continuity, the simultaneity of certain actions, and the timing of utterances and other actions. The action tradition takes communicative intent as its point of departure, and interactions proceed through a variety of communicative acts (Grice 1975; Gumperz 1982; Schiffrin 1987; Tomasello 2003). It includes display behaviour, eye gazes and other types of communicative signalling, as well as utterances (Argyle 1975). But foremost in the approach is an endeavour to understand the prominent role that needs to be given to 'context' (cf. Stalnaker 1978). We will defend the view that context is a cognitive prime which takes the form of a 'mental model' and appeared very early in animal evolution as a means for functional adjustment to the environment (Craik [1943] 1967; Johnson-Laird 1983, 1993). This difference in focus implies that cognitive organisation and social structure are part of the knowledge base of the action analyst. He realises that he deals with conventions and that the social world as we know it is 'constructed' and not objectively available or describable from a sentence perspective (cf. Berger and Luckmann 1967; Geertz 1983; Searle 1995). An action orientation leads to a fundamentally different approach to communicative behaviour. The major implications of the approach will be spelled out now. We will start with an exposition on the theory of mental models, and thereafter introduce main concepts of the theory of language use proposed by Clark (1996).

3.2 The theory of 'mental models'

Sentence grammars are constructed in analogy to the natural sciences, to logic, to proposition theory, to information-processing theories, and others. However, founding a linguistic model on theories of other sciences is a dangerous undertaking, as the past hundred years in linguistic theorising demonstrates. Neither the natural sciences, nor logic or proposition theory can be used as a firm basis for the construction of a language use model.

3.2.1 Mental models

If 'sentences' cannot be taken as units from which to describe the world, how should the relation between speech and the real world be perceived? Craik ([1943] 1967) provided an alternative view in his discussion of the nature of scientific explanation. He argued that sense data (the Cartesian view) is too limited a source for guidance in real life, and he proposed that rather it is 'mental models' people hold about the real world that guide them in their actions and interactions. This notion was further taken up by Johnson-Laird (1983), who developed a basic theory of mental models. In his presentation, language users build mental models of the real and interactive world they participate in. They also build models of discourse worlds, which may be real or imaginative, but are constructed in a similar way. The latter are 'embedded models'.

All living beings with a central nerve cord are capable of building a 'mental model' of the world that surrounds them, and it is such a mental model that determines success or failure of real-world activities. Mental model build-up therefore must be fast and effective. The price for failure is high, it is either starvation or sudden death. Model construction is further based on background knowledge, and on notions of what is 'possible' and 'permissible'. Our study of the particle *le* sees uses of the particle as a special way to influence the state of an addressee's current mental model (a real world model or an imbedded discourse model). The various chapters of this book will illustrate the way in which the particle *le* functions in relation to these models, given certain narrowly defined contexts (procedural discourse, children's stories, conversations). In this section we will focus on the process of mental model build-up, and on the notions of 'relevance' and 'update semantics'.

3.2.2 Mental model build-up

The construction of a current mental model is based on lower-level processing which in the course of time has developed as an adequate mechanism for the rapid build-up of mental models. There are, however, a number of constraints that restrict the construction of a mental model. Johnson-Laird argued that the construction of a model takes place on the basis of a finite set of conceptual primitives (person, kinship, shape, colour, motion, and others), which give rise to a corresponding set of semantic fields (each occupying a part of the lexicon). In each semantic field there is a limited number of 'semantic operators' (time, space, possibility, permissibility, causation, intention) that are involved in the build-up of more complex concepts. As an example, if people watch an event 'they focus their eyes on it for an interval of time, with the intention of seeing what happens'. We take it that the 'intention' criterion also allows the recognition of another person's 'intent', which is the basis for mutual understanding of all living beings (cf. Grice 1975; Tomasello 2003). This leads to a rather general question as to the intent that is recognised when the particle le is used in Chinese. We define that intent as 'co-ordinate now' on the content being signalled.

In constructing models of situations, 'possibility' and 'permissibility' are evaluative criteria. A model can be accepted because it is 'possible', given a person's knowledge of the world. However, it will also need to pass a 'permissibility' test, given a person's understanding of the moral demands in his social environment (Johnson-Laird 1983: 414). If any of these tests fail, the model will not be accepted and a recalculation process will start, during which lower-level input mechanisms will receive special attention and the processing will be scrutinised in more detail. The strength of the present formulation is that it is based on an explicit model of psychological and behavioural functioning, taking evolutionary developments across species into consideration, and specifying changes as regulated by explicit procedures. After interpreting a message, interpreters calculate the implications of the identified message content. An interpreter can then decide to act or to take time to reason further. 'Reasoning' and 'decisions to act' are therefore inherent to the functioning of mental models, and it is that which makes them excessively powerful representations of cognitive activity (cf. Johnson-Laird 1983: 399ff.). In our analysis of the function of the particle le in Chinese we will demonstrate that the particle is not directly linked to action (as in commands) but rather to co-ordination on background frames that are available in cognitive processing. We will call those frames the structure of shared common ground.

3.2.3 Relevance, background and update semantics

In 'mental model' build-up, 'relevance' is created by the 'interpretation function'. A verbal expression is vocalised under the expectation that its projection will be recognised and can be meaningfully related to the addressee's current mental model. The interpretation function calculates the extent to which a projected message can be cognitively incorporated. It looks for something that in a given situation is both 'possible' and 'permissible'. 'Possible' implies that the calculation is possible given certain real-world limitations and background understandings or expectations. 'Permissibility' checks the social controls that have been agreed upon in the society.

The notion of 'project' further allows the introduction of the idea of 'background' or 'common ground'. The shared perceptions and believes in a group or culture are stored as background knowledge. Apart from 'projects', this background knowledge contains information on historical facts, social conventions, norms and procedures (how to do things) (Clark 1996; Longacre 1996). It further has a local, person-oriented component, and a global, culture component. This background knowledge is the source against which verbal projections are made and is used by the interpretation function to make sense (what is possible and permissible) out of what is being signalled. Projection and interpretation presuppose the existence of shared common ground (Clark 1996; see also section 3.3).

The presence of shared background knowledge, however, does not guarantee that the intended relation between a projection and an intended interpretation is made. Signalling is as a rule under-specified. Each language user is treated by the interactant as a forensic expert, a person who can make much out of little and sometimes out of almost nothing, like a head nod or a cough. Therefore failure is common. Many interpretation procedures, however, are routine. They developed over time as successful ways of getting things done. When a mistake is being made, this becomes manifest from the display behaviour of the message intender (who may look surprised, worried, happy, or disappointed). This display behaviour acts as feedback and allows the interactants to agree as to the project being hinted at (cf. Clark 1996; Johnson-Laird 1983).

The semantic theory that handles 'updating' is a form of model theoretic semantics in the sense that the truth function is between an utterance (participatory act) and a model. No validation is sought in terms of the reality status of referents. A set of recursive procedures relates projected information to a mental model. In 'update semantics', furthermore, there is for each situation only one mental model and each new utterance is evaluated in terms of its relation with the current model. There is therefore no need for selection among a variety of possible models (worlds). Model construction is controlled by a small set of semantic operators, which can be seen as the end result of practical experiences in everyday situations. When it rains there is no need to spell out the effect 'you will get wet' since this information is available as common causation in the world knowledge that continuously feeds information during the construction of a mental model.

In empirically valid data the focus is on the relation between utterances and mental models, as produced and constructed by interactants. Mental models can only be constructed when they are supported by information stored in background knowledge, which functions as a real-world encyclopaedia. The interpretation function of the model that tries to make sense out of what is being said is crucial. The way in which that function handles expressions with the particle *le* thereby becomes the central question in our research. We will seek the answer in a 'common-ground co-ordination' operation, the background of which we will describe in the next section.[3]

3.3 A theory of language use

In this section we will introduce some of the central concepts of a theory of language use as proposed by Herbert Clark (1996). This theory further details the nature of an action theory of language. We will discuss respectively the notions 'joint activities', 'joint actions', 'joint projects', and introduce conversations as 'extended joint projects'. In the next section (3.4) we will discuss 'common ground', and 'joint construals'. This theory is discussed as background knowledge for understanding what unites the various uses of the Chinese particle *le*.

3.3.1 *Joint activities*

In an action approach, verbal interaction is a *joint activity*, a form of 'joint action' (Clark 1996). In conversations, signalling behaviour can be observed as running back and forth between the interactants. It is a 'joint activity'. In this section we will introduce the notions 'activity role', 'activity goal', 'co-ordination', and 'boundaries'. In a 'joint activity' the interactants in each case are involved in something different. A person presenting himself before a service counter becomes a 'ratified participant' in a 'joint activity' when he remains consistently within his 'activity role'. He is expected (under an obligation) to select an item on display and pay for it. The activity role of the salesperson is a different one. He is under an obligation to sell the goods on display at the indicated price. When a friend is present, he can be a 'side-participant'. He too may stand in front of the service counter or stall, and have the potential of becoming a full participant. A bystander is an eavesdropper and not a ratified participant in any interaction. He does not have an activity role (Clark 1996: 14, 34).

Participation in a joint activity is *goal*-directed. It is focused on the achievement of a 'dominant activity goal' (Levinson 1992). As part of the overarching dominant goals there may be other goals, such as 'procedural goals'; that is, the goal of going through the various moves fast and efficiently. There also may be 'interpersonal goals' when attending to contacts with other participants and being polite or impressing them. Finally, they may have 'private agendas' when working the situation for their own benefit and for instance being extremely polite but actually trying to get rid of somebody. Joint goals furthermore need to be *public*. Lining up or presenting oneself before a service counter creates a public goal that can be recognised by all concerned. 'Personal goals' remain 'off record'. Trying to impress someone is self-defeating when stated explicitly. It is hidden from view (Clark 1996: 34–5).

A fundamental aspect of a joint activity is *co-ordination* of action. One form co-ordination can take is the use of 'conventional procedures'. In a business transaction part of the exchange is regulated this way. Verbal expressions are directly related to these procedures. They are developed over time to make the execution of the business transaction smooth and efficient. We will address non-conventional procedures in the next section on 'joint actions' (Clark 1996: 35–6).

A shopping expedition may consist of a sequence of smaller 'joint activities'. Each 'joint activity' has a *boundary* that needs to be 'jointly established', as is the case in a business transaction, a conversation or a party. Participants in an activity will need to come to believe that they are participating in the same activity. A 'boundary' therefore will tend to appear at the 'entering' side of a 'joint activity' as it does at the 'exiting' side. A more extensive central body of interactions is often established by the interactants in between these. The business transaction mentioned above can be taken as an example. The customer entered into the joint activity by positioning himself publicly in front of the stall, and the interaction was terminated via an exchange of goods and money, which was the dominant goal of the 'joint action', followed by the customer taking the goods and moving away from the stall. Language is organised in such a way as to facilitate the management of these boundaries. A 'conversation' is frequently 'entered into' via a 'greeting' and 'exited' from via a 'pre-ending' and a 'goodbye'. All major languages can be expected to have procedures for 'entries' and 'exits' in and out of a variety of 'joint activities' (Clark 1996: 36–8).

The various distinctions introduced in this section are as follows:

- activity roles
    'ratified participant'
    'side participant'
    'bystander'
    'eavesdropper'
- activity goals
    'dominant activity goals'
    'procedural goals'
    'interpersonal goals'
    'personal goals'
- activity co-ordination
    'conventional procedures'
- activity boundaries
    'jointly established'
    'entering'
    'exiting'

The implications of this exposition for an understanding of the uses of the particle *le* are as follows. In each case, a 'joint activity type' needs to be recognised. We did so by selecting as data sources 'procedural discourse', 'children's stories' (narratives), and 'conversations'. In each instance, we need to be able to identify the 'activity roles', and 'activity goals' (dominant goals, procedural goals, interpersonal goals), and understand the need for 'boundary negotiation' and 'activity co-ordination'. Against this background it becomes understandable that the particle *le* became associated with the idea of marking a 'boundary', or a 'break', or 'interruption' (Huang 1988; Thompson 1968). However, as this discussion shows, there is far more involved than a 'boundary' alone.

3.3.2 *Joint actions*

'Joint activities advance mostly through joint actions.' In this perspective, 'verbal interaction' is a form of *joint action* and includes such things as 'asking questions, making requests, making assertions, making references'. In a 'joint action', individual actions need to be co-ordinated. That is why such actions are called 'participatory actions' (Clark 1996: 60). Speech acts therefore are 'participatory actions'. The need to co-ordinate on verbal interaction with another participant is absent in 'autonomous actions'.[4] This analysis makes clear that speaking does not consist of a series of 'autonomous actions'. This is most obvious in conversation where interactants take turns and react co-temporally on each other's actions. It is also true for lectures. In organising the content of talk, the speaker is aware of the audience and tries to organise the content of his talk in an accommodative way. He intends his audience to follow what he is talking about. While talking, he therefore observes his audience and adjusts his speed of presentation and organisation in accordance with the feedback signals he receives. However, there is a clear difference, the content of the speech is not 'being negotiated'.

Why would people co-ordinate? Quoting the work by Schelling (1960) and Lewis (1969), Clark (1996: 62) argues that people co-ordinate in order to solve co-ordination problems. In joint actions, there are common interests or gaols and people need to co-ordinate in order to satisfy these interests or reach those goals. For co-ordination a cue, also called a *co-ordination device*, is needed (Lewis 1969). 'Co-ordination devices' can take the form of explicit agreement, precedent, convention or perceptual salience. What these have in common is 'joint saliency'. They create 'mutual expectations' among participants. Three further aspects of co-ordination are 'solvability', 'sufficiency' and 'immediacy'. The person choosing the 'cue' (co-ordination device) assumes that his 'cue' can make the addressee converge on the solution of the co-ordination problem he has in mind. He also assumes that the hint he gives is sufficient for the addressee to solve the problem and can do so immediately, or without much delay.

This discussion suggests that in 'verbal interaction' the crucial feature is the 'co-ordination of individual (participatory) actions'. This implies co-ordination of *content* and *process*. 'Content co-ordination' involves uniting 'plans' and 'aims'. Process co-ordination stresses the need to co ordinate actions and to make the resulting 'joint actions' fit a wider 'joint activity'.

'Plans' are executed through harmonisation of the 'physical' and 'mental' means available.

This discussion suggests that the particle *le* in Chinese is a 'co-ordination cue (device)' that requests the addressee to pay special attention to the exchange 'process' at that point in the interaction, and to co-ordinate on the 'content' provided. The speaker holds the view that in the 'joint action' or in the 'joint activity', at the particular point at which the utterance with *le* is used, the information-processing needs special attention. The speaker also finds that the 'co-ordination' can take place on the basis of the 'content' being provided at that moment. We can formulate this line of thinking as hypothesis H1:

(H1) Verbal interactions are 'joint actions' in a 'joint activity'. The particle *le* in Chinese is a 'co-ordination device', which signals that the speaker wants 'information processing' to be co-ordinated at that point in the 'joint action' or 'joint activity'. He assumes that the 'content' he provides is 'sufficient' for the addressee to 'solve' the intended co-ordination issue 'immediately'.

The particle *le*, in this view, is an 'index', which is conventionally used as a 'co-ordination device'. The 'co-ordination issue' is related to a 'shared goal' in a 'joint action' or 'joint activity'. The content selected by the speaker is taken to be sufficient to allow the addressee to solve the co-ordination issue he has in mind immediately. The theory suggests that uses of the particle *le* are somehow related to 'goal attainment' in 'joint activities'. Our data chapters will provide the details of this relationship, and clarify the co-ordination moments that can empirically be attested.

3.3.3 *Joint projects*

Clark (1996: 191) defines a 'joint project' as 'a joint action projected by one of its participants and taken up by the others'. In this section we will address the 'co-ordination' in projects, the nature of 'joint purpose', and the idea of a conversation as an 'extended joint project'. For any 'joint project' participants need to go from a state of not being engaged to being engaged, after which disengagement again follows. Every 'joint project' therefore has at least three parts (Clark 1996: 201–2):

1 *Entry* into the joint project
2 *Body* or main part of the joint project
3 *Exit* from the joint project

In social interaction, an 'entry' often takes the form of a 'greeting' or an 'opening' of some sort. Thereafter a piece of activity follows which counts as the 'main part' of the joint project. A meeting can function as a joint project example: it is opened, conducted, and closed. After exiting from the joint project, the participants are disengaged and free to enter into other projects.

'Co-ordinating' on a 'joint project' involves three project-related features (Clark 1996: 202):

1 Participants
2 Entry time
3 Content

When entering into a joint project, co-ordination involves the recognition of the 'status' certain participants have in the 'joint project' and the 'roles' they will most likely play. The 'entry time' for a 'joint project' is often set by an outside source. This is at least the case for parties, shops, schools and most institutional environments. In personal interactions the entry time needs to be negotiated by the participants themselves. 'I'll meet you at the pub at four.' Given a certain entry time, *synchronisation* between project participants is necessary, and synchronised behaviour is 'normal' behaviour. 'Content', finally, refers to the individual actions that each of the participants is going to take in the 'joint project'. Under normal conditions, ratified 'participants' will 'synchronise' their behaviour with the 'entry time' of the project, and the 'content' of their actions will match the project they are involved in. The question we can ask is what the relation of the particle *le* is with instances of 'participant role', 'synchronisation', and 'content'.

'Joint projects' and the 'purposes' of these 'projects' are not always established in a matter-of-fact way. The establishment is the result of 'negotiation'. The negotiation process can result in four different states (Clark 1996: 204):

1 Compliance
2 Alteration
3 Declination
4 Withdrawal

'Compliance' is the result when the project proposed by A is taken-up as proposed by B. The purpose of a project can also be 'altered' when the interactants agree on a 'modified purpose' they are able and willing to comply with. 'Declination' results when the person being addressed either is 'not willing' or 'not able' to take up the project. In a 'withdrawal' from a project the addressee can ignore a question leading to a new project or change the topic (Clark 1996: 204).

On the basis of this analysis Clark (1996: 205) concluded that 'adjacency pairs' follow from these options and can be seen as 'minimal joint projects':

> Their form comes from what the participants are trying jointly to do and how well they succeed...

'Minimal joint projects' are shaped by the interacting participants, and that explains why preferred responses often are highly elliptical whereas dispreferred responses are linguistically marked as grammatically more complex. 'Alteration', 'declining' and 'withdrawing' are all quite complex undertakings that reflect the mental processing of the participants. Our data will need to make clear the extent to which uses of the particle *le* are related to 'joint projects' (entry, body, exit; participant role and status, entry time, content), 'project purpose' (identification, ability, willingness, mutual belief), and 'project take up' (compliance, alteration, declination, withdrawal).

3.3.4 Extended joint projects

Conversations are generally regarded as complex activities and as a consequence not very well understood (cf. Wardhaugh 1985). Clark (1996: 205ff.) recognises the difficulties related to the notion of conversation, but, in his framework, is capable of pointing out that it is in effect an 'extended joint activity', but one which the interactants create while engaging in it. The interactants do not know in advance what they actually are going to do. 'Extended joint projects' can be seen as a combination of 'minimal joint projects' and, following conversation analysis, three forms of minimal projects can be distinguished (cf. Clark 1996: 206–12; Eggins and Slade 1997: 30),

1   Embedded projects
2   Chaining
3   Pre-sequences

When setting up a 'minimal joint project', speakers often cannot envisage what the obstacles are that a respondent has to deal with. They therefore simply move ahead and let their addressees work out the problems they encounter. This often leads to sequences in which a question is responded to with another question in order to clarify some of the preparatory conditions related to the initiating remark, and thereby a minimal 'embedded' project is created. The second distinction, 'chaining', can be seen as the result of projecting a minimal project. A question projects an answer, but since this is often an assertion, it in turn leads to assent. Clark (1996: 208) gives the following example:

> *Jane:*   do you know when he he'll be back in
> *Rod:*   he's around now, u:m I don't know where he is, at the moment
> *Jane:*   oh.

Rod's response is part of a question–answer pair. His answer, however, initiates an assertion–assent pair. Other three part chains are shown in Table 3.1. 'Chains' of more than three parts are also possible. For instance an 'offer'

Table 3.1 Examples of three-part chains

Chain	Part 1	Part 2	Part 3
Test question–answer–verdict	What's pi?	3.14159.	Correct.
Offer–agreement–compliance	Want some cake?	Yes, please.	Here.
Request–compliance–thanks	I'll have cake.	Here.	Thanks.
Favour–thanks–acknowledgement	Here's your bag.	Thanks.	No problem.

Source: Clark (1996: 208).

projects 'agreement', which projects 'compliance', which projects 'thanks' (Clark 1996: 208).

'Pre-sequences' (Schegloff 1980) are announcements of what is to follow. In this way, the speaker prepares the addressee for what is coming next and thereby allows him some extra time to prepare. An example of a pre-question is (Clark 1996: 209):

> Ann: oh there's one thing I wanted to ask you
> Betty: mhm-

'Pre-questions' create space for preparatory conditions. Other pre-sequences are 'pre-announcements', 'pre-invitations', 'pre-requests', and 'pre-narratives'. A 'pre-announcement' is intended 'to gain consent to make an announcement, a pre-invitation to make an invitation, a pre-request to make a request, and a pre-narrative to tell a story' (Clark 1996: 210).

Concluding, 'embedding', 'chaining', and 'pre-sequences' are different ways of constructing a 'local project'. These are opportunistic ways for creating a more 'extended joint project' and therefore are the basic building blocks for larger conversations.

3.4 Common ground

'Common ground' is a form of self-awareness (Clark 1996: 120). It is a shared basis for communication and can be reflected upon (Clark 1996: 94–5). 'Everything we do is rooted in information we have about our surroundings, activities, emotions, plans, interests' (Clark 1996: 92; cf. Johnson-Laird 1983). 'Joined projects' are similarly rooted. 'It is our common ground and the *sine qua non* for everything we do with others', and this includes language use (Clark 1996: 92). The essential feature of common ground is that it is shared or 'believed to be shared'. Common ground is built over time and has two aspects: *communal common ground* and *personal common ground*. The first relates to the cultural community a person belongs to, the second to his personal experiences with other people in that community. We will discuss these concepts in some more detail in sections

3.4.1 and 3.4.2. Thereafter we will discuss the cognitive status of common ground, and try to detect the implications for the various uses of the particle *le*.

3.4.1 Communal common ground

Communal common ground can be thought of as a large mental encyclopaedia (Clark and Marshall 1981; Clark 1996: 106). Apart from general aspects of *human nature*, this encyclopaedia contains information on *cultural facts*, *conventions*, *norms* and *procedures*. Community members, during communication, base their inferences on this encyclopaedia and the 'cultural facts', 'conventions', 'norms' and 'procedures' stored there. Without it communication is not possible. 'Cultural facts' are those that provide background for the historical and current facts in a community. The basics of science and literature, geography, television networks, newspapers, etc. are part of that section of the encyclopaedia. A society's 'conventions' are those regulations that are merely a matter of doing things in a certain way, such as shaking hands, driving left or right, wearing certain clothing at certain occasions. For a participant in the society, however, driving left or right and shaking hands is also the 'norm'. These conventions regulate his behaviour. 'Procedures' detail the routines of everyday life and also provide the scripts for joint activities such as how to have a meal in a restaurant (cf. Schank and Abelson 1977).

3.4.2 Personal common ground

'Personal common ground' is based on 'joint perceptual experiences' and 'joint actions'. The first of these can be established in three ways: by 'gestural' indications, through the 'behaviour' of an actor in an event, and as a salient 'perceptual event' (Clark 1996: 112–13). A 'rain shower' is a 'salient perceptual event'. We already saw that the particle *le* must be used when such events are reported, as in example (1) on p. 5: *Xia yu le* ('It's raining'). When a colleague at the office walks in the direction of the door his 'behaviour' can be observed, and the 'personal common ground' can be adjusted accordingly. X is going out now. 'Gestural' indications are 'conventional' and 'immediate', often accompanying 'verbal actions'.

'Joint action' forms another basis for 'personal common ground'. Going out together or meeting at a party and talk, are events that count as 'joint actions'. Together with 'perceptual events' (it might have been raining heavily during that particular day), 'gestural events' and 'participant behaviour', they are stored in memory and form a log of personal experiences. The memory log thus contains traces of:

- 'joint actions'
- 'perceptual events'

- 'gestural events'
- 'participant behaviour'

In that memory log, a distinction is also made between 'intimates', 'friends', 'acquaintances' and 'strangers'. The extent of 'common ground' varies considerably between degrees of acquaintedness. This also illustrates that 'common ground' is not given, but needs to be built up with each person. During build-up, much can be inferred from circumstantial evidence. There is natural evidence from a person's 'physical appearance', and some of that evidence is displayed deliberately through dress or behaviour. Other evidence is perceptual input from the 'place or setting' being visited at that moment. Pieces of evidence are 'cumulative'. Over time, 'common ground' is build with various persons, and 'the depth of that ground varies'.

Against this background we can imagine how, during a conversation, the 'common ground' of the participants accumulates. By asserting certain things the interactants intend to add the content of what is asserted to the common ground (cf. Stalnaker 1978). In order to understand the progress of common ground, Clark (1996: 43) divides common ground into three parts:

1 *Initial common ground*
   This is the set of background facts, assumptions, and beliefs the participants presupposed when they entered the joint activity.
2 *Current state of the joint activity*
   This is what the participants suppose to be the state of the activity at that moment.[5]
3 *Public events so far*
   These are the events the participants assume to have occurred in public leading up to the current state.[6]

Initial common ground. In a buying-and-selling situation, the initial common ground is the perceptive input from the settings and the objects being displayed. These will create certain expectations as to the kind of setting this is, the procedures to be followed, the activity roles involved, and the rights and obligations of the people taking up these roles. In proceeding from the initial state, a script of events to be expected is activated (Goffman 197; Schank and Abelson 1977). Furthermore, 'rights' and 'obligations' reflect the value cluster of the culture as well as the legitimations that are used to ratify a particular way of doing things (Berger and Luckmann 1967).

Current state of the activity. When the buying-and-selling situation progresses, certain things change. A shopping basket gets filled, a person presents himself before the counter. The scene changes. However, it is not this kind of predictable change that attracts the use of the particle *le*. In Chapter 2 we observed that several authors proposed that signalling a 'boundary' or 'interruption' is the main function of the particle *le*. What they seem to say is that the particle *le* is used when an 'interruption' of the 'normal' event flow occurs. Both Huang (1988), Huang and Davis (1989), and Li and Thompson (1981) hinted at this. 'Current relevance' in this line of thought then signals that there is an 'interruption' of some sort in the progression of the 'current state of the activity'. What we need to lay our hands on then is the nature of this 'interruption'.

Public events so far. Participants in a 'joint activity 'are aware of the incremental steps and of the major phases of the activity. They keep both an *annotated record* and an *outline record* of joint events. The 'annotated record' traces 'joint events', and groups them into purposeful sequences. When goods have been selected it is time to go to the counter and pay. The 'outline record' can be used to rethink what happened so far (Clark 1996: 47–9; cf. van Dijk 1977). A question that arises here is the relation of the particle *le* with these distinctions. Does the particle *le* index the 'annotated record', or rather the 'outline record', or perhaps both?

3.4.3 *Assertion*

One grammatical feature associated with the use of the particle *le* in an interaction is the force of *assertion* (Wu 2000). 'Assertions' are intended to bring a change about in the 'current common ground'. In the historical development of function assignment this force became associated with uses of the particle *le* (Wu 2000; see also Chapter 4). An 'assertion' is a strong way of stating that something is the case (cf. Grice 1975). Stalnaker (1978: 315) spoke in the same vein when he opened his paper with, 'Let me begin with some truisms about assertions.' Thereafter he listed four aspects of 'assertions':

> First, assertions have *content*; an act of assertion is, among other things, the expression of a proposition; something that represents the world as being a certain way.
>
> Second, assertions are made in a *context*; a situation that includes a speaker with certain beliefs and intentions, and some people with their own beliefs and intentions to whom the assertion is addressed.
>
> Third, sometimes the content of the assertion is *dependent on the context* in which it is made, for example, on who is speaking or when the act of assertion takes place.
>
> Fourth, acts of assertion *affect*, and are intended to affect, the context, in particular the attitudes of the participants in the situation; how the assertion affects the context will depend on its content.
>
> (Stalnaker 1978: 315; italics added)

The idea of 'the world being a certain way' is indicated by the asserted part of the expression. The 'context' mentioned by Stalnaker, we take to mean 'common ground'. This assumption is not without reason, since Stalnaker explicitly comments on this notion in his paper in terms of 'common knowledge' or 'mutual knowledge' (Stalnaker 1978: 320). We therefore also take this to mean that a new piece of 'common ground' is being asserted. This can be relatively easily observed during phases of 'build up of common ground' when participants assert pieces of 'personal common ground' such as names, region of origin or profession.

Not all pieces of common ground are equally justified. They vary as to their quality of *evidence*. Evidence can be of different types; it can be 'perceived', 'assumed', 'believed' or 'known'. The strength of the evidence can also vary. 'Perception' can generally be claimed to provide 'strong evidence', on the basis of which it can be inferred that another person 'knows' something. Accumulation of 'knowing' leads to a 'feeling of knowing' and to a 'feeling of others knowing'. Both have shown to be very accurate (see Clark 1996: 98, 111, and the various sources quoted there). 'Assumptions' and 'belief' are based on personal ('I assume') and communal ('we believe') experiences.

3.4.4 *Common ground and* le

The discussion so far shows that 'common ground' has a 'cultural component' and a 'personal component'. The first provides agreement on 'human nature', 'cultural facts', 'conventions', 'norms', and 'procedures'. The latter complements the former with personal relationships and information that is accumulated during actual interactions. The 'initial common ground' develops into the 'current state of the activity', whereas 'public events so far' have been stored in memory. The memory log also contains traces of 'joint actions', 'perceptual events', 'gestural events' and 'participant behaviour'. Together they form the basis for successful communication. All interaction presupposes the existence of an 'initial common ground'. This latter observation is reminiscent of claims for a 'previous state' or 'pre-constructed domain', which we encountered in Chapter 2 (cf. Bisang and Sonaiya 1997).

We noted that the particle *le* is frequently used in 'assertions' (Wu 2000; see also Chapter 4). Its usage therefore is dependent on the 'context', and intended to 'affect' that context. The question then is 'in what way' does it affect the 'context'/'common ground'? We seek an answer in the relationship of the particle *le* with the common ground (cultural and personal), and will focus on the connection with the 'current state of an activity' and 'public events so far'. Are there certain moments at which 'common-ground co-ordination' with the particle *le* is conventionally requested, and, if so, 'why' at the points at which they occur and not at others? We can further ask what the relationship is between uses of the particle *le* and the 'evidence' for the 'assertion'. Can the assertion be based on 'perceived', 'assumed', 'believed' and 'known' pieces of evidence, or are there limitations for establishing a relationship between the particle *le* and 'common ground'?

3.5 Conversations

Conversations can be seen as 'extended joint projects', as the sequencing of 'minimal joint projects'. 'Minimal joint projects' are 'locally managed' and 'opportunistic'. The latter concepts try to grasp the idea that a conversation is not planned, but 'emerges' as one goes. Co-ordination is 'local', and proceeds from one 'minimal project' to the next. Furthermore, the progress is under 'joint control'. A 'project proposal' can be 'altered', 'declined' or 'withdrawn' from, and needs 'commitment' to become a 'joint proposal'. In this section we discuss what it takes to be 'committed', how we see 'politeness' and 'autonomy', and how 'topics' enter into the 'conversation'. We begin with a closer look at the structure of conversation and discuss 'continuity and organisation'.

3.5.1 Continuity and organisation

Conversations, just as actions, are 'continuous' and perceived as having a certain 'organisation', both at the level of the 'minimal project' and at the global 'joint project' level. 'Continuity' implies that the co-ordination proceeds from one 'minimal project' to the next. In a conversation the interactants need to co-ordinate on:

1. the co-ordination problem,
2. the solution, and
3. the moment of response.

And they need to do so moment by moment, and from one phase to the next. Each interaction and each phase needs to be timed. Speaking early or answering late also reveal personal characteristics in relation to the current co-ordination problem (Clark 1996: 82–4).

How is the body of a conversation 'organised'? 'Conversations tend to divide into sections' (Clark 1996: 330). The sequence is from not being engaged to being engaged and not being engaged again. This implies that there is always an entering section and an exiting section in a conversation, with the body of the conversation in between. When we compare 'personal conversations' and 'business conversations', the latter appear to be more structured. 'Business conversations' tend to have an 'informative phase' and a 'performative phase'. During the latter 'new facts' ('Okay, I'll buy this one') are created to which the participants have committed themselves (Steuten 1998). What emerges as a 'personal conversation' is a sequential order of 'minimal joint projects', which also can take the form of 'embedded' minimal projects, 'chaining', and 'pre-sequences'. Upon 'entering', an 'opening' section emerges and on 'exit' a 'closing' section (Clark 1996: 331). We can list the various distinctions as,

Personal conversations
Opening
  'Minimal joint project'
  'Minimal joint project'
  . . .
  [embedded minimal project]
  [chaining]
  pre-sequences]
  . . .
Closing

Each 'minimal project' poses a co-ordination problem. When that is solved, a moment of response must be selected.

3.5.2 *Projects and commitment*

A conversation, as an 'extended joint project', crucially depends on the establishment of *joint commitment* (Clark 1996: 289ff.). Proposing a 'joint project' and establishing a 'joint commitment' are two different things. Since 'joint projects' serve 'joint purposes', for A and B to be 'committed' to a 'joint purpose' four requirements must be fulfilled:

1 Identification.
2 Ability.
3 Willingness.
4 Mutual belief.

First, a 'joint purpose' needs to be 'identified' by the project participants. The project participants must be 'able' to do their part in reaching the project goal, and they must be 'willing' to do these parts. Finally, participants need each to 'believe' that their mutual belief as to goal attainment, ability and willingness is part of their common ground (Clark 1996: 203). These are the normal conditions under which a project operates.

There can be, and often are, complications. An addressee may be 'able' but 'unwilling' to share sensitive information, or he may be 'willing' to help out but 'unable' to provide a requested piece of information. In certain social situations 'joint commitment' is regulated by convention. When going to a shop to buy shampoo, for example, the salesperson is 'institutionally committed' to accepting the customer's money in exchange for a piece of the shop's merchandise. In family and friendship relations 'commitment' can be expected but it needs to be negotiated anew for each 'proposed project'. 'Commitment' cannot be expected or claimed in personal encounters with 'strangers'. Such encounters are handled as exercises in 'politeness'. 'Conversations' then are 'joint projects', emerging, and based on 'commitment' by each of the participants.

3.5.3 Politeness

One way to 'encourage commitment' to a 'proposed project' is through *politeness* (Brown and Levinson 1978). 'Politeness' deals with face and with the way it is jointly established, whereas 'face maintenance' is a condition for a smooth interaction (Goffman 1967). 'Politeness' is a central aspect of interpersonal management and is therefore always part of project negotiation (Gu 1999; Dik 1997). The particle *le* can be involved in interpersonal management. A common example is (3.1):

(3.1) [response to invitation]
   Tai keqi le!
   Too polite *le*
   'You don't need to do that!'

Examples as this suggest that special attention is needed for the way the particle *le* affects the management of interpersonal relationships.

3.5.4 'Self-worth' and 'autonomy'

In an interaction, each participant's 'self-worth' and 'autonomy' are involved. An act by A can lower either A's or B's 'self-worth' or 'autonomy'. Examples of these four effects potentially created by A are, respectively, 'criticism' or 'challenges', 'orders', 'apologies', and 'promises' (Clark 1996: 293–4). In schematic form this can be presented as:

Act by A lowers 'self-worth' or 'autonomy' of:

	A	B
'self-worth'	'apology'	'criticism' or 'challenge'
'autonomy'	'promise'	'order'

A question that presents itself is the extent to which the particle *le* can relate to these four contextual effects. Will we find the particle *le* in 'orders', which implies the lowering of an addressee's 'autonomy'? And the answer to that must be negative in principle.[7] And what about lowering of 'self-worth' and 'autonomy'; will a speaker be inclined to use the particle *le* in an 'apology' or a 'promise'? At first sight such uses do not seem to be uncommon. Lowering self-worth is part of Chinese polite culture. 'Challenges' are a form of confronting moves, as we will see, and they too can be marked with *le* (Chapter 7).

3.5.5 Topics

It is often assumed that conversations are organised around *topics*. It is, however, extremely difficult or even impossible to come up with a technical

Table 3.2 Contrasts between essays/speeches and conversations

Essay/speech	Conversation
1 Highly planned	Opportunistic; emergent; locally managed
2 Unilateral control	Joint control
3 Assertions	Various acts

definition of what a 'topic' is (cf. Wardhaugh 1985: 139). Clark (1996: 341) observed that essays and speeches consist mostly of assertions and are really 'what the writer or speaker is talking about'. The contrast with conversations, he states, is at three levels (see Table 3.2).

'Topics' are inferred by interactants and are not necessarily explicitly indicated as a segment of a particular expression (Wardhaugh 1985: 139). They often are hinted at and constructed, shifted and changed as part of the ongoing interaction (cf. Eggins and Slade 1997: 30; Fauconnier 1997). This discussion seems to allow two assumptions. Uses of the particle *le* do not easily occur in 'essays' or 'speeches' (cf. Li and Thompson 1981). The answer seems to be that we are dealing with 'highly planned' 'assertions' under 'unilateral control'. When used in conversations, we expect the particle *le* to occur during moments of 'negotiation', when co-ordination is requested. What we do not know, however, is the kind of acts in which it tends to occur. This is what our study will focus on.

3.5.6 *Joint construals*

When there is a co-ordination problem what is needed is agreement on what is being asserted as part of the common ground, and that implies 'joint construal'. In order to clarify this notion further, we will discuss, in this section, 'action ladders', 'uptake', and 'display', and their relation with uses of the particle *le*. Clark (1996: 147) illustrated the idea of an 'action ladder' by discussing what happens when person A calls an elevator. In doing so A is taking five different actions (see Table 3.3). These five actions are co-temporal, says Clark they begin and end together. The levels, however, have an internal relationship that can be described as 'upward causality', 'downward evidence' and 'upward completion'. The latter concept is relatively straightforward. Actions are completed from the bottom level up through the hierarchy. Between the levels there is a relation of causality, which is purposeful. A puts his finger on the button in order to depress it, which he does in order to activate the button, in order thereby to call the elevator in the expectation that in this way he can make it to come down. Upward completion, furthermore, entails downward evidence. If the elevator comes down A (or someone else) pressed a button, or, when A sees that the light of the button goes on, he knows that he pressed it and expects that an elevator will come.

We noted that speech takes the form of 'joint action'. When the idea of a

Table 3.3 Example of an action ladder

Level	Action in progress from t_0 to t_1
5	A is getting an 'up' elevator to come
4	A is calling an 'up' elevator
3	A is activating the 'up' button
2	A is depressing the 'up' button
1	A is pressing the right index finger against the 'up' button

Source: Clark (1996: 147).

Table 3.4 Example of a joint action ladder

Level	Speaker A's actions	Addressee B's actions
4	A *proposes* a joint project w	B *considers* w
3	A *signals* that p	B *recognises* that p
2	A *presents* signal s	B *identifies* s
1	A *executes* behaviour t	B *attends* to t

ladder is applied to a joint action what results is a 'joint action ladder'. In a joint action ladder there is 'joint action' between both A and B at each level (for a comparison see Table 3.4). The 'joint ladder' too has the features of 'upward causality', 'downward evidence' and 'upward completion'. A must get B to attend to his voice, to 'identify' the signal he presents as meaning something for him, and B will have to 'recognise' what A signals and 'consider' what is being 'proposed'. The proposal regards a 'joint project', which in speech can take the form of a 'minimal joint project'. A special form of a 'proposal' is an 'assertion'. The asserted content becomes part of the conversational record and can be appealed to as common ground (Clark 1996: 118, 120).

How can interactants reach a 'joint construal'? Clark (1996: 192) argues that 'display' is the key. Through 'display', interactants can indicate how they interpret a construal and settle on a 'joint construal'. A speaker means something by his utterance but he can never be completely sure how the addressee is going to take it, to interpret it. The speaker needs 'confirmation' that the addressee has recognised his construal as intended (cf. Clark 1996: 139). When an information exchange actually takes place, the implication is that there is silent agreement on project 'take-up'. The addressee has 'considered' what is being proposed and the act of 'answering' implies project 'take-up'; that is, for instance, the case in a getting-acquainted situation. Answering a question about 'place of origin' implies that the project 'having a getting-acquainted conversation' is 'taken up'. By answering a question, the speaker 'displays' a piece of personal information, and thereby signals that he 'recognised' speaker intent. By revealing that information he 'took up' the 'joint project' of 'getting acquainted'. He might not do so wholeheartedly, but that is an issue of 'willingness'.

How does 'joint construal' relate to uses of the particle *le*? When an answer is given to a question, that acts as 'project take-up', and the particle *le* is not needed, or better, in such 'normal' situations is out of place. It is still to be determined, however, what 'special effect' uses of the particle *le* create and at what level they operate. The particle *le* is being processed at levels 1 and 2. At level 3, a request for common ground co-ordination can be recognised. It seems then that the content of the assertion will determine what is being intended (proposed), a 'joint project', 'interpersonal management', or possibly something else. 'Joint construal' can involve a 'co-ordination problem'. We therefore need to pay special attention to such occurrences in our data, and see how recognition of the 'co-ordination problem' is being 'displayed'. This is of particular importance, since as far as we know 'joint construal' has received no attention so far in the linguistic literature.

3.5.7 Genre

Now we come to the idea of conversation 'genre'. It has been argued that a distinction must be made between *personal* interactions and *institutional* interactions (van Dijk 1997; Fishman 1972). 'Institutional interactions' are 'scripted' social practices; 'personal interactions' are also scripted, but to a far lesser extent (Levinson 1992). Eggins and Slade (1997: 19–20) contrast 'casual' conversations and 'pragmatic' conversations. They observe that pragmatically motivated interactions have a clear pragmatic purpose, and such interactions take place between two people with complementary roles (salesperson and customer, for example). 'Pragmatic conversations' also tend to be short, whereas a 'casual conversation' can go on for hours and often involves 'multilogue' interactions between various people who often form alignments either in support of certain participants or in disagreement with them. They also observed that 'informality' and 'humour' characterise 'casual conversation', whereas 'formality' generally characterises 'pragmatic conversations'.

In the study of 'business conversations' a distinction is made between 'performative' conversations and 'informative' conversations (Steuten 1998). In a 'performative conversation' 'new facts' are created. The latter interaction type changes the interpersonal world by creating a 'new agenda' for future action. In business communications such 'new facts' are often confirmed in writing. This can be seen as a technique for making the 'joint agenda' legally binding. In 'informative conversations' no new things are created. In such interactions existing knowledge is distributed (Steuten 1998: 62).[8]

The oppositions between the 'personal' and 'institutional' conversation genres, as discussed by these authors, look as follows when listed:

Personal interactions
Casual conversation
Informative conversation
Non-scripted
Multilogue
Non-pragmatic purpose
Long
Informal
Humour
Alignment
Distribution of information

Institutional interactions
Pragmatic conversation
Performative conversation
Scripted
Dialogue
Pragmatic purpose
Short
Formal
No humour
Role complementarity
New facts / new agenda

Despite the clear tendencies revealed in this list, a further distinction is suggested when we focus on the opposition between 'information' and 'new facts'. To begin with, the distribution of information is also an important feature in business conversations. In an institutional setting, such as a hotel and its reservation desk, distribution of information regarding the location, availability of rooms in a certain period, the price and what is included in that price, are expected issues in the negotiation process (cf. Steuten 1998: 60, for the data). A client might need this information in order to be able, or feel comfortable, to make a booking decision. The following interaction illustrates how a certain piece of information – in this case the precise location of the hotel – can be distributed,

Customer: Could you tell me, are you the hotel next to the conference centre?
Hotel: Yes, we are right next door.

(Steuten 1998: 66)

In this dyadic setting, the roles are complementary and the information therefore is not equally distributed. The caller, through an enquiry, arranges a more equal distribution of information; both parties know that the exchange of that information is part of a 'wider project', potentially involving a choice from the services the hotel has to offer. The exchange of the requested information creates a piece of solid ground on which to move forward. This view does not include autonomous actions such as 'watching TV' or 'preparing food'. It is suggested that 'information distribution' is the common feature of all dyadic communication. In 'business transactions' and 'business conversations', it is supplemented with decisions to act and commitments to future action (an 'agenda').

These examples also illustrate a more general principle. All communication is driven by *difference* (Berger and Luckmann 1967; Eggins and Slade 1997; Kress 1988). One way of reducing this difference is to distribute information more equally. The purpose for doing so, as strongly argued by Berger and Luckmann (1967), is 'universe maintenance', the creation and maintenance of common ground. Examples are 'getting-acquainted' encounters when information as to name, place of origin, profession, dispositions, and other personal traits is exchanged. In such settings the amount and quality of information will still always remain asymmetric, but the more equal distribution creates a common ground for the development of the exchange and for further interactions. This principle is also illustrated by 'gossiping', a subtype of 'casual conversation', the purpose of which is 'establishing and maintaining group membership' (Eggins and Slade 1997: 273ff.). In our view, gossiping too is in essence a form of 'information distribution', but in this interaction type the information flow is about a third person with whom both interactants are familiar to a certain extent.

In the 'genre' schema quoted above, we did not list *storytelling* as a separate entity. That is because stories are told in shared social contexts and are part of wider conversations. Stories are told to

> entertain an amuse ... and give the participants the opportunity to share experiences and to display agreement.
>
> (Eggins and Slade 1997: 229)

When telling a story people share their experiences and reactions to events with others, and in this way the social world of a community is recreated and evaluated (Eggins and Slade 1997: 229). Support for this view can be found in the Chinese practice of storytelling in traditional tea houses located in the centre of a village where storytellers recreated the essence of Chinese culture (the cultural common ground). A similar claim can be made for Chinese musical theatre (opera) and puppet plays performed at seasonal junctions opposite the temples of local deities. Eggins and Slade (1997: 236–8) further distinguished the subtypes of *narratives, anecdotes, exemplums,* and *recounts.* 'Narratives' culminate in a crisis and are followed by a resolution. In an 'anecdote' the resolution part is missing and replaced by an emotional expression of amazement, frustration, or otherwise. 'Exemplums' try to make explicit how the world should or should not be, and 'recounts' involve the retelling of events. Clark (1996: 346) also mentioned *jokes* as a special genre, a piece of fiction that needs to be recognised as such. 'The punch line of a joke tells the audience when the joke proper has ended and the response should begin' (Clark 1996: 350). It describes 'an episode that did not actually happen' (Clark 1996: 360).

Our conversational data are less extensive and limited to relatively short interactions between a variety of social actors. However, they allow the distinction between 'setting an agenda', 'construal' of events, and 'having an argument'. The various conversational genres discussed so far can be listed as follows:

Personal conversations
   'minimal joint actions'
   'setting an agenda

'event construal'
'having an argument'
'narrate'
'tell an anecdote'
'provide an exemplum'
'retell an event'
'tell a joke'
Business conversations
  'informative conversations'
    'distribute information;
  'performative conversations'
    'establish new facts'
    'setting an agenda'

As this overview shows, 'creating new facts' and 'setting an agenda' can be done between private persons and between a customer and a business organisation. The mechanism is the same, but the implications are different. In business transactions an exchange of goods and services for money is involved. The exchange between private persons usually is of a different nature, less formal. A personal agenda can be set for joint action, for instance, such as 'going to the movies'.

The crucial difference between the various listed genres is the extent of scripting. Casual conversations are emerging and opportunistic (Clark 1996). 'Personal conversations' depend heavily on the personal background of the interactants, and the role of the particle *le* in such environments is therefore more idiosyncratic and more difficult to predict. However, we will show that the notion of 'common-ground co-ordination' holds in such interactions, as it does in the other discourse genres we analysed.

Written stories, in our view, are the counterparts of narratives but in a different medium. The main difference with the practice of storytelling in its different manifestations is the absence of an actual social situation, which creates an immediate cultural environment as a shared common ground. This, however, has grave consequences. Written stories develop without 'co-ordination' and 'joint commitment' (Clark 1996: 346). Writers invent stories to 'entertain and amuse', but need to imagine a certain audience (readership) with a specific cultural background. 'Children's stories' narrate exemplary personal experiences and reactions to events and thereby create, recreate and evaluate the social world of the child's community. Children's stories in this sense are a source for the building of community membership, comparable to the traditional storytelling in teahouses.

3.6 Conversations and *le*

We feel that the claim in the literature that the particle *le* cannot be used in expository text (Li and Thompson 1981) has acquired a stronger basis after the exposition of the concepts 'joint activities', 'joint actions', 'joint projects' and 'joint construals' in this chapter. It is possible now to relate uses of the particle *le* in 'personal conversations' to 'joint control' or 'negotiation', to 'emergence' and 'local management', and to a variety of 'participatory acts' ('discourse acts'). These distinctions all support the basic idea we are defending that the Chinese particle *le* is a 'common-ground co-ordination cue'. At this point, however, we can more specifically enquire as to the type of 'minimal joint project' or 'conversational genre' in which the particle *le* is used, and try to determine why 'local management' considers the use of the particle *le* necessary. Given this characterisation of conversations, we can also ask in which kind of 'participatory acts' or 'discourse acts' the particle *le* tends to appear. For that purpose, we have a 'move typology' available, which should allow the identification of certain move types as sensitive to uses of the particle *le*, while at the same time rejecting others. We will come back to this issue in Chapters 8 and 9. There too we will address other distinctions the data in the coming chapters will reveal. We will start with examples from procedural discourse, follow that up with an analysis of written stories, and finally, in Chapter 7, endeavour an analysis of conversational data. Before doing so, we will continue now first with an analysis of the development of the particle *le* in historical records.

4 The historical development of the particle *le*[1]

In this chapter we will trace the course of the development of the particle *le* through history to reveal its origin and the evolution of its functions. With regard to the particle's origin, there is controversy in the literature over whether the Mandarin particle *le* has the same origin as the verb suffix *-le*. While scholars such as Wang (1947), Liu (1985), Cao (1987), Huang and Davis (1989), Shi (1990), Liu *et al.* (1992) and Mei (1994) think that both LEs have their origin in the lexical verb *liao* ('to finish'), Chao (1968: 246) suggests that the particle *le* is probably a weak form of *lai* ('to come'), a hypothesis followed by scholars such as Mei (1981), Anderson (1982) and Sun (1996). We take the position that the particle *le* has developed from the verb *liao* ('to finish'), and will focus our discussion on its development. As for the arguments against the *lai*-origin claim, readers are referred to Wu (2000). In the following we will first discuss the development of the particle *le* in texts from the tenth century on to show that the modern use of the particle *le* has developed from the early use of *liao*, or *liao* + *ye*. Then we will present evidence from *Ponyok Nogoltae (Fanyi Laoqida)*, a Korean textbook of Chinese in the early sixteenth century, and synchronic data from Shantou dialect to support our claim for the diachronic development of the particle. We will conclude the chapter by examining elements involved in this development that contribute to the pragmatic function of the particle as it is used today.

4.1 The development of the particle *le*

In Chinese *liao* as a verb, meaning 'to finish', is found at the end of the Eastern Han (AD 25–220) (Pan and Yang 1980: 15), and around Wei, Jin and the Northern and Southern Dynasties (AD 220–581) when, along with other verbs meaning 'finish', such as *jing*, *qi*, *yi* and *bi*, it started to occur after V(O) in the form of V(O) + completive to indicate the completion of the situation indicated by V(O). When the structure V(O) + completive first occurred after the Eastern Han (AD 25–220) there were two constraints on the pattern. First, the completives *jing*, *qi*, *yi*, *bi* and *liao* usually occurred in an utterance-final position, but not in a discourse-unit-final (hence discourse-final) position (Cao 1987: 10; Liu *et al.* 1992: 112). Second, what preceded the completives was normally an event, or a non-stative situation; that is, something which could be finished, since these completives still maintained their meaning of 'finish' or 'complete'. The structure was often used in an event sequence, marking a boundary between events (Thompson 1968), as shown in texts from around Wei and Jin (AD 220–316),

(4.1) [examples with various uses of 'finish' in early texts]
 a. (Zhang Jiying) zuo shu qu jing, fu qin yue
 (name) play several tune 'finish', stroke zither say
 'After he had played a few tunes, (Zhang Jiying) strummed the zither and said...'

 b. Ju qi shi qi, huan zhi Shizun suo
 all beg food 'finish', return to Buddha place
 'After they had begged for food, they returned to where Shizun (the Buddha) was.'

 c. Qiren shi yi, outu yu di
 The-person eat 'finish', vomit to ground
 'After eating, the person vomited on the ground.'

 d. Wang yin jiu bi, yinde zi jiequ
 surname drinking 'finish', then self leave
 'After drinking, Wang excused himself.'

 e. Xiang cuiqu xiequ liao, shen buke guo yanliu
 Want urge copy 'finish', careful mustn't over stay
 '(I) want to urge you to finish copying it, be sure not to delay.'

Later on *liao* gradually replaced other verbs with the same function, and became the most frequently used completive in late Tang (AD 618–907). The structure V(O) *liao* then emerged (Cao 1987: 11; Liu *et al.* 1992: 111–12).

When it first occurred, the completive *liao*, though having lost its status as an independent verb, still maintained its lexical meaning. As demonstrated by the above examples, *liao* with the meaning of 'finish' marked an interruption or boundary in the event line (Thompson 1968; Huang and Davis 1989), or the sequence of events, but it was unable to mark the end of the event line as it was not eligible in a discourse-final position. However, this started to change around the Tang Dynasty (AD 618–907). In that dynasty, during the first stage of the slow process of the grammaticalisation of *liao*, the two constraints mentioned (mark boundary in the event line, not eligible for marking the end of the event line) started to relax: *liao* began to occur with stative situations as well as in discourse-final position. These are significant changes, which finally led to the emergence of the particle *le* in modern Chinese.

The completive *liao* was already used quite frequently with stative situations in Bianwen – 'a popular form of literature (generally on Buddhistic themes) with alternating prose and rhymed parts for recitation and singing', which was flourishing in the Tang Dynasty (Sun 1996: 4). In his table of 'distribution of *liao* in temporal and main clauses in 10th-century (bianwen) vernacular texts', Shi (1989: 102) reports that 'of the 18 tokens of *liao* in main clauses..., 6 are found to predicate states'. That is to say that *liao* predicating states accounts for 33 per cent of the total use of *liao* in the main clauses studied. In the example below, *liao* follows adjectives indicating stative situations:

(4.2) [examples of uses of *liao* after stative verbs in *bianwen* texts]
a. **Zhi dai nan nü ankang liao, aniang fang shi bu youchou.**
until male female safe–healthy LIAO, mum then begin not worry
'Mum will not stop worrying until the children are safe and well.'
b. **Zhangzhe shenxin huanxi liao, chi qi baogai yi rulai.**
elderly body–mind happy LIAO, hold his parasol visit 'will-come'
'When the venerable elder is content in mind and body, he takes the parasol to pay a visit to Buddha.'

As a stative situation with no natural termination points is unbounded (Li and Thompson 1981: 185) it can't be finished, so to speak. What can be finished or completed in this case is the entry into the relevant state (Comrie 1976: 19–20). Consequently, in these examples, *liao* does not indicate the finishing or completion of a situation but refers to the actualisation of the situation. In (a) and (b) *liao* is used after adjectives designating the states of affairs of 'being safe and well' and 'being content' to signal the inception of the states concerned, marking a deviation from their current or normal states in the speaker's mental model of the situation. This was a significant step in *liao*'s development to the particle, as from then on *liao* was associated not only with events but also with stative situations.

The above examples demonstrate that as early as the Tang, at least in stative situations, *liao* had lost its lexical meaning 'to finish', and took up the function of marking the inception of a deviation from the normal. During the same period, as well as occurring with stative situations, *liao* started to occur in discourse-final positions with or without *ye* – a particle expressing assertion. For example:

(4.3) [examples of uses of *liao* in discourse final position; *bianwen* texts]
a. **bian dao: 'wo hui fofa liao ye'.**
then say: 'I know way of Buddha LIAO YE'
Then said: 'I now understand the way of Buddha.'

b. Nan nü chengzhang, xu wei hunyin liao.
male female now grown, should make marriage LIAO
'As the children have come of age, it's time for them to marry.'

c. Shanglai diyi, shuo bu hui zhong de liao ye...
come-up first, say not can value virtue LIAO YE
'The first thing to say is that people no longer care deeply about virtue.'

(4.4) [examples of uses of *liao* in discourse final position; *Chuandenglu*[2] text containing conversational exchanges]

a. yu zhu shangzuo shuopo liao ye.
to each master say-through LIAO YE
'I've already disclosed it to Your Eminences.'

b. Lunqi wen: 'Yi shu hai kai hua ye wu?'
Lunqi ask: 'one tree yet flower YE WU'

c. Shi yue: 'Kailai jiu yi.'
Master say: 'Flower come long YI'

d. Seng yue: 'Wei shen hai jiezi ye wu?'
monk say: 'not know yet fruit YE WU'

e. Shi yue: 'Zuoye zao shuang liao.'
Master say: 'yesterday-night suffer frost LIAO'
Lunqi asked: 'Is the tree in flower yet?' The master said: 'It has long been in flower.' The monk said: 'I wonder whether it is fruiting yet?' The master said: 'It was attacked by frost last night.'

In the above examples, *liao* not only marks the state of affairs indicated by what precedes it but also takes a discourse-final position with or without YE, placing special emphasis on the state presented. And where *liao* is followed by YE, an assertion marker, the state of affairs is further placed into focus. Consequently, this use of *liao* is related to cognitively important points in the speaker's mental model of states of affairs in the respective joint projects. In (4.3a) and (4.4a) both 'my understanding of the way of Buddha' and 'having disclosed it to Your Eminences' mark the speaker's goal-attainment moments. In (4.3b) the state of affairs 'being time (for them) to marry' represents an important stage in people's lives, and 'people not knowing how to value virtue' in (4.3c), a deterioration point in morality in society. In the conversational example, (4.4e) 'having been attacked by frost last night' serves as a counter move to contradict any expectations of fruiting.

The use of *liao* (*ye*) in all these cases is linked to cognitively remarkable moments. If the completive *liao* had been used before to mark a boundary or interruption in the event line only, the relaxation of the previous two constraints on the completive *liao* now enabled it to mark not only a boundary in the line of state of affairs, or the episode line, but a peak episode. This is actually similar to how the modern particle is used today, as we will demonstrate in more detail in the following chapters.

The combination of *liao* and *ye* in a discourse-final position is crucial to the development of the modern particle *le*. Liu (1985: 130–2) examined the use of *liao* in *Zhutangji*[3] (AD 952) and found that all the uses of *liao* occurred in three patterns VP *liao* VP, VP *liao*#, VP *liao ye*# (where # indicates a pause between utterances):

(4.5) [examples of uses of *liao* in *Zhutangji*, according to Liu (1985)]
A. VP *liao* VP
a. Heshang jian liao yun:...
monk see LIAO say
'*The monk saw { } and said:...*'

b. ... Si shan qing liao you huang,
four mountain green LIAO again yellow
'*The four mountains turned yellow after being green.*'

B. VP *liao* #
a. Guo jiang liao, xiang xingzhe yun:...
cross river LIAO to traveller say
'*After crossing the river, { } said to the traveller:...*'

b. ... Dongshan shou liao, you zhan shou yun:...
name accept LIAO, again stretch hand say
'*Dongshan, after accepting { }, stretched his hand and said:...*'

C. VP *liaoye* #
a. Duiyue: gong heshang shangliang liaoye...
reply with monk discuss LIAOYE
'*{ } replied: "{ } have already discussed with the monk."*'

b. Chi fan liaoye.
eat meal LIAOYE
'*{ } have already eaten.*'

Liu further observed that a follow-up utterance is compulsory in (B) and that therefore the use of *liao* in both (A) and (B) are in fact the same: the utterance containing *liao* cannot stand alone and has to be followed by another utterance. In other words, *liao* in (A) and (B) is non-discourse-final. This is in contrast with (C), which can be discourse-final and a follow-up utterance is only optional. Comparing the two types of *liao* used in the patterns, Liu concluded that the verbal *-le* in modern Chinese is related to the use of non-discourse-final *liao* in (A) and (B), whereas the particle is related to the use of discourse-final *liaoye* in (C). Liu's observation is confirmed by the existence of the equivalent of the modern particle *le* in many northern dialects whose phonological form is a combination of *liao* and YE in those dialects.

Following Liu, we take the position that the structure of V(O) *liaoye* is the environment from which the modern particle finally developed. When *liao* was used in the pattern long enough, *liao* was able to establish its utterance-final position, leading to its replacing *ye* or merging with *ye*. Although we found that *liao* in this pattern is not always followed by *ye* in examples from other sources, we believe that the combination of *liao* with *ye* is crucial in this process. It was *ye*, which was discourse-final, that helped *liao* to occur in and hold on to the discourse-final position; and it was also *ye*, an assertion marker, that incorporated an assertive force into the particle, which is missing in the lexical meaning of the verb *liao*. The use of *liao* without *ye* in the discourse-final position may be explained by regional differences in the development of the particle.

By the Southern Song (1127–1279) in *Zhuzi Yulei*, a classified collection of conversations of Master Zhu (AD 1270), LE is used in discourse units with a variety of grammatical structures, comparable to those in which the modern *le* is used. It was also in this period that the pattern V-*le* O *le* occurred, marking the completion of the development of *le* (Cao 1987: 13). Early Song (960–1279) is also the period when the perfective *le* starts to take its position between V and O, resulting in the pattern V-*le* O *ye*.[4] However, this happened only in utterances involving transitive verbs with an object. For utterances containing intransitive verbs or adjectives the V-*le* O *ye* pattern was simply irrelevant. In such sentences *liao* remained at the sentence-final position preceding *ye*, whereby its function as a discourse-final particle was further strengthened. When the use of *liao* in stative situations combined with its discourse-final position, it, in time, extended to asserting a new state of affairs, and thereby its function came to coincide with that of *ye*. In the discourse-final position *liao* thereby became associated with the assertion of a changed situation (Cao 1987).[5] Gradually *liao*, the incipient particle, replaced *ye*, or, in some northern regions, merged with *ye*. This happened over a period of several hundred years and across all the patterns with *liaoye*, including V-*le* O (*liao*)*ye*.

4.2 Evidence from *Ponyok Nogoltae*

This account of the development of the particle *le* has found support in Kim's (1998) investigations into the linguistic signs LE, *lai* and *ye* in *Ponyok Nogoltae* (c.1510). With the help of Korean translations and phonetic transcriptions, Kim presents a clear picture of the distribution and semantics of the linguistic signs LE and *ye* in this source.

Frequent occurrences of -*le* and *le* in Kim's data show that the two grams were fully developed in the sixteenth century. An overwhelming number of particle *le* are found in the pattern V LE, where V is either an intransitive verb (or a transitive verb with a topicalised object), or an adjective. The pattern obviously comes from V *liaoye*. While all the LEs in this pattern have a particle function, some of them may be interpreted as the combination of verb-*le* and the particle *le*, and can be seen as the legacy of the historical development of *liao* into these two grams (cf. Chao 1968; Wang 1947; Lü 1991; Zhu 1984; Li and Thompson 1981). Meanwhile, Kim's data also reveal that *ye*, LE*ye* and *le* co-existed in the sentence-final position at that time, characterising a period of transition. The following examples in this section are based on Kim (1998). The Chinese transcription should be taken as representing sixteenth-century Chinese. For the Chinese text see Wu (2000).

A: V *le* – V *ye*
A considerable number of sentences with similar semantic content are marked with either *liao/le* or *ye*. For example:

(4.6) [three comparative examples of uses of *liao* and *ye* in *Ponyok Nogoltae*, c.1510]
a. jinri wan liao
today late LIAO
'It's got late.'

b. lin wan ye
[just before] late YE
'It's almost late.'

c. ming xing gao liao
bright star high LIAO
'The morning star has risen high.'

d. Shen er gao ye
Ginseng little high YE
'The Shen constellation is already high.'

e. ritou luo liao
sun fall LIAO
'The sun is setting.'

f. zhe zaowan ritou luo ye
now soon sun fall YE
'Now the sun is setting.'

B: V *le* – V LE*ye*
Similarly, a certain number of sentences in the same pattern are marked with either *liao/le* or *liao ye* / LE*ye*:

94 *Historical development of the particle* le

(4.7) [three comparative examples of uses of *liao* and *liao ye* in *Ponyok Nogoltae*, c.1510]

a. tuo duo dou da liao
camel load all put LIAO
'The load are all loaded now.'

b. tuo duo dou da liao ye
camel load all put LIAO YE
'The load are all loaded now.'

c. zhe duanzi ye mai liao
this damask too buy LIAO
'I have bought this damask, too.'

d. zhe duanzi mai liao ye
this damask buy LIAO YE
'I have bought this damask.'

e. biji chi-liao shi wo ye liao-liao
around eat-LIAO time I too finish-LIAO[6]
'When it is time to eat, I'll be also finished.'

f. biji dao nali xun-liao dian shi, na liangge daolai-liao ye
around arrive there 'look for'-LIAO inn time, that two-M arrive-come-LIAO YE
'Around the time when we get there and look for an inn, those two will arrive.'

C: V-*le* O *le* – V-*le* O *ye*/LE*ye*
Finally, some sentences with the verbal -*liao*/-*le* are found to be marked by either liao/*le* or *ye*:

(4.8) [two comparative examples of uses of verbal -*liao*/-*le* and final *liao* or *ye* in *Ponyok Nogoltae*, c.1510]

a. zhe dianli dou bi-liao menzi liao, pa you shenme ren rulai?[7]
this inn-in all close-LIAO door *liao*, fear 'there is' some person 'go in'-come
'When this inn has closed all its doors, who could come in?'

b. wo xie-liao zhe yige qi liao[8]
I write-LIAO this one-M deed LIAO
'I have written this contract.'

c. ta ye chi-liao fan ye
3p also eat-LIAO meal YE
'He will have finished eating.'

d. chi-liao jiu ye
absorb-LIAO wine YE
'We have drunk up.'

Although no cases of the pattern V-*le* O LE*ye* are found in Kim's data, such a pattern does occur in *Xixiangji*, 'Romance of the Western Chamber' (cf. Cao 1987: 14):

(4.9) [two comparative examples of uses of verbal -*liao* / -*le* and final *liao ye* in *Romance of the Western Chamber*]

a. Yingying yi yu-liao bieren liaoye
name already give-LIAO other person LIAOYE
'Yingying has already been engaged to someone else.'

b. yanjiande shou-liao zhao'an liaoye
eye-see-DE receive-LIAO compromise LIAO YE
'Apparently she has sided with them.'

These examples give us a vivid picture of the transition period from *ye* to *le* or LE*ye* in early Ming (1368–1644), a period during which the three grams were still used almost interchangeably in similar contexts, though both -*le* and *le* had already fully developed. However, the overwhelmingly greater number of -*le* and *le* suggests that the transition was reaching its last stage and *ye* was about to fade out. When *Chunggan Nogoltae* (Chongkan Laoqida), a new edition of *Ponyok Nogoltae* (c.1510), was published in 1795, the sequence of LE*ye* became *le*. In the new edition, except for one case of V-*le* O *ye*, all previous occurrences of *ye* were replaced by *liao* / *le* or had disappeared.

It is reasonably clear that between late Tang (618–907) and Ming (1368–1644) *ye*, *liao ye* / LE*ye* and *liao* / *le* co-existed, serving as the marker of major boundaries in the episode line until the latter two gradually replaced *ye*. However, the result of the process and the time the whole process took seem to have varied with dialect regions, perhaps due to the influence of local dialects. For instance, the phonological value of the cognate of Mandarin *le* in many northern dialects was the reduction of the sequence *liao* and *ye* (Liu 1985), while in other regions the equivalent of Mandarin *le* was a weakened *liao*. On the other hand, sources produced in the southern dialect regions show that *ye* almost disappeared in late Song (960–1279) (Cao 1987: 14). However, it is frequently found in Yuan and Ming materials probably because these materials were more related to the language used in the northern dialect regions.

96 *Historical development of the particle* le

The final step of the grammaticalisation of the lexical verb *liao* into *-le* and *le* – the phonological reduction of [liau] into [lə] – didn't take place until the nineteenth century after both *-le* and *le* were fully developed and had replaced *ye*. There are two pieces of evidence for this claim. The most recent is from Kim (1998). According to him, the phonetic value of the linguistic sign LE, representing both the verbal *-le* and the particle *le* in *Chunggan Nogoltae* (1795), was [liau], which means that the phonological reduction of LE (*liao*) didn't happen until at least the end of the eighteenth century. If despite this evidence one may still query whether the phonetic value of a word in the Korean textbook of Mandarin is for the character reading or for the actual pronunciation of the word in context, Ohta's observation makes it absolutely clear that the pronunciation of (at least some) *le* in the early nineteenth century was exactly the same as that of the lexical verb *liao*, i.e. [liau]. Ohta (1958: 317) finds that in *Ernü Yingxiong Zhuan* (Daughters and Sons), written in late Qing (1644–1911) when the sentence particle *a* immediately follows either the particle *le* or the lexical verb *liao*, it is written as *wa*. This is only possible when the last sound of both *le* and *liao* is [u], indicating that the pronunciation of such occurrences of *le* at that time was still [liau], the same as the lexical verb *liao*. On the basis of his observation, Ohta proposes that the phonological reduction of LE from [liau] to [lə] was not completed until after 1880. Ohta's evidence, in its turn, reconfirms Kim's position that the phonetic value of the word in the Korean textbook of Chinese is not for the character but for the pronunciation in context. These two pieces of evidence constitute the most direct argument so far against the view that the particle *le* originated from the phonological reduction of the lexical verb *lai* between the twelfth and eighteenth centuries (Sun 1996: 101), and demonstrate convincingly that the two LEs do have the same origin.

4.3 Evidence from Shantou dialect

The origin of *le* from *liao* is supported not only by the use of LE in texts from the ninth century on, and the subsequent development of LE into *le* proposed above, but also by evidence from some living dialects in which both the old use of *liao* and the modern use of *le* co-exist. The diachronic changes of *liao*, for example, can be seen synchronically in Shantou dialect. The sign LE [liau] in Shantou dialect has retained various Middle Chinese and Early Mandarin uses of *liao* while still having the same functions as modern Chinese *le* and *-le*. It has seven different uses (Shi 1996: 43), of which I will mention only four for the present discussion: LEa, LEb, LEc and LEd.

LEa: lexical verb
LEa is a verb meaning 'to finish', similar to the verb *liao* in the Northern and Southern Dynasties (420–581), but with the focus on the exhaustion of the substance concerned rather than on the end of the process. In the following

examples, the Shantou dialect character readings are given in Mandarin, as we did with the historical examples, whereas the corresponding Mandarin version is added between brackets:

(4.10) a. Shantou: xi hai wei liao, qie wei kai men
   {Mand.: xi hai mei wan ne, xian bie kai men}
   play yet not LE, yet not open door
   'The play has not finished yet, don't open the door yet.'[9]

   b. Shantou: qian shi-liao wei?
   {Mand.: qian huawanle meiyou?}
   money use LE not
   'Has the money been used up or not?'

LEb: completive
LEb is a completive, similar to the completive *liao* in Tang (618–907):

(4.11) Shantou: di chu dianying liao, sidian zheng laiqu chezhan hai buhui[10] man
   {Mand.: kan ta yichang dianying, sidian zhong dao chezhan qu ye bu chi}
   see CL movie LE, four-point exact come-go station still not late
   'We will still be in time if we go to the station at four after seeing a movie.'

LEc: verbal *-le*
LEc is the modern verbal *-le*, for example:

(4.12) Shantou: xue-liao bannian hai ling wu kuai jiashizheng
   {Mand.: xue-*le* bannian hai lingbushang ge jiashizheng}
   learn LE half year still receive no piece licence
   'He's been taking driving lessons for six months, but still hasn't got his licence.'

LEd: particle *le*
LEd is the modern particle *le*; for example:

(4.13) a. Shantou: long shi-liao fan liao
   {Mand.: dou chi-*le* fan *le*}
   all eat LE meal LE
   'Everyone has eaten.'

   b. Shantou: yiren jiaren banzou you liang-san nian liao
   {Mand.: tamen yijia banzoule liangsannian *le*}
   they family move away have two three year LE
   'It's been two or three years since their family moved.'

c. Shantou: shui ai kun liao
[Mand.: shui kuai kai *le*]
water soon boil LE
'The water is about to boil.'

As indicated, the different uses of LE in Shantou dialect have the same pronunciation [liau], only the tone being different in different contexts. On the basis of their semantic and phonological (tones and tone changes) closeness and distribution, Shi (1996: 47) traced both the verbal LEc and the particle LEd back to the completive LEb, and then back to the same origin of LEa, the cognate of the verb *liao* in Middle Chinese. If Shi is correct, the relationships between the seven synchronic uses of LE in Shantou dialect have, in fact, made visible the path of the diachronic development from the verb *liao* in Middle Chinese to the modern particle *le*, from 'complete' to 'completive', and from there to verb suffix and to 'particle' *le*.

4.4 Conclusion

In this chapter we have first examined the early use of the lexical verb *liao* before the tenth century, its use as a completive around the tenth century and the path of its subsequent development into the verbal -*le* and the particle *le*. Then we presented diachronic data from *Ponyok Nogoltae* (*c.* 1510) and *Chunggan Nogoltae* (1795) and synchronic data from the Shantou dialect to support our proposed development path for the particle. We concluded that the particle *le* in modern Chinese has the same origin as the verbal -*le* – the lexical verb *liao* in Middle Chinese. The function of both verbal -*le* and the particle *le* are semantically related to the lexical verb *liao*, meaning 'to finish', depending on which way the situation is viewed. Looking backward, *liao* points to the verb and indicates the completion or cessation of the action indicated by the verb, or to the pre-culmination point of an event, which is the function of the verbal -*le*. Looking forward, it points to the state of affairs resulting from the action completed or ceased; in other words, to the post-event state (Chang 2001).

The development of the particle from the verbal *liao* has undergone the following stages:

lexical verb *liao* > completive *liao* > discourse-final *liao ye* > the particle *le*

During this development two factors are essential: the use of *liao* in stative situations and with the assertion marker *ye*. The first factor has enabled *liao* to mark a boundary between states of affairs, or episodes, whereas the second has a number of implications. *Ye*, as an assertion marker, has helped *liao* to establish its discourse-final position and contributed two essential elements to the particle's function: a strong assertive force and the sense of immediacy. The sense of immediacy arises due to the fact that the force of an assertion always operates at the speech time in interactions, though the content of an assertion may be related to different time-frames. While the assertive force towards the state of affairs marked by *liao* signals the content as cognitively remarkable, the speech-time relevance imposed by the act of assertion appeals to the addressee to react now on the content asserted. Also, the discourse-final position created discourse space needed for the addressee's reflection and response. The original *liao ye* with all these features, explored by speakers in interactions through time, has finally evolved into the particle in its modern shape, which functions as an index to remarkable moments in the shared 'common ground' of interactants. By this we mean a deviation from the expected norm or a return back to it, and a signal of appeal to the addressee to reset his personal 'common ground' accordingly. It is the details of this latter claim that we will further explore in the following chapters.

5 Action-picture stories

In this chapter the occurrence of the particle *le* in 66 action-picture stories (Frauman-Prickel and Takahashi 1985; Romijn and Seely [1979] 1986) is reported.[1] Action stories illustrate everyday procedures and events, and detail the various steps to be followed; that is, the various 'actions' or 'doings' to be carried out in an indicated sequence. In most of the picture stories an 'instructor' indicates to an 'apprentice' which 'actions' to perform, and those actions are also illustrated by the accompanying pictures. Together the action sequence constitutes a generally known 'procedure'. The data show that when a 'problem' develops in a procedure, the 'instructor' marks that 'problem' with the particle *le*. If a 'problem' already exists in the common ground (is already activated), the 'solution' to that problem is also marked with the particle *le*. These uses we take as in agreement with the common-ground co-ordination hypothesis for the particle *le*. When a 'procedure' follows a normal flow of events, the particle *le* is not used. We take this to be an indication that there is no ground for marking with the particle *le*. There is nothing 'special' to co-ordinate on at that point.

The chapter first introduces the action-picture stories and describes the various interactions that compose them (5.1). A global description of occurrences and non-occurrences of the particle *le* and verbal *-le* in procedural discourse follows. A first analysis of verbal *-le* is also given in that section (5.2). The third section (5.3) details the various occurrences of the particle *le* in 'openings', 'progress reports', 'instructions', and other discourse units. We will argue that verbal *-le* and the particle are complementary uses in a process of marking 'peak events'. Whereas marking with verbal *-le* is a mechanism which allows the speaker to guide the interactant/reader as regards event development, the particle *le* is a 'common ground co-ordination device', requesting the addressee to take note of a particular piece of 'outstanding' common ground and co-ordinate on it, thereby creating or re-creating 'shared common ground'.

5.1 The data

The 66 action-picture stories detailed various everyday 'procedures'.[2] The English version of the text accompanying the pictures was translated into

Chinese by a university educated native speaker from China and checked on accuracy during processing by the second author.[3] The various actions constituting a procedure were portrayed by pictures, which provided details of the action involved and created an action sequence. The pictures and the details of actors and objects involved were a help and guide in the imagination process. The various actions, when verbally expressed, were done by an 'instructor' and executed by an 'apprentice' (language student), who was instructed to pretend to execute the actions, performing them as 'virtual reality'. The text could also be read by one person, who then became both 'instructor' and 'apprentice', and this way learned how to interpret (and verbalise) basic instructions, such as *Dakai shuilongtou* ('Open the tap'), *Naqi feizao* ('pick up the soap'), etc. in Chinese.

The 'verbal interactions' between the person taking up the role of 'instructor' and the person taking up the role of 'apprentice' were instances of 'joint projects'. The 'apprentice' needed to orient his behaviour on the verbal (and sometimes also physical) directions of the 'instructor'. Given the nature of the relatively simple actions needed (for instance, 'open a tap', 'pick up the soap', 'put the kettle on the fire'), both were able to do what they were supposed to do. Both also needed to be willing to imagine that they were interacting in virtual reality, and mutually believe that they were involved in a joint project (Clark 1996). The 'verbal interaction' detailed the various steps of an 'autonomous project' ('washing your hands', 'sewing on a button', 'preparing a cup of tea', etc.). In a limited number of cases instructions to do something took the form of directions in a 'scenario'. 'Autonomous projects' and 'scenarios' differ as to the background schema employed. The schema of an autonomous project is conventional and relatively strict, not allowing much leeway in the various steps. The background schema of a 'scenario' is not as specific. What is given is a 'starting point' ('a dirty room') and a 'goal' to be reached ('a clean room'), whereas the 'path' to reach the goal is not strictly conventional and predictable but open to 'personal choice' (hiring somebody or not) and change of circumstances (something falls down, and that mishap also needs to be addressed). 'Scenarios' belong to the build-up of 'personal common ground'.

A first count of the various occurrences of both verbal *le* and the particle *le* showed a total number of 216 cases. Each of the 946 lines was analysed as consisting of one or more 'discourse acts' ('participatory acts'). This is in agreement with our conception that these interactions are 'joint projects', and, following Longacre (1996), allow the distinction of a 'preparatory procedure', 'main procedure', and a 'final procedure, each allowing the differentiation of an 'entering', 'body', and 'exiting' phase.[4]

It was possible to break down each story into (a combination of) a limited number of 'sections' or 'minimal joint projects'; namely, a 'problem' or 'goal', 'instructions', 'progress reports', 'verbal interactions', 'warnings', and 'conclusions'. Table 5.1 gives an overview.

The data in this table show that 'instructions' were the main type (62 per cent) of discourse acts that made up the action-picture stories. The second

102 Action-picture stories

Table 5.1 Discourse acts used in the 66 picture stories, according to discourse type

Discourse acts	Opening	Instructions	Progress reports	Verbal interactions	Other	Total
Picture stories	74 (7%)	672 (62%)	232 (21%)	65 (6%)	43 (4%)	1,086 (100%)

main group of verbal behaviour was formed by 'progress reports' (21 per cent). We will further detail the various discourse act types below.

5.1.1 Instructions

Sixty-two per cent of the discourse acts were *instructions*. The instructions were in Chinese, whereas the procedural 'script' provided the interpretation grid for what was being said. Even though the various tasks can be (virtually) executed, in our study we did not actually study people performing the tasks. Our goal was to locate the various moments in the text which were selected by the translator of these action stories as sensitive to the use of the form LE, where the focus first of all was on occurrences of the particle *le*.

In 11 of the 66 stories the text consisted of a series of 'instructions' only. These detailed the procedural steps of an everyday task, such as 'washing your hands', the full text and the Chinese in pinyin romanisation is given here:[5]

'Washing your hands'
1.1   You're going to wash your hands
      Ni zhengyao qu xi shou
1.2   Turn on the water
      Dakai shuilongtou / Ba shuilongtou dakai
1.3   Pick up the soap
      Naqi feizao
1.4   Wash your hands
      Xi shou / ba shou xiyixi / yong feizao xi shou
1.5   Put the soap down
      Fangxia feizao
1.6   Rinse your hands
      Chongyichong shou / ba shou chongyichong / ba shou chongxi yixia
1.7   Turn off the water
      Guanshang shuilongtou / ba shuilongtou guanshang
1.8   Pick up the towel
      Naqi maojin
1.9   Dry your hands
      Magan shou / cagan shou / ba shou cagan
1.10 Put the towel on the towel rack
      Ba maojin guazai maojinjia shang

The opening line (1.1) of this story indicates the task that needs to be performed. The remaining nine lines are 'instructions' that detail the various steps to be followed. Each instruction is then supposedly executed as intended. For instance:

1 [instruction]
  Turn on the water
  Dakai shuilongtou / Ba shuilongtou dakai
2 [execution]
  the apprentice (virtually) turns on the water

The apprentice, under the conditions described above, makes an 'open the tap' movement to imitate the actual flowing of water. A 'reader' imagines that he is doing so. Furthermore, pictures are cues suggesting an action or situation rather than full and reliable depictions. They are in this sense like language. The background frame of the event controls the processing order. The pictures help to activate the underlying schema (cf. Fauconnier 1997).

5.1.2 Opening lines

All action-picture stories had a 'title' indicating the nature of the upcoming procedure. The 'opening line', the first line of the story, either contained the first 'action' to be performed, or oriented the 'apprentice'/'reader' as to the 'joint project' s/he was going to participate in. When we counted the number of discourse acts in 'opening lines', we found a total of 74 acts, constituting 7 per cent of all text. An example is the 'opening line' of story 1 with the 'title' *Shui jiao* ('Going to bed') which read:

1 It's ten p.m. You're watching TV.
   Xianzai shi wanshang shidian, ni zhengzai kan dianshi

The opening line in this story sets the time of the action (10 p.m.), and introduces the 'activity' the 'animator' ('reader') is expected to be involved in. The accompanying pictures further help to create a feeling of 'shared common ground' by providing details of the appearance of the main character and the way he is positioned in front of the television. By orienting himself on the 'opening line' and imagining the situation, the 'animator'/'reader' is involved in a 'joint construal' (cf. Clark 1996).

5.1.3 Progress reports

One-fifth (21 per cent) of the discourse acts reported 'progress' in the story. One type of 'minimal joint project' for a progress report is the sequence 'instruction' followed by the 'execution' of that instruction, which again is followed by a 'description of consequences', an indication of the 'effect' of the action after it is executed. An example is:

1   'Fasten your seatbelt.'
    Koujin anquandai
2   [the apprentice fastens his seatbelt]
3   'It's too tight.'
    Tai jin le

This type of 'progress report' details the 'effect' of the execution of an action, and, as this example shows, the particle *le* can occur in such progress reports. The 'effect' detailed here is a mismatch between instruction goal and the result obtained – a 'deviation', as we will argue shortly. 'Progress reports' 'update' the 'animator'/'reader' as to a certain 'outstanding feature' in the development of the story. In 17 stories (26 per cent) no 'progress reports' were used. In 88 per cent of the remaining 49 stories, 'progress reports' did not exceed 40 per cent of the total number of discourse acts. In the remaining 12 per cent of these stories (those containing 'progress reports'), however, these reports constituted more than 40 per cent of the total story text. In half of these (6 per cent) that percentage was higher than 61 per cent. These data show that the majority of the stories were strictly or mainly procedural. A minority, however, relied heavily on 'progress reports'. This was particularly the case in 'scenarios' containing a 'starting point', a 'goal' to be achieved, and a 'path' that is not fully scripted. 'Scenarios' are more like 'stories', telling the participants what happens around them during a 'goal-directed' activity.

The 'progress reports' took the form of 'statements' (cf. Halliday [1985] 1994). The 'updating' detailed either:

1   the 'effect' of the execution (cf. the 'seatbelt' example);
2   the 'next step' in the development of the situation;
3   the 'acts' being performed by another situation participant (one interacting with the main story character);
4   'verbal acts' by story characters.

We will illustrate each of these. We begin with providing another example of an 'effect'. The instruction 'Put the kettle on the stove' (*Ba hu fangzai luzishang*), was followed by the progress report 'The water is boiling' (*Shui kaile*).[6] An example of a 'next step' is the situation description 'You're watching TV' (*Ni zhengzai kan dianshi*) of story 1 'Going to Bed', which is followed by 'The program is finished' (*Jiemu bosongwanle*).[7] 'Third party acts' are: 'The doctor takes your temperature' (*Yisheng gei ni liangliang tiwen*), 'She checks your eyes' (*Ta jiancha nide yanjing*), 'She checks your ears', *Ta kankan nide erduo*, etc. 'Progress reports' can also detail 'verbal acts' directed at the main character, as in 'She asks you: "What seems to be the problem?" *Ta wen ni: "Ni juede nar bu shufu?"*'. In incidental cases the 'reply' is also given as a 'progress report', as in 'You reply: "I have a headache." *Ni shuo: "Wo touteng."'*. The latter case could also have been given in the form of an 'instruction', 'Reply: "I have a headache." *Huida: "Wo touteng."*'

5.1.4 Verbal interactions

'Verbal interactions' constituted 6 per cent of all discourse acts and occurred in 28 of the 66 stories. In these stories, several story characters appear and they 'enter into' and 'exit from' one or several 'minimal joint projects'. The first occurrence of a 'minimal joint project' of this type was in the 'taking the air plane' story when the stewardess addressed the main character who acted as passenger. The following exchange developed:

1   [stewardess]
    Are you comfortable?
    Ni juede shufu ma?
2   [main character]
    Yes. Thank you.
    Hen hao. Xiexie.
3   [stewardess]
    Enjoy your flight.
    Zhu nin lüxing yukuai.

This 'minimal joint project' can be identified as 'checking passenger comfort' as part of a wider 'joint project', 'taking care of passengers'. The stewardess enters into the 'project' by 'questioning comfort', the passenger takes it up by 'asserting comfort', and the stewardess exits from it via a 'well wishing'. The sequence thus is: 'question, 'answer', 'exit phrase'.

The number of stories in which story characters holding 'participatory roles' interacted verbally was 13. In these 13 stories, instructions were used to guide both the 'behaviour' and the 'speech' ('verbal actions') of the 'story characters'. For instance, a 'thief' being pursued by a 'police officer' entered into an 'arrest the suspect' procedure, which developed as follows:

1   [policeman in pursuit]
    'Stop! Thief! Stop!'
    'Zhanzhu! Zei! Zhanzhu!'
2   [instruction]
    'Drop your gun. Drop the purse.'
    'Rengdiao shouqiang. Rengdiao pibao.'
3   [execution of instruction]
    Thief drops gun and purse.
4   [instruction]
    'Hold up your hands.'
    'Juqi shou lai / Ba shou juqilai.'

5   [execution of instruction]
    Thief holding up his hands.
6   [instruction][appeal]
    Say: 'Don't shoot.'
    Shuo: 'Buyao kai qiang.'
7   [execution/reaction]
    The officer does not shoot.

This schema makes clear that the simulated interaction between 'thief' and 'policeman' is guided by the 'instructor', who creates the impression of a sequence of 'verbal' and 'non-verbal' actions:

[policeman]
1   Shouts: 'Stop!'
[Thief]
2   Drops gun and purse.
3   Holds up hands.
4   Says: 'Don't shoot!'

The original seven steps of the 'policeman', the 'instructor', and the 'thief', are presented as four pictures, each describing one of the four actions listed. This shows that the picture stories try to concentrate on the main events and to place the various actions of the instructor into the background.

Instructions to 'speak' further fall into two categories, 'telling to' and 'telling that'. Examples are 'Tell them to stand closer together' (*Gaosu tamen zhande kaojin yixie*) during a picture taking session, and 'Tell her that...' as in 'Tell her that you will be late' (*Gaosu ta ni wan yidian cai neng huiqu*). The 'tell them to...' form is an 'instruction to act' and is followed by a 'doing', 'moving closer together', whereas the 'telling that...' form is an 'instruction to speak', which is followed by transmitting a piece of verbal information.

Thirteen of the 66 stories involved 'participatory roles'. These stories are listed in Table 5.2. The 'participatory roles' listed show 'verbal interactions' between 'intimates' (husband and wife, sharing much cumulated 'personal common ground'), and individuals in a variety of institutional settings (airline, police, bank, hairdresser, public transport, doctors, fire brigade, post office, and school). In addition, persons known by name engaged in conversation in two stories. In story 47, 'Eating out', Nina and Nancy talk about what to order while studying the menu. In story 51, 'A Sunday drive', the children Lanlan and Lingling appeal to their father to stop the car and eat – both 'minimal joint projects' between known situation participants. Verbal interactions in the remaining stories were those by the main story character being instructed to say something, as in story 15. 'Opening a present', when he is instructed to say, 'Beautiful, thank you very much! *Zhen piaoliang! Duoxie, duoxie!*'

Table 5.2 Action stories which contain an institutional setting

Story	Story characters	Participatory roles
13 Taking the plane	Passenger	Stewardess
14 Stop! Thief! [robbing a woman]	Thief	Police officer
19 A phone call	Husband	Wife
24 The bank [getting money]	Client	Employee
29 Haircut	Customer	Hairdresser
31 A rough bus ride	Passenger	Driver
42 At the doctor's office	Patient	Physician
43 A dental appointment	Patient	Dentist
44 Fire [calling 911]	Citizen	Fire brigade
48 At the post office	Customer	Clerk
55 Taking a test	Students	Teacher
56 Sick at school	Student	Nurse
59 Going to the library	Student	Librarian

5.1.5 *Procedures and schema*

A 'procedure' and its execution are forms of goal-directed behaviour. It is the execution phase of a plan or schema. Longacre (1996) presented the schema of this discourse type as:

1 problem or question,
2 preparatory procedure,
3 main procedure, and
4 final procedure.

The 'problem' or 'question' is the issue that needs to be addressed. In the action stories, the 'question' often is an 'everyday procedure'. However, as part of storytelling, certain 'problems' were created, as we will see shortly. The 'preparatory steps' of the procedure make the objects that are necessary for a successful execution of the 'procedure' available. The 'main procedure' is organised in such a way that the 'goal' of the project can be reached. The 'final procedure' has its own organisation and is functionally related to the 'main procedure'. The 'schema' of the action story 'Washing your hands' follows here to illustrate the distinctions made.

The schema/superstructure of the 'Washing your hands' task was analysed as follows:

Problem: 'You need to wash your hands'

Preparatory procedure:
[assumed to have taken place; soap and towel are present; water bill has been paid]

Main procedure: 'Washing your hands'
Entry   [open tap; pick up the soap]
Body   [washing hands, rinsing]
Exit   [close tap; put down the soap]

Final procedure: Drying your hands [use towel]
Entry   [pick up towel]
Body   [drying hands]
Exit   [put towel back]

This is a regular and everyday-type procedure. For each step an 'instruction' was used, which was executed in the world of the 'joint imagination'. The particle *le* did not occur in this procedure. However, as already noted, it did occur in 'progress reports', and the nature of such uses will be explored in the next section.

5.2 Action stories and occurrences of *-le/le*

Having characterised the action-picture stories, we will first look now at the distribution of the form LE across the various stories. We will begin by specifying the linguistic environment in which verbal *-le* and the particle *le* were used (5.2.1), continue with an analysis of the stories in which the particle *le* was not used (5.2.2), explore occurrences of verbal *-le* (5.2.3), and study the conditions under which that form is used in a piece of narrative discourse (5.2.4).

5.2.1 Occurrences of verbal -le and particle le

A collection of all the examples in which the form LE was used showed that there were 216 instances of that form (verbal *-le* or particle *le*). This figure, however, is only approximate. Alternative wordings were not counted.[8] For each picture only one wording was accepted for the statistics. As a rule, the first translation line provided the data for the count. As shown in Table 5.3, the categories used in the counting were: idiomatic forms (4 per cent), V-*le* followed by an object or some form of quantification (21 per cent), occurrences of verbal *-le* in clause-final position (35 per cent), cases of the particle

Table 5.3 Occurrence of LE in the 66 picture stories, according to structural type

	Type					
	Idiom	V-le O	V-le	V le	*Mod* le	*Total*
Occurrences	8 (4%)	46 (21%)	76 (35%)	72 (33%)	14 (7%)	216 (100%)

Note
Mod = modus; *keyi* ... *le*, *dei* ... *le*, *gai* ... *la*, etc.

le in clause-final position (33 per cent), and all those instances in which the particle *le* was in construction with some element other than the main verb (7 per cent). The particle *le* in clause-final position occurred in 72 cases or 32 per cent of the counted utterances with LE.⁹ Examples of the most frequent occurrence types of the particle *le* are:

'Progress reports'
6.8   *Tai da le, tuodiao dayi*: 'It's too big. Take it [the coat] off.'
33.6 *Ni chu han le*: 'You're sweating.'

When the instruction *Chuanshang dayi* ('put on the coat') is executed, the effect cannot be observed; this is all virtual and therefore is given in a 'progress report': *Tai da le* ('It's too big'), which is followed by another 'instruction', *Tuodiao dayi* ('Take the coat off'). The sequence is 'instruction'–'progress report'–'instruction'. We will see that in each of these cases the particle *le* marks a 'deviation' or a 'solution', which can be recognised as an 'outstanding' piece of common ground in that environment. Two-fifths of the particle *le* examples described an effect of some sort. Other examples are 4.4 *Dun le* ('It's dull'), an 'involuntary effect'; 13.6 *Tai jin le* ('Too tight'), a mismatch between goal and reality; 20.12 *Hao le* ('That's ready'), 'goal attainment' in an event sequence, and others.

Example 33.6 *Ni chu han le* ('You're sweating'), illustrates the involuntary effect of a natural process. The process verb *chu han* ('sweating') indicates a 'deviation' from 'normal', and as in 60.1 *Waimian xia yu le* ('It's raining outside'), these 'deviations' are marked with the particle *le*. We also found cases in which the particle *le* was used to index a 'deviation' in a mental process, as in 60.3 *Xiangbuqilai le* ('I can't remember'). Half of the total cases (72) were of the 'process' type. The remaining cases were occurrences of the particle *le* in 'warnings' and 'commands'. This usage will be analysed in section 5.3.

Verb-*le* Object examples are clear cases of verbal -*le* marking. Verbal-*le* occurred mostly in 'progress reports' but also appeared in 'instructions'. Example of these two types of uses are:

Progress report
49.5   *Ta kaole hen duo haochide dianxin* ('He bakes a lot of delicious cookies.')

Instruction
0.10   *Tuodiao hanshan, tuole kuzi* ('Take off your sweater. Take off your pants.')

'Progress reports' can count as contributions to story build-up and are the more natural environment for uses of verbal -*le*. We will detail its function as indexing 'realisation' or 'accomplishment', 'successful completion'. This, however, does not mean that what is indexed by the main verb is actually realised. What is indicated is that the interpretation function of the addressee's mental model (see Chapter 3) should take this indexing as if 'successfully completed'. We will discuss these uses further in section 5.3.

Seventy-six cases, or 35 per cent, were identified as verbal -*le* in clause-final position. They appeared in 'progress reports' and 'warnings' (instructions to avoid negative consequences). Examples are:

Progress report
0.2   *Jiemu bosongwanle* ('The programme is finished.')

Warning
65.9   *Buyao shuizhaole* ('Don't fall asleep.')

In example 0.2 *Jiemu bosongwanle* '[programme broadcast-finish-*le*] the programme is finished', we first of all recognise the particle *le* which requests co-ordination for a 'change' in the shared common ground. That 'change' is detailed as *Jiemu bosongwanle* ('the programme is finished'). Requests for 'avoidance' of 'negative effects' take the form of *buyao/bie* followed by the action indicating the negative effect, as in line 65.9 *Buyao shuizhaole* ('Don't fall asleep'), which we analyse as *buyao {shuizhaole}*, a marking with verbal -*le*, 'avoid the realisation of that effect', and was said as a warning to a person sunbathing. It was intended to make him turnover frequently in order to make him avoid getting sunburned. We will discuss uses such as these further in section 5.3.

5.2.2 Stories in which the particle le *did not occur*

The particle *le* did not occur in 12 of the 66 stories (18 per cent), and it therefore became an interesting question to determine why this should be so. We assumed that understanding this could provide a basis for comprehending occurrences of the particle *le*. The stories in which no particle occurred are listed in Table 5.4.

Closer scrutiny of these stories revealed that they were all strictly 'procedural'. They contained a sequence of 'instructions' on how to do something. We therefore concluded that the particle *le* is not used in 'instructions', in verbal acts that request a 'doing' which is 'immediate' and which is part of 'normal' procedure. In a situation in which the 'procedure' is instructed to develop 'normally', according to the shared and generally or culturally accepted 'script' in which the procedure is cognitively encrypted ('question' to be addressed; 'preparatory' procedure, 'main' procedure, 'final' procedure), the particle *le* is not used. When reflecting on reasons why this should be so we hypothesised that in such 'normal' situations there is nothing that communicatively can relevantly be marked with the particle *le*; there is nothing that 'stands out' in that context and is worth while for

Table 5.4 Action stories without any occurrence of the particle *le*

1	Washing your hands
2	Getting home.
8	Wrapping a present.
11	Sewing on a button.
12	Painting a picture.
15	Opening a present.
24	The bank.
26	Writing a letter.
35	At the laundromat.
38	Taking pictures.
39	Halloween.
45	Washing dishes.

drawing the attention of the addressee to it. Both speaker and hearer know the script, and all instructions confirm what is being expected. This hypothesis also projects a further hypothesis which expects the particle *le* to occur in situations in which the expected 'procedure' is *not* being followed, when a 'deviation' or 'disturbance' of 'shared common ground' is involved. We will investigate these hypotheses further in section 5.3.

5.2.3 *Occurrences of verbal* -le

Verbal -*le* followed by an object occurred 46 times in the action-picture stories (Table 5.3). When all occurrences (including the variant lines) were counted we came to a total of 49 uses of verbal -*le*. It occurred nine times in the first 40 action stories, but was used 40 times in the remaining 25 stories. A closer look at the latter set of stories revealed that they did not strictly count as 'procedural discourse'; rather, the various events were described in a story-style fashion involving third persons and a series of progress reports. A tabulation of the frequency of occurrences of 'verbal -*le* and object' across the various action stories shows that in ten action stories verbal -*le* occurred once, in two stories it cropped up twice, in five action stories it appeared three times, four uses were found in two stories, whereas five and seven uses occurred in one action story each, resulting in a total number of 49 uses of verbal -*le* followed by an object (Table 5.5).

Table 5.5 Occurrences of verbal -*le* in the 66 picture stories

	Number of occurrences						
	1	2	3	4	5	7	Total
Stories	10	2	5	2	1	1	21
Occurrences	10	4	15	8	5	7	49

In order to get a first impression of the nature of uses of verbal -*le* we analysed the story in which verbal -*le* occurred seven times in some detail. That analysis is presented in section 5.2.4.

5.2.4 *A first analysis of verbal* -le

In story 49, 'Christmas', verbal -*le* followed by an object occurred seven times. This action story reports Christmas events as they take place in a certain family. It therefore counts as an example of storytelling. It reports the events of a third party. We give three of the seven occurrences as illustrations:

49.4   Baba zai menshang guale yige hen piaoliang de huahuan
       papa in door-on hang-LE one-piece very beautiful DE wreath
       'Daddy puts a beautiful wreath on the door.'

49.5   Ta kaole hen duo haochi de dianxin
       he bake-LE very many good-eat cookies
       'He bakes a lot of delicious cookies.'

49.7   Lanlan he Lingling zai bilushang guale liangzhi da wazi
       Lanlan and Lingling in fireplace-on hang-LE two-piece big socks
       'Lanlan and Lingling each hang a big sock above the fireplace.'

The uses of verbal -*le* indicate 'realisation' of a 'specific event'. We recognise in these uses the modern version of the historical 'completion' particles (Chapter 4). The marking each time is a choice. The translator could also have chosen not to use 'realisation' (i.e. verbal -*le*) in these cases. For instance, example 49.4 could also have appeared without verbal -*le* as:

49.4   Baba zai menshang *gua* yige hen piaoliang de huahuan
       papa in door-on hang one-piece very beautiful DE wreath
       '*Daddy puts a beautiful wreath on the door.*'

In the accompanying picture the wreath was already on the door, and this allowed the use of verbal -*le*, 'realised'. We see this as the marking of an 'accomplishment', which stands out in its context and is often recognised as a 'peak event'. The same holds for the remaining six examples. In all cases verbal -*le* can be left out without essentially disturbing the reported event. What would be different, however, is the feeling of 'accomplishment' and, by implication, of 'progression'. We therefore identify uses of verbal -*le* as the reporting of 'milestones' in the story. By doing so the narrator tries to create a feeling of 'progression' in the event line. Uses of verbal -*le*, therefore, are directly related to techniques and ways of reporting events.

The seven uses of verbal -*le* further allow us to relate 'accomplishment' to 'goal attainment' in the 'main event' being reported. In example 49.12, for example, two actions occur: *paodao* ('run toward') and *dedaole* ('acquire'). The first of these two indexes a 'preparatory event', whereas the second one indexes the main event, 'actually holding the presents in their hands':

49.12   **Lanlan he Lingling paodao shengdanshuxia**
Lanlan and Lingling run-to Christmas-tree-under
nadaole shengdan liwu
take-get-LE Christmas present
'Lanlan and Lingling rush to the Christmas tree to get their presents.'

In line 49.15 the relation is that between a 'general event description' – *chi shengdan dacan* ('eating Christmas dinner') – and a specific act – *duanshanglaile kaohuoji* ('bringing in the roast turkey'). The relation between marking with verbal *-le* and individual acts has often been mentioned (cf. Li and Thompson 1981), and our data support that analysis. In the context of a Christmas celebration, main events are those that count together as constituting the institutional event:[10]

49.15   **Xiawu quanjia zai yiqi chi shengdan dacan**
afternoon whole-family in together eat Christmas big-meal
baba duanshanglaile kaohuoji
papa carry-up-come-LE roast-turkey
'In the afternoon, the whole family sits down together for Christmas dinner. Father brings in the traditional roast turkey.'

In seven of the 16 lines of story 49, 'Christmas', no verbal *-le* occurred. This, for instance, was the case in the first three examples:

49.1   **...Lanlan he Lingling zheng mangzhe**
Lanlan and Lingling just busy-ZHE
zhuangshi shengdanshu
decorate Christmas-tree
'...Lanlan and Lingling are busy decorating the Christmas tree.'

49.2   **Meige ren dou neng dedao yifen shengdan lipin**
every-piece person each can obtain-get one-part Christmas gift
'There are Christmas gifts for everyone.'

49.3   **Women zai yiqi chang shengdan gequ**
we in one-place sing Christmas song
'We sing Christmas carols together.'

In these three examples the action is in progress, no 'milestones' or 'realisations' are reported. In 49.1 what is indicated is *mangzhe* ('being busy doing something'), and in 49.3 the idea of 'event in progress' is expressed. That

114   *Action-picture stories*

idea is also supported by the accompanying pictures. In example 49.2, *neng* ('can') reports a 'possibility', and this cognitively is incompatible with the notion of 'accomplishment'.[11]

Of the remaining four examples in which verbal *-le* did not occur, example 49.6 described an action 'in progress':

49.6   [reporting action in progress]
(a) **Shengdanjie qianxi,**
Christmas eve
Lanlan gei Shengdan Laoren xie yifeng xin,
Lanlan give Santa Claus write one-envelope letter
(b) **xiwang Shengdan Laoren songgei ta yifen hao liwu**
hope Santa Clause present-give her one-part good present
'It's Christmas eve, Lanlan writes Santa Claus a letter telling him what she wants for Christmas.'

In this line verbal *-le* can be used, resulting in the idea that the letter is 'finished' or 'almost finished', whereas in this instance the letter depicted in the picture was just beginning.

In example 49.9 *rang* ('let, allow, give in') is used, which is not compatible with 'accomplishment' and therefore verbal *-le* cannot be used. The second part of this line is a progress report indicating a 'possibility', which, as we have seen, does not allow the use of verbal *-le*,:

49.9   [story 49, 'Christmas', reporting story progress]
(a) **Baba rang Lanlan he Lingling shuijiao,**
father let Lanlan and Lingling sleep
(b) **ta shuo**
he say
(c) **zhiyou tingghua de haizi**
only-have listen-speech DE children
(d) **cai neng dedao Shengdan Laoren de liwu**
only-then can obtain Santa Clause DE present
'Father brings Lanlan and Lingling to bed, and tells them that if they've behaved well Santa Claus will bring them gifts.'

The remaining two examples report 'preparatory events',

49.10   [Christmas story, preparatory events]
(a) **Wanshang baba bancheng Shengdan Laoren**
evening papa disguise-into Santa Clause
(b) **ba songgei haizi de liwu fangzai shengdanshuxia**
ba give-to children DE present place-in Christmas-tree-under
'In the evening father disguises himself as Santa Claus and puts all the gifts under the Christmas tree.'

49.13 [Christmas story, main event]
(a) **Tamen ganmang dakai hezi,**
they hurry put-open box
(b) **kankan limian shi shenme**
look-look inside be what
'*They open their boxes immediately to see what it is inside.*'

In line 49.10 verbal *-le* could have been used, both *banchengle* ('disguised himself') and *fangzaile* ('put it there') would be fine in this context. However, given the nature of these reports as part of the preparatory procedure of the 'giving presents for Christmas' event, it can be understood why the writer chose not to use verbal *-le* in this instance. The same applies to *dakai hezi* ('opening the box') in 49.13. Verbal *-le* indicating 'realisation' can be used, but we are dealing with a 'preparatory event' which makes the use of verbal *-le* less appropriate. It would not be immediately clear why a preparatory event should 'stand out' in its context. The second part of this line, *kankan* ('take a look'), is of short duration and also preparatory, no verbal *-le* was used.

We can conclude that verbal *-le* marks a 'peak event' in a story line. 'Main events' are more easily selected as 'peaks' than 'preparatory events'. Speakers use markings with *-le* to guide addressees through an event series. The 'peaks' function as 'milestones' in the story. The historical development analysed in Chapter 4, showing event final marking with *liao* indicating 'inception' of an event to develop into modern verbal *-le*, makes the various uses illustrated in this section transparent.

5.3 Distribution of the particle *le* and action-story structure

A cross-tabulation of 'participatory acts' ('discourse acts'), and the form *-le/le* or the particle *le*, shows that the latter occurred most frequently in 'progress reports' (Table 5.6). It occurred in 106 'participatory acts' of that interaction type (9.9 per cent of the total number). Verbal *-le* was also used most

Table 5.6 Occurrence of verbal-*le* and *le* in 66 picture stories, according to type of discourse act

	Discourse act type					
	Opening	Instruction	Progress report	Verbal interaction	Other	Total
Le	9 (0.8%)	0 (0.0%)	106 (9.9%)	10 (0.9%)	4 (0.0%)	1,074 (100%)
V-*le*	5 (0.5%)	15 (1.4%)	30 (2.8%)	0 (0.0%)	3 (0.0%)	1,074 (100%)

Note
The data report occurrences of verbal *-le* and the particle *le* in the action-picture stories.

frequently in that discourse type, but to a much smaller extent however (n = 30 or 2.8 per cent of all discourse acts).

The particle *le* did not occur in 'instructions'. Verbal -*le* did, however (15 cases were counted). For a first exploration of the function of the particle *le* in the action stories, we selected 73 cases of the particle *le*, and studied them in their context. We selected transparent cases; that is, those in which the particle *le* was used in clause-final position, was preceded by a 'stative' verb, or by a non-verbal element. Such cases generally are agreed upon as representing the particle *le*, and we wanted to see the function these clear cases had in the action-picture stories before proceeding with greater numbers and more complex uses.

We will start our analysis with a look at 'project openings' (5.3.1), and then focus on 'progress reports' (5.3.2). We take up instructions in section 5.3.3, and look at uses of the particle in 'verbal interactions' in the following section (5.3.4). We then distinguish 'instigating events' (5.3.5), and also focus on 'warnings' (5.3.6), on ways in which the particle *le* is used in story 'endings' (5.3.7), and look at 'idiomatic uses' (5.3.8). Then we turn to uses of the particle *le* in narratives (5.3.9), and end with the relation between the particle *le* and time expressions (5.3.10). We conclude the chapter with a summary.

5.3.1 Openings

The particle *le* was used in four titles. We list them here as a first point of orientation:

10 *Sheng bing le* 'Getting sick'
44 *Shi huo le* 'Fire!'
56 *Sheng bing le* 'Sick at school'
61 *Xia yu le* 'It's raining'

All four indicate a 'deviation' from 'normal'. People on average are healthy, 'being sick' is considered a 'deviation', and so are the remaining two cases, a 'fire' and 'rain'. We will see shortly that the particle *le* is used most frequently to draw the attention of addressees to 'changes' or 'developments' that need special attention since they are not 'normal' or 'as expected'.

Opening lines

In the action-picture stories the particle *le* occurred in nine opening lines. An analysis of these occurrences revealed that the particle *le* was used in these nine stories under three conditions:

1 speaker pointing to an 'involuntary effect' (Mann and Thompson 1988) that needs to be addressed by the addressee;
2 suggested 'solution' to an earlier problem;

3 speaker indexing a 'new' or 'upcoming event' under the assumption that the addressee understands the implications and acts accordingly.

We found four instances of an 'involuntary effect', one case of a 'suggested solution', and four cases of an 'upcoming event'. We will discuss them in that order.

Involuntary effects

We distinguish between 'perceived problems' and 'event–reaction pairs'. 'Involuntary effects' are outside the control of both speaker and addressee. They often create a 'problem', or are 'perceived' as creating a 'problem', which the person being addressed supposedly is not aware of, and is expected to address. The examples are given in Table 5.7.

The 'weather change' 60.1 (*Waimian xia yu le!* 'It's raining outside') is a 'common event', and generally perceived as a 'deviation', as 'disturbing' an ongoing 'activity' or 'joint project'. Other examples are 63.3 (*Xia xue le* '[fall snow *le*] It's beginning to snow') and 64.2 (*Huran qi wu le* '[sudden rise fog *le*] Suddenly you enter a patch of fog'). The 'solution' to the 'rain problem' is scripted, and 'procedures' are available to deal with it: 'Find an umbrella', 'Put on rain clothes', or 'Wait', respectively. The various 'repairs' for the 'rain', 'snow' and 'fog' situation are both 'cultural' and 'personal'; they are part of the 'personal common ground'.

The remaining three problems relate to a person's individual or social situation. This implies that the 'problem' hinted at by the speaker is a 'perceived' problem, a 'problem' which cannot be claimed in objective terms but exists in the eyes of the speaker. However, the speaker assumes that there is a 'community-wide' justification for him saying this. He is not acting on his own, he assumes that he is invoking shared norms (and this should put the addressee under pressure to act), and he therefore expects the addressee to address the problem and solve it in agreement with the shared value system.

Table 5.7 Particle *le* marking a problem in the opening line(s) of a story (n = 6)

Opening line	Involuntary effect
29.1 Your hair is getting long. You need a haircut. *Ni de toufa chang le. Dei li fa le.*	Hair too long
34.1 Boy, your house sure is dirty! *Fangjian tai zang le. Dasaodasao ba!*	Room dirty
57.1 It's already 10 o'clock. You're late for class! *Shidian le. Ni chidaole!*	Late for class
60.1 It's raining outside. *Waimian xia yu le!*	Weather disruption

118 *Action-picture stories*

Suggested solution

In 29.1 *Ni de toufa chang le* ('Your hair is getting long'), the perceived 'deviation' is followed by a 'suggestion' for 'repair'. *Dei li fa le* '([must tidy-up hair *le*] You need a haircut'). In this case, the speaker suggests a 'solution' to a 'problem' and does so by using the particle *le*. The particle in this example is in construction with *dei* ('must'), which makes the 'suggestion' stand out as an 'advice'. 'It would be better for you, given the current circumstances, to go and have a hair cut'. An alternative formulation could have been an instruction, such as *Qu li fa qu* ('go and have a hair cut'). We will address 'Instructions' in section 5.3.3. We also will see shortly that indexing a 'solution' is a crucial component in understanding uses of the particle *le*. This is the first instance in which we encounter that possibility.

The second Chinese translation for the 'suggestion' for 'repair' had the form of an action marked with the particle *ba*: *dasodasao ba* ('you better clean up'). As in 'instructions', direct actions or 'doings' do not allow the use of the particle *le*. The particle *ba*, however, can be used to do precisely that, to negotiate an action the speaker considers necessary, demonstrating the functional differentiation of the various particles in Chinese. This alternative usage highlights the question for our study: 'what is the functional domain for the particle *le* in Chinese discourse.[12]

Upcoming events

The third type of example which attracted the use of the particle *le* was 'upcoming events'. The speaker signalled the 'upcoming event' in order to draw the attention of the addressee to it, thereby allowing him to reset his mental model (frame), and prepare for action. The relevant cases are listed in Table 5.8.

We see these 'upcoming events' as potentially 'breaking' the regular flow of everyday events. This view is in agreement with Thompson (1968), Huang (1988) and Huang and Davis (1989). However, in an interactive perspective there are other distinctions to consider, such as event 'goal', 'opening' and 'closing', type of 'control', 'participant status', and the extent of variation in 'practices' (cultural, institutional, individual). The examples found illustrate three possibilities:

1 'Seasonal festivals': the event 'goal' is culturally determined and historically legalised (Berger and Luckmann 1967); 'opening' and 'closing' are set as a day or days in the national calendar, participant status is a matter of free choice, leading to a wide variation in family oriented practices.
2 'Institution' (school) controlled events tend to have clearly defined 'goals', whereas participation of registered institution members is required, 'time' and 'place' are set by the institution.

Table 5.8 Particle *le* marking an upcoming event in the opening line(s) of a story (n = 4)

Opening line	Problem
40.1 You're going to have a Thanksgiving Dinner! *Nimen yao chi Gan'enjie Dacan le!*	Thanksgiving dinner
41.1 You feel that you could use a cup of tea *Ni xiang he cha le.*	Being thirsty/need a break
54.1 There's a test tomorrow. You need to work hard all evening *Mingtian yao kaoshi. Jintian dei ao ge ye le.*	Test
55.1 Everybody is in the classroom waiting for the exam *Ni he tongxuemen dou zuozai jiaoshi.li, kaoshi jiu yao kaishi le.*	Exam will begin

3 'Everyday events': one of a series of common practices, each scripted; individual and family-wise variation in practices.

All 'practices' tend to vary both within cultures and across cultures. Given observable differences in the way people participate in events, and in the way events are practised, each still can be seen as going through an 'opening', which confirms the event as open and initiates an event flow, and a 'closing', when the event is considered terminated, ceases cognitively to exist, and can thereafter only be remembered. The questions then are who 'opens' and who 'closes', 'how' is this done, and what is a person's participant status? In the case of 'seasonal happenings', there might be an official 'opening' and 'closing', but not all community members necessarily participate or are aware of its existence. Individual families or family members will synchronise their behaviour in agreement with local or personal circumstances and practices. 'Preparatory actions' are performed outside the time-frame set for the event. The main event is considered 'opened' when there is a minimal number of 'participants' present. For most participants the event is considered 'closed' when the main procedure is terminated (cf. Gumperz 1982).[13]

In 'institutional settings' (tests and exams at school) 'goals' are generally well defined and known to the participants; both the time and procedure are formally set (often in writing) and strictly adhered to. The status of all participants is known and achievements are recorded and regularly evaluated. There are sanctions for non-participation. Finally, each day 'individuals' create their own series of everyday behavioural practices, each with their own 'goal' and 'preparatory procedure'. Activating a 'preparatory procedure' ('putting the kettle on the fire') signals that a certain procedure (for instance 'making tea') is activated, and the 'main procedure' of 'drinking tea' will follow. Adult family members typically manipulate events freely. There are 'synchronisation forces', though. Breakfast tends to be in the morning, but has tended to move to lunchtime during the weekend.

In an 'interactive view', when one person finds reason to alert another person to some 'upcoming event', and he is authorised to do so, he starts from a full understanding of the event, its surrounding circumstances, 'goal' definition, and the addressee's and others' involvement and 'participant status'. Assertions with the particle *le* can alert a person, but they do not characterise a state of affairs as such. A speaker alerts an addressee by saying 'take note of this', 'this has consequences for you', and expects the addressee to be able to work out the implications and consequences. S/he assumes background knowledge (shared common ground). In each instance, a 'reframing of reality' is being urged. And reframing requires (mental) preparation, followed by a decision, which may lead to action, the execution of some 'procedure' (preparatory, main, final).

This situation is very clear in the case of the Thanksgiving Dinner, 40.1 *Nimen yao chi Gan'enjie Dacan le!* ('You're going to have a Thanksgiving Dinner!'). When such a major event is brought up, and the addressee had not yet set his mind to it, he needs to reframe, and consider the implications. If he decides to activate the Thanksgiving script, and act in agreement with local, regional, or national custom, he needs to prepare ('buy presents', 'buy food'; 'cook and set the table'), in order to make the execution of the 'main events' of the procedure' ('Christmas presents', 'enjoying the food together') possible.

This 'breaking into' or 'deviation' from normal is also the case with the upcoming test in 55.1 *Ni he tongxuemen dou zuozai jiaoshi.li, kaoshi jiu yao kaishi le* ('[you and classmates all sit-in class-*li*, exam follow will start *le*] Everybody is in the classroom waiting for the exam'). The announcement of the 'upcoming event', 'exam', requests the addressee to prepare his mind and be ready for what is to come. In line 54.1 the test itself is not brought into focus. It is mentioned as a shared fact: *Mingtian yao kaoshi* ('[Tomorrow must test] You are having a test tomorrow'). In this case the test information is provided as background knowledge, which allows focusing on the implications the test has for the addressee's personal common ground, his activities that evening *Jintian dei ao ge ye le* ('[Today must endure one night *le*] You need to work hard all night'), a related 'preparatory event' (the test being the 'main' event). This example makes clear again that the application of the particle *le* is not automatic, but 'speaker', 'goal' and 'purpose' oriented (cf. Chang 1986).

Example 41.1 *Ni xiang he cha le* ('You feel that you could use a cup of tea'), is marked with the particle *le* to indicate that this is an 'upcoming event', a 'break' into, or 'deviation' from, 'normal' procedure. The opening line could also have been given in a form without *le* to avoid such a 'break in' effect: 41.1 *Ni xiang pao yibei cha* ('[you think soak one-cup tea] You feel that you could use a cup of tea'). However, that in this instance the idea of 'break in' or 'deviation' is correct, is demonstrated by four similar examples occurring in story 53, 'Doing Homework', and story 58, 'Late for class', respectively. The text provided by the translator for these instances was: 53.5 *Huran ni xiang chi pingguo le* ('[suddenly you think eat apple *le*] Suddenly you feel hungry for an apple'); 53.7 *Ni you xiang kan dianshi le* ('[you again want watch TV *le*] Suddenly you realise that your favourite television program is on'); and 53.11 *Yihuir ni you xiang ting yinyue le* ('[shortly you again think listen music *le*] Some music would be nice'). The example in story 58 was *Ni huran xiang chi tang he qiaokeli le* ('[you suddenly think eat sweets and chocolate *le*] Suddenly, you feel hungry for something sweet'). The latter four examples all had a 'break-in' marker in the form of *huran* ('suddenly'), and *you* ('again').

We conclude that the analysis of the particle *le* in 'openings' showed that the particle is used to either mark a 'deviation', an 'involuntary effect', or an 'upcoming event'. All three deal with 'problems' that need to be addressed by the person spoken to. In the case of 'involuntary effects', the related 'problem' can be 'individual' or social'. The particle *le* in an 'upcoming event' signals a need for reorientation of the addressee at that point, and expects the addressee to reframe the situation, make a decision, and prepare for further action. A 'solution' to a 'problem' can also be 'suggested' and marked with *le*. However, the basic idea remains the same: the addressee is expected to co-ordinate his common ground on the information being provided, reset his mental model accordingly, and work out the consequences.

5.3.2 Progress reports

Having established that in 'openings' of action stories there are 'peak events' that mark 'deviations', and 'solutions', we first looked at 11 stories in which the particle *le* occurred once (not counting opening lines). We limited our data in this way in order to,

1 study clear cases of uses of the particle *le* in its cognitive environment,
2 go forward step by step rather than jump into a mass of uses of the particle and share in the general confusion,
3 see if the first analysis stands or is refuted.

The step-by-step procedure showed that among the 11 cases encountered, seven indexed 'involuntary effects', whereas one was an 'upcoming event', and in three cases the idea of a 'solution' could be recognised. All within the confines of the 'deviation' and 'solution' hypotheses. We start with a listing of the involuntary effects (Table 5.9).

As in the previous analysis, the 'involuntary effects' imply an addressee related 'problem' (individual, social), which, in the speaker perspective, the person spoken to should address. The seriousness of the effects observed, and therefore the need to react to the problem, varied considerably. We found

Table 5.9 Particle *le* indexing an involuntary effect, progress reports (n = 7)

Story/line	Involuntary effect	Problem
3.10	It's stuck in your throat!	*Yaowan qiazai sangzi.li le.*
4.4	The point is dull.	*Bijian dun le.*
5.4	You spilled some of it on your plate!	*Youxie daozai diezi.li le.*
6.8	It's too big!	*Tai da le.*
7.2	You spilled some of it on the table!	*Sadao zhuozi.shang le.*
64.2	Suddenly you enter a patch of fog!	*Huran qi wu le!*
65.11	You're perspiring all over!	*Ni hunshen shi han le*

'life threatening' situations, as in 3.10, *Yaowan qiazai sangzi.li le* ('It's stuck in your throat!'), when a normal body function is blocked. And mere 'disturbances' of a regular situation, as in 7.2, *Sadao zhuozi.shang le* ('You spilled some of it on the table'), when milk is spilled. The reactions by the addressee therefore also varied in intensity. The remaining 'deviations'/'problems' attested were: 4.4 *Bijian dun le* ('[pen-point dull *le*] The point is dull)' ('not being able to write'); 5.4 *Youxie daozai diezi.li le* ('[have-some drop-on plate-in *le*] You spilled some of it on your plate'); (spilling cereals); 6.8 *Tai da le* ('[too big *le*] It's too big!') (a mismatch ['problem'] between plan and execution [coat too big]); 64.2 *Huran qi wu le* ('[sudden rise fog *le*] Suddenly you enter a patch of fog!') (a 'problem' due to a circumstance change); and 65.11 *Ni hunshen shi han le* ('[you whole-body is sweat *le*] You're perspiring all over!') (a 'problem' of 'getting too hot').

The weather example ('fog' in 64.2) can be treated in the same way as the 'rain' example in the previous section. 'Fog' is a 'deviation' from 'normal' circumstances, and this deviation is so 'salient' that the co-ordination marker *le* must be expressed. The 'dull pencil' example is like the 'hair' example. The resulting 'problem', however, is 'self-inflicted'. By using a pencil it ends up dull. The 'predictability' of this effect implies that techniques have been developed to solve the problem (finding and applying a pencil sharpener). Addressee responsibility is also involved in the 'sunbathing event'. It is a case of person–nature interaction. The story character lies down in the sun but after a while discovers that it is too hot and starts 'sweating', and 'sweating' (65.11) is a 'deviation' from 'normal' (being comfortable and not-sweating), and is marked with the particle *le*. The remaining part of the story describes how the story character finds a way out of this by moving to a shady place and taking his nap there.

Example 6.8 illustrates the 'misfiring' ('deviation') of a 'trying a coat on' procedure. The 'goal' set by the procedure ('trying on a coat') is reached, but what is being 'attained' is not what is 'intended', 'the coat does not fit'. The intended 'goal' is not reached and that is presented as a 'deviation' which is marked with the particle *le*, *tai da le* ('too big!'). Either the 'person trying on the coat' (looking in a mirror) or the 'person observing the procedure' can signal to the other that something is wrong, and either can propose a 'repair procedure', after which the cycle can be repeated again. The cyclical nature of this procedure makes it different from the preceding ones. Neither 'involuntary effects' nor 'upcoming events' allow second chances.

In the remaining two instances, a similar 'deviation' from 'goal attainment' occurs, but this time the 'problem' is fully self-inflicted in the sense that 'a motor skill fails' and a more or less serious 'problem' results. 'Cereals are spilled' on the plate (they are not in the bowl; 5.4), and 'milk is spilled' on the table (7.2).

These seven 'involuntary effects' confirm our earlier findings. The particle *le* marks 'deviations', 'disturbances' of expected 'normal' or 'everyday' developments (event flow), or 'disturbances' of a procedure. For everyday situations, 'repair procedures' have been worked out and are available as scripts. In non-life-threatening situations, however, the addressee always has the option to decide not to initiate the repair. He can decide not to clean the table or not try on another coat. 'Common sense' ('the will to live') is one form of regulation. 'Societal institutions' such as the 'police force' and the 'judiciary' are others. Given the non-compelling nature of certain repairs, it still remains true that speakers can mark a 'deviation' in the normal unfolding of a procedure or project with the particle *le*. Their intent thereby is to notify the addressee. The latter needs to work out the way in which it is best to proceed, or not to proceed at all.

We already met one instance of a 'suggested solution' to a perceived 'problem'. There were three more solutions in our data and they are listed in Table 5.10. Each of these examples marks the 'solution' to an earlier 'problem'. In story 21, 'Changing a light bulb', the light did not work (an 'involuntary effect' resulting in a 'technical problem'), and now after replacing the bulb it works again (21.10). An earlier 'deviation' has been 'resolved', and now the remark by the speaker helps the addressee to realise that he can remove the problem from his memory file/mental model and act as 'normal' again.

This analysis can also be applied to the remaining two examples. When a 'preparing toast' procedure is started and the toast is ready, the particle *le* is used when the 'goal' of that procedure is reached. As this example shows, 'goal attainment' in a (preparatory) procedure can be marked with the expression *Hao le* ('Ready!'), and can be understood from the perspective of the reset of the addressee's 'personal common ground'. He now can prepare for the next step in the overarching procedure 'making breakfast', placing

Table 5.10 Particle *le* indexing 'solutionhood'; progress reports

Story		Solutionhood
21.10	It works!	*Liang le.*
32.6	It's done!	*Hao le.*
42.14	...take it easy and take plenty of rest.	...*haohao shui yijiao jiu hao le.*

the toast on his plate and putting butter and jam on it. The fourth example developed in a context in which the story character did not feel well (his 'problem'), and went to see a doctor to get his problem 'solved'. The latter projected a behavioural path, which is presented as guaranteeing recovery (. . . *jiu hao le*).

What we found in this section is that the analysis of the particle *le* as indexing a 'problem' or 'deviation' in a procedure, suggesting a 'solution', or alerting an addressee to a 'new event' are confirmed by the data. We found:

1   'solutions' to an earlier 'problem', and
2   'goal attainment' as part of the execution of a 'procedure'.

Both the 'solution' to a 'problem' and 'goal-attainment' we like to list under the term 'solutionhood', following earlier event analyses by Mann and Thompson (1988). The particle *le*, at this point, can be hypothesised as being triggered in one of three ways:

1   'Deviation' from 'normal', or from an 'intended goal'; unidirectional or cyclical.
2   'Upcoming event' requiring a mental model reset.
3   'Solutionhood' bringing an earlier 'deviation' back to 'normal'; (suggest) a 'solution' to a 'problem'; report 'goal attainment'.

This analysis demonstrates that the particle *le* can be used both in situations of 'deviation' and in situations of 'repair' or 'solutionhood'. Both the movement 'away' from 'normal' and 'back' to 'normal' can be marked with the particle *le*. The area of 'deviation' is where Murphy's Law applies. If something can go wrong it will, as some of the action stories illustrate, and in such cases the particle *le* can be used. 'Goal attainment' can be seen as the 'solution' to a self-created 'problem'. This opens a window on the next event. We recognise this as an instance of an 'event boundary', or 'progress so far' (Thompson 1968; Li and Thompson 1981).

5.3.3 *Instructions*

Instructions to act, as a rule, do not take up the particle *le*. However, some instructions make an appeal to cognitive functioning and in such instances the particle *le* did appear in the data. An example is:

9.2   Wake up   *Xing le!*

This finding leads us to hypothesise that a 'doing' in the immediate situation is not compatible with usage of the particle *le*. The particle indexes a 'deviation', or 'solutionhood', and the information being provided suffices to reset the common ground existing between speaker and addressee. Both 'deviation' and 'solutionhood' require 'reflection' on what is implied. They require a mental reset, a reset of the current mental model or personal common ground.

'Instructions', however, did accommodate certain uses of verbal *-le* (see the data in Table 5.6), as the following examples illustrate:

27.11   *Zhengdale yanjing*   'Open your eyes wide'
61.4   *Chengkaile san*   'Open the umbrella'

These two examples are more easily used without the 'reality' marker verbal *-le*, but the current uses stressing the full result of the resultative constructions: 27.11 *Zhengdale* ('[open-large-*le*] open wide'), followed by *yanjing* ('eyes'), and 61.4 *Chengkaile* ('[push-open-*le*] open') followed by the object *san* ('umbrella'), are possible.

One question to be answered now regards the nature of marking or indexing with verbal *-le*. Is this syntactic or pragmatic in orientation? Clearly, the answer in the case of verbal *-le*, as was the case with the particle *le*, must be pragmatic. The various 'instructions' can appear without *-le*. The pragmatic criterion is the wish by the speaker to express 'realisation' or 'accomplishment' of the indexed action at that point: 'do it' and 'do it through and through'. In example 49.4 *guale* ('[hang-realised]' 'puts on'), 'accomplishment' is being reported, and the accompanying picture showed the wreath as fixed on the door. This comparison allows the following schema:

61.4   'direct address'   'instruction'   'a doing'
49.4   'narrative'   'progress report'   'a doing' (reported)

These data suggest two types of uses for verbal *-le*. Verbal *-le* can be related to 'actions' or 'doings' and can be used both in 'instructions' to 'do something immediately' and in 'progress reports' as part of narrating a series of events.[14] It can, in other words, function at two levels – at the action level, the level of the immediate situation, and at the level of 'reporting', which requires cognitive reflection, remembering and reporting of earlier events.

Interestingly, the particle *le* cannot be used this way. It cannot be used in 'instructions' involving direct action, and it cannot be used to mark an 'action' as 'realised'. The particle stands out as doing something more, and that leads us to the second question we must ask: in comparison with verbal *-le*, what, in comparison, is the nature and level of marking with the particle *le*?

In order to be able to hypothesise an answer for that question, we compared the following two examples, a verbal *-le* example and a particle *le* example respectively:

49.4   *Baba zai menshang* **guale** *yige hen piaoliang de huahuan*
       'Daddy puts a beautiful wreath on the door,'
46.12 *Huanranyixin le!* 'It looks quite clean now!'

126   *Action-picture stories*

Example 49.4, as already discussed, indexes 'accomplishment' of an action, and thereby makes it 'stand out' as 'successfully completed'. Example 46.12, in which the particle *le* is used, occurs in the closing line of story 46, 'Cleaning the living room', and reports 'solutionhood'. We therefore hypothesise that both forms of marking are complementary: one marking a 'peak event' in the current common ground, whereas the other marks a 'peak episode'. The 'peak event' is an 'accomplishment' in a foregrounded event, whereas the 'peak episode' marks 'deviations' and 'solutionhood' – change in the structure of the common ground. A 'peak event' is mainly used in narrative discourse and makes story progress possible, whereas the particle *le* is chosen when there is a 'peak episode' (representing a 'deviation' or 'solutionhood') on which the speaker wants the addressee to co-ordinate and requests him/her to reset the shared common ground as indicated.

5.3.4 Verbal interactions

'Verbal interactions' are 'conversational exchanges' or 'minimal joint projects' between two or more story characters holding a certain 'participatory role'. These exchanges are particularly interesting since conversational data are complex and illustrate uses of the particle *le* between identified participants, each holding their own personal common ground.[15] This first encounter with such data is also a test for the hypotheses developed so far. We will see shortly that the hypotheses formulated hold, but need to be appended in order to allow them to cope with the conversational data encountered in the action-picture stories.

In seven of the (14) interactional exchanges the particle *le* (and/or verbal *-le*) occurred. All examples are quotes of direct speech. They are listed in Table 5.11. The data can be analysed as three cases of a 'solution', and two cases indexing a 'problem' or 'deviation'. These distinctions are familiar. In addition, however, we find one case in which something was made 'outstanding', and another in which a 'question' was asked. The latter two possibilities are new in our data and we will pay special attention to them.[16]

The two 'deviation' examples are 44.8 *Wode jia zhao huo le!* ('[my house catch fire *le*] My house is on fire'), and 51.13 *Wo e le!* ('[I hunger *le*] I'm hungry!'). The first of these clearly shows a 'deviation' from 'normal'. Houses in the 'normal everyday world' are not on fire. 'Hunger' too, in our view, is a 'deviation' from what is 'normal' or expected as being 'normal', 'not being hungry'.

'Solutionhood' was expressed by three examples. The doctor–patient interaction, example 42.14, we already encountered in section 5.3.2 (Table 5.10). The same distinction can be recognised in line 48.15 when the 'post office clerk' signals to the 'customer' that the interaction is completed, *banhaole* ('it's fixed'), implying that the 'procedure' has reached the status of a 'solution' (particle *le*). The signalling of 'solutionhood' implies that the customer is expected to leave and make room for the next customer. Similarly,

Table 5.11 Uses of the particle *le* in verbal interactions

Story	Activity roles	Verbal interaction
42.14	Doctor–patient	*Huiqu haohao shui yijiao jiu hao le.* 'Take it easy and take plenty of rest.'
44.8	Main character–fire department	*Wode jia zhao huo le!* 'My house is on fire.'
47.10	Nancy–Nina	*Wo zui ai chi yu le!* 'I like fish very much.'
48.15	Clerk–customer	*Dou banhaole*! 'It's all set, sir.'
51.13	Daughter–father	*Wo e le*! 'I'm hungry!'
55.16	Student–father	*Wo quan zuoduile!* 'Everything went okay!'
56.4	Teacher–student	*Ni zenmo la?* 'What's the matter?'

in line 55.16 the 'son' informs his 'father' that the exam went well, *zuoduile* ('it went okay'). Here too we can recognise 'solutionhood', but as part of information distribution between related personal common grounds.

In the two examples 48.15 *banhaole* ('it's fixed') and 55.16 *zuoduile* ('it went okay'), we wrote [*le*] as if it was verbal -*le*, but our discussion was that of the particle *le*. We did this in order to show that in these instances both verbal -*le* and the particle *le* are involved. 'Realisation' (verbal -*le*) and 'project completion' ('solutionhood') are easily combined. We take it that 'project completion' (that is the particle *le*), is always the stronger; that is, the cognitively more demanding notion. However, both notions reinforce each other and that can explain why we only find one marking [*le*] in such cases (cf. Li and Thompson 1981).

Two examples do not fit and seem to break the hypothesis developed so far. In story 47 two girls visit a restaurant and one of them tells the other, when they are studying the menu card, 47.10 *Wo zui ai chi yu le!* ('[I most like eat fish *le*] I like fish very much'). This is a way in which one of the situation participants makes her 'personal ground' 'outstanding' in an endeavour to make her 'preference' part of the shared 'personal common ground' of that moment.[17] We can bring this under the earlier distinctions by seeing it as a 'deviation' in a category of comparable events. The message can then be read as 'Comparing dishes, look at what my preference is and add this information to our common ground'.[18]

In 56.4, finally, we also encountered a question, *Ni zenmo la?* ('What's the matter?'), when the teacher notices that one of the students in his class does not look very well. He thereby signals that he recognised a 'problem' or 'deviation' and requests to be 'updated'. The answer to that request will potentially bring him 'up to date' with current affairs, and on that basis he

128 *Action-picture stories*

can decide further action (such as sending her to the school nurse, as in this case). This type of question we like to call a 'co-ordinating question'.

Our data so far show that apart from 'deviation' and 'solutionhood' (project completion), the particle *le* can be used to 'make something stand out among equals', and be used to ask about a 'deviation' in someone's 'personal common ground'. We list these four occurrence types for ease of overview:

1   'Deviation' or 'problem' (including 'upcoming events')
2   'Solutionhood'
3   'Making something stand out' (deviate)
4   'Questioning common ground' (about a deviation)

As we argued, 'problems' and 'solutions' are different sides of the same coin. When there is a 'problem' in the 'common ground', the particle *le* is used to request co-ordination on the information presented as a 'solution'. Otherwise, when the 'initial common ground' is 'normal' or 'conventional', the particle *le* is used to signal a 'deviation' or 'problem' of some sort. All four usage types, however, confirm that the core function of the particle *le* is 'signalling the perceived need for common ground co-ordination at that point in the interaction'. 'Making something stand out' already indicates that there is something being communicated that needs co-ordinating. In 'questions' there is not a request in the direction of the addressee to update herself/himself; rather, the speaker signals that s/he (the speaker) requests 'being 'updated' because s/he misses a piece of information in the 'shared common ground'. S/he is 'willing' to co-ordinate but would like to know 'what to co-ordinate on'. We can conclude, then, that so far the seven examples of 'verbal interactions' discussed in this section remain within the unifying analysis proposed.

5.3.5 Event–reaction pairs

Event–reaction pairs consist of two ordered events – an 'instigating event' and a 'reaction' – which have different origins (cf. Clark 1996: 194). The 'reaction' in the following examples is an 'emotional reaction' and self-directed.[19] Four event – reaction pairs that contained the particle *le* were attested in the action stories. They are listed in Table 5.12.

The four 'instigating events' all created sudden (realisations) of 'involuntary effects' which were not intended and developed out of the control of the speaker, or were the result of inattentiveness, negligence, or distraction by the speaker. In 16.12 the ice cream was left out of the refrigerator and melted: *Bingqilin ronghuale!* ('[ice cream melt-change-*le*] Oh no! The ice cream melted'). This was shocking when discovered, and a 'sudden' development at the moment of discovery. In 17.10 the baby who is being fed suddenly 'vomits': *Ah, kan! Ta tuchulaile!* ('[Oh look, she spit-out-come-*le*] Oh

Action-picture stories 129

Table 5.12 Particle *le* indexing the 'endpoint' of a procedure; event–reaction pairs

Story	Event	Reaction	Translation
16.12	Ice cream melted	A! Bingqilin ronghuale!	Oh no! The ice cream melted.
17.10	Child vomits	A, kan! Ta tuchulaile!	Oh look! She's spitting it out!
43.4	Tooth aches	Tengsi wo le!	It hurts!
58.12	Being late	Aiya! Kuai shang ke le!	Oh, no! Break time is over!

look! She's spitting it out!'); and in 43.4 the 'instigating event' is a sudden penetrating pain caused by a 'toothache': *Tengsi wo le!* ('[pain-die I *le*] It hurts!'). Example 58.12, finally, is a 'co-ordination problem', and since it involves time also a 'synchronisation problem': 'I'm being late', *Aiya! Kuai shang ke le* ('[Oh no, fast go-up class *le*] Oh no! Break time is over!'). Since 'time' is not directly visible, the person must either realise the 'synchronisation problem' himself or be notified that there exists such a 'problem'. In this case, he realises what time it is, and reacts in an ashamed way about his 'failure' to 'synchronise'.

The 'identification' and 'recognition' of the 'sudden' 'instigating event' evokes an 'emotional reaction'. The speaker thereby expresses 'negative evaluation' of the 'involuntary effect'. What s/he signals is that there is a 'problem'. We therefore count these examples as special cases of 'problems' or 'deviations'. Since the expressions are self-directed, the speaker her/himself is supposed to be resourceful enough to solve the 'problem' s/he finds her/himself in. However, these emotional expressions can attract the attention of other situation participants, and these latter may feel obliged to join in and help. That is the nature of human 'empathy'.

Now it may occur to some readers that earlier examples of 'rain falling' (*Xia yu le* '[fall rain *le*] it rains') and 'fog arising' (*Qi wu le* '[rise fog *le*] It's foggy'), can be interpreted in a similar way. That is indeed the case. A lone car driver may sigh, *A ya, qi wu le!* ('Oh no, it's getting foggy'). There is a crucial difference, however. Requests for co-ordination are assertions directed at an addressee as 'participant' in a 'joint project'. 'Emotional expressions' can only be used in direct relationship to the 'instigating event' occurring. They do not allow transposition to a later time. A third person informing his colleague that it is raining does not do so by using the emotional expression *Ah ya, xia yu le!* ('Oh no, it starts to rain!'). He will use the expression *Xia yu le* ('It's raining now'), knowing that this piece of background information will make the addressee co-ordinate and allow him to react in a way that fits his 'personal common ground'.[20]

5.3.6 *Warnings*

'Warnings' are 'assertions' or 'instructions' of what to 'avoid' or 'not to do'. An example is 18.3 *Buyao geshang ziji* ('Don't cut yourself!'). The expression

Table 5.13 Uses of *xiaoxin* 'be careful' (n = 5)

Story/line	Negative instruction	Translation
7.14	***Xiaoxin**. Buyao zai sale!*	Be careful. Don't spill again!
18.3.	***Xiaoxin**. Buyao geshang ziji!*	Be careful. Don't cut yourself!
18.12	*Zhehuir ke dei **xiaoxin** dianr le!*	Be careful this time.
	Buyao zai ba zhege shuaihuaile!	Don't break this one!
25.9	*Ba panzi fangzai zhuozi.shang,*	Put the plate down, but careful!
	***xiaoxin** dianr.*	
30.6	***Xiaoxin**. You xie lanni.*	Careful! There's some mud!

xiaoxin '[small-heart] be careful' is in comparison a 'pre-warning', signalling that attention is needed for the current 'project' (for instance for 'crossing the street'). The 'pre-warning', *xiaoxin* ('be careful') occurred five times in the action stories (Table 5.13), four times it was used in the form '*xiaoxin*' and one time the particle *le* was added. The particle *le* form occurred in line 18.12 *Zhehuir ke dei xiaoxin dianr le!* ('[this-time sure must careful a-little *le*} Be careful this time'). In this example, however, the particle *le* is in construction with the modality index *dei* ('must'), which requests a mental reset and preparation for future actions. We observed such a use before in the 'suggested solution' of line 29.1 *Dei li fa le* ('You need a hair cut'). This way the force of immediacy is taken away from the 'pre-warning' and room is created for 'reflection', and the 'immediacy' is bracketed.

Three times the 'pre-warning' was followed by a 'warning' (7.14, 18.3, 18.12). We will come back to these in a moment. One time an 'instruction' to do something preceded the use of the 'pre-warning', 25.9 *Ba panzi fangzai zhuozi.shang, xiaoxin dianr* ('Put the plate down, but careful!'). These examples make us sensitive to a possible event chain, 'instruction', 'pre-warning', 'warning' (*buyao/bie*...). The following 'chain' options can be distinguished:

Event chain
'instruction', 'pre-warning', 'warning' (*buyao*...)
'instruction', 'pre-warning' (25.9)
   'pre-warning', 'warning' (7.14, 18.3, 18.12, 30.6)
   'pre-warning',
      'warning'

Four of the five examples can be linked to two 'chains': one is 'instruction', 'pre-warning', and the other 'pre-warning', 'warning'. In example 30.6 *Xiaoxin. You xie lanni.*' ([careful, have some mud] 'Careful! There's some mud!'), the 'warning' is 'indirect'. It is created through pointing to a substance (on the road) which had better be avoided.[21]

The three remaining examples in which the 'pre-warning' is followed by a 'warning', point at 'doings' to be 'avoided'. This is illustrated by example

18.3 *Buyao geshang ziji* ('Don't cut yourself!'). The 'warnings' in the remaining two examples, 7.14, *Buyao zai sale!* ('Don't spill again!') and 18.12, *Buyao zai ba zhege shuaihuaile!* ('Don't break this one!') also assert 'negative effects' (*sale* ['spill-*le*'] and *shuaihuaile* ['throw-break-*le*']). Both are final remarks in the story and we take them to represent the particle *le* which requests common-ground co-ordination in such a way that repetition (*zai* ['new again'], *you* 'repeat again') of a previous disturbance in future actions can be avoided.

The two 'negative effects' are also marked as 'realised' with verbal -*le*. However, as these examples show, the 'realisation' in these two examples can also be recognised as forms of 'deterioration' (the particle *le*), *sale* ('spill it'), and *shuaihuaile* ('break it'), respectively. They therefore are directly related to the state of the 'shared common ground' at that moment, and therefore take the form of an advice to reset the common ground in such a way that the potential 'distortion' does not occur.[22]

In this section we have observed that 'warnings' can accept marking with verbal -*le*. However, we also observed that in 'pre-warnings' and 'warnings' the particle *le* can be used when a link with existing 'cumulated common ground' is assumed. The common-ground markers in these cases were *zai* and *you* ('again'), as well as *dei* ('must'). They created distance from the immediate situation and allow time for 'reflection' and 'preparation' for the next activity, which will be a repetition of the one that misfired earlier. Without such 'common-ground markers', the activity can only be described directly or with the help of the 'peak' marker verbal -*le*.

5.3.7 Story endings

Examples 7.14 and 18.12, which we encountered in the previous section, were last lines in a picture story. That position encouraged the establishment of a relation with the 'cumulated common ground'. Not considering these two cases of 'final remarks', we found 13 stories in which the 'last line' commented on, or described, the 'endpoint' of the procedure or event being portrayed. The particle *le*, as demonstrated above, would be expected when a 'peak event' (a 'deviation' or 'solution') could be signalled. In four endings *le* occurred. Of these, three indicated 'project completion', whereas the fourth was an evaluation of a project result. They are listed in Table 5.14.

Line 25.12 opens with an evaluative remark *Tai bang le* ('Great!'), and this way draws the attention of the addressee to a 'project solution'. In the second part *Xiuhaole* ('You fixed it') that 'project solution' is further spelled out. Example 44.15 *zongsuan ba huo pumiele* ('at least the fire has been put out') can be similarly analysed. It asserts 'project completion', the 'solution' to a previous 'problem' (particle *le*). The fire brigade arrived and extinguished the kitchen fire. Example 46.12, *Huanran yixin le!* ('It looks quite clean now!'), we already discussed; it is a clear case of 'project completion' or 'solutionhood'. The originally dirty room now looks as new!

132 *Action-picture stories*

Table 5.14 Particle *le* in goal–reaction pairs

Story/last line	Chinese	English
25.12	Tai bang le! Xiuhaole!	Great! You fixed it! [solution]
41.16	Chade weidao haojile.	It tastes great! [solutionhood]
44.15	...danshi zongsuan ba huo pumiele.	...but at least the fire has been put out [solution]
46.12	Huanran yixin le!	It looks quite clean now! [solution]

The fourth and final example of a 'story ending' 41.16 (tasting a cup of tea), *Chade weidao haojile* ('[tea *de* taste good-extreme-*le*] It tastes great!'), is an evaluative remark expressing appreciation. It can be recognised as a 'peak event'. The form -*jile* indicates the extreme pole (-*ji* ['extreme', 'pole']) of a positive evaluation (*hao* ['good']), and thereby qualifies as a special case of making something 'stand out' as extreme in a series of events (cf. Clark 1996: 194).

5.3.8 *Idioms with* le

The last example draws our attention to idiomatic forms, combinations of an index of something 'extreme' and the particle *le*. Our data contain three more such idiomatic forms. They are all evaluative remarks. We listed all four, including example 41.16 just discussed, in Table 5.15 for ease of overview. The 'outstanding effects' in these examples, apart from -*jile* ('extreme'), were created in 34.16 with -*duole* in *haoduole* ('[good-much-*le*] much better'), with -*huaile* ('bad') in 49.14 *gaoxinghuaile* ('[happy-bad-*le*]') so good that it went bad, that is even farther than happy, 'very very happy', and with -*toule* ('[penetrate-*le*]') in 51.16 *Xie dou shitoule* ('[shoes all wet-penetrate-*le*] Your shoes are all wet!'). The first index of a negative extreme was *huai* ('bad'), which was used to create a strong positive effect, whereas the second 'deviation peak' was created through the use of the term *shi* ('wet'), which itself is already a 'deviation' and 'outstanding', and will need to appear with the particle *le* as in *Xie shi le* ('My shoes are wet'). In this case it is made even more 'outstanding' by the addition of -*tou*, *shitoule* '[penetrate-*le*]; fully-*le*', 'wet through and through'. This last example also counts as an 'instigating event' – 'reaction' chain. Like the 'ice cream' example, the process itself takes some time, but on discovery of the 'effect' the reaction is emotional. *Aiya! Xie dou shitoule!* ('Oh no! My shoes are all wet!')[23]

5.3.9 *Telling a story*

In section 5.1.3 we observed that a small number of the action-picture stories relied heavily on 'progress reports'. These action stories took the form

Table 5.15 Idioms with *-le* in evaluative expressions

Story/ last line	Project	Chinese	English
34.16	[Cleaning the house]	Kanshangqu *haoduole*	'It looks much better!'
41.16	[Making tea]	Cha *de* weidao *haojile*	'The tea tastes great!'
49.14	[Christmas presents]	Tamen dou gaoxing*huaile*	'They feel very happy!'
61.16	[Bad weather]	Aiya! Xie dou *shitoule!*	'Your shoes are all wet!'

Table 5.16 Uses of the particle *le* in story 51, 'A Sunday Drive' (scenario)

Story	Example	Translation
51.6	*Hongdeng liang le! Ba che tingxialai.*	'The light turns red! Slow down.'
51.8	*Lüdeng liang le! Xiang you zhuanwan.*	'The light turns green! Turn right!'
51.12	*Tamen laidao yitiao linyindao.shang le.*	'They come now on a country road with nothing but trees at both sides.'
51.13	*Lingling he Lanlan you dian e le...*	'Lingling and Lanlan are a little hungry.'
51.13	*Wo e le!*	'I'm hungry!'

of a regular adventure. In this section, we would like to take a closer look at story 51, 'A Sunday Drive', in which the particle *le* was used more frequently than in any other story (five times). These five cases are listed in Table 5.16.

The first four of these examples of the 'Sunday Drive' are 'updates' or 'progress reports'; that is, information provided by the 'narrator' to the 'apprentice'/'reader'. The fifth example is a case of 'verbal interaction' between 'story characters'. In lines 51.6 and 51.8 the Sunday drive is 'disturbed' by a 'traffic light'. We therefore see 51.6, *Hongdeng liang le!* ('The light turns red!') and 51.8 *Lüdeng liang le!* ('The light turns green!'), as a 'problem' and a 'solution' respectively in traffic flow. The third example of the use of *le* is a 'progress report' detailing a new phase in the trip: 51.12, *Tamen laidao yitiao linyindao.shang le* ('They come now on a country road with nothing but trees at both sides.') Clearly, this development is marked as a 'peak event', which we can recognise either as 'making the area outstanding', and thereby 'creating a new situation' for the participants, as 'goal attainment', or as 'project completion'.

In example 51.13, finally, we find two uses of the particle *le* with *e* ('being hungry'). The first of these is a 'progress report', two of the story characters (the children) got hungry, and the 'storyteller' requests the 'animators'/'readers' to co-ordinate on that. 51.13, *Lingling he Lanlan you dian e le....* ('Lingling and Lanlan are a little hungry'). The second use is a verbal interaction between one of the children and their father, *Wo e le* ('I got hungry'). The latter seems to have got the message (has 'taken up' the 'proposed project'), for he stops the car and they go looking for a nice picnic spot.

We can conclude that the distinctions made so far work in the 'Sunday Drive' story we just analysed. We found marking with the particle *le* in 'progress reports' for the indication of, respectively,

1   a 'problem' and its 'solution' (traffic flow);
2   'project completion' as a case of 'solutionhood';
3   a 'deviation' from 'normal' (hungry) ('progress report');
4   a 'deviation' from 'normal' (hungry) ('assertion' 'direct address').

All four cases can fall within the 'deviation', 'solutionhood', and 'being outstanding' in a series hypothesis. The remarkable difference is that between 'progress reports' and 'direct address'. In the first case, the 'storyteller' updates the 'reader' and requests co-ordination on that point; in the second case a story character reports a 'deviation' to a situation participant and requests the addressee to co-ordinate on that these are two levels of 'imagining', as we will see in the next chapter (cf. Clark 1996).

5.3.10 *Projects and time*

When the particle *le* is related to a time expression, it can be identified as a 'change of state' (Li and Thompson 1981: 246). It must be clear by now that we reject such an interpretation and the question therefore arises as to how time expressions can be treated under a unified theory of 'peak events' and 'co-ordination of common ground'. We therefore surveyed all action stories for time expressions and found six with *le*. We list them in Table 5.17.

Time progresses constantly, and natural time (progression through the day and into the night) is a perceptual source. In stories such information is missing. It is no surprise then that the six cases listed all represent a time update by the instructor as to the time passed so far, allowing the animator to reorient himself, co-ordinate his common ground with the content of the assertion, and work out the consequences. We therefore conclude that the moments in time marked with *le* are marked as 'peak events'.

A pragmatic analysis of time allows at least four distinctions; namely, natural or *cyclical time* (that is, the changes of day and night), *calendar time* (the function assignment to the seasons in terms of days, weeks and months), *clock time* (the precise counting of time in minutes and seconds, and hourly intervals), all of which are used in technologically developed societies to detail the calendar time. The fourth distinction we want to add is *institutional time*, the way in which institutions synchronise their operations with cyclical, calendar, and clock time and assign them functions (opening time, closing time, working time, coffee break, tea time, etc.) (cf. Comrie 1976).

Table 5.17 Pragmatic marking of clauses containing a time index (n = 6)

Story	Chinese	English
52.8	Zhongwu le, taiyang shaide ni hunshen shi han.	It's noon now and the sun is so strong you sweat all over.
53.14	Aiya! Zenmo yijing shidian le!	Wow! It's already ten o'clock!
54.14	Shijian bu zao le, gai shui jiao le!	It's already late, you need to go to sleep.
57.1	Shidian le! Ni chidaole!	It's already ten o'clock. You're late for class!
57.5	Zhenshi bu zao le, ni paode geng kuai le!	Now you're really late. Run even faster!
60.12	Shijian bu zao le, ni jueding chuan yuyi chuqu!	It's late already, so you decide to put on your raincoat.

When the six uses of a time expression were related to these time distinctions, it turned out that three cases were related to cyclical time, whereas the remaining three cases indexed institutional time:

52.8	*Zhongwu le*	Cyclical time
53.14	*Zenmo yijing shidian le*	Cyclical/task time; homework
54.14	*Shijian bu zao le*	Cyclical time
57.1	*Shidian le*	Institutional time; school
57.5	*zhenshi bu zao le*	Institutional time; school
60.12	*shijian bu zao le*	Institutional time; work

Four of these expressions are of the form *bu zao le* ('[not early *le*] It's late already') type. In these cases time is marked as a 'peak event' and co-ordination at that point is requested. Example 54.14, *Shijian bu zao le, gai shuijiao le* ('[time not early *le*, must sleep *le*] It's already late, you need to go to sleep'), makes cyclical time stand out. It is time to go to bed. The latter 'obligation' is marked *gai* ('should') which implies an appeal to common ground and can easily be chosen as the content for a co-ordination request. Two of the remaining examples signalled a 'synchronisation problem', a mismatch between personal time and institutional time (cf. Gumperz 1982). In example 57.1, *Shidian le! Ni chidaole!* ('It's already ten o'clock, you're late for class'), a student is 'being late' for class: later in the same story, example 57.5, *Zhenshi bu zao le, ni paode geng kuai le* ('[really not early *le*, you run-DE even fast *le*] Now you're really late. Run even faster'), he has another delay and is even later. In the worktime example 60.12, *Shijian bu zao le, ni jueding chuan yuyi chuqu* ('[time not early *le*, you decide spear rain-clothes out-go] It's late already, so you decide to put on your raincoat'), the main character is delayed due to a long search for an umbrella.

In story 52, 'At the beach', line 52.8. states *Zhongwu le, taiyang shaide ni hunshen shi han* ('[noon *le*, sun shine-DE you whole-body is sweat] It's noon now and the sun is so strong you sweat all over'). The indexing of the midday sun through the use of the time-word 'noon', makes that moment in time 'stand out', and activates the animator's knowledge of the increasing and decreasing strength of the sun. In 53.14, *Aiya! Zenmo yijing shidian le!* ('[how already ten-point *le*] Wow! It's already ten o'clock'), the main character has a synchronisation problem with cyclical time. He wonders how it is possible that it is already that late! It's time to sleep, but homework is far from finished!

5.4 Conclusion

Procedural discourse as represented by the action-picture stories demonstrated that the particle *le* is not used in 'normal' or 'regular procedures'. 'Deviation' of a procedure, and its counterpart 'restoration', attracted marking with *le*. When we tried to understand why this is so, what first came to mind was that a 'deviation' from the 'normal' or 'expected' order can count as a 'peak event' and needs the attention of the addressee (cf. Chang 1986; Li and Thompson 1981). When a 'deviation' occurs, the latter needs to prepare for what is going to happen next, or what he needs to do next, which may imply a 'repair procedure'. We grouped all instances of 'repair' under the notion 'solutionhood'. We then came to the conclusion that the particle *le* is used in situations in which the speaker finds reason to appeal to the interlocutor to reset their shared common ground, either as the result of a 'disturbance' or of a 'repair', and calculate the implications.

The nature of the 'procedural disturbance' could be described as either a 'deviation' or 'problem' in the execution of the procedure ('glass broken'), or an 'involuntary effect' ('bulb burned out'). Major (social) events (festivals, exams) also could be marked as 'deviations' and as 'new situations' or 'peak events'. In 'procedural discourse' the latter took the following form:

peak event
'deviation'; 'problem'
  'involuntary effect'
  'upcoming major (social) event'
'solutionhood'
  'repair' or 'solution' to earlier 'problem'
  'project completion'

Restoration of the original situation ('bulb replaced') falls under 'solutionhood'. A restoration procedure by necessity is 'goal'-oriented. Procedures are not performed without 'goals' in mind. 'Peak events' of the above-mentioned types (marked with the particle *le*), we could locate at various points in the action stories. In 'titles' (story 44, *Zhao huo le* ['Fire!']), in 'opening lines' ('*Ni de toufa chang le* ['Your hair is getting long']), in

Action-picture stories 137

'progress reports' (4.4, *Bijian dun le* ['pencil point dull']), in 'warnings' (pro-active; from now on avoid the previous involuntary effect), (7.14, *Xiaoxin. Buyao zai sale!* ['Be careful. Don't spill again!']) and 'story endings' (46.12, *Huanran yixin le!* ['It looks quite clean now!']). All stories in our data ended 'happily', a preceding 'negative effect' was restored and a 'solution' was found.

We also encountered a limited number of 'verbal interactions' (section 5.3.4). The 'peak events' in these everyday situations, apart from 'problems' and 'solutions', also showed special uses of the particle *le*. We found three: 'something outstanding (deviating) in a series', 'questioning common ground', and 'idiomatic expressions'. Questions with *le* (*Zenmo le?* ['How come this is so?'] ['What's the problem?']) are a means to request being updated as to a 'problem' in the shared common ground. The question is 'Please update me on this'. 'Idiomatic expressions' were used in evaluative remarks, and are the result of common association between 'peaks', an 'outstanding'/'deviating' piece of common ground and the particle *le*. These special uses in person-to-person conversations suggest that we might find different uses when more data of personal interactions are studied (Chapter 7).

When special attention was given to the relation between time and uses of the particle *le* it became clear that time is related to conventional ways of doing things. We rise early in the morning and do not go to school at night. When conventional synchronisation is disturbed, situation participants recognise the situation they are in (at that moment), and, when reminded, will look for means to remedy the non-conventional asynchronic situation they find themselves in.

The overview of uses of LE allows three conclusions. In 'direct address' the attention of the addressee is drawn towards a particular common-ground situation which in the first instance we called a 'peak event' or 'information peak'. The addressee is requested to co-ordinate the shared common ground on the basis of the information provided, and is expected to work out the consequences, which may be acting on the new situation. In a given common-ground situation the particle signals a newly 'realised' common ground structure. Verbal *-le* marks event 'realisation'. This is the modern version of the historical 'completion' particles. In the realm of storytelling verbal *-le* is used to mark milestones in story progress. When both verbal *-le* and the particle *le* act upon the immediate situation, the first distinction (verbal *-le*) commands progress in the event line, whereas the second distinction (the particle *le*), as common ground co-ordination marker, requests the reset of the current mental model. In quite a few instances the 'event peak' (verbal *-le*) and the 'situation peak' (particle *le*) coincide, and in such instances this is marked as a 'co-ordination point', and only one *le* is used in Chinese. Such 'co-ordination points' combine a 'progress report' and an 'assertion' of a new state of affairs, defined as either a 'deviation' or a 'solution'.

6 Children's stories

In the previous chapter we related uses of verbal -*le* and the particle *le* to 'peaks' in information flow, and 'peaks' as changes in the structure of the common ground, respectively. We observed that common-ground-related 'peaks' ('deviations', 'solutions') function at the project level, whereas verbal -*le* marked 'peaks' ('realisations') in event flow to guide the reader through the story line, from one 'accomplishment' to the next. In this chapter we take a closer look at ten relatively short children's stories to see if the hypotheses formulated hold. We claim that the hypotheses are in essence confirmed by the data of the children's stories. The chapter will first provide more details about the stories we used (6.1), and thereafter take a special look at the 'art of storytelling' in an endeavour to understand the nature of 'imagining', a story's notional structure, and aspects of 'writing style' (6.2). Our analysis of the various uses of the particle *le* in relation to that notional structure is presented in section 6.3. The various occurrences of verbal -*le* are discussed in the next section, where we also endeavour a comparison with the various uses of the particle *le* (6.4). A conclusion of this part of the analysis is presented in the closing section (6.5).

6.1 Data

The ten children's stories under discussion are rewritings in Chinese of non-Chinese (English-language) originals, published in Taiwan in the mid-1970s as part of a literature programme for younger children undertaken by the Mandarin Daily Publishing Press. Children's stories were not part of the Chinese cultural tradition and this explains the reliance at that time on foreign models in the Chinese experience and in our work.[1] Each of the stories is accompanied by pictures elucidating the characters and the events. The first exploration was a count of all the *le* forms in the stories. The result (Table 6.1) shows that there were 69 occurrences of *le* in the stories. Sixteen of these (2.3 per cent) were on the basis of linguistic criteria identifiable as cases of the particle *le*. Twenty-eight cases (41 per cent) were uses of verbal -*le*. Clearly verbal -*le* is used more frequently in the children's stories than we found for the action-picture stories (Chapter 5), and that finding is in

Table 6.1 Number of occurrences of verbal *-le* and the particle *le*; children's stories

Stories	V-le	V LE	V le	Total
10	28 (41%)	25 (36%)	16 (23%)	69 (100%)

direct support of the idea that in the action-picture stories 'instructions' were the main 'discourse act' type used. In 25 cases (36 per cent) the form *le* followed directly after a verb at the end of a clause or utterance and could not be immediately identified. It could either represent verbal *-le*, the particle *le*, or both. In order to clarify these uses, we developed a set of criteria based on the findings in the previous chapter (Table 6.1).

In the following, we will first take a closer look at storytelling and at the organisation of narrative discourse.

6.2 Storytelling

In order to understand the relation between the particle *le* and storytelling, we considered it opportune to investigate storytelling in somewhat more detail. We will look at the work by Clark (1996), Longacre (1996) and Bal (1997), respectively.

6.2.1 Imagining

Clark (1996: 360ff.) observed that all fiction requires a joint pretence, and he distinguished three levels of imagining. The first requirement is that both narrator/writer and audience/reader pretend that a story is being told. This further requires at level two the acceptance of the reporting of events in a world of imagination. That world is either close to the real world of everyday experience, and is still reflecting real-world experiences, or is a supernatural world in which new constituting principles can be at work. Each of these two worlds is embedded in some real-world model and that world's associated background conventions (cf. Johnson-Laird 1983). The interaction of the story characters then takes place in a third layer of pretence:

Layer 3 story characters interacting
Layer 2 a reporter is telling a reportee the events in layer 3
Layer 1 ...jointly pretend that actions in layer 2 are taking place[2]
Layer 0 'verbal interaction' between members of the audience

When writing a story, the author cannot make assumptions about his readers' knowledge in the same way as is possible in storytelling to an audience or in conversation. It is at this point that in written stories pictures, when well executed, provide a separate channel of information in which environmental and personal characteristics can be depicted and details of events given that stimulate the imagining process. They also help to create shared common ground between writer and readers, and stimulate a reader to get engrossed in the world of the story characters (Clark 1996: 360ff.).[3]

At the third layer of imagining, a story tends to pass through a number of phases. In the opening phase, the story characters and their behavioural characteristics are presented. Events then tend to move into a deterioration cycle creating 'suspense', after which a restoration cycle can be expected that brings things back to normal. Suspense in children's stories is generally related to the emotions of excitement, fear, and anger, which are associated with adventures, the main genre in these stories (Bal 1997; Clark 1996: 360ff.).

6.2.2 Notional structure

Longacre (1996) distinguished seven steps in the build-up of a story or narrated event: 'exposition', 'inciting incident', 'mounting tension', 'climax', 'resolution', 'lessening tension', and 'conclusion'. The deterioration cycle of a story can be identified with 'inciting incident', 'mounting tension', and 'climax', whereas the restoration cycle is typically composed of 'resolution', 'lessening tension', and 'conclusion'. Labov and Waletzky used the term 'coda' for the last step.[4] These distinctions are listed again here:

Notional structure of a story
Exposition
Deterioration cycle
   inciting incident
   mounting tension
   climax
Restoration cycle
   resolution
   lessening tension
Conclusion/coda

These notional structures are 'conventional', they can neither be considered fixed structures that always need to be followed, nor universal schema in the sense that in each culture the practice of storytelling will take this form. Given the nature of the particle *le* as a common-ground co-ordination device, we expect such uses to be particularly prominent in the deterioration and restoration cycle and the 'coda', whereas verbal *-le* will be expected for markings of 'key events' throughout.

6.2.3 Writing styles

When we now focus on the task the narrator/writer faces when creating common ground between himself and the audience/readers, it is clear that he somehow needs to introduce the 'story characters', some of their relevant background features such as 'goals' or 'aspirations', and 'activities' or 'events' in which that actor habitually participates. The writer also needs to feed his readers information as to the way events develop, and he can choose to introduce events through the eyes, thoughts and feelings of one of his characters and thereby create what is often called 'narrated monologue'. The fourth distinction is that of 'dialogue' or 'verbal interaction'. The distinctions we made so far are:

1   Building common ground
2   Reporting story progress
3   Narrated monologue
4   Dialogue/verbal interaction

In actual narrative texts, the styles intermix, but readers are very well capable of feeding the information provided accurately to the right mental model component (background settings, story line, thoughts and experiences of a character, interactions between characters). We like to illustrate the distinctions with examples taken from the story *Xiao Chuanfu* ('The Little Boatsman'):

The building of common ground

When introducing a new story character, the narrator builds up a piece of shared common ground. In the following example, he opens the story by telling the reader what kind of person the story character is:

(6.1)   [narrator introducing the main character and his habits]
    a. **Xiao chuanfu Bubu,**
    little boatsman Bubu
    b. **meitian yaozhe yitiao xiguachuan,**
    every-day row-ZHE one-stripe watermelon-boat
    c. **zai yunheli mai xigua.**
    LOC canal-in sell watermelon
    '*The little boatsman Bubu is a watermelon seller and he sells these from his boat.*'

Thereafter he specified personal preferences of the character and thereby created expectations in the readers as to upcoming events:

(6.2)   [narrator introducing the main character and his aspirations]
    a. **Ta hen xiwang,**
    he very hope
    b. **you yitian,**
    there-be one-day

142   *Children's stories*

       c. ziji ye neng you yitiao jiantouchuan.
       self too can there-be one-stripe sharp-head-boat
       d. yinwei jiantouchuan bi xiguachuan piaoliang.
      because sharp-head-boat compare watermelon-boat beautiful
      '*He hoped very much that one day he could also own a stylish gondola, because a stylish gondola is more beautiful than a watermelon boat.*'

The influence of the accompanying picture, showing Bubu on his watermelon boat and not far away from that boat a stylish gondola, can be felt here in the use of *ye* 'also'. Readers picking up this 'longing' might develop a feeling of 'hope' or 'sorrow' for this character. 'Hope' that he may succeed in obtaining one, and 'sorrow' for him having this 'illusion' which might not work out.

Reporting story progress

In a story it is mainly the 'key events' that are reported, the dramatic highlights; that is, events that have a strong influence on the development of the story line. These are typically the turning points – moments at which the situation changes, or a story line is broken. Such moments are depicted in relative detail in a scene, whereas unimportant events (with less impact on the story line) are reported more densely (cf. Bal 1997: 80).[5] The following scene does not seem to be a 'key event' in any objective sense. However, it is presented by the writer as such. He thereby creates two effects, the story remains focused on the interactions between the main story characters, and the successful completion of a social convention, a marriage ceremony, is introduced in this way:

(6.3)   [narrator reporting on current events]
       a. **Nü'er jiele hun,**
       daughter tie-LE marriage
       b. **xinli hen kuaile,**
       heart-in very happy
       c. **jiu ba xinlang baoqilai qinyiqin.**
       then BA bridegroom pack-up-come kiss-one-kiss
      '*After getting married, the daughter is very happy, she takes the groom in her arms and kisses him.*'

The marriage ceremony is mentioned as something that was 'realised' before the current scene. The details of the marriage can be imagined, but are not reported in any detail. It is being reported as 'story progress', as 'successful completion' of the institutional event: *jie hun* ('marrying'). It can now be understood why the bride is so happy, and attention can be focused on the foregrounded events 'picking him up' and 'kissing him'. Both events are supported by full colour pictures, depicting the bride as huge and the bridegroom as small, creating a humorous effect.

Narrated monologue

After introducing the main character, the writer introduced current developments through the eyes and thoughts of the main character, who made the following observations:

(6.4) [narrator allowing main character to make certain observations]
    a. Ta shuo:
    he speak
    b. 'Wode qianmian jiu you yitiao jiantouchuan,
    I-DE front then there-is one-stripe sharp-head-boat
    c. chuanshang chamanle xianhua,
    boat-on insert-full-LE fresh-flower
    d. yiding shi yao song xinniang dao jiaotang qu jiehunde.'
    certainly be will send bride to church go marry-DE
    'He said: "The gondola in front of me carries lots of fresh flowers, that surely is one going to bring a bride to the church to get married."'

The reported *shuo* ('speak') is 'speak to oneself', and introduces the inner speech of the story character, which in this case represents his personal observations as to the kind of events going on around him. In this way the reader is informed about the current situation through this character's eyes. In the 'c.' line, the current situation is described as a boat loaded with flowers, not a few, but a lot (*man* ['full']). The writer also chose to mark this description with verbal *-le*, and thereby created an 'information peak', which made the 'boat' and its 'flowers' 'stand out' in the developing scene (the event foregrounded through the eyes of the main character). The writer could have chosen not to use verbal *-le* and use *chaman* [insert-full] instead, without changing the nature of the event but missing an opportunity for especially drawing the attention of the readers to this part of the scene.

Dialogue

'Verbal interaction' between story characters creates 'dialogue' in the story. In the gondola story this happened once, the quote is:

(6.5) [narrator introducing verbal interaction between story characters]
    a. Fuqin shuo:
    father said
    b. 'Yaoshi meiyou ni,
    if there-is-not you
    c. wode nü'er jiebuliao hun le.'
    I-DE daughter knit-not-realise marriage LE
    'The father said: "Without you, my daughter would not have gotten married."'

In this dialogue, the father makes a point of thanking the addressee, Bubu, for his help (getting them out of the water). He does so by creating a hypothetical situation in which the addressee is absent and describes the consequences. This remark is directed at an 'interpersonal goal', and is recognisable as an 'interpersonal management' technique – a way to show gratitude for other people's actions.

When we take these few examples from one story as indicative of the kind of environments in which the particle *le* and verbal *-le* in stories operate, we get the following impressionistic schema:

Writing style	le	-le
1 Building common ground	–	–
2 Reporting story progress	–	+
3 Narrated monologue	–	+
4 Dialogue/verbal interaction	+	–

This schema suggests that verbal *-le* will be most frequently used during the reporting of events and in narrated monologue. The particle *le*, in contrast, is used during 'verbal interactions' of story characters at a point in the restoration cycle at which common-ground co-ordination serves a purpose. It seems reasonable to assume that this reasoning will also apply to the deterioration cycle. Our data will have to show to what extent this first impression can be maintained.

6.3 Uses of the particle *le*

We will now take a closer look at the occurrences of the particle *le* in the ten stories by focusing on the number of occurrences of the particle and looking for examples that might falsify our common-ground co-ordination hypothesis. When an information 'peak' is asserted, the 'addressee'/'reader'/'story character', in this view, is requested to reset the shared common ground. We will discuss the various uses in the order of the number of occurrences in a story. In two stories the particle did not occur.

6.3.1 Two zero uses

It is just as revealing to see why the particle *le* is not used as it is to see why it is used. We found two stories in which the particle *le* did not occur at all. These stories were *Da Zhentan* ('The Great Detective'), and *Jingcha Bobo* ('Uncle Policeman'). We will discuss these two stories first. It is relatively easy to see why the particle *le* did not occur in the 'Uncle Policeman' story. The policeman instructs his readers (expected to be children) what to do, given certain circumstances, and what not to do. Here is an example of the kind of 'instruction' he gave:

(6.6) [child driving in the back seat of a car]
'Buyao ba tou shendao chechuangwai.'
not-must BA head stretch-out car-window-out
'Don't stick your head out of the (car) window.'

The policeman's 'directives' are intended to add conventional wisdom to the common ground. They represent recurring and common events, which the addressees should learn to handle properly. The policeman tells the children what the rules they need to obey in a given situation are, and he assumes thereby that the information he gives is not yet part of the shared common ground, or not well established yet. This nature of a directive excludes the use of the particle *le*.[6]

In the second story, *Da Zhentan* ('The Great Detective'), the actors are 'crooks' and 'policemen'. Common knowledge tells the readers that these types of actors do not easily interact. In this story, too, there are no direct 'verbal interactions' between these actors in their respective roles, other than the one party arresting the other. Before it gets that far, interactions take place between 'disguised' policemen and 'crooks'. The disguised policemen act as 'newcomers' and do not share 'personal common ground' with the 'bandits'. We see this as the main reason for the absence of any situations in which the particle *le* can be used purposefully. It does not seem to make much sense to appeal to co-ordination of common ground, when no shared event has started yet. Here is an example of the kind of interaction that occurs between the number one 'crook' and one of the 'disguised' policemen:

(6.7) [policemen disguised as artists knock on the door]
'Qing kaikai men! Qing kaikai men!'
please open-open door! please open-open door
'Open the door please! Open the door please!'

This is a conventional 'request' for 'entrance', between strangers, a common action in everyday life. When used between friends, persons who share a common ground, an urgent request implying some sort of a 'problem' can take the form *Kai men le, kai men le!* ('Open the door now, open the door!'). The situation in this story is just conventional, and under that assumption excludes the use of the particle *le*. The writer then continues the story with:

(6.8) [crook answering the knocking on the door]
(a) Da qiangdao xionghenhende shuo:
great bandit ferocious-hate-hate-DE say
(b) 'Shei zai waitou qiao men!'
who at outside knock door
'The robber said with a ferocious voice: "Who is there knocking on my door?"'

The 'a.' clause reports details of the verbal behaviour of the 'criminal', whereas the 'b.' part quotes his verbal response to the still unknown person knocking at the door. Requesting an out-group person's identity is common everyday behaviour too, and, as a rule, is not treated in the first instance as an 'incident'. However, the bandit could have created an 'incident' situation by saying '*Shei zai waitou qiao men le?*' ('Who knocks on my door?') thereby indicating that he wanted to upgrade his personal common ground with the identity of the person knocking.

6.3.2 'Peaks' and 'tension'

We encountered one story in which the particle *le* occurred in an idiomatic expression *-jile*, which expresses the idea of an 'extreme' state of affairs. This form suggests that in this case we are dealing with a 'peak event' or 'peak episode' of some sort. The form *-jile* occurred in the 'restoration cycle' of the story *Kuaile de Tanzhang* ('The Happy Inspector'); that is, after the tension build-up in that story was resolved. We will introduce the build-up of that story first, before presenting the expression with *-jile*.

In this story, as was the case in the story *Da Zhentan* ('The Great Detective'), there were no direct 'verbal interactions' between the characters, in this case a 'policeman' named *Da Erduo* ('Big Ear'), and a group of 'train passengers' having the appearance of 'crooks'. We can point to this to explain the absence of uses of the particle *le*. The lack of verbal interactions and common ground build-up between story characters excludes the use of the particle *le*. Now let us see how this story develops. In the relatively lengthy opening part of this story 'tension' was built up by having the main character participate in a number of threatening situations. Here is an example:

(6.9) [writer reporting the inspector's experiences on his trip]
    a. Da Erduo shangle huoche,
    Big Ear board-LE train
    b. jiu kandao cheshang laile xuduo qiqiguaiguai,
    then see car-on come-LE quite-many very strange,
    feichang kepa de ren,
    extremely frightening DE persons
    c. dajia dou daizhe shoutiqin.
    all each carry-ZHE violin
    '*When Big Ear boarded the train, he noticed that quite a few very strange and extremely frightening people, all carrying a violin case, had boarded too.*'

In this descriptive episode, the writer updates the readers as to what kind of situation the main story character (the inspector) is in. Two events are described. The writer reports that the main character (*Da Erduo* ['Big Ear']) boarded a train, and then, through the eyes of *Da Erduo* ('Big Ear') detailed the situation further. There are quite a few creepy creatures surrounding him, each carrying a violin case. This 'tension' is resolved, when it turns out that all the strange-looking people surrounding the inspector during his trip actually are the inspector's colleagues, and have all come to congratulate him on his birthday. Here is how the writer breaks the tension:

(6.10) [writer describing a 'peak event' in the story]
(a) Ta xia yida tiao,
he come-down one-big fear
(b) zhengzai dasuan yinggai zenmo ban,
just-now consider must how act
(c) nayidaqun ren huran dou zhaixiale hei yanjing,
that-one-big-group person sudden each grasp-down-LE black glasses
(d) laqi shoutiqin lai.
pull-up violin come
'*He was startled, and just thought what best to do now, when those people suddenly took off their sunglasses and started to play their violins.*'

In this 'event', the story characters take of their glasses and thereby reveal their true identity, at the same time also removing the 'threat' of their presence.[7] In the episode that follows, the interactants start celebrating the inspector's birthday party, they go to the beach, eat birthday cake, and ice cream. This day, the story concludes:

(6.11) [writer reporting change in main character's feelings]
a. Da Erduo kuailejile.
Big Ear happy-extreme-LE
'*Big Ear was extremely happy.*'

This description contrasts with the feeling of 'unhappiness' and 'tension' in the preceding part of the story. The idiomatic form *-jile* ('extreme') coincides with this 'conclusion' of happiness, and therefore, in our view, changes the structure of the common ground. The feeling of unhappiness related to the disturbance of his birthday party and the fear he experienced during his trip have given way to an extreme state of happiness. Without *le* the expression *Daerduo hen/zhen kuaile* ('Big Ear was very/really happy'), would be possible here but lacks the contrast and related change in common ground structure.

6.3.3 *Individual cases of* le

In four stories, the particle *le*, not counting any of the LE (-*le/le*) cases still to be discussed, occurred once. Three of these are cases of verbal interaction between story characters, and in one case the request for common ground coordination is directed at the readers, as we will see. These four examples of uses of the particle *le* we will discuss one by one. We begin with the

148 *Children's stories*

interaction between the story characters in the story *Da Jiangjun* ('The Great General') which runs as follows:

(6.12) [writer introducing a new situation]
    a. 'Da Jiangjun, ni tai hao le.
    Great General you too good LE
    b. Jintian shi wode shengri,
    today be I-DE birthday
    c. ni hai mei wangle song wo jiduo hua.'
    you yet not-there-is forget-LE present I few-ear flower
    '*Great General, how good of you. Today is my birthday, but you did not forget to bring me some flowers.*'

The event that triggered this reaction was the general, entering the house with a pot of flowers on his head that got there accidentally by falling from a balcony. However, these flowers were perceived by his wife as a present. She thanked him wholeheartedly (another instance of personal management), and in this case used an expression with the particle *le*. She could have chosen to say *Ni zhen hao* ('Really nice of you'), but chose to use *Ni tai hao le* ('How good of you!'), thereby indicating that she perceived the situation as a 'solution' to one of her 'fears', her husband forgetting her birthday. For expressing 'appreciation', the expressions *ni tai hao le* ('[you too good *le*] How good of you') is available. It implies a request to the addressee to co-ordinate on the content of the assertion 'I am really happy about this'. You are such a good husband (cf. Dik 1997; Gu 1999).

In the second story, *Yonggan de Jingzhang* ('The Brave Sheriff'), the writer, or a bystander, is warning the hero to be careful:

(6.13) [writer introducing a new situation]
    a. 'Xiao Huanxiong, xiaoxin!
    Little Racoon little-heart
    b. Liangge da liumang yao zou ni la!'
    two-piece big rogue want hit you LA
    '*Little Racoon, watch out! Those two hooligans are going to hit you!*'

The 'warning' following the pre-warning *xiaoxin* ('look out'), is related to a perceived 'problem', a perceived 'intent to do bodily harm'. The 'warning', however, takes the form of 'perceived intent' *yao . . . le* ('are going to. . .'), and this gives the addressee time to prepare, to 'reset' his mental model of the current situation accordingly and prepare for action. The content of the assertion is that there are two hooligans around who are at the point of hurting him. Little Racoon was already warned about these two in the opening phase of the story. He was mentally prepared, so to speak, to co-ordinate on the warning and the content of the assertion.

In the third story, *Youqi Shifu* ('The Master Painters'), the painters are involved in a 'painting the house' project, and when they have finished *youqihaole* ('[paint-good-*le*] finished painting'), finished the 'joint project', they discover that something went wrong:

(6.14) [writer introducing a new situation]
  a. Fangzi youqihaole,
  house paint-okay-LE
  b. zixi yikan,
  detail one-look
  c. chu cuor la!
  produce mistake LA
  '*When the house is finished and they take a closer look, there's a mistake!*'

The 'c.' clause marks a serious 'problem', which can either be taken as 'narrated' or as 'narrated monologue': 'There is a mistake!', or, 'We have made a mistake!' The mistake we recognise as a 'deviation' or 'problem' as identified in Chapter 5. In this story the 'problem' is made into a 'peak episode' marked with the particle *le*, which must result in a reset of common ground, 'our project is not finished yet, and we must prepare for the consequences'.

The fourth story in which the particle *le* was used once was *Chuanzhang Bobo* ('Uncle Captain'), and opened with:

(6.15) [writer introducing a new situation]
  Da huochuan yao guo qiaodong le.
  big goods-boat want pass bridge-hole LE
  '*The big freighter is going to pass under the bridge.*'

The writer chose to open this story with the announcement of an upcoming event, *yao ... le*, and the previous uses of the particle *le* suggest that this happening will be a 'deviation' of some sort; and that indeed is what is the case in this instance. By marking this conventional episode (a boat passing under a bridge) with the particle *le*, the writer appealed to shared common ground, but also created 'tension' as to what might be going to happen there. The 'tension' was also created by the picture in which a pig-like creature on the bridge had fallen asleep but was holding a fishing rod with a hook hanging out dangerously!

6.3.4 *Two cases of* le

Two uses of the particle *le* were observed in the adventure story *Da Sheyingjia* ('The Great Photographer'). The first was used in direct address between story characters, whereas the second instance was used in the closing line of the story:

150 *Children's stories*

(6.16) [writer introducing a new situation]
    a. **Shizi mama dahou yisheng shuo:**
    lion mama big-roar one-sound said
    b. **'Ba nage xiaowawa fanghuiqu,**
    BA that-piece little-baby place-back-go
    c. **women hui jia la!'**
    we return home LA
    '*The lion mama said with a big roar: "Put that doll back, we're going home!"*'

The writer first detailed the voice setting of the character who was going to speak, and then used a quote to introduce her interaction with the members of her family. She signals a 'deviation' from 'current events' (playing around), *hui jia la!* ('time to go home'). She thereby 'disturbed' that activity, and her children, the direct addressees, are supposed to co-ordinate on their mother's assertion and prepare for leaving. The last line of the story introduced a permanent 'change' of attitude and read as follows:

(6.17) [writer making concluding remark]
    a. **Cong nayitian yihou,**
    from that-one-day thereafter
    b. **Laoshu Danzi de danzi**
    Mouse Timid DE courage
    c. **jiu bu zai namo xiao le.**
    then not again so little LE
    '*From that day onward, Mouse Timid's courage was no longer that little!*'

A person who was very scared of lions at the beginning of the story is no longer scared. Another example of *le*'s wrapping up function was provided by one of the concluding lines of the *Xiao Chuanfu* ('Little Boatsman') story. In that line it was said:

(6.18) [writer making concluding remark]
    Bubu jiu biancheng yige
    Bubu then change-into one-piece
    yao jiantouchuan de chuanfu le.
    row sharp-point-boat every-day DE boatsman LE
    '*Bubu then became a proud gondola owner.*'

The preceding events resulted in a 'change of status'. Bubu ended up as a proud gondola owner and on moonlit nights rowed his romantic passengers through the canals while also singing for them.

6.3.5 *Four cases of* le

Four uses of the particle *le* were found in one story. That is, not counting repetition and not counting instances of LE (-*le*/*le*) occurrences. As are the other stories, this is an adventure story in which one of the characters has a dangerous habit – climbing on top of high mountains, but getting scared when it is time to come down. In such cases, the help of *Da Pa Shan Jia* ('The Great Mountain Climber') is sought, and here is how he reacts when climbing towards the cow waiting on top of the mountain:

(6.19) [writer reporting verbal interaction between story characters]
    a. 'Tai mafan le.
    too troublesome LE
    b. Yihou wo zai ye buguan nide shi le.
    hereafter I again too not-care you-DE things LE
    c. Jintian shi zuihou yici!'
    today be most-later one-time
    'This is too much. Next time I won't help you anymore. Today is the last time.'

The opening line in the interaction, *Tai mafan le* ('This is too much') is meant to impress on the addressee the trouble she caused. 'Take note of it that this situation is unacceptable to me.' We like to see this as another endeavour of 'interpersonal management'. This 'impression management' is followed by an assertion of a 'deviation': 'Don't count on me next time.' That too is something the addressee is requested to co-ordinate on, since it influences future interactions.[7a]

Having said this, the situation they are in on top of the mountain suddenly 'deteriorates':

(6.20) [writer reporting 'inciting incident']
    a. Huran ta jiaodixia yihua,
    suddenly he foot-under one-slip
    b. zhanbuzhu le.
    stand-not-hold LE
    'Suddenly he slipped, and could not hold any more.'

Here a serious 'deviation' in the climbing procedure is reported, the Great Mountain Climber slips and they both fall down! Clearly, a 'deterioration cycle' starts. However, the main character, through sheer supernatural effort, manages to avoid a total disaster. He then is very angry and says:

(6.21) [writer reporting verbal interaction between story characters]
    a. 'Yihou wo zhende zai ye bulai
    hereafter I really again too not-come
    guan nimen de shi le.'
    take-care you-people DE things LE
    'Hereafter I really will never care about your situation anymore.'

152 *Children's stories*

However, the next day the situation repeats itself and the naughty neighbour climbs to the top of the mountain again. When called to the rescue our 'mountain climber' says angrily:

(6.22) [writer reporting verbal interaction between story characters]
    a. 'Zhen taoyan!
    really hateful
    b. Yihou wo zhende zai ye buguan nimen de shi le.
    hereafter I really again too no-care you-people DE things LE
    c. Jintian shi zuihou yici!'
    today be most-after one-time
    '*How hateful! Next time I won't help anymore. Today is the last time!*'

In direct address the 'Great Mountain Climber' first signals that he is fed up with the situation: *Zhen taoyan* ('I'm fed-up with this'). Thereafter he repeats that he changed his attitude (a deviation), signalling that his earlier remark was not an empty threat. The addressee should co-ordinate on this and this time reset the 'shared common ground'.

6.3.6 *Five cases of* le

The story *Xiao Chuanfu* ('the Little Boatsman'), was introduced in section 6.2.3. where we saw that the storyteller first introduced the main character, by giving his name and telling of his daily way of earning a living. We were made cognisant of the character's wishes for the future – in this case, the ownership of another type of gondola which he considered more beautiful. Then, the environment is introduced through the eyes and thoughts of the main character and takes the form of 'narrated monologue'. The writer, or the main character in narrating, then reports the following development:

(6.23) [writer reporting developments as unfolding]
    a. Keshi nü'er de shenti tai zhong le,
    but daughter body too heavy LE
    b. yishang chuan ba chuan caifanle.
    one-ascend boat ba boat step-turn-LE
    '*But the daughter is too heavy, as soon as she sets foot on the boat it capsizes.*'

The use of *keshi* ('but; contrary to expectations') prepares the reader for something unusual to happen, for what we have called a 'deviation' of some sort – in this case a mismatch between the body size of the bride and the size of the gondola she is going to board. This 'deviation' in the story line creates a feeling of 'mounting tension', and it is here that we see the particle *le* being used to mark the 'deviation' which is 'standing out' in the particular environment of 'boarding a gondola'. The effect of the actions unfolding in the scene is reported in the 'b.' line, 'the boat capsizes' and it will be understood that the participants end up in the water. At least that is what the pictures help to visualise. The writer then addresses the reader directly by asking 'What to do now?', and draws a conclusion:

(6.24) [narrator reporting a project disturbance]
Ta bu neng dao jiaotang qu jiehun le
she not can arrive church go marry LE
'*She cannot go to the church for her marriage now.*'

The writer states this point explicitly in order to establish a 'climax', which in this case is a clear 'deviation' from the original plan. The readers are requested to co-ordinate their common (story) ground respectively. The readers now realise that 'there is a problem'. The original 'goal', going to the church to get married, no longer holds. Now, 'what to do about it'. The writer continues with:

(6.25) [writer reporting developments as unfolding]
a. Hai hao, hai hao,
still good, still good
b. Bubu yaozhe xiguachuan guolai jiu ren le
Bubu row-ZHE watermelon-boat pass-come save people LE
'*Okay, okay, there comes Bubu to the rescue.*'

This way, the build-up 'tension' is lessened, and a 'solution' to the current 'problem' is in sight. This 'solution' or 'restoration' is introduced as a 'rescue mission' by Bubu, the main story character. We can recognise this new 'episode' as something 'outstanding in its context, the first step in a resolution cycle. The readers are requested to reset their common ground accordingly. The 'intent' of the main story character is to come to the rescue, and, as the pictures show, he is close by now!

Later in the story, when the 'resolution cycle' is completed, it is time for the showing of gratitude. We have already introduced this piece of dialogue, and the use of the particle *le*, in the section on 'Storytelling' (p. 143) and repeat it here for convenience:

(6.5) [narrator introducing verbal interaction between story characters]
a. Fuqin shuo:
father said
b. 'Yaoshi meiyou ni,
if there-is-not you
c. wode nü'er jiebuliao hun le.'
I-DE daughter knit-not-realise marriage LE
'*The father said: "Without you, my daughter would not have gotten married."*'

We noted that this is a case of 'interpersonal management'. The father raises the status of Bubu to that of 'rescuer'. This therefore allows an interpretation of 'gratitude', since the 'event record' of both interactants has the information that he was present, rescued the bridal party, and the marriage was successfully concluded (cf. Clark 1996).

This verbal expression of gratitude is followed in this story by the material gift of a gondola, which fulfils Bubu's wish and changes him into a proud gondola owner:

(6.26) [writer introducing events that lead to a new situation]
    a. **Xinniang de fuqin songgei Bubu yitiao jiantouchuan.**
    Bride DE father present-to Bubu one-stripe sharp-point-gondola
    b. **Bubu jiu biancheng yige yao jiantouchuan de chuanfu le.**
    Bubu then change-into one-piece row sharp-point-boat DE boatsman LE
    'The father of the bride presented Bubu with a stylish gondola. Bubu then became a proud gondola owner.'

The writer first introduced the event of presenting a gondola, and thereafter spelled out the consequences, a change of role pattern, which is a change in Bubu's personal common ground. This change is presented as the 'conclusion' of the story, and marked with the particle *le*, to request the reader to co-ordinate on that piece of information, and store the 'conclusion' in memory as a 'lesson', since this is the purpose of 'storytelling' as already observed by Aristotle.[8]

6.4 Uses of verbal *-le*

In the previous chapter we defended the idea that Chinese verbal *-le* is used by speakers/writers to mark activities that are 'outstanding' in their context, which can count as 'peak events' in the foregrounded environment. These 'peaks' designate 'realisation', 'accomplishment', or 'successful completion', or when 'negative' in content designate forms of 'deterioration' (cf. *wangle* ['forgotten']). We thereby maintained that uses of verbal *-le*, like those of the particle *le*, are in first instance pragmatically motivated.[9] At first sight, uses of verbal *-le* in the children's stories support this analysis. In the two following examples verbal *-le* is respectively related to 'accomplishment' and 'deterioration'. The first example we already introduced above:

(6.10) [writer describing a 'peak event' in the story]
    (a) **Ta xia yida tiao,**
    he come-down one-big fear
    (b) **zhengzai dasuan yinggai zenmo ban,**
    just-now consider should how act
    (c) **nayidaqun ren huran dou zhaixiale hei yanjing,**

that-one-big-group person sudden each grasp-down-LE black glasses
(d) laqi shoutiqin lai.
pull-up violin come
'He was startled, and just thought what best to do now, when those people suddenly took off their sunglasses and started to play their violins.'

In this example, the narrator sequenced the events 'taking off the sunglasses' and playing their violins', and chose to make 'taking off the sunglasses' the more 'outstanding' of these two by marking it with verbal -*le* and thereby making it into a 'peak event' in the story. Readers recognise this event as a 'peak event' since thereby they now know the identity of the 'sunglasses-wearing' people, and the story gets a totally different meaning. It changes from 'threatening' to 'celebrating'. The use of verbal -*le*, in other words, is also related to the common-ground build-up in the story, and is not merely an 'accomplishment' but also directly related to the 'restoration cycle' of the story, signalling 'lessening tension'. We claim, then, that 'revealing of identity' (by taking off the sunglasses) is reported as a technique to 'lessen the tension build-up so far in the story'. Of course, 'lessening tension' was not only created through 'taking off the sunglasses', the appearance of violins (rather than guns or rifles) also helped to do so. Nevertheless, the writer chose to mark the sunglasses event.

The writer could have used verbal -*le* in a different way. He could have chosen the second action ('taking out the violins') instead, by marking it as *laqile shoutiqin lai* or as *laqi shoutiqin laile* ('started to play their violins'), or mark both events with verbal -*le*. These still would be possible ways of telling the story. The effect created that way, however, would be different. We'll come back to this in a moment, but let us now take a closer look at the second example which introduces another 'accomplishment' (or 'realisation') which can be related to the notion of 'deterioration':

(6.27) [narrator describing events in Laoshu Danzi's tent who is sleeping]
a. Liangge shizi baobao mei shi zuo,
two-piece lion precious not-have thing do
b. jiu kunaoqilaile.
then cry-noise-start-LE
'The two lion children had nothing to do, and started to weep and make noise.'

The sequencing of events in this example is that the children stop playing and don't know what to do, and then they 'weep and make noise'. That 'realisation' meant a 'deviation' from the then 'normal' flow of events (i.e. 'playing around') in *Laoshu Danzi*'s ('Mouse Timid's) tent. It meant a disturbance of the 'normal' flow of events. Marking the 'realisation' of this kind of behaviour can be taken as either a 'narrated event' or as 'writer and reader interaction'. We will address that difference in the next section. Our observation at this point is that the behaviour of the children 'deteriorated', and since it is marked as a main event, the readers anxiously await further developments. Developments in the 'b.' line could have been marked as *kunaole qilai* [weep-make noise-*le* up-come], an alternative for the *kunaoqilaile* in the example. At first reading these two ways of marking with -*le* seem to have the same effect. In the next section, we will take a closer look at the possible side effects phrase-final-marking with verbal -*le* can have, but first we explore further ideas on verbal -*le*.

In this section we have suggested that in storytelling there is a common strategy to mark one of the events in a series as a 'peak event' and not mark both. That is not a fixed rule however. Sometimes it might be necessary to mark all events in a series, or to mark related events, as in the following example:

(6.28) {narrator reporting story progress}
(a) Hai you nage sheyingji
further there-was that-piece film-machine
(b) yinwei dipian yongwanle,
because film use-finish-LE
(c) jiu gala yisheng ziji guanshangle.
follow click one-sound close-down-LE
'And then there was the film camera, it ran out of film, and with a loud click closed itself down.'

In this example both the 'running out of film' and the machine 'closing down' are marked with verbal -*le* and the particle *le*, creating a sequence of two 'deviations' requesting the readers' 'special' attention. The effect of such double marking, when there is a cause–effect relationship between the two parts, is that the event as a whole stands out sharply in the context. Double marking, as this example shows, is also available as part of the storytelling strategy.

6.4.1 Contrasting views on verbal -le

At this point is seems appropriate to introduce some contrasting views on the nature of Chinese verbal -*le*. Li and Thompson (1981: 185–216) specified the verbal -*le* marker as 'perfectivity', and characterised it as events that are being viewed in their entirety or as a whole, and they added that this viewing as a whole is possible when an event is temporally, spatially, or conceptually bounded (1981: 185). Chang (1986: 68, 119, 242ff.) criticised this analysis as incomplete by observing that not all 'bounded' quantified and specific events require the use of -*le*, and that what is involved is more than 'syntactico-semantic conditions underlying Li and Thompson's claim' (1986: 60). This criticism would also apply to proposals made by Chan (1980), who allowed inchoative *le* to combine with permanent states, and perfective -*le* with events, processes, and transitory states. The proposal by Chang (1986) is a tripartite hypothesis for the functions of the Mandarin verbal suffix -*le*:

1. 'Realis marker', denoting an action/event that had happened, has happened, or is happening.
2. It functions as the overt marker of a 'peak event' within a segment of discourse.
3. It serves to explicitly mark anteriority of an action/event in relation to another. The anteriority can be temporal or logical.

To this general characterisation he added that monosyllabic action verbs in both 'peak' and 'non-peak' clauses often require the presence of verbal -*le* as a means of 'realis' marking (Chang 1986: 115). Also, anteriority is explicitly marked when the verbs in a series do not suggest the sequence and/or 'when special emphasis on the order of the events is called for'. He also observed that verbal -*le* tends not to occur in classical or set phrases, or in background events. The latter observation is of particular importance, since it supports our claim that the particle *le* is operative at the background level and at that level only.

Before proceeding, we will make a few remarks on the distinctions made. To begin with, the notion of 'peak event' indicates 'the peak clause of a discourse segment'. This concept Chang took from Hinds (1979), who defined it as 'a sentence of particular semantic importance within a segment'. Longacre defended a similar view and used the notion 'peak episode', which he defined as:

> any episode like unit set apart by specific structure features and corresponding to the climax or denouement in the notional structure.
> (Longacre 1996: 37)

The two concepts 'peak event' and 'peak episode' describe different levels of cognitive organisation of a narrative text. The 'peak event' is a local distinction, whereas a 'peak episode' points at outstanding developments at the notional level. Longacre's definition is further restrictive since he focuses on the 'climax' mainly. If we take this limitation away, we can identify 'peak events' with uses of verbal -*le*, whereas 'peak episodes' are marked with the particle *le*. They 'stand out' as 'milestones', not in the event line but in the notional structure, which are points at which common-ground resets are perceived as necessary. Examples of the latter in the previous chapter were 'deviations' and 'solutions' in a procedure. We identified these as 'information peaks' and 'co-ordination points' in the previous chapter, and will continue to do so in the data chapters until the distinctions have become transparent.

'Peak events' as used in Chang (1986) are characterised as 'the peak clause in a discourse segment'. This, we find, is a system distinction that operates

158 *Children's stories*

independently of cognitive organisation, actual interactants and event structure. Rather, we see a contextualised relationship between interactants, an utterance and a cognitive structure or common ground, and therefore want to modify the notion 'semantic importance' as used by Hinds (1979) in this sense. A 'peak event', we will claim, is selected by the speaker/writer and made 'outstanding' as the 'realisation' of an 'action', 'activity', 'event', 'process', or 'behavioural pattern'. It must be seen in relation to preceding and expected events, and to the story line. With the latter distinction we are referring to the relation the 'peak' maintains with moments of a 'deterioration cycle' and a 'restoration cycle'. We now will look at some examples of the three uses of verbal *-le* first, and then continue with a comparison of verbal *-le* and the particle *le* as found in the children's story data.

Realis marking

We reported several instances of realis marking with verbal *-le* in Chapter 5, when we first explored uses of verbal *-le* in the action-picture stories. The children's story data also contain several instances of this usage. However, we first like to give a 'verbal interaction' example observed in a supermarket. A Chinese girl in that market used the following expression while putting a chocolate bar in the shopping basket held by her boyfriend:

(6.29) [verbal interaction in supermarket]
  Wo maile zhege.
  I buy-LE this-one
  '*I want this. / I'll buy this.*'

The 'joint project' 'buying things in the supermarket' was situationally given. Both interactants had taken up the activity role of 'shopper' and behaved accordingly. The remark reports progress in the shopping expedition, and indicates the goods one of the interactants wanted to obtain in that 'buying project'. By placing the goods in the basket, the girl signalled to her boyfriend that that was what she wanted to buy and by implication that she wanted him to pay for the chocolate as well.[10]

Now let us turn to the examples or realis marking in the children's stories. We found three types of marking and will discuss these in this section:

(6.30) [narrator reporting story progress]
  (a) **Di'ertian zaoshang,**
  next day early-on
  huoche daole Taiyangcheng.
  train arrive-LE Sun City
  '*The next morning, the train arrived at Sun City.*'

(6.31) [narrator reporting story progress]
(a) **Ta ba xiaomeimei de bangbangtang**
he BA little-sister DE lollipop
qiangqu chile,
rob-go eat-LE
(b) **rang xiaomeimei pade zhi ku.**
let little-sister frighten-DE straight cry
'*He stole a girl's lollipop and ate it, making the girl cry out of fear.*'

(6.32) [narrator introducing story characters]
Dajijiao de linju shanyang guniang,
Big-horn DE neighbour goat girl
ta jiali yangle yitou taoqi de niu.
she house-in raise-LE naughty DE cow
'*At the house of Big Horn's neighbour miss goat, they had a naughty cow.*'

The three verbs in these examples all are monosyllabic: *dao* ('arrive'), *chi* ('eat'), and *yang* ('to raise'). Marking with verbal *-le* activated the idea of 'realisation', 'goal attainment', and made the result 'stand out' in the context given: 'the train got there', the crook 'ate or was eating the girl's lollipop', and at the goat's house they 'had' a naughty cow. There are a few differences however, given the nature of each of the activities. The stative nature of *yang* ('raise [at home]') implies that in example (6.32) the story line could be either *yang* or *yangle* with, as indicated, the difference that 'goal attainment', 'having successfully raised the cow' would be missing. In example (6.31) the use of *qiangqu chi* ('took it from the girl to eat it') still has the option of getting it back, whereas *chile* implies that he was actually eating the lollypop. In example (6.30) leaving out verbal *-le* would result in *Di'ertian zaoshang, huoche dao Taiyangcheng* ('The next day the train will be at Sun City'), which would be a train schedule announcement. The nature of *dao* ('arrive at destination') has an implicit endpoint, and without verbal *-le* the idea of 'realisation' is missing. However, the phrase *Di'ertian, huoche dao Taiyangcheng,...* could be the first part of a longer narrative piece ending for instance with *Da Erduo xiale che* ('where Big Ear got off'). The latter information could also appear as *Da Erduo xia che le* ('where Big Ear got off'), when the storyteller wants the reader to co-ordinate on the endpoint of the 'train trip' event in the main character's personal common ground, and prepare for what is to follow (see 'Peak event' section following).

Peak event

When we now look at a longer stretch of narrative discourse and locate examples of verbal *-le*, we find expressions such as:

160 *Children's stories*

(6.33) [narrator describing events in the tent, the owner of which is sleeping]
a. Shizi baba ba Laoshu Danzi de wuxianqin naqilai,
lion baba BA Beaver Brave DE guitar pick-up
b. luan tan yiqi,
wildly play one-while
c. changle jishou ge.
sing-LE few-piece song
'The lion daddy picked up Mouse Timid's guitar, wildly played a while and then sang a few songs.'

The 'singing songs' activity in the 'c.' clause was chosen by the narrator for marking with verbal -*le*. He thereby assigned it the status of 'peak event'. This can be understood when we realise that the order of presentation is from 'preparatory steps' (picking up the guitar, and touching the strings), to main event 'singing a few songs while playing the guitar'. The 'goal' of picking up the guitar is 'to play and sing', and the 'attainment of that goal' – the actual singing of a number of songs – was marked with verbal -*le*, which seems an easy-to-defend narration strategy, 'asking attention for main points' in the story line.

'Peak events' also create 'story progress'. In the children's stories we could identify a few cases of this usage. It seems to be a typical storytelling device. Here are two more cases:

(6.34) [narrator reporting story progress]
(a) Shi guniang ba Laoshu Danzi baoqilai,
lion girl BA Rodent Brave hold-up-come
(b) tiaole jichang wu.
jump-LE several-session dance
'The lion girl picked up Mouse Timid and danced with him for a while.'

(6.35) [narrator reporting story progress]
(a) Ta guyi qu cai nijiang,
he on-purpose go step mud
(b) jianle laotaitai yishen.
splash-LE old-lady one-body
'He on purpose went to spat mud, and made an old lady's clothes all dirty.'

In the 'picking-up' and 'dancing' sequence, clearly the 'goal' of the 'main event' – 'dancing' – was reached, and this was marked with verbal -*le*. The second example shows an activity 'splashing mud' which has no particular 'goal' in itself, but this time was used to create a negative effect, splashing mud on the clothes of a passer-by, and this way was made to 'stand out' as 'realised' through marking with verbal -*le*.

Anteriority marking

The third use of verbal *-le* is 'marking anteriority'. Chang (1986: 100, 110) described the relationship between a series of events in terms of a time relationship and a cause–effect relationship. When each step in an event series is marked with verbal *-le*, he argued, a 'peak event' interpretation can be changed into a 'cause–effect' relationship. The example Chang discussed (1986: 100, 110–11) was the event series 'being admitted to high school', the family 'setting of firecrackers', and consequently 'being immersed in happiness for several days'. Each of these events was marked with verbal *-le*:

(6.36) [writer reporting personal experiences]
a. Dang wo jiaoxing kaoshang-le
when I luckily admit-LE
Bei-shi yisuo shili gaozhong
Taipei-city one-M municipal high-school
b. jiali ranfang-le yichuan bianpao
home-LOC set-off-LE one-M fire-cracker
c. zuzu gaoxing-le haoji tian.
thorough happy-LE several day
'When I was, luckily, admitted into a municipal high school in Taipei, my folks set off a string of firecrackers and we were thoroughly immersed in happiness for several days.'

In a temporal view, what is communicated is that these events happened as different entities and are set apart. In a cause–effect reading, Chang argued, 'cohesion' is created through recognition that 'being admitted to high school' causes the family to 'set off firecrackers' and 'indulge in happiness'.

'Cohesion,' Chang supported by the linguistic concept of 'collocation'. Halliday ([1985] 1994: 308–39) observed that 'cohesion' operates in four ways: by 'reference', 'ellipsis', 'conjunction', and 'lexical organisation'. Whereas 'reference' and 'ellipsis' in Halliday's model are relatively straightforward, he is more specific about the remaining two distinctions. 'Conjunction' takes the form of 'elaboration', 'extension', and 'enhancement', which result in categories such as 'apposition' ('in other words') and 'clarification' ('in short'), 'addition' ('and', 'also') and 'variation' ('instead', 'except'), as well as 'spatio-temporal' ('then', 'before'), 'manner' ('likewise', 'thus'), 'causal-conditional' ('in consequence', 'then'), and 'matter' ('here', 'there', 'elsewhere') distinctions. 'Lexical cohesion' takes the form of 'repetition', 'synonymy' ('sound' and 'noise') and 'collocation' ('smoke' and 'pipe'). As these indications show, both Chang and Halliday rely heavily on linguistic and logico-semantic distinctions.[11]

In our model, 'cohesion' is the recognition of individual events as parts of shared common ground and shared knowledge of 'individual' and 'joint projects'. We observe that both the cause (admittance to high school) and the

162 *Children's stories*

effect (firecrackers, happiness) are culturally conditioned. The relationship can therefore also be described in terms of an 'achievement' and 'response' pattern. Such a characterisation brings out more clearly that we are dealing here with human achievement and human reaction patterns (practices) as part of a wider cultural common ground. First a family member achieves some remarkable result, and that feat triggers a family response in terms of 'setting off firecrackers' and 'being immersed in happiness for several days'. The 'goal' of passing the high school entrance examination was 'achieved', and the response patterns of 'setting off firecrackers', and 'being immersed in happiness' were 'realised'. All three were marked with verbal -*le*, which made them stand out as wholes, as three independent events. The underlying concepts are part of the shared common ground existing between the writer and his readers.

In the children's stories there were quite a few examples of 'anteriority' marking, and the relationship between the various events varied greatly, but all can be related through common ground knowledge. Here is an example from the children's stories that introduces 'anteriority', temporally related events:

(6.37) [narrator describing events perceived by main character]
a. Chuan zai yisuo da fangzi de qianmian
boat at one-location big house DE front
kaole an,
lean against-LE shore
b. jiu you yiwei fuqin,
then there-was one-M father
fuzhe jiu yao dang xinniang de nü'er
supporting-ZHE then will be bride at DE daughter
zouchulaile.
walk-out-come-LE
'The boat was moored in front of a big house and the father walked his bride-to-be daughter to the boat.'

In this scene, the temporally related events, the arrival of a 'marriage gondola' and a father, 'walking the bride-to-be to the boat' are presented. They stand in a functional relationship to the wider institutional event or scenario 'getting married'. The boat was ordered and has a scripted 'goal', transporting the family to the church. The arrival of the 'marriage gondola' and 'boarding the boat' are each preparatory events that enable the trip to the church. They therefore must be seen here as 'enabling events', not 'main events', in a 'getting married' script. The two events in this story are mooring a 'marriage gondola' and getting it successfully moored at the right place, and 'the boarding of the boat' – the father helping the bride. This situation is also visualised in the accompanying pictures. The 'moored boat' and the 'bridal group' preparing for boarding are separate ('enabling') events and both are marked as 'realised' with verbal -*le*, which is a technique for keeping events separate as realised units. Each event can be imagined as having passed through various event-specific phases or parts. The expression *kaole an* ('moored') in this story (narration of events) is by necessity understood as 'anterior', as one does not endeavour to 'board' a boat when it is not there yet. By presenting the 'mooring' as 'realised' (with verbal -*le*), it can be imagined that the event went through an initiating phase (coming to shore), main phase (mooring) and final phase (preparing for taking on passengers). This is all expressed by *kaole an* ('moored'), an event presented as actual in the immediate situation (foregrounded), which creates expectations for a related follow-up event.

The event *zouchulaile* ('walked her out') similarly went through a preparatory phase (putting dresses in order etc.), and a main phase ('walking her out'). In this narrative both the *kaole an* ('mooring') and the *zouchulaile* ('walking her out') were marked with verbal -*le*, thereby making them into the two main events to be considered at that point in time. However, the writer could also have chosen the form *zoule chulai* to express the idea of the father having walked out his daughter onto the quay. We therefore conclude that the form *zouchulaile* is marked not only with verbal -*le* to indicate 'realisation' but also with the particle *le* to indicate a change in the structure of the common ground, which needs co-ordination by the addressees / readers.

Example (6.9) also reported progress in a train trip, we repeat it here for convenience. When the inspector, *Da Erduo* ('Big Ear'), moves south for a special appointment the narrator reports progress as:

(6.9) [narrator reporting story progress]
 a. **Da Erduo shangle huoche,**
    Big Ear board-LE train
 b. **jiu kandao cheshang laile xuduo qiqiguaiguai,**
    then see car-on come-LE quite-many very strange,
    feichang kepa de ren,
    extremely frightening DE persons
 c. **dajia dou daizhe shoutiqin.**
    all each carry-ZHE violin
 '*When Big Ear boarded the train, he noticed that quite a few very strange and extremely frightening people, all carrying a violin case, had boarded too.*'

By reporting the act of 'boarding' as 'realised' or 'successfully completed', the idea of 'anteriority' is created. 'Boarding a train', it is understood, is not a particularly interesting piece of information or a final 'goal' in most stories. Reporting that 'goal' as a foregrounded event leaves the reader wondering 'and what next'? That information the narrator provides by reporting what the story character involved in this situation observes after having boarded the train. And what he sees is *laile xuduo qiqiguaiguai de ren* ('quite a few very strange and weird looking people'). In this case, the idea of the passengers 'being on board' is expressed via the verb *lai* ('to come'). By using 'realis' marking with verbal *-le*, the idea, that they were there is expressed. 'Anteriority', then, is created as a result of understanding what the implications are of certain events, and by event sequencing. The reader expects to be able to build a meaningful relationship between what is being reported and what his/her background knowledge tells of what is 'possible' and 'permissible'. S/he expects to be able to build a coherent mental model from the information being provided. The conclusion of this way of presenting the data is that it is not necessary to claim an 'anteriority' construction in Chinese, or, stronger, that there is no anteriority construction. The idea of anteriority is the result of cognitive activity in building a mental model of what is going on in the real or in an embedded world or worlds.

6.4.2 *Verbal* -le *and/or particle* le

We observed that 36 per cent of the uses of the particle *le* directly followed a verb and the question of the status of that marking thereby became problematic: is it verbal *-le* or the particle *le*, or perhaps both? We argue that co-occurrence of a 'peak event', and a 'co-ordination point', which requires an adjustment in the structure of the common ground, seems quite natural. The form *zouchulaile* ('walked her out'), for example, requires modification of the common-ground structure and at the same time represents a 'peak event' marked by verbal *-le*. In order to make this double marking more transparent, we will now first take a look at two examples which illustrate a 'deteriorating cycle'. They are taken from the story *Yonggan de Jingzhang* ('The Brave Sheriff'). In that story, the main character is the courageous sheriff Little Racoon of Gold City. The first example describes an 'inciting incident', which ends with phrase-final verbal *-le*:

(6.38) [narrator introduces inciting incident]
    a. You yitian,
    there-is one day
    b. ta zhengzai xie yizhang baogao,
    he just-now write one-piece report
    c. huran pengde yisheng,
    suddenly bang-DE one-sound
    you ren ba bangongshi de men zhuangkaile.
    there-is person BA office DE door strike-open-LE
    '*One day, when he was just writing a report, suddenly someone with a big bang bumped into his office.*'

This is a piece of the introductory part of the story and belongs to layer 2, a reporter telling a reportee the events in layer 3. In this message, the reader is requested to co-ordinate on a piece of outstanding content, a door being 'bumped open', which is not the 'normal way' of opening a door. The co-occurrence of the particle *le* and verbal *-le* in this instance is an 'inciting incident', a distinction at the notional level of story structure. This double marking is also explicit in the second example, when the person bumping into the office, Mr Big Antler, wants to report an incident, which he describes as:

(6.39) [narrator allowing the tension to mount]
 'Dakuaitou gen Daweiba dou
 Big Piece Head and Big Tail both
 dao Huangjinzhen laile!'
 to Gold City come-LE
 'Big Head and Big Tail are in Gold City!'

In this 'verbal interaction' between Mr Big Antler, the one who bumped into the office, and the sheriff Little Racoon, we recognise both the particle *le* and verbal *-le*. The particle requests adjustment of the common-ground structure, whereas the content of the co-ordination is expressed as *laile* ('[come-realised], are here in town'). The common-ground co-ordination request regards a 'deviation' from normal, which requires the sheriff to act, and that is what he does in this story: he goes out to arrest the two hooligans.

There were 12 other examples (in addition to those quoted already in the numbered examples) of verbal *-le* and the particle *le*. They are listed in Table 6.2. A majority of these examples represent 'deviations' from 'normal'. The captain is on the wall and his boat is gone, *kaizoule* [drive-gone-*le*]; trousers are damaged, *goupole* [hook-broken-*le*]; hoodlums beat each other unconscious, *dahunle* [beat-unconscious-*le*]; a boat capsizes, *caifanle* [step-turn over-*le*]; a camera stops running when it runs out of film (a 'problem'), *guanshangle* [close-down-*le*]; and the story characters fall from the mountain they climbed, *diaoxiaqule* [fall-down-come-*le*]. Movement generally represents a 'change' of scene (*pai dianying qule* 'went [there] to make a movie'), but other 'movements' imply a 'problem' as in *you paodao shantoushang qula!* ('again climbed on the mountain!'). In example (3) a form of 'solutionhood' is presented in a rather remarkable way. The captain gets back to his boat by being thrown through the air and ending up in his pyjamas hanging on the washing line (*diaojin ... qule* [fall-enter ... go-*le*]). This is an embedded world where different realities apply, but is still a case of 'solutionhood'. 'Solutionhood' also is the issue in *youqihaole* [paint-good-*le*], when in one story the painters agree that the job is finished now, and *laoqilaile* [scoop-come-up-*le*] when characters who ended up in the water are rescued with an oar by Bubu, the Little Boatman. A 'beginning' of a 'new event' finally is reported in (9) *paixialaile* [record-down-come-*le*], said when a camera is accidentally set into motion, a 'change' from 'non-activity' to 'activity'. This discussion suggests that in narratives in most instances phrase final LE can be

166 *Children's stories*

Table 6.2 Other verb *-le/le* sequences in ten children's stories (n = 12)

Chinese form	English translation
1 '...*kaizoule*...'	'[my boat] is gone!...'
2 *kuzi goupole.*	the hook left a hole in his trousers
3 *diaojin shengzishang de shuikuli qule.*	fell into the trousers of his pyjamas that hang on the line
4 *Fangzi youqihaole.*	now the house is ready
5 ...*ziji ba ziji dahunle.*	...knocked each other unconscious.
6 *ba chuan caifanle!*	And made the boat capsize.
7 ...*dou laoqilaile.*	...scooped them out of the water.
8 *zhao banma pai dianying qule.*	and went [there] to shoot zebras.
9 ...*dou paixialaile.*	...started to record [everything].
10 *yinwei dipian yongwanle, jiu... ziji guanshangle.*	because the film was finished, it then shut itself down.
11 '...*you padao shantoushang qula!*'	'again climbed on the peak of the mountain!'
12 ...*dou diaoxiaqule!*	...and both fell down!

taken as representing verbal *-le* marking an event as 'realised', whereas the particle *le* pushes the foregrounded event into the background to serve as the new common ground from which the upcoming events will proceed. It's a kind of consolidating process in verbal interactions, forcing a modification of the structure of the common ground.

6.5 Conclusion

This chapter introduced the art of storytelling and tried to determine the role that the particle *le* plays in such forms of imagining. We also looked at uses of verbal *-le* in this discourse type. In the previous chapter 'outstanding moments' triggering the use of the particle *le* were identified as 'deviations' and 'solutions' and as expressions of 'excessiveness' marked with *tai* ('too much'), *zui* ('excessive') and *-ji* ('extreme'). In 'narrative discourse' these distinctions could also be recognised, but in addition it was possible to relate various moments of 'change' to the phasing of the story, and to notional story structure, the creation of a 'deterioration cycle' and a 'restoration cycle'. When used in the 'building of common ground', the particle *le* can index new events such as a 'marriage party' or a camera starting to run, expressed as *zouchulaile* ('walked her [the bride] out onto the quay'), and *paixialaile* ('started to record'), respectively. In other stories, the particle *le* was used in relation to 'inciting incidents', 'mounting tension', and 'climaxes'. 'Resolutions' and 'lessening tension' could also be selected for marking with the particle *le*, and thereby became moments at which common-ground co-ordination was requested. Incidentally, the particle *le* appeared in the 'exposition' part of a story, and also in the 'conclusion' or 'coda, where it marked an attitude 'change' or a 'role change'. These 'changes' all were related to the structure of the common ground.

In 'dialogue' situations at layer 3, characters also attended to 'interpersonal goals', were involved in 'interpersonal management'. We found such examples as *Ni tai hao la!* ('You're too good'), *Tai mafan le* ('Too bothersome'), and *Yihou wo zai ye bu guan ni de shi le!* ('Next time I won't help anymore'), showing 'appreciation' and 'disdain' for the other person's behaviour.

The common-ground co-ordination requests at these various layers were always 'asserted', and formulated in such a way that the co-ordination could be 'immediate'. In the children's stories, the content of the co-ordination was 'outstanding' by itself, either because the action involved was 'deviating' (*yao zou ni la*: 'people want to beat you up'); *men zhuangkaile*: ('the door was being bumped open'); (*zhanbuzhu le*: 'he cannot hold and they fall down'); (*buneng dao jiaotang qu jiehun le*: 'can no longer get married'). Restoration of the normal order, as we observed in some of the technical procedures in Chapter 5, did not occur in that sense in the children's stories. Experience and good deeds change the personal common ground, and readers are expected to learn from that. An example of a reported 'change' in the 'coda' was *Tade danzi bu zai namo xiao le* ('afterwards he was no longer so timid'). In one story, the particle *le* was used in the opening line. This usage underlines that, outside the exposition part of the story in which common ground is build-up, the particle *le* is chosen to mark an 'outstanding' piece of common ground. When no previous information is available, therefore, the particle *le* is taken as marking such an 'outstanding' piece, as in *Da huochuan yao guo qiaodong le* ('the big freighter will be passing under a bridge'). The idea of 'mounting tension' at this point is not expressed but supported by the pictures accompanying the text: a big boat, a small bridge, and a sleepy fisherman positioned on that bridge. The various uses are summarised in Table 6.3.

The 'new' technical event was a camera which started to record events and could be used later to prove that certain events actually happened. The social event described was a marriage party which was actualised as *zouchulaile*

Table 6.3 Particle *le*: 'common-ground co-ordination'

Layer 4	(a) Interaction between narrator and story character
Layer 3	(b) 'Verbal interaction' between story characters (dialogue)
Layer 2	(c) Interaction between narrator and readers
	• exposition part: 'new' technical/social events
	• deterioration cycle
	• restoration cycle
	• conclusion / coda
Layer 1	(d) Direct address by narrator of readers (who are jointly pretending)
Layer 0	'Verbal interaction' by members of the audience (non-story-related)

('walked her [the bride] out onto the quay'), and functioned in the context of common-ground build-up, the 'actualisation' of a marriage party. It was not part of any disturbance. That followed later and what was disturbed was the just-introduced 'marriage party' itself.

In the ten pieces of narrative discourse studied, verbal *-le* was primarily used in 'progress reports' (layer 2) to indicate that certain events were 'realised' or should be taken as 'realised'. This is done in order to create 'milestones' in the story line to guide the readers from one main event to the next. However, we found that verbal *-le* can be used for the same effect in 'narrated monologue', when the writer uses the observations of the main character to bring certain events to the fore. We therefore identified all events marked with verbal *-le* as 'foregrounded' events, whereas the particle *le* is used to request a 'background', or 'common ground' reset.

The particle *le* could also be recognised in cases involving co-occurrence with verbal *-le*. In such cases, the particle *le* signals a modification of the structure of the common ground on an issue which is marked by verbal *-le* as 'realised'. These moments in which foreground and background distinctions get intertwined need to be related to story build-up and to the notional story structure. They indicate 'deviations' and 'solutions' as well as 'beginnings' and endings'. Illustrations of these are, respectively, *kunaoqilaile* ('they started to cry and make noise'), *laoqilaile* ('scooped them out of the water; rescued them'), *paixialiale* ('started to record'), and *ziji guanshangle* ('closed itself down'). Such uses also relate to the notional structure of the story and can index distinctions as 'inciting incident', 'mounting tension' or 'climax'.

7 Conversations

In Chapter 5 we observed that the particle *le* was used to report 'deviations' and 'solutions' in a procedure, whereas in narrative discourse (Chapter 6), we demonstrated that the particle *le* indexes modifications in the structure of the common ground, which apart from 'deviations' and 'solutions' also included 'additions' to the common ground. What form, then, will these earlier notions take in conversational exchanges? Conversations are composed of 'minimal joint projects', which emerge in the course of interaction and combine to form 'extended joint projects' (Clark 1996). We therefore expect that in a conversation the particle *le* will be used to attract the addressee's attention to modifications in the established shared common ground at various minimal project types. Conversations, however, are not structured as procedures and narratives are, but show *ad hoc* development. Therefore the central question at this point becomes the way in which the structure of the shared common ground is modified in conversations.

This question can be detailed in at least three constituting issues: the 'conversation type' (personal or transactional), the kind of 'minimal joint project' in which it functions, and the kind of 'move' in which it occurs.[1] We already observed that business transactions, like procedures and narratives, are conventional and structured. Personal conversations and their *ad hoc* development, however, given their *ad hoc* nature, will develop in different ways, and the question is how do the uses of the particle *le* relate to these? Can the particle *le* occur in all phases of everyday conversations, in openings, pre-entries, embedded projects, the main body, pre-closings, and closings? Can it be used in 'initiating' moves mainly, as we would expect on the basis of the previously analysed material, or does the particle *le* also occur in 'attending', 'continuing', and 'reacting' moves?[2] These are questions we will address in this chapter, the organisation of which is as follows. First we introduce the conversational data, which form the basis for the analysis, then discuss the notion 'move structure' (7.2), and outline the various forces that drive conversations. We distinguish three interaction types (7.3), analyse conventional expressions, which have developed in relation to 'problems', 'solutions' and 'procedures' (7.4), and continue with a discussion of uses of the particle *le/la* in a special group of conventional constructions, expressions of 'politeness' (7.5). Hypothetical constructions are taken up in (7.6), and a redefinition of enumerative uses of *la* is given in (7.7). A 'summary' that allows rapid consultation of main findings concludes the chapter.

7.1 The data

The data reported in this chapter were taken from the Chinese conversational text Chinese 600, published in 1976 in Taipei, Taiwan. These conversational stories totalled 40 in all and dealt with a wide variety of subjects. The form *le/la* or *-le* occurred 210 times in these conversational texts. The breakdown is shown in Table 7.1.

This table demonstrates that the particle *le/la* was far more frequently used in these texts than the verbal marker *-le*. We therefore can say that the signalling of an intended update or reset of the shared common ground did occur more often than the reporting of 'progress' in a foregrounded event. When we look at the distribution of these elements across the various texts another difference appears (Table 7.2). The data show that verbal *-le* occurred in 55 per cent (n = 22) of the texts and never occurred more than five times in one text. The frequency of the particle *le*, in contrast, had a much wider distribution. In a majority of the texts (62 per cent) the particle *le* occurred between one and five times. However, in 32 per cent of the 40 texts (n = 13) the particle appeared between six and ten times, leaving one text with a number of occurrences of the particle higher than ten (12 actually). As claimed in the chapter on narratives, verbal *-le* and the particle *le* are related, though cognitively different, phenomena. The particle attracts attention to the common-ground structure, whereas verbal *-le* reports progress in foregrounded events, that is in events for which a particular background setting holds.

Table 7.1 Occurrences of the forms *-le* and *le/la* in Chinese 600

Text	le	-le	Total
Chinese 600	179 (85%)	31 (15%)	210 (100%)

Table 7.2 Number of occurrences of *le/-le* across conversation text units

Chinese 600	Interval				Total units
	0	1–5	6–10	11–15	
le	1	25	13	1	40
lo	18	22			40

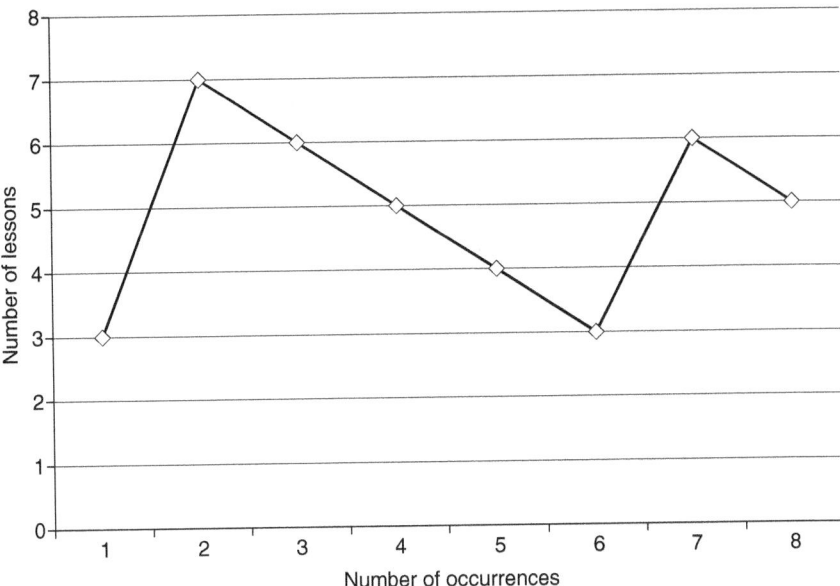

Figure 7.1 Number of occurrences of the particle *le* in a conversational text (horizontal axis) versus the number of lessons in which it occurred.

A closer look at the one extreme case of 12 occurrences of the particle *le/la* in one lesson revealed that in that text five occurrences were used in an enumerative series. Not counting these five, the total number of occurrences was reduced to seven. The total number of occurrences of the particle *le* in the various conversational pieces, is graphically represented in Figure 7.1. The graph has two peaks, meaning that there is no clear pattern discernible. After a peak of two occurrences in one lesson, the number of text units containing more than two (three to six) uses of the particle decreased gradually. However, seven and eight uses of the particle *le* occurred in six and five conversational units respectively. We therefore need to conclude that the nature of the conversation concerned and the type of activities being developed therein are the most likely crucial factors that influence the use or non-use of the particle *le/la*. It is not possible to make a clear generalisation as to the number of uses of the particle *le* in the 40 conversational texts we analysed without going into more detail as to the nature of these texts.

7.2 Move typology

Eggins and Slade (1997: 191–213) modified the systemic grammar tradition in more functional terms, and developed a move typology in which they worked out these various distinctions (cf. Halliday [1985] 1994). They began by opposing 'opening moves' and 'sustaining moves'. The first takes either the form of an 'attending move' or 'initiates' an exchange, whereas 'sustaining moves' can either 'continue' an earlier move or 'react' to one. 'Continuing speech' can take the form of a 'monitoring move' when the state of the interactive situation is being checked, of a 'prolonging move' when further information is projected, or of an 'appending move' when the speaker loses the turn but manages to regain it and creates a relevant expansion of his prior move (Eggins and Slade 1997: 195–200). 'Reactions' can further be subdivided as 'responses' and 'rejoinders', and each can be either 'supporting' or 'confronting'. For instance, a 'reply' is a 'supportive' response, whereas 'disagreeing' is a 'confronting' response. Similarly, 'tracking' is a 'supportive' rejoinder which tries to establish what is going on, whereas 'challenging' is a 'confronting' rejoinder. Both do not bring the exchange to an end but prolong it (Eggins and Slade 1997: 200–13). 'Rejoinders' are set apart from 'responses' in that they tend to 'interrupt, postpone, abort, or suspend the initial speech function sequence' (Eggins and Slade 1997: 207). This first discussion of move structure we can represent as follows:

```
            Open     Attend
                     Initiate
Move
            Sustain  Continue
                     [monitor; prolong; append]
                     React
                             Respond [support; confront]
                             Rejoinder [support; confront]
```

'Attending moves' take the form of 'salutations', 'greetings' and 'calls'. They prepare the ground for interaction by drawing the attention of an addressee or addressees (Eggins and Slade 1997: 193). A Chinese example of an 'attending move' in a business environment is the practice in most Chinese-speaking communities to greet customers with *Huanying guanglin* ('Welcome') and *Xiexie guanglin* ('Thank you for your visit'). 'Initiating' moves actually 'get the interaction under way' and are generally 'assertive' moves. They can be further detailed as an 'offer' ('Would you like some more wine?'), 'command' ('Look'), 'statement of fact' ('I met his sister'), 'statement of opinion' ('This conversation needs Allen'), 'factual question' or 'opinionating question' (with a why-interrogative, or a polar interrogative). Examples of 'factual questions are 'What are you doing?' and 'Is he in London now?' Opinionating questions can be illustrated with 'What do we need here?' and 'Do we need Allen in this conversation?' (Eggins and Slade 1997: 193–4).[3]

When there is a 'continuing speaker', moves can be seen as 'monitoring', 'prolonging' and 'appending'. 'Monitoring' moves deal with the state of the interactive situation by checking that the audience is following, or by inviting another speaker to take the turn (Eggins and Slade 1997: 195). In a 'prolonging' move the continuing speaker 'adds to the exchange by providing further information, whereas in an 'appending' move the speaker lost his turn but manages to regain in and contributes to it (Eggins and Slade 1997: 196).

The logico-semantic relations existing between various 'continuing' and 'reacting' moves are described as 'elaboration', 'extension' and 'enhancement' (cf. Halliday [1985] 1994). In 'elaboration' a move 'clarifies, restates, or exemplifies an immediately prior move' (*'He is a bridge player'*). An 'extension' 'adds to the information in an immediately prior move, or provides contrasting information'. Talking about a mutual friend an 'extension' is *'But he has dinner parties all the time'*. An 'enhancement', finally, 'qualifies or modifies the information in an immediately prior move by providing temporal, spatial, causal, or conditional detail'. An example of an 'enhancement' is *'Cause all you get is him bloody raving on.'* (Halliday [1985] 1994; Eggins and Slade 1997: 197–8).

The supporting and confronting poses of 'responding' and 'rejoining' allow further distinctions, which we list in the following schematic representation:

Reacting move:
Respond:
    Support [develop; engage; register; reply]
        Develop [elaborate; extend; enhance]
        Reply [accept; comply; agree; answer; acknowledge; affirm]
    Confront:
        Disengage
        Reply
        [decline; non-comply; disagree; withhold; disavow; contradict]

Rejoinder:
    Support
        Track [check; confirm; clarify; probe]
        Response [resolve; repair; acquiesce]
    Confront
        Challenge [detach; rebound; counter]
        Response [unresolve; refute; re-challenge]

A 'supportive response' can be intended to 'develop' the contribution, to 'engage', 'to 'register' or to give a 'reply'. A 'reacting move' which intends to 'develop' the exchange, can take the form of an 'elaboration', an 'extension', or an 'enhancement'. To 'engage' signals that a 'joint project' can be taken up, as when a 'greeting' is answered with a 'greeting'. To 'register' implies giving 'feedback' and backchannelling moves, as well as more evaluative reactions such as *Zhende*? ('Really?') When the 'reacting move' is a 'reply', it can take the form of an 'acceptance', 'complying with what was said', 'agreeing', giving an 'answer', 'acknowledging' the other's contribution, or to 'affirm' the previous move. This short overview is just meant to make the reader familiar with some of the basic distinctions used in move-structure analysis. We will use these terms in the analysis where applicable, and then at that place give the definition of the relevant terms as used by Eggins and Slade (1997).

7.3 Three interaction types

The data allow a distinction between 'personal conversations', 'business conversations', and 'business conversations' in which the client brings in some 'personal demand or request'. Business conversations illustrated in these conversational pieces (four conversations) are of the 'expert' type; an institutional expert (for example, a nurse in a hospital) explains to a client the rules that need to be followed in the institution being visited. The person who brings in personal demands already knows the rules and uses these when positioning her/himself within the institution (six conversations). In one conversation, both institutional and personal interactions were observed. An example of a personal contribution in an institutional setting is a tourist trying to book a room in a hotel thereby bringing in personal preferences. 'Personal conversations', finally, are free from institutional constraints and concentrate on common-ground construction or the equalisation of knowledge (31 conversations). Conversations of the latter type, being the largest group, also attracted the largest number of occurrences of the particle *le*. The breakdown is shown in Table 7.3.

In personal conversations 140 cases (78 per cent) of the particle *le* cases were counted. Its use in personal/business conversations (n = 27; 15 per cent), and business conversations (n = 12; 7 per cent) was far less. These latter interactions, furthermore, were mainly conventional in character, as we will see shortly. In personal conversations, one person proposes a 'joint project' ('having a conversation'), and by 'responding' the other person takes it up. However, further distinctions are necessary. A situation participant can project a 'construal' of the addressee's current activity, and that can become the focus of a 'minimal project'. Conversational projects, however, can take quite different forms, such as 'negotiating an agenda', and being involved in an 'argument', as our data show. These 'verbal interactions' are constituted by actions (for instance, Offer–agreement–compliance,[4] or Accusation–rebound and challenge), as the term 'interaction' suggests. This again reveals the 'action' nature of verbal interaction. Interactions are not proposed

Table 7.3 The particle *le* according to interaction type in Chinese 600 (n = 179)

Chinese 600	Business	Business/personal	Personal	Total
le	12 (7%)	27 (15%)	140 (78%)	179 (100%)

as projects: 'Let's negotiate an agenda', or 'Let's argue'. In list form, the discussion so far looks like this:

Interaction types
Personal conversation
    Joint projects
    Construals
    Negotiating an agenda
    Engaging in an argument [about a proposed project or agenda]
Business conversation
    Scripted joint project
Business/personal conversation
    Scripted joint project
    Personal demands/preferences

Pragmatic or business conversations must have dominant goals and a series of idealised steps to achieve those goals. Business conversations of the hotel-reservation-desk type develop in three phases (see Chapter 3):

1 Seeking agreement
2 Decision
3 Binding acceptance

The idealised steps for the creation of these phases were given as:

    A: DIRECTIVE – suggestion of some activity
    B: COMMISSIVE – agreeing to the activity

    A: Decision or material action

    B: STATUTIVE act – establishing time and place
    A: ACCEPTIVE – agreeing to that time and place
    (Steuten 1998)

For personal conversations no such idealised steps have been developed, and most likely also cannot be developed due to the fact that 'differences' between interactants are the crucial feature that drives interactions (Kress 1985; Eggins and Slade 1997). However, we observed that four conversation-related activities can be distinguished, proposing a joint project, construing reality, negotiating an agenda, and being involved in an argument. They will be discussed in that order.

176 *Conversations*

1 Proposing a joint project

Conversational projects or agendas do not need to be proposed explicitly. These issues are often implicit, as in:

- Asking someone's name
- Asking the way
- Asking an acquaintance if he has time

They can, however, be explicit as in a request such as:

- Shall we go shopping

When a person is addressed by a stranger, circumstantial features will help to determine how this should be taken. In a hotel environment, 'getting acquainted' is a socially accepted form of interaction:

(7.1) [A addresses B in a hotel where they both are staying for the night]
       Yang: [initiating move: attending]
       Nin guixing?
       you precious name
       'What's your name, if I may ask?'

By answering this question B takes up the 'joint project' of a 'casual conversation', even though the issue of such an enterprise is mentioned nowhere or explicitly hinted at. It is understood by social convention being that way (Chinese 600/1:1):

(7.2) [B answers A's question]
       Zhang: [reactive move: responds: answer]
       a. Wo xing Zhang.
       I name Zhang
       [initiating move: 'attending']
       b. Nin guixing?
       you precious name
       'My name is Zhang. What is yours.'

By asking a reciprocal question, the joint project is established and both parties will undertake the enterprise of building common ground (see section 7.3.1).

When in a public place, a stranger takes the freedom to address a passer-by, this verbal intrusion can take the form of 'asking the time', or 'asking the way'. Both are expected and socially accepted forms of unsolicited interaction. At such a moment, the background of the person being addressed is as of that moment unknown. When his/her background makes him/her capable of answering the question and s/he is willing to do so, exchanges like the following can develop (Chinese 600/1: 4):

(7.3) [Stranger A addressing local person B]
A: [initiating move: attending and request]
Qingwen dao youzhengju zenmo zou?
request-ask arrive post-office how go
'*May I ask how to go to the post office?*'

B recognises the question not as an endeavour by a stranger to test his knowledge but as an endeavour by A to get help for reaching a planned destination. That is the conventional goal description of such encounters. By answering the question, B signals that he understands this purpose and is willing and capable of helping in this project. The project can remain impersonal but has the potential of becoming more involved, developing into a 'joint project', as we will see later in the discussion.

Each verbal move is related through inference to a project goal. When a boyfriend asks his girlfriend (Chinese 600/1: 12):

(7.4) [boyfriend addressing girlfriend]
A: [initiating move: attending and request]
Jintian wanshang you kong ma?
today night have free time MA
'*Are you free tonight?*'

The addressee recognises this question as an endeavour to set up an agenda for going somewhere, which is demonstrated by her reply:

(7.5) [girlfriend answering question]
A: [reactive move: acknowledging question]
Ni you shenmo haode jihua ma?
you have some good-DE plan MA
'*You do have a nice plan {for going somewhere}?*'

The initiating question is replied to with an exploring counter-question that acknowledges the purpose or intent behind the question being asked. The nice plan being referred to later is revealed as 'going to the cinema', and that agenda we will meet again below.

In another example, the question 'Do you have time' is immediately followed by an explication of the intended project (Chinese 600/1: 9):

(7.6) [one colleague addressing another]
A: [initiating move: acknowledging question]
Neng buneng chuqu pei wo mai dianr dongxi?
can not-can out go accompany I buy few things
'*Can you go with me to buy a few things?*'

The addressee is now immediately aware of the kind of activity expected of her and she can prepare her reply accordingly.

2 Construals

Construing reality is not straightforward and without problems. When a person's current activities, body posture and/or facial expression are construed by another situation participant as representing something, that may or may not be what is actually the case, or what the 'doer' is 'doing' or willing to admit that he is doing. An example of an endeavour to construe another person's activity is (Chinese 600/2: 3; our translation):

(7.7)   [construal of activity]
  Wang: [initiating move: construal, exploring]
  Shi bu shi zai xie qingshu he?
  be not be LOC write love-letter HE[5]
  '*Are you writing a love letter?*'
  Wu: [reactive move: 'rejection' and 'counter-construal']
  a. Bie kai wanxiao la!
  do-not make joke LA
  b. Wo shi zai xie jiaxin ya.
  I be LOC write home-letter YA
  '*Don't make fun of me! I'm just writing a letter home!*'

In his reactive move Wu confronts Wang's assumption, thereby showing that he *disagrees* with him on the construal, and asserts his own version of his activity. His commitment to this construal and his emotional involvement become manifest in the voice-setting and the marking with the emotional particle YA. The move sequence took the following form:

Wang: 'construal'
Wu: 'rejection' and 'counter-construal'

The construal had the form of an assumption. The speaker could not be sure that what he construed was actually the case and he therefore sought confirmation with the 'doer'. The latter obviously disagreed with him and presented a counter-construal, which had the form of a straightforward assertion. The 'rejection' part of the exchange had the form of a 'directive', an instruction of what the addressee should or should not do: *Bie kai wanxiao* ('Do not make fun of me'). The use of the co-ordination device *le* presupposes the assumption on the side of the speaker of the existence of common ground between them, whereas the directive implies that the addressee should know better and correct his perception of the situation.

3 Negotiating an agenda

In personal conversations with thematic indications such as 'planning for a trip', 'planning an outing' and 'proposing to go to the movies', endeavours are made to set an agenda, a plan for future action. In business conversations three steps are distinguished: *negotiation*, *decision*, and the formal creation of a *new fact* (Steuten 1998). In personal interactions, no statutive acts for establishing new facts are established; this is a matter of trust. The following example is from the opening phase of an outing proposal (our translation):

(7.8) [proposal to go for a trip on the weekend]
Wang: [initiating move: plan and seeking support]
a. Zhoumo xiang chuqu lüxing,
weekend think go-out travel
b. ni you xingqu ma?
you have interest MA
'*I plan to go out in the weekend. Are you interested?*'

Wang, in his initiating move, tables a plan and requests the addressee to take it up as a 'joint project'. The latter reacts with (Chinese 600/1: 13; our translation):

(7.9) [reaction to proposal to go for a trip at the weekend]
Sun: [reactive move: supporting and declining]
a. Xingqu daoshi you,
interest certainly have,
b. jiushi que qian.
only-be lack money
'*I would like to, but I have no money.*'

Sun reacts by simultaneously supporting and declining the project. This reaction prompts Wang to focus on the supporting part (Sun's 'a.' utterance) and assert that 'being interested' is in principle enough to sustain the project. Wang does this as follows:

(7.10) [proposal to go for a trip on the weekend continued]
Wang: [supportive reply: 'focus' and 'assert solution']
a. Zhiyao you xingqu,
only-need have interest
b. na jiu haoban le.
that-case then good-manage LE
'*Being interested, will be enough.*'

The 'reacting move' is a 'supportive reply' implying 'partial acceptance'. Wang focuses on the piece of common ground that can lead to agreement,

180 *Conversations*

and then 'asserts' that it can function as the 'solution' to the 'problem' they encountered. As we would expect, the latter 'concluding' assertion is marked with the particle *le*. It is a proposal for the joint construction of shared common ground.

4 Engaging in an argument

When somebody requests a 'favour' (for example 'please pour me a cup of tea') and this request is refused, an 'argument' may develop as in the case in our data. Arguments are the result of 'disagreement'. In this case, the 'disagreement' is a practical one, involving a 'refusal' to take up a requested 'participatory role', and the break-down of a proposed 'joint project'. Arguments can develop into a 'dispute' when the people know each other well and social obligations related to the role relationship are involved (Plantin 1996: 10). The following exchange is the one referred to. It runs as follows (our translation):

(7.11) [wife reacts to husband refusing to make her a cup of tea]
Fang: [confronting move: negative construal]
Ni zhege ren zhen fengjian.
you this-piece man really feudal
'*You're from the Middle Ages.*'

In a 'confronting move', the wife (Fang) questions the 'being of this time and age' status of her husband, who reacts by rebounding the assertion. He does this by questioning the grounds for the negative construal and challenging its appropriateness (cf. Eggins and Slade 1997: 207ff.) (Chinese 600/2: 14; our translation):

(7.12) [reacting to verbal abuse by wife]
Chang: [confronting move: 'rebounding' and 'challenge']
a. Ni zenmo suibian ma ren ne,
you how follow-ease curse person NE,
b. tai buxiang hua la.
too not-like speech LA
'*Why do you curse me, this is outrageous!*'

The particle *le/la* was used in the 'challenging' part of the exchange. The move sequence was:

Fang: 'confronting' move
Chang: 'rebounding' and 'challenge' LA

The 'challenge' forces the addressee (the wife) to take a position. This is a form of co-ordination of personal common ground and a move that would fit the development of a dispute.

7.3.1 Building common ground in casual conversations

Knowledge differences drive personal conversations forward. The Chinese 600 texts allow recognition of the following five types of common-ground differences between interactants:

1 *Personal common ground*
2 *Project-related problems*
3 *Expertise differences: equalising common ground*
4 *Differences in disposition*
5 *Information differences*

We will illustrate each of these differences and, at the same time, relate these uses to occurrences of the particle *le* in an endeavour to clarify its use in the context of cognitive differences.

1 Personal common ground

In conversations with thematic indications such as 'getting acquainted', 'getting further acquainted', and 'meeting an old friend', the main goal of the exchanges is to build 'personal common ground' or update an outdated 'personal common ground'. Contributions to common-ground build-up tend to be straightforward assertions. An example is:

(7.13) [building personal common ground]
    Yang: [initiating move: question]
    Nin zai nar zuo shi a?
    you in where do job A
    'What is your profession?'
    Zhang: [reply move: answer]
    Wo shi jiao shu de.
    I be teach book DE
    'I am a teacher.'

In such exchanges, matters such as family names, place of origin, professional background, personal habits, etc. are dealt with in a 'conventional' way, and do not require marking with the particle *le/la*. There is no 'deviation' or something 'outstanding' to co-ordinate on. The particle *le* was used, however, in this kind of conversation as a means to appeal to 'shared communal common ground'. The above quoted exchange, for example, was reacted to as follows (Chinese 600/1: 1; our translation):

(7.14) [building personal common ground]
    Yang: [support: reply: a. 'acknowledge', b. and c. 'affirm' (common ground)]

182   *Conversations*

>   a. Ah, laoshi!
>   Ah, teacher
>   b. Jiaole bushao nian le ba!
>   teach-LE not-few year LE BA
>   c. Yiding shi taoli man tianxia la!
>   certainly be peach-plum full world LA
>   *'Ah, a teacher! You must have taught quite some years already, and have pupils everywhere!'*

In this reacting move, the speaker (Yang) first displayed that he understood the information provided, and showed that he recognised the importance of that piece of personal common ground (the interactant is a 'teacher'!). The 'a.' utterance shows *admiration*. In the 'b.' and 'c.' utterances Yang used the particle *le*. In the 'b.' line this was followed by the uncertainty marker *ba* (*ba: bu* ['not' + particle *a*]), which softens the assertion. In both cases the speaker demonstrates that he is a member of the 'Chinese cultural common ground', and understands what it means to be a 'teacher' in that cultural environment.[6] By saying this, the speaker does not bring in a new piece of 'information'; rather, he 'construes' the addressee's 'participant status' as perceived through the assumedly shared cultural common ground. The 'construal' has an interpersonal goal and is a form of interpersonal management. Given the respected position of teachers in Chinese culture, it is a form of 'praise'. The 'praise' intent of the move might make Mr Zhang decline the 'praise', but our text did not show that response. Silence or facial expression can be imagined as a form of acceptance of the situation, and recognition of the addressee's intent.

'Construal' was also involved in the conversation which addressed the 'participant status' of a third party. Knowledge of situation participants regarding a third party's personal common ground may differ considerably. Interactants may agree or disagree on that person's personal background, and this is still independent of what is actually the case. In the following opening sequence of a conversation, 'construal' and 'contradiction' of that construal occurred:

(7.15) [discussing a third party's personal common ground]
>   Hu: [initiating move 'construal']
>   a. Ai,
>   ai
>   b. Lao Li dagai yijing chaoguo Wang Laowu de nianling le ba.
>   old Li probably already passed Wang Lao-wu DE year LE BA
>   *'Ai, Li's age probably has already passed that of Wang Lao-wu's, hasn't it?'*

The person called Li is a friend of the interactants (Hu and Huang) and is therefore referred to as Lao Li ('Old Li; friend Li') in the Chinese text. The first speaker opens the conversation believing that their mutual friend Li has reached a certain age by now (and should be thinking about getting married). He assumes (*ba*) that their friend Li is at a crucial age now, and brings that 'construal' into the conversation with the intention to exchange views with the addressee (Huang) with regard to Li's 'not-being-married-yet' social status. The age being asserted is presented as 'deviant', surpassing the upper limit of a bachelor's age, which is 35. The reaction by Huang was (Chinese 600/1: 10):

(7.16) [discussing a third party's personal common ground]
  Huang: [confronting move: disagree and contradict]
  a. Lao Li hezhi sanshiwu,
  old Li how-stop thirty-five,
  c. sishi chutou la.
  forty starting LA
  '*Li is far older, over forty.*'

Huang asserts that he is sure that Hu represented Li's personal common ground erroneously, and therefore confronts that 'construal'. He does so by first expressing 'disagreement' with what has been asserted (*hezhi*: 'where stop at; far beyond'), and second by asserting a different personal ground for the mutual friend. In this case, both the 'initiating assumption' and the 'contradicting assertion' involve the use of the particle *le*. In a shortened form the exchange looks as follows:

Hu: 'construal' LE BA
Huang: 'contradiction' LA

Both uses of the particle *le* involve an urging for common-ground co-ordination between the interactants. The request was one for co-ordination of common ground regarding a third party's personal ground, and the interaction can be seen as an endeavour to make it into shared common ground. In the first personal common ground example we discussed that was different, shared cultural common ground was indirectly asserted as a form of 'praise'.

2 Project-related problems

In a conversation between friends, when the conversational project has already been established, certain issues can be brought up as 'problems' in an endeavour to seek some advice or support for the planned activity. Here is an example (Chinese 600/2: 1; our translation):

(7.17) [talking about moving to Taiwan]
  Wang: [prolonging move: 'enhance']
  Keshi dao xianzai hai meiyou zhao fangzi na.
  but until now still not-have look-for house NA

'But I haven't found a house yet.'
Li: [reactive move: 'appeasing' and 'supportive question']
a. **Fangzi tai rongyi la!**
house too easy LA
b. **Ni dasuan zhao shenmo yang de fangzi na.**
you plan search what type DE house NA
'Houses is no problem! What kind of house are you looking for?'

Wang, in his prolonging move, tables a 'problem', to which the attention of the addressee is drawn (NA: NE + A), It is understood as being part of the previously introduced project 'moving to Taiwan'. Li, a local person, can be considered an expert (see p. 203) in matters like these, and his reactive move signals that the problem, given that time and location, is not something serious. He asserts that it is *tai rongyi* ('[too easy] a piece of cake'), and with *la* (*le + a*) requests Wang to update his common ground accordingly, thereby making it into an 'appeasing move'. In the second supportive move (the 'b.' utterance) Li asks Wang what kind of house he is looking for. We take this remark as indicating that he is willing to consider the problem raised as a 'joint project'. The move sequence was:

Wang: prolonging move: enhance: 'problem' NA
Li: reactive move: 'appeasing' LE and 'supportive question' NA

The particle *le/la* is used in the 'reactive move' to set Wang's mind at ease and urges him to co-ordinate on the assertion that finding houses in Taiwan belongs to the easy to-do category of things. As a co-ordination device, the particle *le* requests the addressee to co-ordinate his shared common ground in agreement with the assertion being made, 'this is easy'.

3 Expertise differences: equalising common ground

People's expertise is built up over a large number of years and as a consequence of increasing age, wider learning and experience, interactants differ as to the content of their personal common ground. 'Expertise differences' therefore are one of the strong driving forces in human communication (Berger and Luckmann 1967; Kress 1985). It was this kind of difference that was involved in conversations with thematic indications such as 'seeking advice'; 'deciding what to buy'; 'discussing sight-seeing in Taiwan'; 'discussing Chinese literature'. Here is an example related to knowledge of a food-related issue (our translation):

(7.18) [Talking about food]
Wu: [initiating move: stating 'problem']
a. **Tiantian mai cai,**
day-day buy food

b. zhen bu zhidao gai mai shenmo hao.
really not know need buy what good
'In buying food, I really don't know what to buy?'

In his 'initiating' move, Wu introduces a PROBLEM. He considers this a shared problem and is interested in hearing how other people solve it. Here is Wang's reaction (our translation):

(7.19) [talking about food]
Wang: [respond: engage: 'assert' shared cultural common ground]
a. Women Zhongguoren zui zhuzhong sexiangwei le,
we China-man most consider-important colour-fragrance-taste LE,
[developing: 'extension']
b. suoyi an zhezhong yuanze zai peishang yingyang,
so according-to this-type principle further accompany nutrition
c. jiu cheng le.
then okay LE
'We Chinese pay special attention to the matching of colour, taste and fragrance, so if you stick to this principle and also make it nutritious, then that's it.'

Wang, in his reply, first focuses on the shared common ground and 'construes' one particular common-ground feature as 'outstanding', as a 'deviation' from other cultural ways of preparing food (*zui ... le*). Thereafter he extends on it by stating that adding attention to 'nutrition' will basically solve the problem. An extending move adds 'further supporting or contrasting details' (Eggins and Slade 1997: 203). The expression ... *jiu cheng le* ('and then okay *le*') finishes this extending move off, and signals that what has been presented should be a 'solution' to the problem introduced by Wu. With the latter remark, we encounter again one of the functions of the particle *le* first formulated in Chapter 5 in the action-picture stories, that of marking 'solutionhood'. The exchange then continues with (Chinese 600/1: 13; our translation):

(7.20) [talking about food]
Wang: [sustaining moves: 'register' and 'extends']
a. Sexiangwei wo daoshi hai dong,
colour-fragrance-taste contrast-be still understand
b. keshi shuo yingyang wo jiu waihang le.
but speak nutrition I then outsider LE
'Yes, the colour, fragrance and taste thing I grasp, but I do not quite understand the nutrition thing.'

In his 'sustaining move', Wu, in reaction to the information provided, wants it to be registered that co-ordination of his common ground on the colour, taste and fragrance issue is not a problem. Registering moves contain 'feedback' and 'evaluative reactions' (Eggins and Slade 1997: 204). He admits, however, that his knowledge on the second issue, nutrition, is limited. For this purpose, he uses a 'prolonging' move and 'extends' on the registered common ground by 'adding', as new information, that with regards to one piece of that common ground he is not knowledgeable. In this way, Wang indicates a PROBLEM, 'limited expertise', and thereby appeals to Wu, as someone with a higher expertise level, to help him SOLVE it.

As demonstrated in the previous chapters, it is the cognitive notion of a 'problem', something 'deviant', which can attract the use of the particle *le*. There must be something in the information flow that is worth co-ordinating on. The case is that the information provided in the clause following *jiu* describes a new situation or a cognitively new situation which requires a common-ground reset. There is no compelling syntactic mechanism involved here. The claim by Li and Thompson (1981: 256) that *jiu* in this example marks a relation 'between general or future time mentioned in the sentence and the changed situation' is difficult to defend, and in our view not tenable. The idea of time is a western grammatical concept being projected onto Chinese grammar. By doing so the relation between a common-ground 'problem' and its 'solution' is missed. The change involved is a change in common-ground structure, as we will argue more extensively shortly, and not merely a change in the situation, which in fact can be anything.

To conclude, after a problem was introduced in the conversation, the particle *le* in this example was used to:

- 'construe' a piece of cultural common ground as 'deviation' (*zui* ... *le*);
- (conventionally) mark a 'solution' to a 'problem' (. . . *jiu cheng le*);
- mark a new 'problem': lack of expertise (TOPIC *wo jiu waihang le*).

The remaining part of the conversation then shows how an endeavour is made by Wang to solve the last problem by sharing his expertise, and thereby allow Wu to build a personal common ground that contains more of the elements already mastered by him. We like to call this an example of 'equalising personal common ground'.

4 Differences in disposition

In the growing-up process, and during interaction with other people and cultural objects, people develop 'preferences' or 'dispositions'. They develop hobbies, choose a sport of their liking, acquire a preference for a certain type of music, develop religious preferences and reading habits. All of these issues return in the conversational texts as differences in personal common ground. They are not necessarily the main topic of the conversation. Music preferences, for instance, can come up in a situation in which a person has an extra ticket and is looking for a friend who might be interested in going to the concert concerned, and in that context a person's musical preferences may surface. In the following example, the situation is straightforward, the main issue that surfaces is the hobby of one of the participants:

(7.21) [guessing a hobby]
    Li: [initiating move: a. 'opinion', b. 'elaborate']
    a. Ni zhexie huochaihe zhen piaoliang,
    you these match-box really beautiful
    b. souji zhexie feile bushao shijian ba.
    collect these waist-LE no-little time BA
    'These matchboxes are very beautiful; you must have spent a lot of time to collect them.'

The 'initiating move' in this conversation is in reaction to visiting a collectors' market or a similar event. It consists of a positive evaluation, which counts as an attending move, and a related 'construal' in which Li, in response to perceptual input, 'elaborates' on the opening move by assuming (construing) that the addressee has spent quite some time on collecting the items on display.

(7.22) [guessing a hobby]
    Wang: [reactive move: engage and affirm]
    a. Shi he,
    so-be HE[7]
    b. wo jiu xihuan zhexie xiao dongxi.
    I just like these little thing
    'Yes, I just love these little things.'

Wang displays agreement in his reply, and 'asserts' that collecting these things is something he likes. This is part of the build-up of shared common ground and is not an environment for the use of *le*, as we demonstrated. Li then develops the conversation with (our translation):

(7.23) [guessing a hobby]
    Li: [support: develop: elaborate: 'assert' (common ground)]
    a. Wo xiang,
    I think
    b. souji huochaihe gai shi nide shihao la!
    collect match-box must be you-DE hobby LA
    'I think collecting matchboxes must be your hobby!'

Wang's reaction prompts Li to assert that 'collecting matchboxes' must be the addressee's 'hobby'. As in the example discussed in the section on 'personal common ground', this 'construal' is based on shared personal common ground. The speaker later turns out to be a stamp collector himself. As a 'construal' it is also a request for confirmation by the addressee. The use of *gai* ('should be') further indicates that the speaker is guessing, and this kind of 'construal' therefore is easily marked with the particle *la*. The conversation continues (Chinese 600/1: 11):

(7.24) [guessing a hobby]
    Wang: [reactive move: 'affirm']
    Keyi zhemo shuo.
    Can so say
    'You might say so.'

Wang does affirm it, and it thereby becomes part of the shared personal common ground and a secure basis for further development of the discourse. In shortened form the exchange developed as follows:

    Li: 'construal'   (...*feile bushao shijian ba*)
    Wang: 'affirm'   (*shi he*)
    Li: 'construal' LA (*gai ... la*)
    Wang: 'affirm'   (*keyi zhemo shuo*)

The relation between 'construal' and the particle *le* is an essential step in the creation of common ground and therefore a crucial moment in the development of a discourse. 'Affirmation' or 'confrontation' needs to follow in order to create a firm basis for that common ground (cf. Eggins and Slade 1997: 202).

5 Information differences

One way of getting informed about current events is by reading newspapers. People reading or not reading newspapers will have different information levels. The same is true for people reading different parts of daily newspapers. In our text, one conversation is built around the latter issue, as illustrated by the following exchange:

(7.25) [discussing differences in news awareness]
    Wang: [reactive move: counter question and response]
    a. Zhe you sha xiqi?[8]
    this has what strange
    b. Wo shi zai baozhi.shang kandaode.
    I be at paper.up read-reach-DE
    'Nothing special, I have just learned it from the newspapers.'

Awareness of an information difference is handled by Wang via a matter-of-fact referring to the newspapers. This in turn makes Xia wonder how come he did not see the piece of international news being referred to (Chinese 600/2: 12):

(7.26) [discussing differences in news awareness]
    Xia: [rejoinder: confront: 'rebound']
    a. **Wo ye zhengtian kan bao,**
    I also whole-day read paper,
    b. **zenmo mei kanjian zhexiang xiaoxi ne?**
    how-come not-have see-perceive this-item news NE
    read the newspapers all day long too, why didn't I see this news.

Xia 'affirms' his reading behaviour and then 'wonders why' he missed that particular news item. The conversation then continues with an exploration of reading habits:

(7.27) [discussing reading habits]
    Wang: [support: reply: 'factual question']
    Ni dou kan nayiban?
    you all read which-one-page
    'What page do you usually read?'

Xia answers this exploring question with:

(7.28) [discussing reading habits]
    Xia: [reactive: 'answer']
    Wo shi meiban dou kan.
    I be every-page all read
    'I read every page.'

That answer prompts Wang to observe that Xia should know more than he (Wang) does, rather than the other way around (Chinese 600/1: 12; our translation):

(7.29) [discussing reading habits]
    Wang: [concluding move: 'elaboration' / 'conclusion']
    Na ni zhidaode gai bi wo duo la!
    that-case you know-DE must-be compare I more LA
    'Then you must know more then I do!'

The 'prolonging move' is a new 'construal', a new 'cognitive fact' from the speaker's reasoning, just like a new physical situation. The *gai shi nide shihao la!* ('This must be your hobby!') example in (7.22) comes to mind here. The move sequence in this part can then be represented as:

Xia:	'wondering why'	(*zenmo mei . . . ne?*)
Wang:	'question'	(*. . . kan nayiban?*)
Xia:	'answer'	(*meiban dou kan*)
Wang:	'construal' LA	(*na, ni zhidaode gai bi wo duo la*)

190 *Conversations*

The 'construal' in this case is based on information provided by the conversation participant. The particle *le/la* is also used by Wang to 'confront' an earlier claim of 'not knowing'. If that is the case, you should know more than I do!

7.3.2 *Business conversations*

The business conversations that clearly illustrated a conventional action or reaction pattern were:

1   'Dinner in a restaurant'
2   'Haggling in the market'
3   'A traffic control officer stopping a speeding car'
4   'Medical treatment in a hospital'

The 12 remarks involving the use of the particle *le* listed for this category all were conventional ways of reacting in a given situation. We can distinguish two uses, 'setting the rules' or 'reminding someone as to the existence of rules', and 'conventionally applying the rules'. When a nurse explains to a patient how to proceed when seeing a doctor in the policlinic, she is explaining the procedures to be followed in that institution. An example is (Chinese 600/1: 18):

(7.30) [a nurse explaining procedure to policlinic patient]
      Nurse: [reactive move: answer: 'explain procedure']
      a. Hushi xiaojie hui anzhe haoshu jiao hao,
      nurse miss will according number call number
      jiaodao ninde haoma,
      call-to you-DE number
      b. jiu gai nin kan le.
      then turn you see LE
      '*The nurse will call the numbers according to the order of registering. When your number is called, you may go to see the doctor.*'

The addressee is requested to co-ordinate his behaviour (*le*) with the asserted procedural steps, indicated here as a sequence [nurse calls] *jiu* [your turn] *le*. The explication regards procedural structure, background knowledge that guides actual behaviour. It formulates the 'solutionhood' part of the procedure.
   A case of 'breaking the rules' is illustrated in the following traffic scene:

(7.31) [police officer stopping a car]
      Driver: [initiating move: 'clarification request']
      Zenmo la, fasheng shenmo shi le ma?
      what LE happen what thing LE MA
      Driver: '*What's wrong, something happened?*'

The driver, in a common event–reaction pattern, signals that he does not know what is going on. His first reaction *Zenmo la?* ('What's wrong?') we have seen before in Chapter 5 when the teacher said to the student looking sick, *Ni zenmo le?*, in an endeavour to be updated on what was wrong. In this case it is the driver who wants to be 'updated' on 'what's wrong'. The second question is identical in structure and tries to achieve the same with different words: 'Please fill me in on this.'

In response, the police officer 'asserts' what went wrong, and thereby clarified what motivated him to stop the car (Chinese 600/1: 16):

(7.32) [police officer stopping a car]
Officer: {reactive move: 'assertion' / 'deviation'}
Nide chezi chaosu la!
you-DE car exceed-speed LA
Officer: '*You were speeding.*'

The policeman 'asserts' a piece of information that is a 'deviation' from the shared cultural common ground of traffic rules: 'you were driving too fast'.

Our next example comes from a 'restaurant' situation. We found three expressions with *le*, all were controlled by the institutional role bearer (waiter or waitress) and could be said to any guest initiating a particular action. Here is an example (Chinese 600/1: 7):

(7.33) [waiter to arriving guests]
Waiter: {attending move: greeting; directive}
a. Nin laile, xiansheng,
you come LE, sir,
b. qing libian zuo.
request inside sit
'*Welcome, sir, come in and have a seat, please.*'

As the translation of this event–reaction item suggests, the remark *Nin laile* ('you have come') in this situation is an 'attending' move, a 'greeting'. It asserts that a 'joint project' is recognised. It is an 'assertion' of the existence of shared common ground, as we have seen in a few other examples. With his 'greeting', the speaker (waiter) also asserts that he will take up his 'participatory role', in the understanding that the person being addressed will do so as well; that is, take a seat inside and give his order.

Another example from this dialogue is an action-response pair (Chinese 600/1: 7):

(7.34) [waiter responding to an action by the guests]
Waiter: {reactive move: evaluative; assertion}
a. Na tai hao le,
that too good LE

b. **zhe shi women de nashoucai.**
this be our DE speciality
'*Couldn't be better. This is our speciality.*'

In this turn, the waiter expresses his satisfaction with the progress of the joint project of 'ordering food' so far. He thereby signals that an 'outstanding' choice has been made. As a 'solution' it can also count as a 'pre-closure' or the 'closure' of the ordering event.

Our next example is from the sphere of 'haggling'. According to Chinese custom 'haggling' is common practice in environments such as the wet or vegetable market. In the following buyer–seller exchange, the customer tried to lower the price, only to being rebuked by the salesperson as going too far. The customer made the following move (Chinese 600/1: 10; our translation):

(7.35) [customer trying to get a lower price]
Customer: [prolonging move: 'propose solution']
a. **Huan ge jia sibaiwu**
change piece price 450
b. **jiu keyi le.**
then okay LE
'*I'll give 450 okay?*'

The customer, in a prolonging move, uses the particle *le* to signal that the common-ground structure will be that of a 'solution' if the price mentioned will be accepted. For that purpose he proposes a new price, and signals to consider that an opening for a 'deal'. This latter content is expressed by . . . *jiu keyi* ('and then it is all right'). The salesperson, however, in his next turn, shows that he is not willing to consider the proposal and come to a decision at this point. His 'declining' expression is *Nin xiansheng zhen hui kai wanxiao* ('[you sir really know-how-to joke] You must be joking!'). The customer then gives it another try with a somewhat higher price, and they meet common ground on an in-between position.

7.3.3 *Business/personal conversations*

A person enacting a script related to a particular institutional environment can, at a certain moment, introduce aspects of his 'personal common ground'. The conversations in which personal contributions were marked with the particle *le* were:

1   'Checking into a hotel'
2   'Ordering food in a restaurant'
3   'Asking the way'
4   'A traffic control officer holding a speeding car'

5 'Time to take up a project'
6 'An employee falling ill'

For instance, the following exchange occurred in a 'checking in' situation:

(7.36) [guest checking into a hotel]
   Guest: [prolonging move: 'assertion']
   Wo zui pa pa louti le.
   I most afraid climb stairs LE
   Guest: *'I'm particularly scared of climbing stairs.'*

At this point in the business conversation the guest brings in a 'personal preference, something that is 'deviant' (*zui ... le*), and makes the hotel employee co-ordinate on that. The employee thereafter tries to appease the customer with a 'counter assertion' (Chinese 600/1: 3; our translation):

(7.37) [guest checking into a hotel]
   Employee: [reactive move: counter assertion]
   a. Women zher quanbu dou shi zidong dianti,
   we here completely piece-by-piece automatic elevator
   b. fangbianjile.
   convenient-extreme-LE
   Employee: *'We have elevators, all automatic, extremely convenient.'*

The employee's assertion is intended to take the guest's fears away. He does so by asserting that the hotel has nice elevators and that there is no need for concern.

Preceding this exchange, the guest expressed his concern as regards the price for a room offered (Chinese 600/1: 3; our translation):

(7.38) [guest checking into a hotel]
   Guest: [reactive move: a. rejoinder: 'track' b. confront: reply: 'pre-decline']
   a. Liubai kuai?
   600 dollar
   b. Tai gui le ba!
   too expensive LE BA
   'Six hundred? Say yourself, that's too much!'

The guest in this turn first 'tracks' and thereby foregrounds the price mentioned, and then 'construes' that price as 'deviant'. By using the particle *ba* ('is it not'), the speaker appeals to the addressee's understanding: 'Say yourself', this is 'deviant' in comparison with prices elsewhere or the kind of room on offer.[9]

Personal involvement also develops in the traffic rule violation incident, when the police officer does not give an instruction but asks a question instead, which is taken up by the rule-violating driver with a *Dui la!* ('Yes, indeed!'), and hereafter the policeman concludes the conversation (Chinese 600/1: 3; our translation):

(7.39) [policeman talking to traffic offender]
    Policeman: [concluding move: rejoinder: support: 'appease']
    Xiangxin ni zheci yiding hui jizhu la!
    have-faith you this-time definitely will remember LA
    'I can rely on you to remember this, right?'

We encountered this usage in the children's stories when the particle *le* was used in the last story line to reset the shared common ground. The police officer expresses that he is sure that from now on the driver will 'remember what is right' and behave according to the rules (the expected common-ground structure). We can recognise a case of 'solutionhood', given the earlier 'deviation', which is asserted in this move as (*yiding*) *hui jizhu* '(surely) will remember', whereas the policeman with *le* appeals to the existence of shared cultural common ground, in this case the set of traffic rules as they are locally defined and implemented.

Our third example of personal elements in a business conversation comes from the restaurant environment. Ordering food is always a personal choice, so we list the following expression in this section. The particle *le* was used (Chinese 600/1: 7; our translation):

(7.40) [guest ordering food in a restaurant]
    Guest: [reactive move: assert 'goal attainment']
    a. **Sange cai yige tang**
    three-piece dish one-piece soup
    b. **jiu gou le.**
    then enough LE
    'Just take it that three dishes and a soup is enough.'

This is the guest's response to the waiter's question as to what he would like to order. The guest signals that he expects the waiter to co-ordinate his common ground on the assertion that he (the guest) considers three dishes and a soup enough for the occasion, and takes that as the structure of the shared common ground for that transaction.

'Asking the way' was another conventional environment in which personal involvement was expressed via the common-ground co-ordination marker *le*. We take it that, when taken up as a 'joint project', a pragmatic conversation will develop in which there are clear information goals and a limited amount of information can be exchanged. The particle *le* was used among others in the following (Chinese 600/1: 4):

(7.41) [local person giving directions to a stranger]
   Local person: [supporting: develop: 'elaborate']
   a. **Zuo che bu tai yuan,**
   sit car not too far,
   b. **zou lu**
   walk road
   ke jiu yuan le.
   however then far LE
   '*It is not far by car, but for walking it really is too far.*'

The speaker in this example asserts his personal experiences and/or perception as regards the distance to the post office from the place they are now. 'My assertion is, by bus it is not far, walking however is too far.' Walking there would be 'deviant' given my understanding of the common-ground structure as it relates to this locality.

In an office setting, one situation participant (employee) discovers that he has a 'problem' with the actual time of the day. He expressed this as (Chinese 600/1: 5):

(7.42) [employee addressing other employee]
   Employee: [initiating move: 'co-ordination question']
   Qing wen xianzai jidian zhong le.
   request ask now how much-point clock LE
   '*Hey, what time is it now?*'

We recognise this as a common way to signal a 'problem' in the shared common ground, and request to be 'updated'. Synchronisation with clock time is a necessary condition for job performance in a company, as well as for the establishment of an 'agenda' or 'joint project'. It is revealed in the subsequent exchange that his watch stopped. It is also revealed later that he needs to synchronise his behaviour in connection with a 'joint project', which is already planned: 'meeting someone at the station'.

The last example is also taken from a working environment. The speaker is a company manager who feels a need to update himself as to the current physical well-being of an employee (Chinese 600/1: 17):

(7.43) [manager addressing employee]
   Manager: [initiating move: co-ordination question; confirmation question]
   Ni zenmo le? Bu shufu ma?
   you how LE; not comfortable MA
   '*What's the matter with you? Not feeling well?*'

In his initiating move, the manager first signals that he wants to be updated as to the 'problem' in shared common ground existing between him and the addressee. In his follow-up question he signals that he has some idea about that (*bu shufu* ['not feeling well']), but would like the addressee to confirm this assumption, to fill him in on this.

7.4 Conventional responses

We claim that the particle *le* is a common-ground co-ordination device, which relates to the current common-ground structure. It is therefore to be expected that the language has developed conventional responses for 'solutionhood' and the existence of shared common ground (supportive moves).

7.4.1 Supportive replies, appeal to common ground, and feedback moves

Replies 'are the most negotiatory of the responding reactions' (Eggins and Slade 1997: 205), and therefore fit the idea of negotiation of common ground well. 'Supportive replies' are reactive moves that can show acceptance, compliance, agreement, acknowledgement or affirmation (cf. Eggins and Slade 1997: 202). In our view, these are all indications of acceptance, acknowledgement, agreement, affirmation, etc. of common-ground structure. We found two types of replies that involved the use of the particle *le/la* and were directly related to the confirmation of shared common-ground structure. These were:

1 *Dui le/la*
2 *Dangran le/la*

Related uses were:

3 *Yiding le*
4 *Wo dong le*

The first of the latter two, *Yiding le* ('Agreed') is a confirmation of shared common-ground structure, whereas the latter, *Wo dong le* ('I see'), we see as a feedback move, also confirming the current common-ground structure.

1 Dui le/la

The use of *dui le* is very common. Our data provided seven cases. The range of uses varied between affirmation, agreement, acknowledgement, confirmation and acceptance. These uses, however, all relate to the confirmation of common-ground structure. Here is an example:

(7.44) [casual conversation]
      Jiang: [reactive move: answer]

a. **Xiatian xihuan youyong,**
summer like swim
b. **dongtian xihuan pa shan.**
Winter like climb mountain
'In summer, I like swimming, in winter, mountain-climbing.'

Jiang reveals part of his personal common ground, to which Wang reacts with (Chinese 600/1: 14; our translation):

(7.45) [casual conversation]
  Wang: {support: reply: agree: 'assert'}
  a. **Dui le,**
  right LE
  {continue: prolong: 'self disclosure', 'report experience'}
  b. **yiqian wo ye ai pa shan,**
  before I too like climb mountain
  c. **padao shanding.shang**
  climb-to mountain-top.on
  d. **yu juede yuzhou de weida he ziji de miaoxiao.**
  more feel universe DE greatness and self DE small
  'Oh yes. Before I too liked mountain climbing. On a mountain, one feels the greatness of the universe and the insignificance of the self.'

Wang's response is built-up in three steps. First, his reply *Dui le* ('Oh, yes') indicates recognition of shared common ground, which allows him to take the turn and bring in his own experiences. Thereafter, he clarifies his own involvement in that common ground, and after introducing an activity related circumstantial setting ('when on the mountain'), he develops the conversation further by giving an opinion. The function of the supportive reply, in our view, is to confirm to the interlocutor the extent of shared common ground as regards the issue or activity involved.

2 Dangran le/la

Another frequent conversational reply is *dangran le* ('of course'). In our view, this reply makes a direct appeal to shared common-ground structure, and claims that the common-ground structure is there as a matter of fact: 'Everybody knows'. Our data contained three examples. In one case, the reply was simply *dangran la!* It was part of a move sequence that tried to construe the autonomous activity of the addressee:

(7.46) [opening part of a casual conversation: construal]
  Wang: {support: reply: 'accept'}
  a. **Zhemo shuo,**
  so say

b. **ni shi zhen zai xie jiashu lou.**
you be really at write home-letter LOU
'*Well, then you are really just writing a letter home.*'

Here, Wang finally accepts the 'construal' of Wu's personal and autonomous activity. The latter thereupon signals that he considers this no more than natural (Chinese 600/2: 3):

(7.47) [opening part of a casual conversation: construal]
    Wu: [support: reply: 'confirm']
    Dangran la!
    of-course LA
    '*Of course!*'

The confirmation regards the nature of their shared common ground. '*Of course, I'm doing what I said I was doing!*' You were deviant, not I. Wu's reply could have been a simple *dangran* ('of course!'). By adding the common-ground marker, *le/la*, it became clear that there was an earlier 'deviation' in the discussion, which is now brought to a 'solution': '*How could you have thought otherwise.*'

3 Yiding le

The expression *yiding le/la* ('certainly') also relates directly to shared common-ground structure and confirms its existence as shared. Its use in a 'confirmation' move, for instance after an appointment has been made, is common in everyday conversation. Our data contain one example. There it is used to 'confirm' the existence of a piece of shared common ground. The example has been quoted already (example 7.14) when 'construals' were discussed. It is repeated here (Chinese 600/1: 1; our translation):

(7.14) [building personal common ground]
    Yang: [support: reply: a. 'acknowledge', b. and c. 'affirm' (common ground)]
    a. Ah, laoshi!
    ah, teacher
    b. Jiaole bushao nian le ba!
    teach-LE not-few year LE BA
    c. Yiding shi taoli man tianxia la!
    certainly be peach-plum full world LA
    '*Ah, a teacher! You must have taught quite some years already, and have pupils everywhere!*'

As observed, in his reactive move Yang makes the appeal in order to show that he shares the Chinese communal common ground with the new acquaintance, and respects his position in that culture. The 'construal' with *yiding* ('certain') reveals the speaker's conviction that the common-ground structure must be this way.

4 Feedback and 'Wo dong le'

When one of the interactants in a conversation does not have certain information in his knowledge base, or is not sure about a piece of information, s/he needs to inform her/himself or request an update in order to have a basis for further communication on the subject. The example is a casual conversation between neighbours about some religious practices:

(7.48) [casual conversation on religious practices between neighbours]
He: [prolonging move: request elaboration]
Namo Tianzhu jiaotang he Jidu jiaotang you shenmo fenbie ne?
that-case Catholic Church and Protestant Church have what differnce NE
'*Then, what is the difference between the Catholic and the Protestant Church?*'

He's prolonging move is a request for information. The answer by Zhu provides some of the information requested:

(7.49) [casual conversation on religious practices between neighbours]
Zhu: [reacting: reply: 'answer']
a. Tianzhujiao shi jiujiao,
Catholic faith be old-faith
b. juxing zongjiao yishi de ren jiao shenfu,
perform religion ceremony DE people is-called priest
c. suoxing de zongjiao lijie jiao Misa.
performed DE religion protocol is-called mass
'*The Catholic faith is the old faith, the person who presides over the liturgy is called Priest. The religious service is called mass.*'

He thereupon seems to realise how the related knowledge base is organised. He then signals that things have become clear to him:

(7.50) [casual conversation on religious practices between neighbours]
He: [respond: support: reply: 'acknowledge']
a. A, wo dong le!
A I understand LE
[support: develop: elaborate: 'assert' fact]
b. Xiang mushi, zuo libai, zhelei de mingci shi shuyu Jidujiao de.

200   *Conversations*

   like minister do service this-kind DE name be belong-to Protestant-
   faith DE
   '*Oh, I see! Words such as minister, Sunday service, and the like are part of the Protestant religion.*'

'Has become clear' is the 'solution' to the earlier 'problem' of 'not being clear about an issue'. We see this as another way of indicating that *He* now understands how the shared common ground is organised, and in order to show this *He* thereafter produces an assertion as a test to see if he really has got it right. *He* passes the test. Zhu reacts to it positively (Chinese 600/2: 9):

(7.51)   [casual conversation on religious practices between neighbours]
    Zhu: [supportive reply: 'acknowledge']
    Dui la!
    correct LA
    'That's right!'

Again, *Dui la* is used to acknowledge that the structure of the shared common ground, as presented, is now correct.

7.4.2 Goal attainment

A second group of expressions involving the particle *le/la* is related to the signalling of 'goal attainment'. The data provided seven conventional combinations involving the particle *le/la*. These were:

1   *tai hao la*
2   *...(jiu) hao la*
3   *...jiu keyi le*
4   *...jiu shi le*
5   *...jiu cheng le*
6   *...jiu xing le*
7   *...jiu suan le*

Each of these expressions contains three constituents *jiu*, verb, and *le*. The particle *le* explicitly signals that a 'solutionhood' parameter has been set in the current common ground structure, and the addressee is requested to co-ordinate on that. The marker *jiu* ('follow') links the already introduced cognitive target to the status of 'solutionhood'. The frequent nature of this kind of phrasings has made them into some kind of stock expressions. This, however, does not imply that there is a syntactic link between the constituents. The particle *le* in these cases can only be used when there is a 'solutionhood' moment recognisable in the common-ground structure of that moment. We will illustrate each of the seven conventional expressions below.

Tai hao la *and* hao la

The expression *Tai hao la* ('Very good then'), we already observed in a waiter–customer exchange, in which it was used as 'pre-closure' in the taking of an order. In an interpersonal interaction, there can be no 'pre-closure' effect since it is not clear yet which kind of project the interactants are involved in. Let us consider the following example and see where the expression comes in:

(7.52) [old friends meeting and updating their common ground]
  Wang: [initiating move: 'attending' and 'question']
  a. Hen jiu bu jian le,
  very long no see LE
  b. zuijin dou mang xie shenmo?
  most-recent all busy some what
  'I haven't seen you for a long time, what have you been doing lately?'

In the attending move, *hen jiu bu jian* ('long time no see') is asserted. This expression, which is itself a greeting, obtains the character of something 'deviating' when the speaker selects the particle *le*, 'really long time no see', 'haven't seen YOU for a long time'! These people know each other well but may have lost touch with each other.

In (7.53) and (7.54) old friends meet and a conversation begins; through it they update their common ground:

(7.53) [old friends meeting and updating their common ground]
  Zeng: [reactive move: answer]
  Wo zuijin xiujia, suoyi hen xian.
  I most-recent rest-leave, so very free
  'I have been off from work lately and taking it easy.'

In his reactive move, Zeng answers the question and thereby adds information to the shared common ground as a matter of fact. Wang then 'prolongs' the conversation with (Chinese 600/2: 8):

(7.54) [old friends meeting and updating their common ground]
  Wang: ['support: reply: a. 'acknowledge' b. 'affirm']
  a. Xiu jia?
  rest-leave
  b. Na zhenshi tai hao le!
  that really-be too good LE
  'On holiday? Excellent.'

Wang first shows that the update provided by *Zeng* surprises him, and he therefore repeats the surprising part, *xiu jia* ('holidays?'), but also reacts to it in a 'supportive' way with *tai hao le!* Zeng can read from this that Wang, for some yet unknown reason, approves of him having a vacation. Later it turns out that Wang sees this as an opportunity for their going places together.

For the expression *hao le* ('okay now') we found three uses. It can be used as an intervention intended to stop an interaction, it can be used at the end of a proposal and signal that the speaker considers the proposal a 'solution' to an earlier raised 'problem', or it can be used after the marker *jiu* ('then') to signal attainment of a procedural 'goal'. The three uses we found are:

(a) *hao le, hao le*
(b) ... *hao le*
(c) ... *jiu hao le*

Of these we will illustrate (a) *hao le, hao le*, and (b) assertion *hao le*; the (c) type is very much like (b), and we have also met that usage in Chapter 5. We therefore will not illustrate that usage separately.

(a) *hao le, hao le* The expression *hao le, hao le* occurred once in our data. It was used in an 'intervention', in this case by a third party who intended to stop an argument which was going on between two relatives. The intervention was followed by a suggestion for avoiding further conflict (Chinese 600/2: 14):

(7.55) [father intervening in dispute]
Ming: [a. rejoinder: 'intervention'; b. c. extend: 'suggestion']
a. Hao le, hao le.
good LE good LE
b. Xiaci shuohua zhi qian,
next-time speak-words ZHI before
c. xian kaolü yixia shidang de xingrongci ba.
first consider one-while suitable DE descriptive-word BA
'*That's enough! Think of some proper adjective before speaking next time.*'

Ming, the father, at this point decided to break into the conversation, which at that time had the form of an argument, and tried to stop it. 'Enough, enough!' The conventional expression for interventions in Chinese is *hao le* ('okay now; enough'). Repeating it once as *hao le, hao le* has the iconic effect of expressing strong urgency. The break in conversation is obviously a 'disturbance' and requires co-ordination by the addressees (son and daughter-in-law) to reflect on the intervention act, and calculate the effects on their current common ground. The father thereafter initiated a further contribution by suggesting a procedure that potentially could avoid further conflict.

(b) ... *hao le/la* The expression ... *hao la* was used in a 'developing move', and in a 'reply move'. Both are reactive moves in a particular situation. The 'developing move' brings in new information, whereas the 'reply move' is a conventional responding reaction (Eggins and Slade 1997: 202, 205). The following example illustrates a 'developing move', which is meant to solve an earlier raised problem (Chinese 600/2: 1; our translation):

(7.56) [friends talking about moving to Taiwan]
Li: [appending move: 'offer']
a. **wo kan,**
I see
b. **nin yao juede wode fangzi hai heshi de hua,**
you if consider I-DE house still suitable DE case
c. **jiu zu women jia de fangzi hao la!**
then rent our family DE house okay LA
'Well, if you think my house is suitable, then why don't you rent this house!'

Earlier in the conversation, the non-local person, Wang, had raised a problem. He wanted to move to Taiwan, but could not find a house to rent. In this 'developing move', Li offers Wang a way out by offering one of the houses of his family. The expression . . . *hao la* ('well, that should do it'), is an offer that in the perspective of the speaker is a 'solution' to the 'problem' under discussion. The addressee now needs to consider the proposal and either accept of reject it. His reaction was outright positive (Chinese 600/2: 1):

(7.57) [friends talking about moving to Taiwan]
Wang: [reactive move: 'acceptance']
Na ke zai hao ye meiyou la!
then sure more good also not-have LA
'It couldn't be better!'

The acceptance of the offer takes the form of *ke zai hao ye meiyou la* ('there can't be any better'), and thereby reinforces the 'solution' moment which was introduced in the common-ground structure by the 'offer'. By praising the 'solution' on offer it will be taken as accepted.

The 'reply move' . . . *hao le* ('. . . okay *le*') is a 'supportive response' (Eggins and Slade 1997: 205). It acknowledges what preceded. If a 'command' preceded, it signals 'compliance', as in (Chinese 600/1: 7):

(7.58) [guest instructing waiter in restaurant]
Guest: [initiating move: 'directive']
Kuai diar!
fast little
'Hurry up!'
Waiter: [reactive move: supportive reply]
Fangxin hao le.
relax okay LE
'Don't worry!'

204 *Conversations*

The supportive reply implies that the directive is understood and will be taken up. It also brings the 'command', which stands out as a 'problem' in that context (a customer is not satisfied), under control. With the expression *fangxin hao le* ('don't worry about it'), that 'problem' is brought to a (temporary) 'solution'.

... jiu keyi le and others

In this section we will illustrate uses of *jiu keyi le* ('that will be okay') as well as *jiu shi le* ('that's it'). Due to space limitation we will not give further examples of *jiu cheng le* ('then you succeeded'), and *jiu xing le* ('then it will do'). The working of these constructions is the same. The expression *... jiu keyi le* ('that will be fine') was used three times, one time during haggling in the market and two times during an 'Asking the way' exchange. We provide an example from the latter conversation genre, which, in our view, clearly illustrates the common-ground elicitation function of the particle *le*. In this exchange, the local person decided that he needed additional information in order to be able to give directions:

(7.59) [casual meeting: asking the way]
Local person: [prolonging move: 'enhancing': 'disjunctive question']
Nin yao dao zongju haishi fenju?
you want arrive central-office rather-be branch-office
'*Do you want to go to the Central Post Office or to a branch office?*'

The indication 'enhancing move' (Eggins and Slade 1997: 198) suggests that this move is merely 'qualifying the immediately prior move'. However, it is attractive to look at this move sequence as a *side sequence*, which the local person initiated in order to determine the official business they are involved in (Clark 1996: 242). The person asking the way reacted with (Chinese 600/1: 4):

(7.60) [casual meeting: asking the way]
Stranger: [reactive move: a. 'elaboration'; b. reply: 'probability'; c. 'affirm']
a. Wo zhi shi mai youpiao.
I only be buy stamps
b. Wo xiang
I think
c. fenju jiu keyi le.
branch-office then okay LE
'*I only need to buy stamps. I think the branch office will be alright.*'

In this side sequence, the stranger first 'elaborated' a prior move by clarifying his 'project goal'. Thereafter, he took it as probable (*wo xiang* ['I think']) that one of the two foregrounded targets (the 'central post office' and a 'branch office') was the location for the execution of his 'project'.[10] By using the particle *le*, the stranger created the feeling of 'solutionhood' in the common-ground structure, signalling that according to him they could proceed from there. If the answer had been ... *jiu keyi*, the interaction had been missing the link to common-ground structure.

In the expression ... *jiu shi le* ('...and there it is; that's it'), as in the previous examples, the particle *le* is used to create a feeling of 'solutionhood' in the shared common-ground structure. A previously mentioned cognitive target is identified, *shi* ('be so'), and the expression requests co-ordination on that target. We found three types of cognitive targets, (a) locality ('there it is then'), (b) common knowledge ('that's just it then'), and with a similarly limiting effect in (c) a social practice ('just doing in that way'). We give an examples of each (Chinese 600/1: 4):

(7.61) [casual meeting: asking the way]
  Local person: [gives directions; asserts how to get there]
  a. Nin yanzhe zhetiao malu yizhi zou,
  you along this-strip road straight walk
  b. guo qianmian nage shizi lukou,
  pass front that-piece cross corner
  c. wang zuo yiguai
  toward left one-turn
  d. jiu shi le.
  then be LE
  '*Go straight ahead along this street, cross the crossroad, and turn left; the post office is right there.*'

The target mentioned was the 'post office', a non-movable object. After giving directions, the target destination is marked with *jiu shi le* ('there it is'). The use of the particle *le* requests co-ordination on the 'solution' being offered. When the expression *jiu shi* ('and there it is') is used, there is no recognition of a 'solutionhood', which makes the remark more distant.

The second example is related to 'personal knowledge'. After being praised, the addressee plays the praise down by restricting his knowledge to one particular type – 'common knowledge' (Chinese 600/2: 2):

(7.62) [exchanging information on buying food]
  Wang: [reactive move: 'decline'; 'assertion' and 'focusing']
  a. nar de hua,
  where DE speech
  b. zhe zhi shi putong changshi
  this only be general knowledge
  c. jiu shi le,
  then be LE
  '*Not at all, this is merely common knowledge.*'

Wang in his reactive move 'declines' the praise 'politely', and thereafter asserts that his knowledge should be limited to one particular type, 'common knowledge', as said. The *jiu shi le* ('and that's it') sequence further strengthens the limiting effect of the 'b.' clause, and strengthens the idea of 'downgrading', a politeness strategy, which is the socially accepted practice of interpersonal management. This downgrading changes the structure of the shared common ground.

The third example also contains a 'limiting' expression through the use of *zhishi* ('it is only'), and has as target a 'social practice', 'keep on learning'. When two friends remember their mutual experiences and one is being 'praised', he plays this down with (Chinese 600/2: 18):

(7.63) [casual conversation between schoolmates as to their educational experiences and progress]
Li: [reactive move: 'interpersonal management']
Ni zhenshi guojiang le.
you really-be pass-praise LE
[developing: 'elaboration']
a. Wo zhishi buduande xuexi
I only-be not-stop-DE study
b. jiu shi le.
then be LE
'*You just flatter me. I only keep on learning.*'

Li downplays the praise directed towards him, and limits his achievement by identifying it as 'merely the result of hard work'. The limiting term used in these examples was *zhi shi* ('it is only'), and the expression *jiu shi le* ('that's it') further strengthened that idea, and thereby the structure of the shared common ground changes.

... jiu suanle

In this expression, *jiu* is followed by *suanle* ('count as-realised'), which results in the idea of 'that's it; that's all'. This expression requests the addressee to co-ordinate their common ground in agreement with the content of the assertion (Chinese 600/2: 20):

(7.64) [casual conversation about reading behaviour]
Hu: [prolonging move: extension]
a. Shuo laoshi hua,
speak true speech
b. wo yiqian kan shu,
I before read book
c. zhi xiang duo kan, kuai kan,
only think much read fast read

d. zhishi yong yanjing liuguoqu
only-be use eyes stream-over-go
e. jiu suanle.
then count as-finish LE
'To tell the truth, before when I read I was focused on more and faster, just let my eyes glide over the pages and that's it.'

Hu added to the information already given by admitting that he, when being honest, as regards 'reading', limited himself to scanning pages. The limiting expressions in this example was *zhishi* ('it only is...'), whereas *jiu* introduced the idea of *suanle* ('that's it'). The latter addition affirms it as a change in the structure of the current common ground.

7.5 Politeness

In the previous examples we met at least two cases of interpersonal management through 'downgrading', which can be considered forms of politeness (cf. Gu 1999). The Chinese language has a large repertoire of conventional expressions that developed in the context of regulating interpersonal relationships. Our data contained seven politeness expressions in which the particle *le* was used. Six of these are listed in Table 7.4. The seventh is discussed separately.

We already met a few of these in this chapter and in the previous two. In this section we will illustrate two common phrases used in polite discourse (1) *tai keqi le*, and (2) *Qingjiao*. Politeness is a highly developed art in China and its roots can be traced at least until the early Zhou Dynasty (Oliver 1971). No wonder then that there is quite a variety of conventional expressions of this type. Glossed out of context, these expressions cannot always be easily understood. We therefore give examples in context to illustrate the impact of pragmatic forces on the organisation and form of polite discourse involving the particle *le*.

1 Tai keqi le

One of the most common Chinese politeness expressions is *Nin tai keqi le* ('You should not have done that'). In the following example friends are

Table 7.4 Politeness expressions in Chinese involving the particle *le*

Chinese	English
1 *Nin tai keqi le.*	You are too polite. Don't say that.
2 *Ni ba wo pengde tai gao le.*	You flatter me too much.
3 *Na women lia shi zhi-tong-dao-he la!*	Then, we two are comrades.
4 *Yihou xiang duo xiang ni qingjiao la!*	From now on, I will ask your advice.
5 *Tai xinku le.*	She must be very tired.
6 *Ni zhenshi guojiang le.*	You just flatter me.

talking about Chinese literature and the conversation develops as follows (Chinese 600/2: 6):

(7.65) [friends talking about Chinese literature]
Lin: [prolonging move: 'elaboration']
Xihuan wenxue de ren you fengfu de qinggan.
like literature DE person have rich DE feelings
'*A person who likes literature must be a man of great feelings.*'

When we take this move as 'polite discourse' and a form of 'complimenting', the task of the addressee is to respond to it in an appropriate way, which in Chinese culture means 'downgrading' the compliment. The reply was:

(7.66) [friends talking about Chinese literature]
Wang: [polite discourse: three forms of 'downgrading']
a. Nin tai keqi le.
you too polite LE
b. Wo dui wenxue shi waihangde,
I towards literature be outsider-DE
c. gen ni yibi jiu chayuan le.
with you one-compare them differ-far LE
'*That's too much. I'm just a laymen, interested but I cannot stand in your shadow!*'

Wang declined the praise in three steps. First he used a conventional reply, thereby changing the structure of the common ground: *Nin tai keqi le* ('You praise me too much'). Thereafter he makes two moves to change that structure by further 'downgrading' his expertise. He asserts his status as 'layman', *wo dui wenxue shi waihangde*, and thereafter further downgrades his position in comparison to the addressee by elevating him to a higher status, *gen ni yibi jiu chayuan le*. In this way the position of both participants in the common-ground structure has changed. One lowered himself while endeavouring to raise the other.

2 Qingjiao

Qingjiao ('please instruct me') is a very frequent phrase in polite discourse and used at several places in the text. The example we want to discuss occurred a little later in the same conversation on Chinese literature. After exchanging several polite expressions, the conversation ends with (Chinese 600/2: 6; our translation):

(7.67) [friends talking about Chinese literature]
Wang: [polite discourse: raising the other']
Yihou yao duo xiang nin qingjiao la!

hereafter must more toward you request-instruct LA
'From now on I will turn to you for advice!'

The content of this final assertion is marked with *yao* ('shall, will'), which together with *le* indexes a common-ground 'change' that will affect the speaker's future behaviour. It is an announced change in the addressee's position and thereby a change in common-ground structure

7.6 Assert a hypothetical situation and its consequences

In a conversation, the conversational genre and the extent of shared common-ground forces a contributor to remain within conventional bounds or allows him to use the common-ground setting to signal something that is 'outstanding' and requests a 'change' or 'reset' of the common ground. One way to create a 'deviation' in the background distinctions of the culture is to do this in a hypothetical situation. Here is an example (Chinese 600/2: 9):

(7.68) {neighbours coming to talk about religion}
Zhu: {elaborating move: 'assertion'}
{priests do not marry}
He: {reactive move: hypothetical contradiction}
...
a. Ruguo you yitian shenfu ye keyi jiehun le,
if have one-day priest also may marry LE
b. jiu bu neng suan shi chujiaren la!
then not can count-as be leave-home-person LA
'If one day priests are allowed to get married, you can no longer consider them recluses!'

The goal of the speaker, whose name is He, in the final line of this reported conversation asserts that the current state of affairs may change if priests are being allowed to marry. He 'construes' a hypothetical future situation in which different social practices prevail, and also asserts the consequences of such a state of affairs for the status of priests. Both hypothetical steps are marked with the particle *le/la*. Each step modifies the structure of the shared common ground. The sequence *ruguo keyi ... le* ('if that would become possible'), then *buneng suan ... la* ('one could not count them any longer as [recluses]'). These contributions signal that the structure of the common ground can be manipulated and the consequences worked out.

7.7 Asserting step by step

In the final section of this chapter, the enumerative usage of the particle *le/la* is considered. Chang (1986) argued that in essence this usage is the same as the other uses of *le*, it marks a 'discourse unit' or 'discourse block'. We agree

210   *Conversations*

with him on that. However, his explanation is too mechanical. We like to approach this in terms of a perceived need by the speaker as to making clear to the addressee that co-ordination in these cases is part of the cultural common ground, and that he should take note of that and reset his cultural common ground accordingly. The examples in our data confirm this. The units the speaker marks with *la* are part of the cultural common ground. For instance, in a conversation on sight-seeing in Taipei, the following contribution was made as an answer to a request for information (Chinese 600/1: 19):

(7.69)   [acquaintances talking about sight seeing in Taipei]
Hou: [reactive move: answer]
a. Piru Yuanshan Dongwuyuan he Ertong Leyuan la,
for-example Yuanshan Zoo and Children Playground LA
b. Minquan Donglu de Rongxing huayuan la
Minquan East-road DE Glorious Star Garden LA
c. dou bucuo.
each no-bad
'For example, the Yuanshan Zoo and Children{'s} Playground, the Rongxing Garden at the Minquan East road are not bad.'

Hou selected some of the landmarks in Taipei, as they existed in those days, and marked them with *la* in order to signal that he wanted the addressees to add them to their cultural common ground. We therefore claim that the so-called enumerative *la* marks 'cognitive landmarks', pieces of the (shared) cultural common ground.

Conclusion

We started this chapter with the question as to the kind of modifications in common-ground structure that will be marked by the particle *le* in conversations. To be able to answer that question we first made a distinction between 'personal conversations' and 'business conversations'. The latter are conventionally organised and do not allow much room for personal input. Both types of conversation are emerging phenomena, but personal conversations are 'fully' emergent, moving from one 'minimal joint project' to the next, and therefore are scripted to a far lesser extent. Our data contained information on four types of exchanges that can occur in personal conversations: 'building common ground', 'construals', 'setting an agenda', and participating in an 'argument'. The structure of the common ground is involved in each of these, but in a different way. In building common ground, the structure of that common ground is established. In an already established conversational project (such as 'seeking advice'), 'problems' and 'solutions' are conversational moments that a speaker might select as 'co-ordination points' for the modification of the common ground structure. The 'rejection' of a 'construal', and in 'argumentation' a 'challenge', were examples of 'co-ordination points'. In 'setting an agenda' a 'co-ordination point' was the marking of a piece of information as the basis for getting the proposed 'agenda' (where to go) set. 'Construals' also were used to project pieces of the cultural common ground for some purpose as instances of 'deviation' or 'solutionhood'. When 'construals' changed the structure of the common ground, they were marked as co-ordination points. This was clearest in cases of the hypothetical construal of common-ground structure, which were marked as co-ordination points when contrasted with a previous situation in which either the hypothesised or the normal situations were absent.

Agreeing on common ground is an essential feature of interpersonal interaction. Conventional responses such as *dui le* and *dangran le* are available in Chinese to mark 'recognition' or 'acceptance' of the current common-ground structure. In interpersonal management a speaker can choose to make his own position in the interaction clear or to clarify how he takes the construction by the other speaker. For this purpose, a number of expressions are available that index 'politeness' levels. Finally, 'asserting step by step' is another environment in which the particle *la* can be used to request co-ordination on pieces of cultural common ground. In all cases, co-ordination points index modifications in the structure of the current common ground.

8   Discussion

In this chapter we will condense the findings of the previous three chapters and formulate a general characterisation of the particle *le* in Chinese discourse, thereby taking into account the questions posed in Chapter 3. We will argue that across all exchanges the function of the particle *le* as a 'common-ground co-ordination device' can be maintained. We claim that the 'why' question of the particle's use is a modification of the 'structure' of the common ground as it is represented by the 'mental model', which is constituted at that moment.[1] The 'when' question relates to the moments that interactants in a verbal interaction find suitable, or use conventionally, as 'co-ordination points'. We observed in the previous chapters that moments of 'deviation', 'solutionhood', and certain forms of 'construal' answer the 'when' question. In order to get this into a sharper perspective, we will scrutinise our findings once more in this chapter in order to get this clearer, and better understand the nature of co-ordination-point marking, the main function of uses of the particle *le*, and its relation to common-ground structure. It is the latter notion, we feel, that is crucial for understanding the relationship between the various manifestations of marking with the particle *le*.

The chapter is organised as follows. We will start (8.1) with a statistical comparison of uses of the particle *le* across the three discourse types studied. This is followed by a comparison of uses of the particle *le* in these interaction types (8.2), which leads to a characterisation of the particle *le* in the following section (8.3). In that section, we will detail the nature of 'co-ordination' as represented by the examples studied in this book, and thereafter specify the various linguistic ways in which this is achieved. These two notions are directly related to the structure of shared common ground, and determine how that structure can be influenced, constructed, or otherwise manipulated. We conclude the analysis (8.4) with an overview and by confronting our findings with the data in Chao (1968), which we considered as benchmark data.

8.1 Statistical comparison

Supportive data are of two kinds: statistical and contextual. The statistics (Table 8.1) show that in this study we analysed 495 cases of contextualised

Table 8.1 Comparison of uses of verbal -*le* and the particle *le* in various discourse environments

Discourse type	Verbal -le	Particle le	Total
Procedural	46 (21%)	170 (79%)	216 (100%)
Children's stories	28 (41%)	41 (59%)	69 (100%)
Conversations	31 (15%)	179 (85%)	210 (100%)
All	105 (21%)	390 (79%)	495 (100%)

Note
All discourse-act final uses of -*le*/*le* cases counted as representing the particle *le*.

uses of verbal -*le* and the particle *le* across three discourse types: 'procedural discourse' ('action-picture stories'), 'children's stories' and 'conversations'. The number of uses of the particle *le* in 'procedural' discourse and the 'conversations' analysed was about the same, 170 and 179 cases respectively. The number of occurrences of the particle *le* in the 'children's stories' was much lower (n = 41). The data show a rank order for the particle *le* as (1) conversations (85 per cent), (2) action-picture stories (79 per cent), and (3) children's stories (59 per cent).

These figures confirm the often observed relatively high use of the particle *le* in conversational exchanges (cf. Li and Thompson 1981: 290), but still are too general to suggest reasons for that rank order. Clearly, the 'conversation' and 'procedural discourse' data group together, whereas the 'narrative' data follow at considerable distance. This result can be directly related to the concept 'common-ground co-ordination', since it is not difficult to defend the position that the need for co-ordination is higher in interpersonal encounters in which people know each other well or learn to know each other ('conversations'), and in cases where there is already shared common ground ('procedural discourse'), than in situations in which strangers reportedly are involved in everyday events without interaction, as we observed in some of the children's stories. In one of those stories, *Da Zhentan* ('The Great Detective'), the structure of the common ground was being introduced, and the writer reported a neutral series of events.[2] In conversational settings, interlocutors depend heavily on common-ground structure and co-ordination between the two mental-model structures of the interacting persons. In our model we relate the relatively frequent use of the particle *le* in conversations to the communicative need existing between interlocutors to construct and maintain shared common ground.

The data in Table 8.1 further show that the number of cases of marking with verbal -*le* was just the opposite. We found 21 per cent usage in the procedural discourse pieces, 41 per cent in the children's stories, and 15 per cent in face-to-face conversations. This under the assumption that all discourse-act final uses of -*le* or *le* were counted as the particle *le* in first instance, and no double counting was allowed. Of course, this procedure strongly reduced the percentage of occurrences of verbal -*le*, but allows cross-discourse-type comparison. The rank order for uses of verbal -*le* from high to low was then:

1 Children's stories   41 per cent
2 Procedural discourse ['action-picture stories']   21 per cent
3 Conversations   15 per cent

We associate the relatively high percentage of use of verbal -*le* in children's stories with the need to report story progress, whereas in face-to-face conversations, progress reports are often provided by the perceived developments in the immediate situation or setting. The action-picture stories hold the middle ground. Pictures, providing a partial contextual representation, most likely are responsible for this effect. They are a non-verbal way of creating common ground.

The data for verbal -*le* in Table 8.1 do not reflect cases of marking with -*le/le*. These were all counted as the particle *le*. We did do so because at message-final position, the particle *le* marks a 'co-ordination point', and that assertion is more important than the use of verbal -*le* for marking event 'realisation' (a 'peak event'). Speakers/writers use marking with verbal -*le* in phrase-final position to index 'goal attainment' of some action or process, which as a notional distinction changes the structure of the common ground and requires common-ground co-ordination. Given our orientation on cognitive marking, we therefore decided to keep the data as they are presented here. The statistics are still only indicative and do not express any absolute value or pertinent relationship. Other materials most likely will provide different results. The main line, however, is clear.

8.2 A contextual comparison

In this section we will compare the data of Chapters 5, 6 and 7 in three relatively fast steps to bring out the main findings. The comparison shows that in all three discourse types marking a co-ordination point takes the form of indexing a 'deviation' or 'solutionhood'. We therefore detail the co-ordination function of the Chinese particle *le* as:

> The particle *le* marks a 'co-ordination point' in the process of 'distribution of information'. These co-ordination points index changes in common-ground constituent structure.

What we will have to make clear is the central role of 'distribution of information', and 'constituent structure' of the common ground. These two concepts are fundamental in helping to understand 'when' the particle *le* is used, and to comprehend the way in which uses of the particle *le* regulate the information flow between interactants. In procedural environments, co-ordination points were 'deviations', or their counterpart 'solutionhood'. In narrative discourse these distinctions needed to be further supplemented with 'additions' to common-ground structure, whereas in conversational settings, apart from the notion 'construal' which was a new distinction, they can be recognised as 'confrontation' and 'confirmation'. These additions are related to the nature of co-ordination points in different discourse types, and have to do with the creation of shared common ground.

8.2.1 Action-picture stories

The analysis of 66 action-picture stories in Chapter 5 demonstrated that the particle *le* was *not* used when a regular script was involved and the procedure developed along expected and predictable lines. It was particularly not used in instructions of how to perform the constituting acts of a regular procedure. When we look at these findings from an information flow perspective, the conclusion must be that for a 'regular' or 'normal' flow of events interactants do not feel a direct need to appeal for co-ordination, and therefore do not use the particle *le*. The 'instructor' in the procedure tasks, however, marked 'deviations' as co-ordination points, and expected the 'apprentice' to co-ordinate on that and adjust the structure of the shared common ground accordingly. The 'instructor' also expects the 'apprentice' to understand the consequences of what is being said.[3]

'Deviations' in a procedure were further specified as 'involuntary effects', 'upcoming events' or 'institutional facts', as the deviation counterpart 'solution', and as a 'deviation'/'contrast' in a series. When the speaker wanted to update himself on some 'perceived problem' in the common ground, a co-ordination question was used. We list these distinctions here once more, and provide an example for each of them as a reminder. For the details we refer back to Chapter 5:

Motivations for the use of the particle le in the action-picture stories

1	'Deviation' or 'problem'	*Tai da le, tuodiao day*
	'Involuntary effects'[4]	*Ni de toufa chang le*
	'Upcoming events'[5]	*kaoshi jiu yao kaishi le*
2	'Solutionhood'[6]	*Hao le. Tunxiaqule*
3	'Deviation' in series	*Wo zui ai chi yu le!*
4	'Requesting a common-ground update'	*Ni zenmo la?*

The need for requesting an addressee to reorient himself as to the structure of the shared common ground, as illustrated in the 'action-picture stories', was mainly related to 'progress reports', and only incidentally in 'verbal interactions' and other procedure-related distinctions such as 'instructions', 'warnings' and 'endings'.[7]

The generalisation that holds is that the particle *le* indexes a 'co-ordination point', and requests common-ground co-ordination. Signalling a 'co-ordination point' is intended to result in a harmonisation between the common-ground structures of the interactants. The speaker provides information that should be sufficient for the addressee to perform the co-ordination successfully. Issues that can function as 'co-ordination point' are then both a matter of common-ground knowledge and of subjective selection.

8.2.2 Children's stories

In two of the ten children's stories the particle *le* was not used. It was possible to relate that absence to the lack of interaction between story characters. When there is no shared common ground, and there are only conventional interactions (as between strangers), the particle *le* is not applied. There is nothing to co-ordinate on.[8] In the 'action-picture stories' the particle *le* occurred mainly in 'progress reports'. In children's stories, the particle *le* did occur at all moments of the global story structure, with the exception of the exposition part. The particle *le* indexes a 'co-ordination point', as we said, and in the children's stories these were various moments in the 'deterioration' cycle and the 'restoration' cycle. In all notional parts of the children's stories the particle *le* did occur. The clearest exception to this generalisation was the 'exposition' part of a story. The particle *le* occurred in only one story in the opening part and in that case, by necessity, it indexed an upcoming change in the structure of shared common ground.

As in the action stories, the particle *le* occurred most frequently in progress reports, which are interactions between the narrator and his audience/readers. The particle *le* was used at moments at which a new development took place in the story. Co-ordination points were moments in the 'deterioration' and 'restoration' cycle. 'Deterioration' can be illustrated with cases such as *yishang chuan ba chuan caifanle* ('as soon as she stepped on the boat it capsized'), whereas for 'restoration' we found examples such as *Bubu yaozhe xiguachuan guolai jiu ren le* ('[Okay, okay,] there comes Bubu to the rescue'). For the 'coda' we can quote an example from the same story that read *Bubu jiu biancheng yige yao jiantouchuan de chuanfu le* ('[The father of the bride presented Bubu with a stylish gondola.] Bubu then became a proud gondola owner.')[9] In the latter case, however, we need to conclude that it is not so much a case of 'solutionhood' as a permanent change in the 'structure of the shared common ground' that is being reported. Bubu's wish was to change his participant status by becoming a gondola owner, and when that was realised it changed the structure of the shared common ground.[10] In the conclusion to Chapter 6 we presented the various relationships in Table 6.3. At this point we only need to confirm that in each instance the structure of the shared common ground was modified.

In the exposition phase of the children's stories, common-ground modification took the form of the appearance of a 'new event', in this case a marriage party, whereas in another story the consequences of a technical event were reported and that too formed part of scene development and did not cause a 'problem' or 'deviation'. It is the consequence of the camera being set into motion that was marked with the particle *le*, and thereby the reader was 'updated' on the addition of a 'recording event' to the scene.[11] It is this additional nature of a 'technical event' that was a new insight acquired from the analysis of the children's stories. We can recognise this as a 'side event', which is unobtrusive but still changes the common-ground structure. In retrospect this analysis can also be applied to 'new events', and what they have in common is that they change the structure of the shared common ground.

In Chapter 6 we argued that a writer uses four techniques to allow his story to develop. These were building common ground, reporting story progress, narrated monologue, and dialogue/verbal interaction. We observed that in 'building common ground' in stories the particle *le* can only be used incidentally. Story 'progress' was the main area for uses of the particle *le* as described. 'Dialogue' between story characters could introduce various special events as we have seen. In 'narrated monologue', finally, events do develop synchronously with the 'main event' in which the story character is involved. In such cases a story character reports events developing in front of him, and when he observes things that do not match the 'normal' structure of the common ground he has the option to mark that 'deviation' with the particle *le*.

The children's stories, as observed, allowed the distinction of scene development, the introduction of events that take place simultaneously. We can distinguish between 'main events', 'observed events', 'merged events', and 'side events'. The reader participated in an 'observed' event when Bubu, the watermelon seller, identified a marriage party on one of the quays in Venice, and later got mixed up in that marriage party, which resulted in a 'merged event'. Such a 'merged scene' also occurred in the Great Photographer's story when the tent of the main character, Mouse Timid, was visited by a lion family while he was sleeping. In that story we learned to recognise 'side events' when a film camera was accidentally started and began recording (*dou paixialaile* ['recorded everything']). The 'merged scene' of Bubu rescuing the bridal party by scooping them out of the water resulted in a more complex common-ground situation, and created the need for the regulation of social obligations, the expression of gratitude and 'politeness'.

The children's stories confirmed the idea that the particle *le* in Chinese is a common-ground co-ordination device, and that it marks common-ground co-ordination points, pieces of general common ground that in the perception of the speaker need to be co-ordinated on since they change the structure of the common ground. We found the following interactions or actions as co-ordination points:

'co-ordination points'
1   'Verbal interaction' signalling 'threat'   *yao zou ni la!*
2   Reporting a 'deviation'   *zhanbuzhu le*
3   Reporting 'solutionhood'   *Bubu . . . lai jiu ren le*

4   'New event' 'side event' [start]   ba ... paixialaile
5   'New event' 'side event' [end]   ziji ba ziji guanshangle
6   'Verbal interaction' 'approval'   ni tai hao le!
7   'Verbal interaction' 'disapproval'   tai mafan le!

In verbal interaction a speaker directly addresses an addressee. In the first example, *yao zou ni la!* ('They are going to hit you!'), that clearly is a warning, and this is based on the reading of the intentions of certain situation participants versus a third party. It is a way of recognising the potential implications of the structure of the current common ground. In the latter two types of 'verbal interaction' the goal is human relationships, expressed as 'approval' and disapproval'. Both expressions change the structure of the shared common ground. The particle *le* is frequently called upon in cases of 'deviations' and 'solutionhood'. These are often 'beginnings' of new events and 'endpoints' of 'deviant' events. Interestingly, the particle *le* does not occur in situations in which an event is reported as being 'in progress' (Wu 2005).

8.2.3 Conversations

The action-picture stories and the children's stories both allowed recognition of 'deviations' and 'solutions' and illustrated how these distinctions were related to the 'structure of common ground'. How then did these notions relate to conversational exchanges? Occurrences of both 'deviations' and 'solutions' were confirmed. These took the form of 'confrontation' and 'confirmation'. A special category, however, was 'construal' of common ground. We will study that category first, and thereafter focus on initiating moves, reacting moves, and ways of handling politeness.

Common-ground 'construal'

'Construals' hold a direct relationship with the building of common ground. It is one way of making sense of another person's status as 'situation participant'. It is therefore important from a communication point of view that 'construals' are accepted as part of common-ground structure. 'Construal' of the 'surroundings' constituent of common-ground structure was endeavoured in an initiating move as *Jintian buhui zai xia yu le ba?* ('It won't rain again today, will it?'). The assumption *buhui ... ba* ('it won't be the case, will it') regards the idea of *zai xia yu le* ('raining again'), and this 'construal' was 'confirmed by the addressee with the remark *Qixiang suo shuo yuhou qing* ('The weather forecast said "Clear after some rain"'), and in this way the weather circumstances ('surroundings') for that day were agreed upon and further plans were made on the basis of that assumption.

In everyday life all kind of events are 'construed'. Addressee status was construed when the speaker characterised the addressee's 'participant status' by identifying what he thought was one of the addressee's hobbies. His own hobby later turned out to be *jiyou* ('collecting stamps'), which explains his interest. By marking the construal as a co-ordination point the speaker also signalled a need for 'confirmation' by the addressee. The addressee's 'participant status' can also be construed on the basis of assumedly shared cultural common ground. By doing so the speaker showed his relation with Chinese shared common ground, and such a construal does not need explicit 'confirmation' since it is assumed shared knowledge. When there is no need for confirmation, pieces of 'cultural common ground' can be 'construed' as the basis for argumentation. The construal started from 'something we all know'.[12] 'Construal' can also be related to a 'conclusion' drawn from the information flow. Since the example was 'deviant' in relation to an earlier piece of information, this construal was used in a 'confronting way'; therefore it was marked as 'co-ordination point' since it affected the 'information status' of the interactants, and a realignment of common-ground structure was considered necessary. The final example of construal was the creation of a hypothetical common ground, and asserting the 'deviant' common-ground structure that would follow from that.

In this section we grouped together 'construals' relating to 'surroundings', 'participant status', a 'personal habit', 'cultural common ground', a 'conclusion drawn', and a 'hypothetical common-ground structure'. The construal of 'participant status' was also used to make one's own relation to the Chinese 'cultural common ground' clear, and to present oneself as knowledgeable.

'Initiating moves'

We attested six cases in which the particle *le* was used in an 'initiating move'. Two uses were 'construals', which we have already introduced in the previous section. One of the 'attending moves' was used in a 'pragmatic situation' when a waiter in a restaurant greeted the arriving 'guests' and thereby confirmed the change in the common-ground structure that had taken place, and authenticated their 'participatory roles' as guests in the restaurant. The second example was used between old friends who had not seen each other for some time. This greeting created a special setting of common-ground structure, a reactivation of previous encounters, and was used as a departure point for the conversation that followed. Two initiating moves had the form of a 'co-ordination question'. We analysed this as a 'common-ground co-ordination' request. The speaker wanted to be updated on the structure of the current common ground. In questions co-ordination points can be used this way.[13]

Reacting moves

A special issue was the rejection of our hypothesis that the particle *le* would be used in 'initiating' moves mainly to attract the attention of an addressee

220 Discussion

towards a particular piece of common ground. The data revealed that the particle *le* was used mainly in 'reacting moves', either to 'support' or to 'confront' existing common-ground structure, as we will see shortly. We will first look at 'assertions' of straightforward 'deviations' and then at 'confronting moves', another manifestation of 'deviation' in conversational context.

DEVIATIONS

Straightforward assertions of 'deviations' signal a discrepancy in common-ground structure between the speaker and the addressee. When the speaker is an authority representing the official common-ground structure, by implication the addressee is at fault. His behaviour does not match the agreed-upon structure of the shared common ground. Authority also is involved when a stranger approaches a local person and requests to be directed to a certain location. By posing the question the stranger indicates that he is not familiar (deviant) with regard to local circumstances. The advice being given also can take the form of a co-ordination point, as in 'my understanding of the common-ground structure is that going there by foot would be *yuan* ("too far"), which would take much longer than going by bus'. Another example is when friends are talking about Chinese food and one, the information requestor, declares himself 'deviant' on this issue, which is quite a different situation again. People can choose the way in which they want to position themselves as regards the cultural common ground and its knowledge base, and that positioning itself may become a co-ordination point.

CONFRONTING

In the conversational exchanges we encountered a number of 'confronting moves'. We found five types:

1 'Intervention'   *hao le, hao le*
2 'Rejection'   *bie kai wanxiao le*
3 'Challenge'   *tai buxiang hua le*
4 'Contradiction'   *sishi chutou la!*
5 'Disagreement'   *tai gui le ba!*

The wider context of these exchanges is given in Chapter 7. Here we give the number of the illustrations quoted. In example (7.55) a father intervened in a dispute, between his son and his daughter-in-law with the 'remark': *hao le, hao le* ('stop it, enough'). In (7.7) we found the 'rejection' of a 'construal': *bie kai wanxiao la* ('Don't make fun of me! [I'm just writing a letter home!]'), and a rejection of praise in (7.63): *Ni zhenshi guojiang le* ('You just flatter me')[14] The 'challenge', *tai bu xiang hua la!* '[Why do you curse me], this is outrageous!' was quoted as example (7.12), where the son whose father featured in example (7.55) refused to make his wife a cup of tea and was reprimanded. The quoted 'contradiction' *sishi chutou la!* ('[Li is far older], over forty') comes from example (7.16) where a third party's personal common ground was construed. The 'disagreement' appeared in example (7.38) and was used by a guest checking into a hotel: *Tai gui le ba!* ('[Six hundred?] Say yourself, that's too much!'). Co-ordination points, then, particularly occur at those places where the common-ground structure is not shared or being disputed.

CONFIRMATION

Another type of 'reacting move' was 'confirmation'. The need for 'confirmation' of the structure of shared common ground helps to explain why we find a number of short 'confirmatory' replies in Chinese. We found these examples: *Dui le* as ('Oh yes! [now we are on shared common ground]') in (7.45), as 'That's right!' when agreeing with the interactant as to the content of what was just said in (7.51), or as 'Indeed' when agreeing with a certain interpretation of current affairs, or used as a 'confirmatory' move that the plan being proposed is right ('Now you mention that,...'). There is quite a variety of uses here which all can be related to the basic notion of 'recognition of common ground' as argued in Chapter 7. *Wo dong le* ('Oh, I see! [Words such as "minister", "Sunday service", and the like are part of the Protestant religion]') quoted in (7.50); *Dangran la* ('Of course'), when finally agreement had been reached on shared common ground in (7.47); or longer expressions such as *Na women lia shi zhi-tong-dao-he la!* ('Then, we two are comrades'), listed in Table 7.4 under 'polite expressions'. The politeness in this case existed in the assertion of the existence of 'shared cultural common ground', which is one way of creating 'closeness'.

The second way in which common ground was 'confirmed' was through 're-assertion', the re-confirmation of the existence of 'shared common ground'. This can only happen when there is an official version of the shared common ground which supposedly is shared; but people forget and make mistakes. When they assumedly realise what they have been doing wrong, repair of the formal common-ground structure can be made into a co-ordination point. We also found one case in which the speaker sought 'confirmation' from an authoritative person (nurse) in a hospital procedure (how to see a doctor) as to his current understanding of the procedure. The exchange had the form of a confirmation question, which was confirmed by the authority controlling the procedure in question.

'SOLUTIONHOOD'

Cases of 'solutionhood' were first of all an 'offer' and its 'acceptance'. The person making the offer tries to solve a 'problem', 'acceptance' makes the 'solution' stand as part of the new common-ground structure. By necessity,

222 *Discussion*

'solutionhood' was also involved in the 'negotiation' of a joint agenda. Negotiations tend to move through a series of proposals which are rejected or altered, and when that happens a co-ordination point is created. 'Solutionhood'-related also were a number of fixed expressions that assert 'truth' (*jiu shi le*), 'success' (*jiu cheng le*), and 'possibility' (*jiu keyi le*).[15] They relate to that moment in the current common-ground structure that is being asserted in the directly preceding part of the move.

Politeness

A separate level in the grammar is that which handles personal relationships, the expression of politeness in particular (cf. Dik 1997; Li and Li 1996; Shi 1986). Politeness is the result of addressing interpersonal goals (Clark 1996). In Chinese culture 'hierarchy' and 'politeness' are crucial features in the organisation of social life. In Table 7.4 we listed a few examples. Politeness expression can be made into a co-ordination point, and used as a reactive move in an exchange to play down a compliment. Politeness has to do with the way in which two social statuses in two interlinked common-ground structures relate to each other. As the Confucian tradition dictates that these statuses are almost always not equal, it is this that must have generated a need for positioning routines. We analysed several in the various chapters.

8.3 Characterisation of *le*

After this overview of the various ways in which co-ordination can be activated, it seems appropriate to focus on the particle *le* as a feature of language use. Language use, we observed, relies on the co-ordination of content and (physical and mental) processes (Clark 1996: 60). Uses of the particle *le* in this view can be characterised by specifying the co-ordination process and the content of co-ordination. We will do so in the following sections.

8.3.1 The 'co-ordination' process

In this section we focus on the way in which the co-ordination process is manifested in our data. By implication this endeavour leads us to a discussion of the structure of mental models, which we will take up in Chapter 9. 'Common ground', as we noted in Chapter 3, is a form of self-awareness (Clark 1996: 120). It is a shared basis for communication and can be reflected upon (Clark 1996: 94–5). When we reflect now on the communication type in each of the data chapters, we must conclude that the information flow in each was quite different. In Chapter 5 and Chapter 6 we observed language use in worlds of the imagination. Information flow in these stories was controlled by one source and directed at one recipient or a number of recipients. In the procedural discourse (action-picture stories), the flow of information was from the more authoritative figure (the 'instructor') to the information recipient, the 'apprentice', and was mainly in the form of a series of 'instructions' and 'progress reports'. Moments of 'deviation' were clear cases for choosing a co-ordination point. The interactions in that chapter could also be seen as a form of soliloquy, when the situation participant was taken as both sender and receiver of the information.

In the children's stories too the information flow was from a 'source', a 'writer' or 'storyteller', to 'readers' or an 'audience'. The writer reported his perception of a series of interconnected actions, events, and projects, and in that process signalled co-ordination points at moments of 'deviation' and 'solutionhood'. He also made repeated appeals to assumedly shared knowledge (police, sheriffs, bandits, good citizens, travellers) in the build-up of common ground, in the reporting of events, and in the creation of dialogue. In contrast, in the third data chapter all interactions were 'dialogue', interactional data which took the form of everyday 'conversations'. Those data showed that not only do we need to have cases which can be recognised as 'deviation', and 'solutionhood', but that we also need to distinguish issues of 'construal', 'confrontation' and 'confirmation'. In the following we will further reflect on these differences in order to understand the nature of the co-ordination process better. Before proceeding, the differences in the three data sets, as discussed, are listed:

Co-ordination processes in the three data sets

Data set		Information flow	Interaction type
1	Action-picture stories	Unidirectional	Instructions, progress reports
2	Children's stories	Unidirectional	Reports of 'actions', 'events', etc.
3	Conversations	Interaction	'Conversations'

In conversations the structure of the common ground is 'jointly construed' through a series of 'opening' and 'sustaining' moves, which are either 'attending', 'initiating', 'continuing', 'reacting', or acts of 'rejoining', and in which the particle *le* could be related to moments of 'construal', 'deviation', 'confronting', 'confirmation', and 'solutionhood'.

Procedural discourse and common-ground structure

In Chapter 5 dealing with 'procedures' and simple 'story structure' (scenarios), 'deviations' and cases of 'solutionhood' were moments at which using a co-ordination point marker was communicatively pervasive and was recognisable as an endeavour to get a 'changed' common-ground structure to the attention of the addressee. When we reviewed the various uses we could distinguish four common-ground structure constituents that were being addressed via the choice of a co-ordination point. These were, respectively, 'surroundings', the personal ground of a 'situation participant', the 'procedure' involved, and a 'new event'. Not taking account of instances of verbal interaction, these constituents can be illustrated this way:

Common-ground constituent structure
Surroundings	*xia yu le; shi huo le; fangzi zang le*
Participant status	*sheng bing le; chidaole; nide toufa chang le; wo xiang he cha le*
Procedure	'Deviation': *Yaowan qiazai sangzi.li le; bijian dun le*
	'Solution': *hao le; liang le*
New event	*kaoshi yao kaishi le; shi'er lu che lai le*

When one of the constituents of common-ground structure changed, a moment for co-ordination was perceived in cases such as *Shi huo le* ('We are having a fire!'), a self-report as *Sheng bing le* ('I'm not feeling well') or a procedure-related 'problem' such as *Bijian dun le* ('the point is dull'). In the first of these, the speaker's environment (surroundings) 'changed' (dramatically), and he requested the addressee (the fire department) to take note of that and act in agreement with the tasks and duties of a fire department – that is, as the caller expected. It implied an appeal to communal common ground. A similar scenario can be imagined for a situation in which a person indexes his 'participant status' as 'deviant'. In the third example, the pencil as 'instrument' was crucial for the execution of the procedure, and its failure was a cause for reflection and a search for a 'solution'.[16] Finally, by definition 'new events' change the structure of the common ground, as in *Kaoshi yao kaishi le* ('The test will start now'). That 'event' might be known or expected, but it changed the common-ground structure at that moment, and that made it relevant as a possible co-ordination point. In a different situation such as a formal announcement or soliloquy, the use of *kaoshi kaishi* ('the test now starts') would be fitting. The use of *yao* ('will') in event-related cases has a tendency to evoke a co-ordination point, which can be paraphrased as 'a change of common-ground structure is coming up'. The latter observation implies that co-ordination points are 'chosen' with the structure of the common ground in mind. That structure involves the presence of actors with 'participant statuses'.

The action-picture stories, however, also contained a few examples of 'verbal interaction', and we were obliged to make the distinction between 'transactional'/'pragmatic' and 'personal' interactions to approach such uses (Cooper 1969; Eggins and Slade 1997; Fishman 1972). One of the examples was a 'remembered change', and such changes are more appropriate in a personal ground setting, since transactional interactions, as we observed in Chapter 3, tend to be short, scripted, and directed at a pragmatic goal, whereas personal interactions are informal, non-scripted and directed at the 'distribution of information'. This latter formulation ('distribution of information') also covers the revealing of personal details and common-ground co-ordination questions. In the latter case, the speaker wanted to be 'updated' as to the structure of the shared common ground at that moment – the addressee's participant status.

Common-ground structure in narratives

The data of Chapter 6 (children's stories) confirmed the common-ground constituent structure we claimed for the procedural discourse pieces. In narrative text, however, various 'events' are being reported, and we therefore need to add an 'event' constituent. We will illustrate these distinctions first:

Common-ground constituent structure
Surroundings ...*kai qiche dao yedili qu zhao banma pai dianying qule.*
Participant status *biancheng yige yao jiantouchuan de chuanfu le*
Procedure *chu cuor la!*
Event *Wanshang ta zhiqi yingzhang lai, chi yidianr dongxi, tantan qin, changchang ge, jiu qu shui le*
New event *Liangge liumang yao zou ni la!*

The narratives showed that 'surroundings' can change in two ways, either the environment changes (*xia xue le* ['it starts snowing'], for instance), or the main character goes to a different location, and by implication to a different surrounding: 'he took his car and drove to the wild to film zebras', the example reads. Change in 'participant status' we have illustrated with various examples. The one listed translates as 'Bubu then became a proud gondola owner'. We saw in Chapter 5 that 'procedures' and 'deviations' as co-ordination points were closely related, and the narratives confirmed that. One example (6.14) was that of two painters who were involved in a joint project of painting the outside of a house, and when they had finished were reported as concluding: 'There is a mistake!'

All stories contain 'events'. We can illustrate this with the Great Photographer's activities which were first described as *Ta mangle yizhengtian* ('He was busy for a whole day'), and were further detailed as *Wanshang ta zhiqi yingzhang lai* ('In the evening he set up his tent'), *chi yidianr dongxi* ('ate a little'), *tantan qin* ('played his guitar'), *changchang ge* ('sang a few songs'), *jiu qu shui le* ('and went to bed'). We know now what he did that day and that he is sleeping now.[17] The latter was a co-ordination point involving a change of consciousness. New and upcoming events are a common practice in stories, as we illustrated in the overview in section 8.2.

The children's stories, however, also showed how in 'verbal interactions' common ground is being built-up and how as a general rule that build-up is not a structure for the marking of a co-ordination point. 'Verbal interactions' also showed that in conventional situations, when there is no shared common ground between interactants, there is no room for the marking of co-ordination points. 'Verbal interactions', however, also showed a variety of ways in which the structure of the common ground can be changed. Co-ordination points were a 'change of plan', a 'deviant' situation, and the 'hypothetical' construction of a common-ground structure, which contrasts with the current structure, and the 'deviates' from that structure were portrayed. We also saw this as a technique for the management of interpersonal relations, which elsewhere took the form of the expression of 'approval' and 'disapproval'. We list the additional distinctions we found in verbal interactions in the children's stories for ease of overview:

Verbal interactions
No le
Common-ground instruction   *Bie ba tou shendao chechuangwai*[18]
Request to act   *Qing kaikai men*[19]
Use of le
Announcement 'new situation' upcoming   *Women hui jia la!*[20]
Reporting of deviant situation   *Keshi nü'er de shenti tai zhong le*[21]
'Hypothetical situation' projected   *Yaoshi meiyou ni, wode nu'er jiebuliao hun le*[22]
Management of 'interpersonal relations'   *Ni tai hao le; Tai mafan le*[23]

The hypothetical situation is used here as emerging from the existing common ground and 'contrasting' with it. The same holds for the interpersonal examples; they were used in a context of 'approval' and 'disapproval', and can as well appear without *le*. We are interested, however, in the possibility of co-ordination-point marking in these interaction types, and these examples show that they can be used.[24] However, the marking of a co-ordination point always involves a 'contrast' with the current common ground, which in these two latter cases took the form of 'surprise', an unexpected development in the common ground, and a 'rejection' of help. In the first request no *le* was used, but when the request was repeated, disapproval was expressed by adding the particle *le* and making it into a co-ordination point, which we paraphrase as 'reset the common ground now!'

A remark is needed here as to the notion 'contrast', since this was used by some analysts as the main function of the particle *le* (cf. Li 1990). In that type of approach, however, it indicates a contrast with a previous situation, which is not specified. Also, there are no interactional implications mentioned. The analysis is sentence-based. In the way it is used here it indicates a contrast with the current common-ground structure, but is intended as becoming part of that common ground. This also holds for hypothetical examples used as part of interpersonal management. A thank-you effect, construed through creating a hypothetical situation, becomes part of the shared common ground. It does not hold for other hypothetical examples, however, since those are merely exploring, and when terminated the mental experiment is terminated.

Common-ground structure in conversations

In Chapter 7 we distinguished between 'personal' and 'pragmatic' or 'business' conversations and pointed at the different levels of scripting involved in each of these interaction types. 'Personal' interactions, we indicated in that chapter, are directed at the construction of common ground and the 'equalisation of knowledge'. In the meantime, we have come to see the latter concept as implying a more equal 'distribution of information'. This notion also encompasses 'knowledge distribution', 'differences in disposition', and, more generally, 'differences in personal common ground'. The question we need to address now, as part of our focus on the co-ordination process in this section, is the relation of the four interaction types distinguished (entering into a joint project, construal, negotiating an agenda, having an argument) with common-ground structure. Can we find instances in which each of the common-ground constituents distinguished so far is being called upon?

When we began with 'surroundings', we found interactions with the particle *le* in conversations in relation to 'the weather' and in 'street directions'. When a 'means of transportation' was mentioned, the 'cultural common ground' and 'institutional support' were brought in, which have a feeding relationship to the current structure of the common ground (Clark 1996).[25] Weather changes are 'contrasts' with a previous situation, but change the structure of the shared common ground.

Construal of the addressee's 'participant status' was the most common denominator in our data, and this too was related to 'cultural common ground'. Another way was clarifying the deviant part of one's participant status, which took various forms. Remarkable was construing a status, and thereby bringing in 'cultural common-ground knowledge' about regional influences on speech and behaviour.[26] 'Fears' and 'habits' also were marked as co-ordination points related to a person's 'participant status'. Establishing one's everyday behaviour of 'rising early' as 'a habit' was another co-ordination-point option.[27] Everyday behaviour also can be construed and approached as a 'confirmation question'; that is, as an intonation question which contains a co-ordination point.[28]

The discussion so far allows us to see the process of co-ordination point marking, of common-ground co-ordination, divided into two levels: 'cultural common ground' and 'personal common ground'. The first of these is supposedly 'shared' in communication and contains all non-personal structural items and patterns, and enriches and contributes towards the construction of the perceived current 'participant status' of a speaker by an addressee. The 'shared cultural common ground' is built-up through reciprocal interactions and is stored as 'system knowledge' (Berger and Luckmann 1967). So far, we have distinguished 'weather patterns', 'geographical facts', and 'institutional support factors' (infrastructure, social system, language situation, social practices). 'Participant status' as a co-ordination point was common in our data and was supported by pieces of 'shared cultural common ground'. We can represent these distinctions in a two-way model as follows:

SHARED CULTURAL COMMON GROUND
Weather patterns; geographical facts
Institutional support
[infrastructure] [social system] [language] [practices]

PERSONAL COMMON GROUND [ACTUAL]
'Surroundings'
'Participant status'
[social status] [language] [habits]
'Joint project'

Now if we limit the discussion to 'personal interactions' and we define the interaction process as 'distribution of information', the model can be represented as a tripod in which the 'shared cultural common ground' is the basis on which the two 'personal grounds' interact and become 'personal common grounds':

SHARED CULTURAL COMMON GROUND
Weather patterns; geographical facts
Institutional support
[infrastructure] [social system] [language] [practices]

PERSONAL COMMON GROUND	PERSONAL COMMON GROUND
'Surroundings'	'Surroundings'
'Participant status'	'Participant status'
[social status] [language] [habits]	[social status] [language] [habits]

Distribution of information
'Joint project'

From here on we will focus on the position of 'joint projects' in this model, and the use of co-ordination points, as has been the focus throughout. 'Conversations' are clear cases of a 'joint project'. When an 'opening' move is 'sustained', a 'joint project' is established which is open to development. It is in conversations as 'joint projects' that various uses of the particle *le* were anchored. These 'joint projects' were identified as 'personal exchanges', 'construals', 'setting an agenda' and 'having an argument'. A few 'personal exchanges' were opened with a 'co-ordination question', others with an 'attending move'. This allows the specification for joint project parts as marked co-ordination points as:

'joint projects'
personal exchanges
'openings'
'construal'
'agenda'
'argument'

'Construals', which were marked with the particle *le*, related to 'surroundings' – the most likely status of the weather – and 'participant status'. When a piece of the 'cultural common ground' is made into a co-ordination point, it can be used as the basis for the 'distribution of information'. Other special cases were construing a 'confronting conclusion' and construing a 'hypothetical' construction of the common ground. Further 'construals' were in need of 'confirmation', and were 'rejected' and 'contradicted'. We list the distinctions for ease of overview:

'construals'
'surroundings'
'participant status'
'cultural common ground'
'confronting construal'
'hypothetical common ground'

---

reaction to construal
'rejected'
'contradicted'
'confirmed'

These 'rejection' and 'contradiction' examples show that in everyday conversations information is not ready made, and that in certain cases information is not something that can be simply picked up and transmitted.[29] Rather, it shows that in conversations shared common ground is interactively constructed. We can observe, however, that 'construals' tend to be 'hypothetical' that they await 'confirmation'. The weather assumption was 'confirmed' by the weather forecast for that day. A 'participant status' is 'construed' by each interactant since he needs that information for the construction of appropriate messages. The confirmation is given in various ways by the addressee, through his 'display' behaviour and through his verbal behaviour (cf. Clark 1996). A conclusion is 'drawn', which indicates that it is 'derived' and that it might be wrong in the eyes of the addressee. The use of a piece of 'cultural common ground', however, does not have a 'confirmation' requirement. Being part of the 'cultural common ground' indicates that it is shared knowledge, the result of 'agreement' ('repeated confirmation') among members of society, and that therefore it can be used as a point of departure in a case of reasoning (cf. Berger and Luckmann 1967).

The need for 'confirmation' can be illustrated with uses of the expression *Dui le* ('Now we are on common ground'), or as *Dui la!* ('That is indeed the case, I confirm, you're right now'). These uses stand in contrast to common supportive moves of the form *Dui, dui, dui* ('Yes, yes, right'), which encourage the speaker to go on as s/he is doing. The form *Dui le*, in contrast, is used to show a sudden cognitive 'realisation' and can be used to break into the exchange and force a turn shift, which allows the addition of related personal information. Other examples were *Wo dong le* ('Oh I see') and *Dangran le* ('Of course it is this way, I told you so'). 'Confirmation' can also take the form of 'assertion of belief' that the common ground is shared – but that can occur only in situations in which the structure of the common ground is institutionally controlled.[30]

'Personal exchanges' could be 'opened' with a 'co-ordination question' and with special uses of attending phrases.[31] It also allowed the use of the particle *le* in the assertion of 'deviation' and 'solutionhood'. Two of these occurred in the information exchange phase of a 'public event', a rule violation and a 'disagreement' on the price of a hotel room.[32] The third example was the self-positioning of the speaker as 'deviant' versus the current information flow.[33] 'Solutionhood' took the form of an 'offer' and its 'acceptance', and appeared in fixed expressions such as *jiu shi le* and *jiu cheng le*.[34] We list these findings as well:

Distribution of information
'personal exchanges'
'co-ordination question'
'attending move'
'confirmation'
'deviation'
'solutionhood'

Negotiating an 'agenda' is a form of 'construal' too, but different from the other cases in that it is not merely concerned with the construction of current common ground but seeks agreement on a course of action for which a decision is needed. As we found for 'construals', 'proposals' for setting an agenda can be 'rejected' but also 'altered' or 'reformulated' (cf. Clark 1996: 204).[35] Further, the 'negotiation' can be 'broken into'.[36] 'Deviations' can take the form of asserting an issue as 'deviant' in the sense of 'outstanding' against the current background.[37] We also found the assertion of a 'negative effect'.[38] We list the various distinctions for negotiating an agenda separately:

Negotiating an agenda
'partial acceptance'
'confirmation'
'alteration'
'rejection'
'deviation'

In the 'argument' interaction type, 'confronting moves' were related to a 'challenge' and an 'intervention', which were illustrated with *tai buxiang hua le* ('this is outrageous') and *hao le, hao le* ('enough, enough!'). The forms marked with the particle *le* in the argument we also list separately:

Argument
'challenge'
'intervention'

The conversational data made clear that interaction is a two-way process, and that a move by one of the situation participants always implies a mental (and often also physical) reaction from the addressee. 'Construal' as type was most frequently marked as a co-ordination point, and was related to modifications in the structure of the common ground. This was either the 'perceptual world' (surroundings), the 'social world' (participant status), or the world of 'thought' and 'reasoning' (cultural common ground and confronting conclusion). Co-ordination points were highlighted through the possibility of construing a hypothetical world, in contrast with the current common-ground structure, and letting 'deviant' events develop in that 'created world'. The nature of 'construal' induced the idea of 'rejection' and 'contradiction', but also brought about the need for 'confirmation'. 'Personal exchanges' and 'negotiating an agenda' were in second position as regards the variety of ways in which moves could be marked as co-ordination points. They represent the common-sense sphere of social practices, and illustrated the everyday flow of information between interactants, which took the form of a 'co-ordinating question', and the assertion of 'deviation' and 'solutionhood', which in conversations took the form of 'explaining' what was wrong, showing 'disagreement' with the information offered, and 'positioning' oneself outside the knowledge base needed at that moment. Finally, as a special case of verbal interaction, 'arguments' are an interaction type that one tends to avoid. The example we encountered therefore attracted just a few moves marked with *le*, which we identified as a 'challenge' and an 'intervention'.

8.3.2 *Content of the assertion*

Having analysed the co-ordination process marked by the particle *le* as a two-way process which relates to 'construal', 'co-ordination questions', 'special' moments in personal exchanges, in 'negotiation', and in 'argument', this leads to the question as to how the content of the various 'co-ordination points' is represented. If a speaker wants the co-ordination process to proceed he must choose language materials that he can safely assume to be known by the addressee. It is impossible to co-ordinate on content one is not yet familiar with. Our data show that there are four main ways of marking the content of a common-ground co-ordination request. We list them here in the order of frequency in our data:

1. Verb–object constructions
2. Stative verbs
3. Time words
4. Resultative construction

1 Verb–object constructions

Verb–object constructions are the indexes for the various events that are distinguished in Chinese cultural common ground. These expressions can be called upon to make an 'immediate' co-ordination possible. It can be reasonably expected that the addressee is capable of performing the expected mental operation (common-ground co-ordination) indexed by the particle *le*, and work out the consequences. Four of the story titles of Chapter 5 were marked this way. They indexed 'participant status' and 'surroundings': 10. *Sheng bing le* ('Getting sick'), 44. *Shi huo le* ('Fire!'), 56. *Sheng bing le* ('Sick at school'), 61. *Xia yu le* ('It's raining'). A further example illustrating 'surroundings' was *qi wu* ('getting foggy'), whereas 'participant status' was indicated with *li fa* ('have a hair cut'), *chu han* ('to sweat'), *shang ke* ('go to class'), *hui jia* ('go home'), *jie hun* ('marry'), *jiu ren* ('save people'), *shui jiao* ('go to bed'), *he cha* ('drink tea'), *chao su* ('exceed speed; drive too fast'), *chu cuor* ('produce mistake; there is a mistake') and *fa shao* (['produce heat'] have a fever').

'Participant status' was also involved in upcoming developments which were indexed with modal verbs such as *xiang* ('think; intend'), *yao* ('want; will; must'), *gai* ('should'), and *dei* ('must'). We give an example of each of these: *ni xiang he cha le* ('time for a cup of tea'), *yao shang ke le* ('time to go to class'), *gai shui jiao le* ('time to go to bed'), *and dei li fa le* ('time to have a hair cut'). In each English translation the idea of 'time' can be used to indicate that what follows is future-oriented. What varies is the way in which the need for taking action is indexed. This varies from the presence of strict rules in a person's personal situation, *yao* ('want; will; must'), to the actual application of a rule in some situation, *gai* ('should'), and the presence of community norms that seem to apply *dei* ('must'). Future developments were also indexed by the adverb *kuai* ('soon'), and, in direct interaction, with the conjunction *jiu* ('then'). With *kuai* ('soon') we have *kuai shang ke le* ('I better hurry up [to go to class]'), and with *jiu* ('then'), indicating a direct consequence *kaoshi jiu yao kaishi le* ('the exam will start soon').[39]

We observed that the speaker is requested to change the structure of the current common ground in agreement with the content being indexed by the verb–object construction. That indexed information is part of the addressee's general common ground, and s/he can therefore make the adjustment 'immediately', and then take time to work out the consequences of that adjustment. We can finish the verb–object part of the discussion by concluding that an appeal to change the structure of the common ground takes place on the basis of the information provided by the verb–object construction. The addressee is expected to be able to make the structural adjustment 'immediately', since all such expressions are part of her/his cultural knowledge. The adjustment is immediate, but he needs more time to work out the consequences.

2 Stative verbs

Stative verbs (adjectives) are part of the common lexicon and, when not marked with a degree adverb, index a state of affairs in a comparative way. When marked as co-ordination point, the addressee is requested to change the structure of the common ground accordingly. The examples in our data show that stative verbs marked with the particle *le* were used to index a 'deviation' or 'solution'. We found examples of 'deviations' in 'surroundings': *zang* ('dirty [of a room]'), *yuan* ('too far [of the post office]'); 'participant status': *chang* ('long; too long [of hair]'), *e* ('hungry'), *bu chun* ('not pure [of accent]'), *bu xiao* ('no longer small [of courage]'); and 'procedures': *da* ('big; too big'), *dun* ('dumb [of a pencil]').

'Solutionhood' was related to 'surroundings' with *rongyi* ('easy [to find a house]'), and to 'procedures' as with *hao* ('good; endpoint [of making toast]'), *cheng* ('all right, that's it [of cooking]'), *gou* ('enough [of ordering food]'), and *xing* ('okay; you got it [of getting healthy food]'). In some cases, as for instance *liang* ('bright'), it can indicate both a 'deviation' or a 'solution' depending on the procedure phase involved: *hongdeng liang le* ('the light turns red'), *Lüdeng liang le* ('the light turns green').

Stative verbs then can be marked with the particle *le* when they can index a 'deviation' or 'solutionhood'. They too can take up the adverb *tai* ('too'), and in that combination can (not 'must') take up the particle *le*. Some special expressions with *tai* are *tai bang le* ('great!'), a combination with *bang* ('fine; excellent').[40] In politeness terms we have *nin tai keqi le* ('you're too polite'), *tai xinku le* ('this was too much work'). Finally we have expressions with *zui* ('most'), which can be marked when something is presented as 'deviating' in a series, as in *wo zui ai chu yu le* ('I like fish most'), or *wo zui pa pa louti le* ('I most dislike climbing stairs'). The verbs *ai* ('like to') and *pa* ('be afraid of') are mental state verbs, which in this respect are very similar to stative verbs.

3 Time words

Time words (including *zao* ['early']) used as co-ordination points were discussed in Chapter 5, where we related phrases such as *Zhongwu le* ('It twelve now') to cyclical time and to an understanding of the strength of the sun around that time of the day. Remarks such as *shidian le* ('It's ten already') and *Shijian bu zao le* ('It's late already'), were related to 'institutional time', which made it apparent why they should be marked with the particle *le* and request common-ground co-ordination. All these remarks index the time as it is 'now' and imply an appeal to a future-oriented action. In this sense the use of time words and the particle *le* are prototypical.

4 Resultative constructions

Resultative constructions are core grammatical structures and they appeared widely in the various texts studied. Many of these described 'events' which could immediately be recognised as 'deviations'. Examples are uses such as -*hua* ('melted') in *bingqilin ronghuale* ('the ice cream melted'), -*po* ('broken') in *dapole* ('you broke [the glass]') -*sui* ('in pieces') *shuaisuile* ('[the glass] it's in pieces'), -*huai* ('broken'), *shuaihuaile* ('broke it') -*dao* ('fall'), *ni shuaidaole* ('you fall down'). In other cases the 'deviation' was the effect described by the verb. We found cases of a directional complement with -*dao* ('destination'), as in *sadao zhuozi.shang le* ('spilled on the table'), and complements with *zai* ('be in or at'), as in *yaowan qiazai sangzi.li le* ('the pill stuck in your throat') (cf. Yip 2001).

Other directional complements expressing 'deviation' effects were -*xialai* ('down-come'), *shunzhe nide lian liuxialai le* ('[the drop] is running down your cheek [and is not on target, the eye]'), and *guaxialaile* ('blown off [the leaves are ...]'), an example of a natural event, and also -*xiaqu* ('down-go'), which targeted the 'deviation' *dou diaoxiaqule* ('they both fell down!'). With -*chulai* ('out-come') we had *ta tuchulai le* ('she [the baby] spits it out!'). The form -*qilai* ('up-come') indexed 'deviations' such as *tengqilai le* ('it hurts'), *zhongqilaile* ('it feels swollen'), *xiaqilai le* ('it starts raining again'), another 'natural event', and *kunaoqilaile* ('they started to cry and make noise'). 'Surroundings' were also involved in the events described, with -*guolai* ('cross over-come') *daguolai le* ('there's a big wave coming'). Apart from 'natural events', these 'deviation' examples concerned both 'surroundings' and the speaker or the story character's 'participant status' (cf. Yip 2001).

Other verbs describing a 'deviant' event were *zhuang* ('bump into') together with the ending -*kai* ('open'), *ba bangongshi de men zhuangkaile* ('threw the door of the office open'), *chi* ('tardy; late') in *chidaole* ('[late-arrive-le] being late'), whereas the ending -*fan* ('turn over') was used in the report that combined 'surroundings' and 'participant status' *yishang chuan jiu ba chuan caifanle* ('as soon as she stepped on the boat it capsized'); the ending -*zou* ('go away'), concluding this series, was used in the description of the 'deviation' *wode chuan kaizoule* ('my boat has gone'). A 'new event', finally, changing the structure of the common ground, was introduced with the verb *lai* ('come') through the announcement *Dakuaitou gen Daweiba dou dao Huangjingzhen laile*! ('Big Head and Big Tail have come to Gold City!'). These data then showed various ways of expressing 'deviation' in Chinese, which related to 'surroundings', 'participant status', 'event' description in narrative, and, also in that discourse type, the introduction of 'new events'.

'Restoration' or 'solutionhood' was indicated first of all by the resultative ending -*hao* ('good; okay'), which restored earlier 'deviations' as in *xiaohaole* ('It's sharp!'), said of a pencil that was first introduced as 'dull', *xiuhaole* ('you fixed it! [a broken plate])', *che tinghaole* ('the bus stops'), indicating the end of a rough bus ride, *kaohaole* ('It's done [toast roasted]'), *dihaole* ('It's done [drops in eye]'), *banhaole* ('it's all set [post office procedure]'). We also found individual expressions such as *-mie* ('extinguished'), *ba huo pumiele* ('The fire has been put out now'). These expressions all request co-ordination on the 'endpoint' of an event, against a background in which a 'deviant' situation existed. 'Endpoints' are also indicated by *-wan* ('finish'), as in *jiemu bosongwanle* ('the program is finished'), *jiemu bowanle* ('the program is finished'), *li fa* ('cutting hair') and *liwanle* ('all done [haircut]'), *zuowanle* ('you're done [homework]'). A similar resultative ending was *-shu* ('bind; tie'), as in *dianying jieshule* ('Now the movie is over'). These expressions index the endpoint of ('public events'), which is part of the social common-ground structure and implies that further action is needed, such as 'looking for another program', 'leaving the cinema', 'paying the bill', 'leaving the line' and 'going home'.

'Solutionhood' or 'restoration' cases also involved directional verbs, for instance *chulai* ('come-out') in *chulaile* ('there it is [your chocolate]'), and directional complements with *-shanglai* ('up-come') and *da* ('answer'), we had *dashanglaile* ('you come up with answers'), and with *duan* ('carry as a tray') gave *duanshanglaile* ('brought [the coffee]'), *-xialai* ('down-come') resulted in *faxialai le* ('hands out [the tests]'), and *dou beixialaile* ('you memorised it all'). There also was *-xiaqu* ('down-go') as in *yaowan tunxiaqule* ('it [the pill] went down' [after it got stuck in his throat]), *dou naxiaqule* ('took everything away; cleared the table'), and *-jinqu* ('in-go') in *ningjinqule* ('now all the screws are [screwed] in'). We further found a case of *-qilai* ('up-come') indexing an 'endpoint' in combination with *xiang* ('think'), *xiangqilaile* ('now it comes back to you'), and finally *-guolai* ('cross over-come') and *you* ('swim') in *youguolaile* ('you're through [the surf] now').

We also found several more 'solutionhood'-related verb endings: *-tong* ('go through'), *jietongle* ('connected [of phone]'), *-kai* ('open; disappear'), *huakaile* ('melted down [butter in pan, as intended]'), *-jin* ('go in'), *ningjinle!* ('they are all tight!'), *-bao* ('full') as in *wo chibaole* ('I'm full'), and *-xing* ('wake up') together with *jiao* ('to call') in *jiaoxingle* ('woke them up'). A separate series of 'solutionhood'-related expressions indexed the 'participant status' of a character, as in *yinggai lundao ni le* ('it should be your turn by now'), *mashang jiu lundao ni le* ('it will be your turn soon'), *hen kuai jiu lundao ni le* ('it will be your turn soon now') (cf. Yip 2001).

'Beginnings' such as *kunaoqilaile* ('started to cry and make noise') were grouped under the main category 'deviations' on p. 234. Now we can also see this as a 'side-event' that changes the structure of the common ground. Another start of an (unobtrusive) side-event was ... *dou paixialaile* ('[the camera] recorded [everything]'). Its 'endpoint' was similarly marked as in ... *ziji guanshangle* ('and [the machine] then shut itself down'). Some 'side-events' such as *kunaoqilaile* ('[the children] started to cry and make noise'), *kaihaole* ('[the bill] is ready'), tend to signal the endpoint of the 'main event', 'playing around in Mouse Timid's tent' and 'having dinner' respectively. When the bill arrives, it also signals in many instances 'please pay and leave'. When there is no such interference with the main event, a side-event runs its own course. The camera 'side-event', for instance, happened accidentally and was unobtrusive, but did have an effect on the future development of events in the story. It later reported the events in the tent to the astounded family members.

This overview brings us to the conclusion that uses of the particle *le* occur in common procedures at places where something goes 'wrong', or at places where what has gone wrong is brought to a 'solution'. In addition, however, we learned to distinguish between 'main events', 'public events', 'natural events', and 'side events'. 'Natural events' are a subcategory of the common-ground constituent 'surroundings', whereas 'main events' are what we have called 'joint projects' and 'procedures'. Certain 'joint projects' (watching TV, going to the movies, taking a bus or train) are dependent on external sources, and we grouped them together as 'public events'. When a 'main event' develops there can be 'side events', which do not have to disturb the main event but often influence that event and change the structure of the common ground. This explains why in these cases common-ground co-ordination is requested. 'Natural events', due to their overpowering nature, always change the structure of the common ground. Finally, for resultative verb constructions too, we came to distinguish changes in 'participant status', and these are indexed as co-ordination points when they change the structure of the common ground.

Our data at this point allow the following distinctions for marking with *le*:

Event status and marking with *le*
1 'main events'/'joint projects': 'deviation'; 'solutionhood'; 'time'
2 'public events': 'beginning' and 'endpoint'; 'time'
3 'side events': 'beginning' and 'endpoint'
4 'natural events': 'beginning' and 'endpoint'
5 'participant status': change in common-ground structure

'Main events', like a 'procedure', or a 'train trip', 'car drive', or 'going home' project have a 'beginning' and 'destination' or 'endpoint'. A 'beginning' in real time always implies 'exiting' from another activity, which can be seen as a 'deviation' or 'break away'. *Women hui jia la* ('We're going home') is a break away from a current activity, as we noticed. In 'public events' participants in most situations need to synchronise their behaviour on the 'beginning' and 'endpoint' of the event.[41] 'Time', therefore, is also always a variable. 'Side events' 'happen', they are out of the control of the situation participants and their 'beginning' and 'endpoints' can be reported as part of the changing scene, especially if these are unobtrusive technical events. Events can also be narrated or announced as 'new events'. The same is true for 'participant status', which is a special category as already discussed frequently.

5 Special cases in conversations

In conversations the 'construal' of common ground turned out to be a special issue for interactants. 'Construals' cannot be formed in one of the ways just discussed. They cannot be simply indexed with a time word, a verb–object form, or a stative verb. They are 'construed' from elements in the common ground. When this is a sudden 'recognition' of a participant status, the structure of the common ground changes in the perception of the speaker. Similarly, when a conclusion is 'construed' that too changes the structure of the common ground, and the addressee needs to orient her/himself on the implications of the new construal.

8.4 Conclusion

The 'tripod model', introduced in section 8.3.1 (p. 222), clarifies the relation between cultural common-ground distinctions and the distribution of information between two 'situation participants'. One implication of the notion 'distribution' is that the available information supposedly is unequally distributed, and an update move is necessary. Uses of the particle *le* are special cases of updating (cf. Yip 2001). They mark special points in the information flow, which we called 'co-ordination points'. These represent 'perceived' or 'intended' moments of change in common-ground structure. Such changes take place in a variety of ways and relate to the constituents of common-ground structure. That structure we came to see as constituted by 'surroundings', 'participant status', 'procedures', and 'events' – the latter with various subdivisions such as 'main events', 'natural events', 'public events', and 'side-events', through its inherent force, the 'surroundings' constituent changes common-ground structure, and interactants need to adjust. 'Participant statuses' in contrast are 'construed' and need to be confirmed. They thereby become vulnerable to challenge, rejection, and alternation. 'Procedures' are established as part of the cultural common ground. However, during execution they often go wrong (Murphy's law). 'Mishaps' (deviations) do occur and are often followed by 'restoration' endeavours, which may become targets for marking as co-ordination points. 'Events' happen. They can be reported, but also 'remembered', and in both capacities be made into a co-ordination point. Events can also be 'narrated', either as remembrances or as new construals with new story lines. It is the 'deterioration' and 'restoration' cycle in these story lines that attracts co-ordination-point marking. Narrated events do not develop in real time but in 'story time', and are embedded as narrative models.

In conversational settings there were many instances of 'construal'. When these regard a piece of the shared cultural common ground it can be used to assert. No confirmation is required. 'Construals', when not 'confirmed', can also be 'rejected', 'altered' or 'reformulated'. 'Confirmation' cases, when marked as co-ordination points, can also occur after a period of misunderstanding, or as a way to break into the current issue, indicating 'now we are on common ground'. Our study further showed that co-ordination points can be marked when a situation is perceived as 'deviant'. They can also be used when a common-ground structure is 'hypothetically' construed, in contrast with the current structure. Also a 'transformation' of a current structure can be 'intended' as 'plan' or 'instruction'. The data further demonstrated that the meeting of two worlds, that of 'speaker' and 'addressee', demands techniques for relative positioning of statuses, for interpersonal management.

Constituent	*Common-ground structure*	*Co-ordination point*	*le*
Surroundings	Change forced	+	+
Participant status	Construal, confirmation, rejection	(+)	(+)
Procedures	Involuntary effects	+	+
Events	Remembered	(+)	(+)
Narrated	Deterioration / restoration cycle	+	+
Conversations	Construals: rejection; alteration	+	+
	Confirmation (special cases)	+	+
	'Deviant' situation	+	+
	Hypothetical structure (as contrast)	+	+
	Interpersonal management (special cases)	+	+

As with all such schema the interactive situation cannot be systematically represented. The use of parentheses are indications that further details of the interactive setting are needed in order to be able to determine the actual marking of an interaction point. Those details are provided in the accompanying text, and in the data chapters where the various examples are discussed.

'Co-ordination points' also occurred in questions. We distinguished between two types: 'co-ordination questions' and 'confirmation questions'. In the first type, the speaker requests to be updated as to the current state of the common ground. MA questions marked with the particle *le* seek 'confirmation' on a point of co-ordination. They are the opposite of assertions of co-ordination points. These questions can also take the form of an intonation question.

As a last step in this concluding section, we will relate our findings to the benchmark data in Chao (1968). He distinguished seven types of uses of the particle *le* (see also Chapter 2):

1   Inchoative *le*   *Tang leng le*
2   Command in response to a new situation   *Chi fan le*
3   Progress in a story   *Houlai tian jiu qing le*

4	Isolated event in the past	*Wo zuor dao Zhangjia chi fan le*
5	Completed action as of the present	*Wo huilaile*
6	Consequent clause to indicate situation	*Na wo jiu bu zou le*
7	'Obviousness'	*Zhege ni dangran dong le*

In all cases the particle indexes a 'co-ordination point'. It requests the addressee to bring the various pieces of information into the shared personal common ground. When we apply the notions 'deviation' and 'solutionhood' we get the following picture:

1	*Tang leng le* ('the soup is cold')	'Deviation'
2	*Chi fan le* ('Time to eat')	'Deviation'
3	*Houlai tian jiu qing le* ('later it cleared')	'Solutionhood'
4	*Wo zuor dao Zhangjia chi fan le* (Yesterday I ate at the Zhang's)	?
5	*Wo huilaile* ('I'm back')	'Solutionhood'
6	*Na wo jiu bu zou le* ('Well the I won't go')	'Deviation'
7	*Zhege ni dangran dong le*	?

Five of the seven distinctions can be easily identified as either a more or less obvious case of a 'deviation' or of 'solutionhood'. We identified three cases of 'deviation' and two of 'solutionhood'. What remains to be identified are categories (4) 'Isolated event in the past' and (7) 'Obviousness'. The latter category, as we observed in Chapter 2, should not be given a separate label. The idea of 'obviousness' is created by *dangran* ('of course'). Since the assertion is focused on *dangran*, it requires a context where the addressee's understanding of this was in question, the use of *le* in that context marks a deviation from that assumption. Category (4) can be used as an 'initiating move' in a conversation. However, it can only be said to someone the speaker knows (i.e. when both share an existing common ground). The remark adds a new piece of information to their existing common ground to update it. The marking of this piece of information as a co-ordination point makes clear that a change in common-ground structure is intended. As this analysis shows, all examples can be brought under one overarching view, and we can refer back to our earlier analysis of the particle *le*, 'a co-ordination point, which modifies the structure of the common ground', to give the seven categories distinguished in Chao (1968) a recognisable interpretation.

9 Theoretical implications

Language is used in interaction, and this interaction starts from the cognitive functioning of various situation participants, who at moments of communication interlock their cultural and personal common ground. These latter we see as represented by their current mental models (cf. Clark 1996; Johnson-Laird 1983, 1993). The Chinese particle *le*, we argued, is a co-ordination device. This however is not a linguistic concept, it is borrowed from psychological literature, and defines the general nature of human language, the mutual conversion on a joint project (Schelling 1960; Clark 1996). We need to conclude, therefore, that the Chinese particle *le* has all the characteristics of a 'co-ordination device'; it is not used for general communicative purposes, however, but for specific moments in the adaptation process. These moments we called 'co-ordination points', and in this study we specified the nature of these co-ordination points in procedural, narrative and conversational discourse. They deal in essence with moments of 'deviation' in a procedure, event line, or conversational minimal project. Alternatively, when a 'deviation' was activated, co-ordination points indexed a moment of 'solutionhood'. Moments of 'deviation' in conversational exchanges also could take the form of 'construals', 'confrontation', and 'confirmation'. What remains to be done is to position our study in relation to the so-called theoretical and functional paradigms, and we will do this in the first section (9.1). Thereafter, we will review the hypotheses formulated in the opening part of this book, while still strongly relying on previous research and theoretical modelling, and judge their strength and shortcomings (9.2). In the third section we review common-ground constituent structure and its relation to mental model theory (9.3). Those principles then make it possible to compare our analysis with previous proposals, and indicate where the similarities and differences are (9.4). The main part of the chapter is the formulation of a theory of language use, which, in our view, is an alternative for the study of sentence structure (9.5), and we round off with an overview of findings and issues in need for further study (9.6), before presenting some concluding remarks (9.7).

9.1 A pragmatic approach

Our approach in this study has been 'pragmatic', focusing on the details of 'verbal interaction', the study of language acts in certain contexts (Stalnaker 1978; Spanos 1979; Thomas 1995). In that endeavour we took a 'common-sense' approach, and thereby placed ourselves in the line of work by G.E. Moore, Austin, Grice, Johnson-Laird, and Clark. We took the way people interact in everyday life as the basis for our study and tried to understand how and why people in common everyday situations behave language-wise in the way they do, and obviously have done effectively for a large number of generations (cf. Thomas 1995). We also placed our 'empiricism' in opposition to linguistic analyses that refrain from systematic empirical observations and rely mainly on 'logical reasoning' and the analysis of limited data sets (cf. Chomsky 1966, 1972, 1986, Botha 1989, 1992). It was not difficult to demonstrate that approaches, which do not seriously take context into consideration, are generally untenable or can completely miss the point (cf. Sybesma 1992, 1999). In our 'mental-model' or 'language-use' approach, logic is not absent. On the contrary; but it is placed where it belongs, as the deductive component of the mental model people construct as part of their cognitive reacting to reality (Johnson-Laird 1983, 1993). The language user calculates the consequences of the model s/he constructs when using language to build up and trace 'shared common ground'. It is this ability to calculate consequences that we will meet again when discussing the structure of common ground (9.3).

We share the general criticism of sentence linguistics, in terms of its scarceness of data and its practice of limiting explanation to sentences. A further limiting aspect mentioned is the underlying notion of propositions and a search for objective validity. As demonstrated by Clark (1996) and argued by Lakoff (1987), such views exclude a number of phenomena that are relevant for understanding human communication. It also excludes, as we demonstrated in this book, a fruitful approach to the study of uses of the Chinese particle *le*. We started from the idea of pragmatic organisation, the construction of mental models, and the role of language as a hinting device (cf. Fauconnier 1994, 1997), and approached texts as units organised for some purpose. From that perspective, we tried to determine which purpose the particle *le* and verbal *-le* were playing in such larger units and in interaction. The global organisation of a text or activity was thereby taken as given and the functional contribution of the grammatical markers *-le* and *le* became the focus of attention.

9.2 Two hypotheses

In Chapter 3 we formulated the main hypothesis for our study by recognising that the particle *le* in Chinese acts as a co-ordination device, which focuses the attention of both interactants on the structure of the shared common ground as of that moment. In providing the cue, the speaker assumes that his 'cue' can make the addressee 'successfully' co-ordinate, and that this is 'sufficient' for the addressee to solve the co-ordination problem 'immediately' or without much delay. The working hypothesis took the form:

> (H1) Verbal interactions are 'joint actions' in a 'joint activity'. The particle *le* in Chinese is a 'co-ordination device', which signals that the speaker wants 'information processing' to be co-ordinated at that point in the 'joint action' or 'joint activity'. He assumes that the 'content' s/he provides is 'sufficient' for the addressee to 'solve' the intended co-ordination issue 'immediately'.

Our study further specified the nature of these hints in certain discourse environments, and we came to see that the particle *le*

> indexes a 'co-ordination point' in the process of 'distribution of information'. These co-ordination points signal changes in common-ground constituent structure.

As described in Chapter 8, these changes take the form of 'deviation' or its counterpart 'solutionhood'. In narratives, in addition to marking the main points in a deterioration and restoration cycle, they also can mark beginning and endings or closures of side-events. In addition, in conversational settings changes in common-ground constituent structure take the form of 'construal', 'confrontation', and 'confirmation'. They all are changes in common-ground constituent structure, however, and work out differently dependent on the kind of common-ground constituent that is being modified. The incipient situation hypothesis that emerges from historical research can be supported in this analysis. However, it must be concluded that an incipient situation relates to constituent structure, and not directly to sentence structure. The latter is a human abstraction and therefore the wrong domain (cf. Clark 1996).

As argued in Chapter 3, the origin of this hypothesis is psychological research on co-ordination, its goals and motivation (Schelling 1960; Clark 1996). A co-ordination device 'gives the participants a rational, a *basis*, for believing that they and their partners will converge on the same joint action' (Clark 1996: 65). The Chinese particle *le*, indeed, can serve as a basis for converging when construal issues are the main focus. In other instances however the particle regulates information flow by drawing the attention of the addressee to contrasting moments in the information distribution. This implies that the contrast cannot be described in general terms ('contrast with a previous state'), as claimed by some 'theoretical' thinkers, but needs to be addressed at the level of the project, the narrative, or the conversation and in terms of the kind of contrast involved at that moment (also see Chapter 2).

In Chapter 8 we provided more detail as to the nature of common-ground structure, and the various ways that structure can be called upon or manipulated to explain the various uses of the Chinese particle *le*. Move status, for instance, was not taken into account in formulating the hypothesis, and we therefore specified that relationship in Chapter 8 in terms of 'initiating' and 'reacting' moves, and demonstrated that it is the latter move type that attracted most uses of the particle *le*.

Our second hypothesis had to do with the presence in Chinese of two homophonous markers, verbal *-le* and the particle *le*. Our analysis of the uses of the Chinese particle *le* opened with a study of the historical development of the particle, and in that search we determined that the two forms of *le*, verbal *-le* and the particle *le*, had the same origin and became associated with different levels of usage during the development of the language. Language development we see as the adjustment of the resources of a language to usage practices over time (cf. Biq 2000). This finding is in essence in agreement with similar statements by Huang (1988) and Huang and Davis (1989), who distinguished between domains of language use (event/sentence, and experience).

The analysis of various uses of verbal *-le* showed that it marked 'realisation' of an event, which we identified as a 'peak event' in a story line. Uses of verbal *-le* were first of all related to 'main events' and were less likely to appear in 'preparatory events'. This finding is the first indication that use or non-use of verbal *-le* in Chinese is not the result of a syntactic rule but rather that verbal *-le* appears as the result of interaction between cognitive/pragmatic forces and the intent of the speaker, which is related to his overall interaction goal. We also observed that main-event marking was a technique to guide speakers through the story line, which is another pragmatic rule. Also, there is the idea of an anteriority construction in Chinese, but that distinction too can be seen as the result of cognitive functioning in building a mental model of what is going on in the real, or in an embedded, world or worlds.

After an extensive analysis of language-use data, we further came to see that the 'core pragmatic function' of both verbal *-le* and the particle *le* was the marking of a 'peak' in the information flow. For verbal *-le* this was a 'peak event' in an event chain, whereas for the particle *le* this 'peak' was identified as a 'deviation' (and its counterpart 'solutionhood') in the current common-ground structure. In narrative discourse this 'co-ordination point' took the form of a 'peak episode', a 'deviation' or 'solution' in a procedure or event line, whereas in conversations various forms of 'construal', 'confrontation', and 'confirmation' were involved. Given this analysis, what remained to be determined was the delimitation of what counts as a 'co-ordination point' in everyday interactions. A common configuration in many progress reports was that 'realisation' (inception), marked as verbal *-le*, coincided with a 'co-ordination point' (marked as the particle *le*), and we concluded that in such instances a 'co-ordination point' was being marked. Concluding, we feel that the various pragmatic distinctions made (verbal -*le* not in preparatory events, main events marked with verbal -*le* form the story line, the cognitive/pragmatic status of anteriority marking) support and clarify the one-source hypothesis, which therefore can be maintained.

9.3 Common-ground constituent structure

In linguistic circles the idea of 'joint action' and 'co-ordination' has been recognised as a truism, but is in essence widely ignored and not treated as more than an afterthought. All language functions this way it is said then, but no serious attention is given to what co-ordination implies (cf. Clark 1996: 60). As this study has shown, the use of the Chinese particle *le* can only be understood in the context of verbal interaction and a theory of language use. Crucial to that theory is clarification of the notion 'structure of common ground'. We developed this concept as the basis for an explanation of the various uses of the particle *le*. That structure we presented as a 'tripod' model in Chapter 8, and we repeat that model here in shortened form:

Shared cultural common ground	
Personal common ground	Personal common ground
'Distribution of information'	
'Co-ordination points'	

'Conversations' are forms of 'joint projects' and are based on the 'distribution of information'. In 'transactional' exchanges, too, an information phase can be recognised and 'distribution of information' is an issue. Shared cultural common ground, we further argued, is given, and for distinctions at that level no confirmation is needed.[1] It is already generally agreed upon. 'Co-ordination points' relate to the structure of the currently shared common ground. When that structure changes, or when an interactant wants to change that structure, a co-ordination-point marker is employed in Chinese. The common-ground structure changes through *addition* of constituents, or *change* in constituents, and a speaker can verbally distribute the information that he perceived these changes. Since reality is not given, *construal* might be involved, which needs to be confirmed or rejected. Further, a speaker can endeavour to create a change in common ground. This can be done through the expression of 'intent' (a change of plan), or via the adding of 'remembered' pieces of personal common ground. In this section we will review the constituents of common ground structure and explore how they add to or change that structure. The idea of 'change' has been related to the analysis of uses of the particle *le* from the beginning. We therefore will start with a closer look at that concept in order to illustrate the fundamental differences that exist between our methodology and other functional approaches.

9.3.1 *The notion 'change'*

The notion 'change' is most frequently used in relation to uses of the particle *le*. That is also the case in Li and Thompson (1981: 244), who assigned the Chinese particle *le* the basic communicative function of marking a 'currently relevant state', and defined their first category as 'a changed state'. They see this as a 'change' from an earlier state, and they described this as 'some state of affairs holds now which didn't hold before'. It is, however, far from clear what this distinction encompasses. Their first two examples in fact deal with 'knowledge' states, where they compare *wo zhidao* ('I know') with *wo zhidao le* ('Now I know' {I have learned}). 'Knowing', however, has to do with the structure of cultural common ground and personal common ground. In this case it also is a reacting move. Let us see where the reasoning went wrong. The contextualisation cue was given as the person 'who went to the wrong room once before has been reminded which room the meeting will be held in'. The speaker did 'change', but did so on the basis of 'being reminded' – others explained to him where his current mental model was 'deviant'. By using the expression *wo zhidao le*, he made a 'confirmation' move, indicating that he now was on shared common ground: 'co-ordinate on this, I know how the situation is'.[2]

The limitations of strictly linguistic reasoning in the study of the particle *le* manifest themselves clearly, when Li and Thompson within the same framework of change bring in time examples as *yijing sandian le* ('it's already three o'clock'). This immediately raises the issue of what kind of change this time example represents. Time by nature is in constant change, but they do not discuss the implications of that issue. They could have made a comparison with *yijing sandian* ('it's already three o'clock'), which is what they did with other examples in their study, but at this crucial moment they stopped doing that. What we need to observe, however, is that the pair *wo zhidao / wo zhidao le* stand in a quite different relation to each other than the pair *sandian zhong / sandian zhong le*. Even if we accept an often-chosen way out of this dilemma by the claim that the time phrase should be taken as 'newly realised', this still leaves the question why the particle *le*? A sudden realisation without a relation to the common-ground structure could still be phrased as *yijing sandian* without *le*.

Still under the category 'change', Li and Thompson also listed 'natural events' as *xia yu le* ('it's raining {now}'). This example is most likely a comparison with the situation of 'not-raining', but they do not discuss that explicitly. It falls under their general description of a state that did not hold before. Unfortunately that description is so general that it will fit all types of change in the current situation, and we need to know where the borderlines are. Rain is a *new event* and on that basis most likely has been recognised by all students of the particle *le*. It is also a 'deviant' event, since it disturbs the functioning of other events. Rain therefore changes the structure of the common ground in two ways: as a 'new event' and as a 'deviation' in the common ground. When we agree that 'rain' is a change phenomenon it still needs to be determined why the particle *le* appears in this example. In the case of *xia yu le*, a comparison with an assertion *xia yu is not possible. There is no such form. How then to explain the obligatory presence of the particle *le* in assertions of this type? In our analysis the explanation is pragmatic. *Xia yu le* as a 'new event' and a 'deviation' (or 'solutionhood') changed the structure of the shared common ground and almost by necessity needs to be co-ordinated on.

All three examples[3] discussed so far (*zhidao le, sandian zhong le, xia yu le*) relate to different aspects of common-ground structure, and cannot be treated as one 'grammatical' category 'change' which signals that 'some state of affairs holds now which didn't hold before', descriptively adequate as that may be at first sight. Since we are not told what constitutes a 'state of affairs' and do not know the boundaries, the statement only has limited predictive value. In all three cases the particle *le* indexes a 'co-ordination point', which in the first example is a case of 'confirmation' (solutionhood) and in the latter two examples a case of 'deviation'. In our framework they fall under the general heading of 'distribution of information' between interactants, whereas the co-ordination relates to different aspects of the structure of the common ground (participant status, time, and natural events).

When we now also look at the examples given under the various other headings, it becomes clear that they all are cases of our general co-ordination-point analysis. For convenience we repeat their classification once more. The state of affairs represented by sentences with *le* were given as: A. Is a changed state; B. Corrects a wrong assumption; C. Reports progress so far; D. Determines what will happen next; E. Is the speaker's total contribution to the conversation at that point (Li and Thompson 1981: 244). One of the examples in 'B. Corrects a wrong assumption', was *wo yao he le* ('I want to drink it'). In Li and Thompson's analysis the child in this utterance contradicts the mother's belief that she does not want the soda now. However, the idea of 'contradiction' cannot be made explicit here; a 'construal' can be 'contradicted' but contradicting a 'belief' seems difficult. The child might be reacting to the mother's display behaviour, but that is another matter. In a 'request' sequence *wo yao he* ('I want to drink it'), and when the mother does not react, followed by the 'assertion' *wo yao he le!* ('I want to drink it now please!'), we recognise 'reassertion of intent' for which purpose an explicit signal 'co-ordination needed now' is given. The remark still falls under our general category 'distribution of information' and the idea of 'co-ordination-point' marking.

For the examples under 'C. Progress so far' we can make the same claim; these are cases of 'distribution of information' and marking of a 'co-ordination point' in the information flow between interactants. For example, in *wo xihaole yifu le* ('I have finished (the project of) clothes washing (which you knew I had to do)'), the speaker signals to the addressee that this is a case of 'solutionhood', and such an event state changes the structure of the common ground. The additions between parentheses by Li and Thompson in this example are quite meaningful. First of all the authors identified a 'project', which we called a 'procedure', and added a common-ground notion 'which you knew I had to do'. In this category (C. Progress so far) Li and Thompson also place the example *Ni ji sui le?* ('How old are you?')[4] and comment:

> Because inquiries between people who know each other well typically reflect the speaker's concern with the hearer's progress, questions with *le* always seem more friendly, more involved, and more concerned than the same utterances without le.

Interestingly, Li and Thompson again introduce the idea of common ground here, but their analysis is not based on a further study of that concept. In our view this is a case of a 'co-ordination question'. The speaker wants to be updated on the age of the addressee. The reasons for that may vary widely and cannot be generalised as proposed by Li and Thompson. The claimed close personal relationship can only be partial supported, since an utterance of this type can also take place between a recently introduced stranger and a child of the family. In such an instance, too, however, the speaker, by showing his interest ('I want to be updated on this'), created a feeling of 'shared common ground', which indeed seems 'more friendly, more involved and more concerned' as claimed. The idea of 'progress so far' is not the issue, however. When using the particle *le* a request for sharing common ground is being made.[5]

Category D, 'Determines what will happen next', had the illustration *wo you le* ('I have it') referring to the money to be paid for a taxi. The implication 'you don't have to pay now' is claimed as part of the meaning of the particle *le*. We think this is unfortunate. The expression states 'I have the money, co-ordinate on that'. The others can calculate as a consequence that they do not have to, but that is not part of *le*'s function, even though the two operations, seeking an interpretation for the expression with *le* and calculating the consequences, are connected and often take place almost simultaneously.

Category E, 'Is the speaker's total contribution to the conversation at that point', is called later in the book 'Closing a statement', and one of the examples given is *bao le* ('stop it'), which we encountered in this study as a case of 'intervention', and according to their discussion this seems similar. They also apply the concept to *wo chide tai bao le* ('Let me tell you, I am too full from eating'). The idea of closing a statement here is the result of the utterance occurring at the end of a meal (rather than at the beginning), but the analysis does not have to include that distinction. It is another case of 'solutionhood', which changes the participant status of the speaker in the shared common ground. As this discussion shows, the various categories used in Li and Thompson's analysis are often pointing in the right direction, but focus on different aspects of the sense-making mechanism. Our analysis of the particle *le* as a common-ground co-ordination device in information flow between situation participants can account for all their data. 'Change' in our model does not refer to a change expressed in a sentence, but to the change in the structure of the shared common ground, which the expression indexes.

9.3.2 'Natural events' and 'spatial events'

The first distinction we made in common-ground structure was 'surroundings', which are constituted by 'natural events' and 'spatial events'.[6] 'Natural events' are new events ('rain') and additions to the common ground, or changes ('leaves fallen off') in current common ground. The particle's use in other words is pragmatically motivated. Closely related are 'natural processes', which have predictable paths and outcomes.[7] The few examples we have suggest that these occur at a much smaller scale than 'natural events' and are technology related. The need always to mark these events as co-ordination points and use the particle *le* sign – which cannot be explained by any linguistic theory – we related to the all-encompassing force of the 'deviant' nature of these events.

A second distinction we needed to make was that of movement in the environment, which includes geographical space.[8] Such movement implies a 'change' in spatial orientation, which requires a restructuring of the common ground and activation of a different part of common-ground knowledge – in this case the notions 'wild', 'zebras' and 'filming'. In contrast to 'natural events' we like to call these 'spatial events'.

A third distinction in 'surroundings' we made had to do with the available means of transportation, the infrastructure of a society. By guiding a person through the 'spatial environment' appeals to *jin* ('close by'), *yuan* ('far') and available means of transportation are functional ways of dealing with the issue of distributing information about locales and transportation. When a distance is perceived as 'deviant' in relation to an expressed movement goal, it will be marked as a co-ordination point in the information exchange.[9] Deviations in living conditions ('Boy, your house is dirty'), relate to 'institutional environments'.[10] The number of such distinctions in this section comes to two: deviations caused by 'natural events' or 'natural processes', or those created by movement or 'spatial events', perceived as holding for a 'spatial environment' or for 'institutional environments'.

9.3.3 'Participant status'

Participant status is a crucial distinction in many stories, interactions and most conversations. The structure of the common ground can change in a variety of ways in relation to changes or modifications of participant status. Participants can be added; a status can be assumed, changed, perceived as deviant; intents can change; a participatory role can end. Some examples and comments follow. Self-reports of *'physical deviations'* are *wo e le* ('I'm hungry'), *wo sheng bing le* ('I'm ill'), *wo ganmao le* ('I got the flu'), *wo fashao le* ('I have a fever'), *tengsi wo le!* ('It hurts!'), which by implication change the structure of the shared common ground by changing the participant status of the speaker or a third-situation participant, and imply a deviation in their ability to participate in that situation. The obligatory use of the particle *le* in such cases, when information distribution is the communication goal, as with 'natural events', can be explained as the result of the strength of the 'deviation' involved and the need to 'distribute' that change.[11] The counterpart of these deviations are cases of *'solutionhood'* in which health is or will be restored, as illustrated by the doctor's advice: *haohao shui yijiao jiu hao le* ('take a good night's rest then you will feel fine again').

Physical deviation also can be *'perceived'*, as in *nide toufa chang le* ('your hair is too long'). This observation signals that according to the speaker the addressee's participant status is 'deviant' as regards hair length. Change of *intent* also can create a change in common-ground structure and be chosen as a co-ordination point. It is a means to indicate a sudden deviation from current practice, as in *wo xiang he cha le* ('I had like some tea now'), as in all cases this can be used as a form of information distribution or as a self-expression, a form of soliloquy or self-confirmation.[12] *'Construal'* as a sudden realisation (deviation) of a change in participant status also can be marked as a co-ordination point.[13] A change in common-ground structure (deviation) can also be *anticipated*. The ability to anticipate developments (that is, see consequences of certain actions by situation participants) is part of the human capacity of forming mental models, as we will discuss again shortly.

Common-ground structure can also change through 'addition', as when a new participant *appears* on the scene. This was the case in *Jingcha lai le* ('there comes a police officer') in the thief story. The appearance of the policeman changed the structure of the common ground and created a problem for the thief (but a 'solution' for the person being robbed), given the definition of their respective participant roles in the shared cultural common ground.[14]

In a few cases we also observed a participant *status change*, which was permanent.[15] In incidental cases a change in common-ground structure can be ordered, as in the case of a required change in *consciousness*, which changes the common-ground structure.[16] Items standing out as 'deviant' in a series (*zui ... le*) can be presented as co-ordination points. In the distribution of information these can have the role of an update of personal common ground.[17]

In pragmatic encounters people take up *participatory roles*. When these roles change, as for instance from 'waiting in a hospital's waiting room' to 'being treated as a patient' as in *jiu gai nin kan le* ('then it's your turn'), *jiu yinggai gai ni le* ('it should be your turn'), the structure of the common ground also changes. This is also the case when a pragmatic encounter *ends*, as illustrated by *dou banhaole!* ('All set, sir [in post office procedure]'), or when a person comes under an obligation to participate in one: *dei li fa le* ('you need a hair cut'). We list the various distinctions below:

Change in common-ground structure

Participant status	Source	Example
Physical deviation	Self-reported	*wo e le*
Physical deviation	Perceived	*nide toufa chang le*
Intent change	Self-perception	*wo yao he cha le*
Construal	Realisation by speaker	*gai shi ni de shihao le*
Anticipated deviation	Calculated	*ta tai zhong le*
Addition	Appearance	*jingcha lai le*
Status change	Self-report/reported	*biancheng . . . le*
Consciousness change	Instructed	*xing le*
Deviant item	In a series	*zui . . . le*
Participatory role	Changes; ends	*gai ni le*
Obligation	Public event	*dei li fa le*

Assumed deviations in an addressee's participant status can take the form of a *'co-ordination question'*: *ni zenme le?* ('something the matter with you?'), in which the speaker indicated that s/he wanted to be updated as to the addressee's current participant status.

9.3.4 Procedures and events

Procedures appeared in three forms, they were either 'autonomic projects' and were executed by one person, or they were *'joint actions'* or 'joint projects', in which case they could take the form of a 'pragmatic' interaction. Autonomic projects as a 'fasten seatbelt' procedure (routine) may pass through one or more 'deviant' phases – *tai jin le* ('too tight'), *tai song le* ('too loose') – before being well-executed *xianzai hao le* ('that's better'). As constituents in common-ground structure, procedures bring in their own notional organisation, goal, preparatory procedure, main procedure, final procedure. Procedures can go wrong through involuntary effects.[18] When a deviant situation is restored this too is a change in the common-ground structure, and most will be marked with the particle *le* as a sign of 'solutionhood'.[19] Procedures have an expected common-ground structure, and the endpoint of such interactions is often marked as a co-ordination point, as in *zuowanle* ('I'm done [homework]), *dou banhaole* ('all set, sir') in the post office procedure, or *liwanle* ('all done') at the hairdresser's, since they involve a common-ground change and a new procedure or event will follow. The latter two are examples of 'joint actions' and part of a 'joint project'.

Nor are events all of the same type. When a public service is involved, we called the event a *public event*. Beginnings or endpoints of such events often are marked as co-ordination points for the same reason; they change the structure of the common ground and are often treated as co-ordination points in information distribution. Examples were *jiemu bosongwanle* ('the program is finished') and *dianying jieshule* ('Now the movie is over'). Less public are *institutional events*, which are also controlled by an outside source, and if a starting point is announced – *kaoshi jiu yao kaishi le* ('the test will start now') – that will typically be marked as the co-ordination point. Such an event 'announcement' will change the common-ground structure, and the addressees are supposed to prepare for the upcoming change in their ground. A variant of this is a wished-for common-ground change by which the speaker tries to place an obligation on the addressee as in *dei li fa le* ('you need a hair cut'), *zhehuir ke dei xiaoxin dianr le!* '([this-time sure must careful a-little *le*] Be careful this time').

9.3.5 *Narratives*

Narratives by necessity need to build the story's common-ground structure, and introduce surroundings and situation participants, with their backgrounds and wishes. When the stories describe events, they followed, in this case, the notional structure of western stories by going through a deterioration and restoration cycle. In each of the cycle parts deviations or restorations occurred which were marked as co-ordination points, as in, respectively, *yishang chuan ba chuan caifanle* ('as soon as she sets foot on the boat it capsized') and *Bubu . . . guolai jiu ren le* ('there comes Bubu to the rescue'). In stories a distinction between main events, public events, and side-events was necessary. Deviations tended to occur in main events, whereas side-events were more easily added to the story's common-ground structure. One example was *yingzhangli de shiqing dou paixialaile* ('everything in the tent was recorded'). A disturbance of a public event was *Ta bu neng dao jiaotang qu jiehun le* ('She cannot go to the church for her marriage now').

9.3.6 *Conversations*

Conversations are 'joint projects' which are projected, taken up and brought forward (Clark 1996). In personal exchanges, when common ground exists before the encounter, the accumulated common-ground structure forms the basis for additional moves in the 'distribution of information', which is the main force that drives conversations and the overarching distinction for understanding uses of the particle *le*. We first encountered pieces of conversation in Chapters 5 and 6, and in those pieces it was already clear that discourse type provides special uses of co-ordination-point marking. Interactions in those early chapters were those between doctor and patient, a citizen and the fire department, a clerk and a customer at the post office, and illustrated the distribution of information between a daughter and her father (*wo e le*, 'I'm hungry'), a conversation between friends in a restaurant, and a student updating his father on study progress. In these early stories we also encountered a case of a co-ordination question. The children's stories further provided examples of 'anticipation' of a deviant situation, the use of hypothetical situations, and the management of interpersonal relationships.

The conversational pieces in Chapter 7 were grouped under 'openings', 'construal', 'agenda', and 'argument', where 'openings' illustrated cases in which personal common ground was not yet built-up. The most remarkable cases were those in which in the opening part a conversation participant had already used the particle *le* to make an appeal to shared cultural common ground to construct the participant status of the interlocutor, and thereby also present his own cultural standing. 'Construals' in these conversations were related to 'natural events', 'participant status', and the 'cultural common ground', which confirmed the ideas built-up in the procedural sections and the children's stories. Co-ordination points were those moments in which a construal was 'confirmed', but at the same time were used as a technique to break into the conversation and add to it. 'Construals' also could be rejected, or contradicted, and at such moments were marked as co-ordination points. We also encountered a case of the construction of a contrastive hypothetical common ground. That usage, too, was marked as a co-ordination point.

In personal exchanges the main theme was the distribution of information between persons who shared pieces of common ground. Distribution of information related to 'deviations', 'solutionhood', and cases of 'confirmation'. However, we also encountered co-ordination questions, and attending moves with the particle *le*. The latter made clear that the attending move should be taken as a co-ordination point, and that way it obtained special significance. The conversation involving an argument, in the first instance, had to do with a request to do something (pour a cup of tea), which was refused by the husband – a clear confronting move. That refusal was countered with an offensive move (name calling), which in turn was 'challenged'.[20] That sequence of actions led to an 'intervention' by an elderly family member, the father. The challenge and the intervention we identified as confronting moves, and such moves are forms of 'deviation', and, in line with all forms of deviation, marked as co-ordination points.

In one of the opening pieces of the conversation series a non-local person came to seek advice from a local inhabitant. In that case an appeal was made to the cultural common ground of the local person, who had access to a variety of institutional sources which were not easy to access for a non-local person. In the end an 'offer' for living with the local party was made, and that offer was 'accepted'. Both the offer and the acceptance were marked as co-ordination points.[21] In our general model this can be handled by stressing that an offer proposes a change in the common-ground structure, which allows it to become shared common ground. The acceptance is then a 'confirmation' move which establishes the proposed common ground as shared. Acceptance is not a case of information distribution but a decision, and an 'acceptive', as proposed for pragmatic interactions involving contractual obligations (Steuten 1998).

9.3.7 Time

So far we have left the time dimension outside the discussion. Time in all instances is running time, as related to the natural event, main event or procedure involved. In cases of participant status, however, such time needs to be related to the public event (cf. visiting a dentist) concerned, as in *yinggai gai ni le* ('then it should be your turn'), in which case two related events were being sequenced: 'calling a number' and 'being your turn'. In relation to the institutional event *kaoshi jiu yao kaoshi le* ('the test will start soon'), the time dimension was that of the institution as set for that event, even though the co-ordination process in each case was 'now'.

Our data showed that the content of the assertion can be either in the past, at present or in the future. With time expressions, the time module of the interactant's mental model always tracks current time, and the assertion therefore always is current time with future implications. When embedded models are activated, time expressions track 'narrative time' or 'event time'. In procedural discourse, the time module tracks 'event time', whereas in narratives it tracks narrative time. Time references with *le* can be perceived as 'deviations', when there is a synchronisation problem, a mismatch between a 'current time' situation (looking for an umbrella at home) and clock time or 'normal' developments (being at the office around that time). The assertion always is 'now', but this 'now' in narrative discourse is imagined and the same narrative can be replayed each time a joint imagination takes place. The 'now' in conversations is linked to current time and cannot be replayed in this sense.

This observation is one of the clear indications that the model we are seeking consists of modules, and one of these feeds information on the flow of 'time'. 'Day time' and 'institutional time' can be matched on request against this module and the mental model will calculate the consequences. When an addressee receives a time related expression marked with *le*, he will seek the common ground for hints, which is the most likely source to co-ordinate on. Is it 'tea time', 'the cinema' planned for that evening', or 'dinner', perhaps, that is being indexed by *shijian bu zao le* ('it's late already')? When the personal common ground provides information on possible events, the addressee will be able to work out which event is involved by comparing running time with institutional time. The marking of time itself is simple and direct.

9.4 Previous analyses

In Chapter 2 we divided the various approaches to the analysis of the Chinese particle *le* into four groups: two morphemes and multifunction, two morphemes and two functions, one morpheme and two functions, and one morpheme and one function. The first of these, two morphemes and multifunction, was the work by Y.R. Chao (1968), which we reviewed as benchmark data at the end of Chapter 8. That study was descriptively close to adequate, but its explanatory power remained rather limited as we demonstrated there. The main study of the two morphemes two functions type was that by Li and Thompson (1981), and that work we revisited in section 9.3.1. It is a remarkable study, making most of the necessary distinctions but still lacking a unifying framework which could explain the various uses of the particle *le*.

Other studies along these lines did contribute various insights, but none of these proved capable of presenting an alternative. Andreasen (1981) made interesting observations, but his data were not convincing, to state it mildly. Chang's (1986) analysis was interesting in the sense that it laid the foundation for our study by clarifying the need for the recognition of pragmatic forces in Chinese grammar. His analysis of the particle *le* as a discourse-final-unit marker, however, was limited to narrative discourse, pointed mainly to surface structure phenomena and did not provide an explanatory framework. Van den Berg (1989), also followed the Li and Thompson (1981) analysis, brought in concepts from Functional Grammar as developed by Simon Dik (1997) in Amsterdam. Interestingly, the idea of actuality expressed in that study has historical precedence (Chapter 4), and some of the distinctions made were corroborated by the present study. One of these is the idea that in 'short replies', 'the speaker acknowledges the actuality value of what has just been said' (van den Berg: 1989 158). It was also observed that the particle *le* can be used in countering an 'opinion' and generally marks 'remarkable' moments in event flow. All three observations were supported. However, the absence of a move typology, and a general theory of actuality, limited the predictive value of the study as observed in Chapter 2.

The analysis by Bisang and Sonaiya (1997) brought in the idea of the speaker expressing 'her/his reaction or attitude with respect to a given Preconstructed domain' which 'can be characterized in terms of Conformity or Confrontation'. We can conclude now that the distinctions made are both insightful and useful. Preconstructed domain can be related to the structure of common ground, as discussed in this study, whereas the ideas of Confrontation and Conformity can also be partly supported. However, as stated in Chapter 2, the absence of an interactional perspective limits the theory, as does its reliance on sentence structure (Chapter 2). Another interesting contribution was made by Liu (2001), who approached the analysis in interactive terms. He observed that *le* does not express 'change', that the 'change' is related to a previous situation, that *le* expects a 'background situation', and that *le* forces inferences from general knowledge, whereas 'new' means 'new' for the addressee, and expressions with *le* often are just a reminder. All these distinctions are insightful and supported by our study. The generalisation, however, that the particle expresses 'past tense' does not have much theoretical backing, and as an *ad hoc* solution based on translation data cannot be supported by our study. The Liu study therefore, despite its methodological advances, fails in its general analysis.

The third distinction concerned studies distinguishing one morpheme which was realised at two different levels. For Thompson (1968) that was one of a series of events or the whole series of events. We can recognise here an endeavour to identify the distinction between a main event and an event series, but as we have demonstrated in this study, the pragmatic forces influencing the decision to mark verbal expressions with verbal *-le* are more complex than just making the distinction. Spanos's (1979) study, as we observed in Chapter 2, was the first to take a pragmatic orientation, and he too made a distinction between verbal *-le* marking and phrase *le* marking, but unfortunately his use of Grice's conversational maxims did not contribute to an understanding of the communicative function of these forms. More substantial were the contributions by Huang (1988) and Huang and Davis (1989) who differentiated between 'domain' of use and 'substance', and identified the substance for the particle *le* as 'boundary marking'. As we have seen in this study, that is one of the possible ways of using the particle *le*, but the analysis does not address the choice involved, nor does it clarify other uses. Shi's (1990) analysis proposed 'relative anteriority' as the unifying cognitive distinction that can account for both verbal *-le* and the particle *le*. This idea is very difficult to prove or disprove, but generally is too theoretical to be open for empirical disqualification.

In a number of recent studies different concepts were brought in. Chang's (2001) study related 'event structure' to uses of the particle *le* and verbal *-le*. That approach is promising, but still leaves much to be desired due to a limited data set and the absence of insight into event chains. As demonstrated by Chang (1986), not all events are marked in the same way. With the study by Yang (2003), Grice's conversational implicature surfaced again, but as stated in Chapter 2 in the absence of an interactive view, the idea of perfectivity cannot account for the phenomenon under study. In our last category, one morpheme, one function (cf. Li 1990), 'contrast to previous situation' is claimed as the unitary function of both verbal *-le* and the particle *le*. The idea of 'contrast', indeed, can be supported, as can the conception of a previous situation. These distinctions, however, need to be spelled out in far more detail and have theoretical support. None of this is the case in that study. Such a claim has no empirical support and is theoretically weak. Against the background of these various studies, it feels safe to say that the interactional view we presented provides a more wide-ranging analysis of the phenomenon, and provides insight into the way in which information distribution is handled in Chinese.

9.5 A theory of language use

In strictly linguistic approaches, common-ground constituent structure is not recognised, which in our view is a serious methodological problem (cf. Chomsky 1972, 1986; Botha 1992). In a rational linguistic approach the study of sentence structure is considered the main target, and that source should suffice for the formulation of generalisations (cf. Chomsky 1966). However, the history of linguistic study has shown that categorical grammars do not seem to address the real issues of language use and human communication practices. The points at which these generalisations misfire are seldom investigated, let alone the reasons why they miscarry (cf. Clark 1996; Wu 1998). In our view, then, common ground and its constituent structure are determinants for what to say, when to say it, and how to say it, as an old adage of socio-linguistics tells us (cf. Fishman 1972). We hold the view that understanding the constituent structure of the common ground, and an insight into the process of common-ground co-ordination, will lead us to an understanding of language use and of uses of the particle *le* by revealing the moments at which the particle can, should or should not be used.

The tripod model we developed in Chapter 8, and which was repeated in an abridged form in this chapter, distinguishes two personal common grounds which, in a one-culture perspective, are united through background knowledge, the shared cultural common ground and its various constituents (cf. Clark 1996 and Chapter 3 for more details). Distribution of information we identified as the aim that unites the two personal common grounds in most cases, as was the ability of the interactants, the holders of these personal common grounds, to recognise plans and harmonise them (cf. Clark 1996). Plans encountered in our study were a relatively large set of everyday procedures and events, and a small number of stories, which either addressed the cultural common ground directly or took the reader on a journey through an enticing event chain. The conversational issues introduced ranged from getting acquainted and finding a house, to shopping, haggling, movies, travel, sports, discussing language, literature, music, art, religion, medical treatment, and sight-seeing, to give a rough impression. In the conversational pieces both the personal common ground and issues of the cultural common ground were addressed, and the interactants were united in finding ways to harmonise their differences.

The common-ground distinctions used in our various discussions can be easily harmonised with the theory of mental models (see Chapter 3). In that theory background knowledge feeds the construction of mental models in real time, and allows for the formation of embedded models to accommodate imagining and other forms of non-real-time events. The importance of mental model construction in this context is that it is specific as to the way in which information distribution takes place. It is the interpretation function of each interactant's mental model that relates incoming information to the current model and its background knowledge. The interpretation function checks for what is 'possible' and 'permissible'. At this point in our presentation we can make a direct link from the interpretation function of mental models to the constituent structure of common ground, as we introduced that in the previous chapter and generalised it in this chapter. For what is 'possible' the interpretation function relates the incoming information with running time, current natural and spatial events, and other possible events. For what is permissible this is done by linking that information with actual and possible participant statuses. This mental-model structure we can schematically present as:

Mental model modules
Time
Surroundings
[Natural events and spatial events]
Participant status
Procedures and other events

Let us see now how these components differ in two interlocked mental models. Time, when running time, is in principle synchronic, and as part of the harmonisation of aims and plans is linked to certain ongoing or planned projects. When one of the interactants is out of synchrony for one reason or another s/he can try to 'update' her/himself with a 'co-ordination question', or be reminded that s/he is out of synchrony.[22]

The 'surroundings' module regulates 'natural events' and 'spatial events'. The spatial module also contains information about 'localities', and in most cases also activates the 'participant status' and 'procedure/event' modules. A 'shopping event' obtains detail through information flowing in from the personal and cultural common ground. Most interactions focus on the participant status module, and it therefore seems safe to conclude that participant-status is the central component in mental model construction.

Content co-ordination of plans and aims is particularly opportune in conversations. Procedures and narratives provide their own notional organisation. The question, therefore, is how the notional structure and the plans and aims are represented in this model. In order to shape this we propose to add a co-ordinator to the model, which is positioned between the modules and the background knowledge, and will make the mental model schema look as follows:

Organisation schema of mental model processes
Background knowledge/cultural common ground
[notional structures: procedures and narratives]

CO-ORDINATOR
[plans and aims]

Time
Surroundings
[Natural events and spatial events]
Participant status
Procedures and other events

When joint actions start, as in a conversation, the co-ordinator looks for 'plans' and 'aims', which will include recognition of intent. As soon as language processing starts, the co-ordinator uses 'induction' to create content and looks for ways in which the current model needs to be modified. When the model adjustments have been worked out, the co-ordinator, in a 'deductive' process, calculates if what is constructed is still possible and permissible, and also calculates the effects the model modification has for the joint actions or the current joint project. It is essential that the processes of 'induction' and 'deduction' are differentiated. The language component and the cognitive operations involved can become rather blurred when both induction and deduction are being used to characterise the particle *le* (cf. Clark 1996; Johnson-Laird 1983, 1993).[23]

We identified the Chinese particle *le* as a co-ordination device, and determined that it indicated a change in the structure of the common ground. In the current theory that can be rephrased as an intended change in, or modification of, one of the modules of the current mental model. Changes in the surroundings module and changes in participant status were clear enough cases to support this. Modification concerns cases in which a participant status, which is known to the addressee(s), is selected for marking as a co-ordination point. This view also helps to explain how it is possible that pieces of the shared common ground are being used as co-ordination points. The orientation is from 'new' information, to assertion of known pieces of information, to assertion of pieces of shared background knowledge. We conclude that there are three ways of using the particle *le* in relation to a current mental model:

Assert change in module   *xia yu le; wo e le*
Assertion of already changed item   *ta nianji da le*
Assertion of a piece of background knowledge   *xianzai shi taikong shidai la!*

Participant statuses of known persons are stored in the background knowledge that feeds the participant status module. When the conversation addresses that person, his participant status in the current mental model is activated. However, that person's age is also a matter of construal and can be presented in a certain light, as when it is said *ta nianji da le* ('he is old already'), or in the case of *ta lao le* ('she is old') as discussed by Chang (1986). The background knowledge (cultural common ground) example is *xianzai shi taikong shidai le* ('it is the space age now!'), which is marked as a co-ordination point to drive the message home that we are no longer living in traditional society. These examples suggest that after changes have been incorporated as background knowledge, they can be called upon as the basis for confronting a current situation. This is particularly the case for current aspects of participant statuses, since these are remembered and will be stored as background knowledge. Changes in the surroundings module are not stored that way, even though some occurrences, such as tropical storm Katrina of August 2005, theoretically could be stored in a similar way.

The analysis of conversations presented in Chapter 7 allowed a distinction between personal exchanges, business transactions, and business transactions with a personal touch. That personal touch was created by the distribution of personal information in that business transaction. Plans and aims in the conversations studied were related to personal needs and the exchange of information. We illustrated this with the way a casual conversation was built-up between strangers who met in the early morning in the garden of a hotel. They connected their personal common grounds by providing information about their participant status, names, place of origin, accent, profession, and habits. The plan to make a casual conversation united the exchanges, and the information provided by the interactants was consistent with that aim. Other exchanges were practical, such as negotiating an agenda for going somewhere, seeking advice about a personal issue, and discussing an issue by exchanging opinions. The precise way in which plans and aims in those interactions are harmonised still needs to be analysed. In this study we concentrated on moments at which an explicit co-ordination point was marked.

Another issue is that of managing interpersonal relationships. Many contributions in that area have been made (Brown and Levinson 1987; Shih 1986; Liao 1994; Li and Li 1996). Our model connects two personal common grounds, which in language processing connects the two participants statuses, and we can imagine that a systematic study will address the way in which these statuses interact. But in this study we concentrated on moments at which the particle *le* was used; for example, *ni tai keqi le* ('you're too polite') used, for instance, to play down a form of praise, which fits the more general characterisation of uses of the particle *le* in other areas where it is used as a form of confronting. A wider study of politeness and uses of the particle *le* in Chinese is therefore still necessary.

The language-use model discussed in this chapter is able to regulate the various uses of the Chinese particle *le*, since it is interactive and allows each co-ordinator (the person performing the act of co-ordinating background and foreground knowledge) to relate his mental model to that of an interactant. And when the particle *le* is used in Chinese the same co-ordinator recognises what is expected and tries to harmonise plans and aims by reconstructing the common ground build-up so far. We also feel that such a model can handle all interactive phenomena and can form the basis for a wider theory of human understanding. We understand that quite a few details still need to be worked out. We will make a first contribution in the next section by relating various traditional concepts to the model developed here.

9.6 Some related issues

At the start of our study we found a Chinese advertisement leaflet which opened with the phrase *Ni yao mai fangzi le* ('Okay, you want to buy a house'). At the time we were confused by this usage, but now at the end of our study it has become clear that this 'new' intent changes the structure of the common ground, and also brings in related issues such as financing, insurance, estate agents, etc. In this section, we will address a few issues that are directly related to our study but so far have not been raised explicitly. We will first look at an example of verbal -*le* and the particle *le*, and reflect on the limitations of linguistic analysis.

Verbal -le *and the particle* le: *a comparison*

We learned to recognise verbal -*le* as, in origin, a completion marker (Chapter 4), and in modern usage that element of meaning is still recognisable. Our use of the term 'realisation' is indeed another way of stating the same. The event or activity under review has been brought to realisation. We could therefore also call this the 'genesis marker'. Something has been brought into existence, cognitively speaking. Two of the simple expressions we encountered early in our study were *Wo maile yiben shu* ('I bought a book') and *Wo mai shu le* ('I bought some books'). Initially we were confused as to the status and difference of these expressions. When they are contextualised as being said by a father coming home after a trip to town, both expressions are still equally possible and appropriate. Now, in retrospect, we can say that in the first example the 'realisation' of a book-buying procedure is reported, whereas in the second example a 'new' event is reported (cf. Yip 2001). The particle has also been identified as 'the inchoative *le*', and as specifying 'the inception of a new situation, be it a process or a state, transitory or permanent' (Chan 1980: 44). That analysis works in this case, but unfortunately is not generalisable to cases such as *tai chao le* ('too noisy') and *zajian le* ('well goodbye then'), and cannot predict usage of *le*. In our terminology information is distributed in both cases, but in the latter case a change in the structure of the common ground is also reported.

A complicating factor in this case is that the expression *wo maile shu* is not possible, and this needs an explanation. Our emphasis on pragmatic marking and the cognitive structure of events makes it possible to say that a non-quantified expression when marked as realised cannot be sensibly interpreted. In information distribution, people tend to say what they bought, but not that they have participated in the common act of buying books, for the simple reason that it is not something worth reporting. However, when *wo maile shu* is used in a series of events, *wo maile shu hui jia* ('after realising the book buying I am off to home'), the possibility of having bought something is brought in and the sequence can be reported as meaningful since the buying is not the focus of the information and it can be assumed that something is bought then. Now let us look at the same difference in questions.

Questions

A wounded or sick person can be approached either with *Haole yidianr ma?* ('Are you feeling somewhat better?') or with *Hao yidianr le ma?* ('Are you feeling better now?'). The first question we recognise as being made in the known context of a recovery process, and is an endeavour to explore the extent of that process. The second question addresses the same issue, but from the fresh perspective of the addressee's participant status. Can you confirm to me that you are somewhat better now? These 'confirmation questions' explore the shared common ground, or seek confirmation from the addressee as regards a piece of the supposedly currently shared common ground. They also can take the form of an intonation question: *chile zaofan jiu shang ban le?* ('and after breakfast you go to the office?'). We learned to oppose these questions to 'co-ordination questions' in which the speaker does not seek 'confirmation' but wants to be 'updated': *Ni zenme le?* ('Something the matter with you?'), *Fasheng shenme shi le ma?* ('Did something happen?').

Limitations of linguistic analysis

We already observed that common-ground co-ordination is a psychological distinction. It was discussed by Clark (1996) in the context of a theory of language use. This once more illustrates that linguistics as an autonomous discipline has many limitations. Addition of the notion common ground changes the objective and perspective and the nature of the study of language use dramatically, as we have tried to illustrate in this study. When at this point we bring in the question raised in Chapter 3, does the particle *le* index the 'annotated record', or rather the 'outline record', or perhaps both? – we are forced to answer that it must be the outline record. The particle *le* does not attend to variations taking place in the annotated record; it is a background distinction.

We also asked the question (Chapter 3) as to 'in what way' the particle *le* affects the 'context', and we can conclude now that the particle *le* intends to affect the 'structure of the addressee's common ground'. This statement also potentially clarifies the existence in Chinese, as in other languages, of a variety of conventional techniques for the purpose of affecting the addressee's common-ground structure, such as ... *jiu cheng le,... jiu xing le,... jiu shi le*. We can further conclude that the relationship between uses of the particle *le* and the 'evidence' for the 'assertion' can be 'perceived', 'assumed', 'believed', and 'known' pieces of evidence. If it is perceived, it should be verifiable by others, if assumed it can be rejected, when believed it can be contradicted, and when known it can be used as a piece of evidence in argumentation or advice.

Enumerative la

Enumerative *la* was recognised as a variant of the particle *le* by Chang (1986). We agreed with that, but now can add to this that this usage is based on the assertion of an assumedly shared piece of common ground. Pieces of cultural common ground are the most obvious choice in the first instance. When pieces of cultural common ground are asserted to an outsider of that culture, or to someone who is not familiar with local traditions (an obvious setting for such uses), such assertions introduce the local cultural facts. Let us now see how the usage of the particle *le* relates to the four components of the 'cultural common ground': *cultural facts, conventions, norms, procedures* (Clark 1996). We met the 'procedural' component in Chapter 5 and discovered that it is highly scripted and predictable. As to the other distinctions, we now theorise that 'conventions' are rule-governed and the particle *le* will be used at moments when rules are broken. Norms are set by society and are superposed. Non-adherence will lead to corrective acts, as we also observed in the traffic example in our data. That example illustrated that norms can be reconstituted. These observations can be presented schematically as follows:

1. Cultural facts   Enumerative *la*
2. Conventions   Rule assertions; breaking a rule
3. Norms   Violations and restorations
4. Procedures   Problems/solutions

We supported the use of the enumerative *la* in relation to cultural facts with the observation that it is used in an assertion, which does not need confirmation; that usage is supported by other examples in our data, and is one of the predictions of the language-use model we constructed in this chapter.[24] It is a special form of asserting pieces of the shared cultural common ground. The other examples too are supported by some of our data. We therefore feel confident that the analysis will stand further tests. Our conclusion is that the nature of a common-ground change varies in agreement with the common-ground component involved, as already observed. This, however, does not affect the general or core function of the particle *le* as a co-ordination-point marker.

9.7 Concluding remarks

The findings of our study are listed below in a number of points. All are supported in this chapter or in other parts of the book:

1. We demonstrated that the Chinese particle *le* is a special common-ground co-ordination device; it indexes co ordination points in the distribution of information between interactants (cf. 'hypothesis', Chapter 3).

Theoretical implications 263

2   Historical research (Chapter 4) shows that the particle *le* developed as an indicator of the inception of a new situation. That hypothesis can be maintained when related to common-ground structure, and the implications are explored.
3   The notion 'change' needs to be interpreted not as a change as described in the sentence, but as a change in common-ground structure.
4   The common-ground constituent structure we identified as 'time', 'surroundings', 'participant status', 'procedures', and 'events'. These distinctions were used to develop a language-use model, which is presented as an alternative to traditional sentence structure.
5   We introduced the notions 'co-ordination question' [QW ... *le*] and 'confirmation question' [LE MA]. These question types contain 'co-ordination points' which provide the basis for the distinctions made.
    These questions stand in contrast to simple QW questions and questions with MA, which we see, respectively, as requests for more information and endeavours to explore information held by the addressee.
6   We claim that linguistic studies should be strongly empirical and be based on the recognition of common-ground structure rather than on so-called sentence structure. The latter is no more than a reflection of the possible operations of the human mind.
    The theory of language use developed in this and the previous chapter provides the details for that claim. As observed by other researchers, language structure is the result of conventional ways of marking cognitive relationships. By studying the constituent structure of common ground and its relationship with language elements, so-called linguistic structures become transparent and rule limitations can become apparent.
7   We support analysis of conversations in terms of move structure but indicated that these need to be supplemented with recognition of a notional structure, and therefore be brought into a wider model that recognises plans and aims (cf. Clark 1996).
8   We outlined a theory of language use, based on the theory of mental models, which incorporates common-ground structure (this chapter).
9   We claim that the theory of language use proposed, breaks the barrier between so-called theoretical and applied linguistics. There is no such barrier, just an inadequate linguistic theory. Generative linguistic concepts in particular are highly inadequate for understanding language processing and communication.

Notes

1 Introduction

1 This statement of course does not imply that there are not several very interesting studies of the particle *le* available, foremost among which is the Li and Thompson (1981) study. See Chapter 2 for an overview.
2 Admittedly, there are many instances where the judges agreed as to the use and non-use of the particle.
3 The discussion becomes somewhat more complicated by the presence in the Mandarin variety in use in Taiwan by expressions such as the following:

(1) [bus passenger picking up his mobile phone and repeatedly telling that he is not there yet; the following example is his last and most impatient endeavour to make this clear]
Wo hai mei daole la!
I yet not-there-is arrive -*le la*
'I am not there yet *la*!'

(2) [roommate trying to stop another roommate crying]
Bie kule la!
do-not cry -*le la*
'Stop crying now, I beg you!'

These data suggest that the co-ordination marker *la* in these examples is moving out of its current boundaries to a new kind of usage in Taiwan. This possibly happens under influence of the Minnan marker *la*, the most frequently used utterance final particle in Southern Min and identified as 'a marker of finality of a speech unit in discourse' by Ing Cherry Li in her study of Utterance-Final Particles in Taiwanese (Southern Min in Taiwan) (Li 1999: 28–62). Such finality marking, she observes, can be accompanied by a wide range of attitudinal meanings such as 'strong commitment, emphasis, impatience, or friendliness' (Li 1999: 57). The use of this *la* in Taiwan Mandarin, we therefore see as the effect of the transfer of a discourse act from Southern Min discourse to Mandarin discourse in Taiwan. Given its local character we exclude this kind of uses from our data and will not pay further attention to it in this study.

The Southern Min 'finality' marker *la* possibly also has found its way into Bahasa Indonesia. Expressions such as '*Suda la!*' seem reminiscent of this. Personal communication by the Austronesian linguist Bob Blust during a presentation of the core grammatical function of *le/la* at Cheng Chih University, Taipei, Taiwan on Tuesday, 25 June 2002.
4 We are grateful to the teacher at Tsinghua University, Hsinchu, Taiwan, who observed that the particle *le* occurs frequently in 'announcements' and wondered if it was related or not to that speech-act type.

5 For details, see Chapter 5.
6 Most of the chapters are the result of intense collaboration between the two authors, which took place either in the Netherlands or in Australia in the period between 1998 and 2002. Some chapters carry the clear mark of one author, and such specialised contributions will be indicated when applicable; however, most of the work is the result of intensive collaborative efforts.

2 Previous studies

1 Example overheard at Chung Cheng University, Chia-I, Taiwan, May 2002. The annotation of this example is:

> [Audience in cafeteria, students entering preceded by microphone-carrying announcer]
> **Yinyueji laile!**
> Music-ritual come-*le*
> 'The music is here!'

The text reproduced here was carried around by students, each holding a piece of cardboard on which a character and the final exclamation mark were painted.
2 Li and Thompson (1981: 280), example 139.
3 The blanks containing the figures are possible positions where *le* can be inserted. The first figure in each blank indicates the percentage of respondents who considered the use of *le* obligatory, whereas the second figure represents those respondents who considered the use of *le* at that position optional.
4 'Boundary' marking was the idea of Thompson (1968), who proposed that the core function of *le* is to mark an 'event boundary', which can be either an 'initial' or an 'end' boundary.

3 The particle *le* and the study of language use

1 See our discussion of various studies on *le* in Chapter 2, the work by Charles Li and Sandy Thompson in particular. See also Stalnaker (1978).
2 See the discussion of the example *Wo mai zheben shu le* ('I bought this book/I'll buy this book') in Sybesma (1999: 62), quoted in Chapter 1.
3 Cf. also the exposition by Kamp and Reyle (1993), in the context of Discourse Representation Theory.
4 Obviously, co-ordination of the way the action develops remains essential, and most likely also is the basis for the co-ordination process in human interaction.
5 We changed the *presuppose* of the original text into *suppose* under 2. What is meant is what the interactants think the current state of the common ground is.
6 We changed *presuppose* to *assume* under 3. It is what the interactants think they have done so far. Which steps they have taken so far in the interaction. The state of the activity is at a certain point, as indicated by their memory record.
7 However, for possible exceptions see Chapter 5.
8 This can be information as to the existence of new facts, as when the city government informs the community in writing as to a change in the procedure of garbage collection. The recipients of such information are not party to the decision process. Their role is limited to participation in the execution.

4 The historical development of the particle *le*

1 This chapter is based on Wu (2000). We thank JCLTA for their permission for Routledge to reproduce the major part of the article.

266 *Notes*

2 A book about Buddhist history compiled by a monk, Dao Yuan, at the end of the tenth century, which contains dialogue records of monks on Buddhist doctrines. Most dialogues recorded are in the period of Tang and the Five Dynasties (cf. Pan and Yang 1980: 22).
3 The oldest existing Zen (Chan) history compiled by two Chinese Buddhist monks, Jin and Jun in AD 952.
4 It is possible that the movement also resulted in the pattern V-*le* O *leye* considering *leye* had already acquired some function of *le* by that time. The two patterns could have co-existed for some time until they finally became V-*le* O *le*. However, we have no evidence to substantiate the hypothesis as sources available for vernacular Chinese in Song are mainly from the southern dialect regions. The earliest examples of V-*le* O *leye* we know are from *Xixiangji* (*Romance of the Western Chamber*) in Yuan (1279–1368).
5 According to Cao (1987: 14), *ye* was used with stative situations in Old Chinese and began to be used with changed situations after Wei and Jin (220–439).
6 The annotation by Kim for e. biji chi-liao shi wo ye liao liao, reads:
   e. biji chi-liao shi wo ye liao liao
   around eat INCHO then I also finish PFV/CHANGE
7 The question mark is added according to Liu and Jiang (1995: 268).
8 *Zhe* ('this') is missing in Kim (1998). Cf. Liu and Jiang (1995: 280).
9 In (4.10)–(4.13) the Chinese examples are from Shi (1996), while the English glosses and translations are ours.
10 The original character for this word in the Shantou dialect is a combination of characters *bu* and *hui*. *Buhui* here represents the word only, not the sound.

5 Action-picture stories

1 Romijn and Seely ([1979] 1986) was the first series of action stories containing text and a limited number of pictures. The original series was re-edited as a pictures-only publication (Frauman-Prickel 1985; illustrations by Noriko Takahashi) and published by Prentice-Hall. The Frauman-Prickel version does not contain full texts but suggestions for use only. Forty of the original stories were transformed into a picture-story version, and to these were added another 26 stories, resulting in a total of 66 picture stories. The text of the added 26 stories was written by M.E. van den Berg. The English was corrected by an American lady living in the Netherlands. The stories presented themselves as a set of pictures, one action story per page. The number of pictures varied between ten (two rows of five pictures) and 18 (three rows of six pictures), with an average number of pictures per story of 14. The total number of pictures (and text lines) was 946.
2 In the book they were divided into seven units: *AM-PM, Health and Safety, At Home, Going Out, Holidays and Leisure, At School*, and *Weather*. Each unit was introduced by a model lesson. The remaining lessons were left open as to the kind of text required.
3 Translation by a Chinese professor from Shandong, China, who visited the Netherlands in 1992.
4 'Procedures' or 'social practices', as we have seen in Chapter 3, are part of the 'cultural common ground'. The picture series depicted action sequences of Western culture. This, however, we did not consider a problem. We were looking for moments in the action series that in the eyes of a Chinese translator should be marked with verbal -*le* and/or the particle *le*. The cultural factor should not be of influence at these moments, we reasoned. When someone takes a pill and it gets stuck in his throat, this is not a matter of culture. A Christmas

party is, of course, but the events constituting that party can be reported in Chinese, and we still can observe moments at which verbal -*le* and the particle *le* are used to report a series of Christmas-party-related events.

5   In the original data Chinese characters and the pinyin tone marks were given. This kind of data was left out in the manuscript for ease of production.
6   We will argue that in cases like this the particle *le* is used to mark a procedure-related 'outstanding' piece of common ground the addressee is requested to co-ordinate on. In this example this piece of common ground is detailed as 'goal of the activity reached'. The 'activity goal' was marked with verbal -*le*, *kaile* ('boiling'). In the procedure 'making tea', the next step can now be performed.
7   See the previous note for our view on the co-occurrence of the particle *le* and verbal -*le* in cases such as these.
8   We will count occurrences of all LE cases for certain individual purposes.
9   When all occurrences were counted, and not merely the first-line occurrences, the total number of uses in this category was 78.
10 Of course, if the time-frame is widened, the Christmas dinner itself can become a verbal -*le* target, as in *Chile shengdan dacan yihou, wo guan nide shi* ('After the Christmas dinner, I'll attend your case').
11 However, 'possibility' – in the shape of 'permission' – can take *le*, which can result in the form *keyi le*.
12 See Wu (2005) for a study of the particle NE and its relation to the idea of shared common ground.
13 If community members do not synchronise their behaviour, the event only exists as a cultural event among third parties. Interpersonal communication within (family) groups can set the synchronisation point. Dinner at seven for instance. There can be local synchronisation points as with fireworks organised by the city government or other recognised institutional bodies. There are no clear sanctions for non-participation.
14 In 'direct address', a 'progress report' can be used to report an event that happened before the time of speaking and has a bearing on the current exchange. An example would be *Wo dingle fangjian* ('I reserved a room') when standing in front of a hotel counter. Such a 'progress report' would be part of an already agreed upon business transaction.
15 More extensive conversational data will be analysed in Chapter 7.
16 This does not mean that they are not mentioned in the literature. Chao (1968) gives the example *Dong yisheng zui youming le* ('Doctor Dong is most famous') among the people we have just discussed.
17 'Outstanding' is to be taken as 'something extreme'. The use of *tebie* ('special'), for instance, in *tebie xihuan chi yu* ('I specially like fish') is not extreme enough to make something 'stand out' and attract the use of the particle *le*.
18 Examples like this were listed and commented upon by Y.R. Chao in his grammar (1968). However, he did not relate this usage to the general notion of 'deviation' as we do here.
19 The 'verbal reaction' can be directed at an addressee, but usually is not.
20 A person can use the emotional expression *Ah ya, xia yu le* ('Oh no, it's raining'), and treat the rain outside as an 'instigating event', and in that way he may as well inform the people around him. However, this is not the 'normal' way of doing this.
21 This is another example illustrating that we are dealing here with virtual situations. In an actual situation, the warning alone would most likely already be sufficient. The difference between these two situations illustrates that a pre-warning can either stand alone, or the reason for the warning can be explicit.
22 For the notion of 'deterioration', see Chapter 6. There it will be put into relation with the notion 'restoration'.

6 Children's stories

1. The stories were published in 1974 by the Gwoyeu Ryhbaw Press in Taipei. The rewriting of the stories was done by Lin Lang.
2. It seems reasonable to place direct address of the reader by the narrator also at layer 1.
3. The 0 layer we added as self-evident. Below we find reason to add a fourth layer, a meta-layer in which the narrator interacts with one of his story characters.
4. Reported in Eggins and Slade (1997). These authors do not use Longacre's distinctions. The term 'coda' or 'tail', is taken from music notation practice, where after a repetition the final notes are given in the 'coda'.
5. This is in essence an English version of the text in Bal (1997), the Dutch language source.
6. Also see Chapter 5.
7. The writer chose to create this effect with *zhaixiale* ('took [their sunglasses] off'). He also could have focused on the violin cases and mark their appearance with the particle *le*, but in this instance the main event, the identification of the participants, is the sunglasses episode. The violin cases were a 'final procedure'.
7a The speaker can also imagine that the addressee is present at that moment.
8. Aristotle distinguished 'epideictic rhetoric' (from deliberative and judicial), as being concerned with 'praise' and 'blame' (Kennedy 1991: 47).
9. Forces deriving from the general structure of the language, for instance the need to express result, we also consider in the first instance as pragmatically motivated. We will discuss this issue further in Chapter 9.
10. Interview with the girl after she left the supermarket.
11. We will encounter the logico-semantic relations of 'elaboration', 'extension' and 'enhancement' again in the next chapter when we analyse conversational exchanges.

7 Conversations

1. We will discuss a fourth issue, the kind of information on which co-ordination takes place, in the next chapter.
2. See section 7.2 for a discussion.
3. With minor modifications, the examples are from Eggins and Slade (1997: 194, Table 5.8).
4. See Chapter 3, and Clark (1996: 208).
5. The particle HE is a Taiwanese variant, most likely influenced by the Minnan particle HO. It is a regional variant and not part of *putonghua* ('common speech').
6. The wording Yang used is a reflection of the position 'teachers' hold in Chinese communal common ground, which can be traced back to the Chinese philosopher Confucius (551–479 BC; cf. Oliver 1971).
7. See note 3 on the most likely background of HE as a regional variant.
8. The pronunciation for *sha* in the text is given as *she*.
9. This construal as 'deviant' is countered by the hotel clerk saying 'this is the general price in this area'.
10. Choice-type questions were not distinguished by Halliday ([1985] 1994) as a separate category, and they are also not discussed by Eggins and Slade (1997). They did note, however, that polar (yes/no) interrogatives encode an information

imbalance which does not exist between close friends and relatives since most of the circulating information is already shared. We take it that the choice of one of the alternatives in a choice-type interrogative is a form of 'affirming', making a piece of already activated information part of the 'joint project' which is the exchange at that moment.

8 Discussion

1. For a discussion of the structure of the common ground and its relation to mental models, see Chapter 9.
2. See Chapter 6 for the details.
3. If the effect is not easy calculable, the consequence can be spelled out by the speaker. Generally, for people who know each other well, and are aware of the various activities being undertaken, half a word is sufficient. For an illustration see the example *tai da le, tuodiao dayi* ('too big, take off the coat') discussed on p. 109. Note that the common-ground reset is followed by an action which is to be performed in that changed common ground.
4. For the 'involuntary effects', see Tables 5.7 and 5.8.
5. 'Upcoming events' were listed in Table 5.8.
6. 'Solutionhood' examples were given in Table 5.10.
7. We refer to Table 5.6 for the statistics.
8. When the particle *le* is used in 'conversations' in such situations, the presence of shared common ground is being claimed, and the interaction proceeds from that, generally more friendly, perspective. See the discussion of 'conversations' on pp. 218–22.
9. The 'deterioration' example is taken from (6.23), the 'restoration' example from (6.25), whereas the 'coda' is a quote from example (6.26).
10. For a detailed discussion, see Chapter 9.
11. The 'c.' line spelled out the consequences of the previous action. That was not absolutely necessary. It would have been sufficient if the writer had reported the setting into action of the camera. He could have done that by marking the 'change' from non-action to 'action' with *sheyingji jiu galagalade zoudongqilai le* ('and with a clicking sound the camera started to run').
12. It also was another case of *zui . . . le* usage, a base line and something 'deviant', which we can indicate as standing above this base line and thereby attracting attention.
13. MA questions containing a co-ordination point we identified as confirmation questions, see pp. 227 and 234; simple MA questions as exploring.
14. The part that is missing in the Chinese quotation is given between square brackets.
15. And a few others such as *jiu xing le* ('that will be okay'), see Chapter 7.
16. As said before, for common practical problems ready-made solutions are available.
17. As demonstrated in Chapter 5, verbal *-le* and the particle *le* can be used at various places in this summing up of activities, but do not serve a narrative purpose.
18. 'Don't stick your head out of the car.'
19. 'Please open the door.'
20. 'We are going home.'
21. 'But the daughter is too heavy,...'
22. 'Without you my daughter could not have gotten married.'
23. 'How good of you', and 'Too bothersome'.
24. In the original chapters we discussed utterances with and without the particle *le*.

270 *Notes*

25 We refer to Chapter 3 for a more detailed discussion, and to Clark (1996).
26 The example is *Cong xiao jiu daochu pao, xiangyin ye jiu bu chun le* ('I lived at many places, so my [Cantonese] accent is not pure').
27 *chengle xiguan le*.
28 *Chiwan fan jiu yao shang ban la?* ('After breakfast you go to work?')
29 This is, however, the impression created by teachers. They often present various pieces of information as part of the 'cultural (technical/scientific) common ground' and simply transmit that.
30 See example (7.38).
31 Examples were *Xianzai jidian zhong le?* ('What time do we have now?'), and *hen jiu bu jian le* ('really long time no see').
32 *Ni chao su la!* ('You were speeding') and *Tai gui le ba!* ('Be honest, this is too much!').
33 *Wo jiu waihang le* ('I'm an outsider here').
34 The offer was created through ... *hao la!* and the acceptance with *zai hao ye mei you la!*
35 The examples were, respectively, *na jiu haoban le* ('that will be enough'), *Ni ke bie hai ren la!* ('Stop hurting me!'), *Zhemo shuo ni shi xiangyao wo pei ni yuanzu la* ('You mean I should accompany you on a hiking trip').
36 Uses of *Dui le,* . . . as discussed.
37 *Yuanzu de haochu ke duo la* ('There are many good points in hiking').
38 This took the form *Xiang wo zhemo pang, budao bange zhongtou, wo leide shangqi bu neng jie xiaqi la!* ('I'm so fat, I will be out of breath in half an hour!').
39 Quite a number of other combinations between the conjunctions and the modal verbs are possible, such as *kuai yao* in, for example, *kuai yao shang ke le* ('we need to go to class now!').
40 However, we also find the combination *haobang* ('how good of you [to be able to do that]').
41 In France there used to be cinema performances which were continuous; you could walk in at any time.

9 Theoretical implications

1 As in *Women Zhongguoren zui zhuzhong sexiangwei le* ('We Chinese pay special attention to the matching of colour, taste and fragrance').
2 The example in this case should not be paraphrased 'now I know', as the linguistic change rule would require, but as 'I know'. That is why in our model this is a case of 'solutionhood' in relation to an earlier 'deviation' in personal common-ground structure.
3 These are examples (14), (19) and (20) discussed by Li and Thompson (1981) under the change category.
4 It is not clear to us why Li and Thompson do not use the translation 'How old are you now?'
5 We found examples of co-ordination questions between a teacher and a student, and an employer and employee.
6 The first of these accommodated examples, such as *xia yu le* ('it's raining now'), *qi wu le* ('it's getting foggy'), and verbal reports or descriptive statements, such as *shuye dou guaxialaile* ('all the leaves have been blown from the trees').
7 Examples are *Bingqilin ronghuale!* ('the ice cream melted'), *dengpao shaole* ('the bulb is burned out').
8 An example was *kai qiche dao yedili qu zhao banma pai dianying qule* ('he took his car and drove to the wild to film zebras'), which we last quoted in Chapter 8.

9 As in the quoted example *Zuo che bu tai yuan, zou lu ke jiu yuan le* ('It's not far by bus, but really too far to walk').
10 *Ni de fangzi tai zang le* ('Boy, your house is dirty!'). This kind of deviation will also cover cases such as *tai chao le* ('too noisy'), reported in Huang (1988).
11 The particle *le* can be left out in self-address, *wo e!* ('I'm (really) hungry'), but that can also be seen in a shortened form of *wo hao e!* ('I'm really hungry').
12 For more examples see section 5.3.1. In this section the relation with *huran* ('suddenly') is also illustrated.
13 As for instance in *souji huochaihe gai shi ni de shihao la!* ('I think collecting matchboxes must be your hobby!').
14 Another example of the arrival of new participants was illustrated by the verbal report *'Dakuaitou gen Daweiba dou dao Huangjinzhen laile!'* ('Big Head and Big Tail are in Gold City!'). The often-quoted example, *keren lai le / keren laile* ('The guests are coming / the guests are here'), also fits here (Chao 1968), as does an upcoming appearance such as *ta kuai yao lai le!* ('he will be here soon') (Li and Thompson 1981).
15 As in *Bubu jiu biancheng yige yao jiantouchuan de chuanfu le* ('[The father of the bride presented Bubu with a stylish gondola.] Bubu then became a proud gondola owner').
16 Which took the form *xing le!* ('wake up!').
17 As in *wo zui ai chi yu le* ('I like fish most'), or in clear requests for being attended to – for example, *wo zui pa pa louti le* ('I'm most afraid of climbing stairs'), said in a hotel environment.
18 Such as a motor-skill problem, *sadao zhuozi.shang le* ('you spilled some of it on the table'), in a 'pouring a glass of milk' procedure. Another example of an involuntary effect is a 'joint action' such as 'feeding a child' which can go wrong through an involuntary effect – for example, *ta tuchulaile!* ('she's spitting it out!') by one of the participants, in this case the baby.
19 An example is *xianzai ni keyi xie xin le* ('now you can write your letter').
20 the expression used was *tai buxiang hua la!* ('outrageous!').
21 Made possible in this case with the help of offering (*. . . hao la!*) and accepting (*zai hao ye meiyou la!*) routines.
22 Examples here are *Xianzai jidian le?* ('what time is it now?') and *Ni chidaole* ('you're late').
23 Compare the various identifications of uses of the particle *le* by Li and Thompson (1981).
24 It can also be used to list situation participants, but that will only be possible in situations of shared personal common ground.

References

Andreasen, Andrew, John (1981). 'Backgrounding and Foregrounding through Aspect in Chinese Narrative Literature', Ph.D. dissertation, Stanford University.
Anderson, Lloyd (1982). 'The "perfect" as a universal and as a language-particular category', in Paul J. Hopper (ed.) *Tense and Aspect: Between Semantics and Pragmatics*, pp. 227–64, Amsterdam: John Benjamins.
Argyle, Michael (1975). *Bodily Communication*, London: Methuen.
Austin, J.L. (1962). *How to Do Things with Words*, Oxford: Oxford University Press.
Bal, Mieke (1997). *Narratology. Introduction to the Theory of Narrative*, 2nd edn, Toronto: University of Toronto Press.
Berger, Peter L. and Thomas Luckmann (1967). *The Social Construction of Reality*, Penguin: Harmondsworth.
Biq, Yung-O. (2000). 'Recent developments in discourse-and-grammar', in *New Developments in Taiwan Linguistics*, pp. 357–93, Chinese Studies Vol. 18.
Bisang, W. and R. Sonaiya (1997). 'Perfect and beyond, from pragmatic relevance to perfect: the Chinese sentence final particle *le* and Yoruba *ti*', *Sprachtypol. Univ. Forsch. (STUF)* 50/2: 143–58.
Botha, Rudolph P. (1989). *Challenging Chomsky: The Generation Garden Game*, Oxford: Blackwell.
Botha, Rudolph P. (1992). *Twentieth Century Conceptions of Language*, Oxford: Blackwell.
Brown, G. and G. Yule (1983). *Discourse Analysis*, Cambridge: Cambridge University Press.
Brown, P. and S. Levinson (1978). 'Universals in language usage: politeness phenomena', in E. Goody (ed.) *Questions and Politeness*, pp. 56–311, Cambridge: Cambridge University Press.
Brown, P. and S. Levinson (1987). *Politeness: Some Universals in Language Use*, Cambridge: Cambridge University Press.
Bybee, Joan, Revere Perkins and William Pagliuca (1994). *The Evolution of Grammar: Tense, Aspect, and Modality in the Languages of the World*, Chicago: University of Chicago Press.
Cao, Guangshun (1987). 'Yuqici LE yuanliu qianshuo' (The origin of the particle LE), *Yuwen Yanjiu* 2: 10–15.
Chan, Marjorie K.M. (1980). 'Temporal reference in Mandarin Chinese: an analytical-semantic approach to the study of the morphemes LE, ZAI, ZHE and NE', *Journal of the Chinese Language Teachers Association* 15: 33–79.
Chang, Jung-hsing (2001). 'The syntax of event structure in Chinese', Ph.D. dissertation, University of Hawaii.

Chang, Vincent Wu-chang (1982). 'Le as a discourse-final particle in Mandarin Chinese', MA thesis, University of Florida.
Chang, Vincent Wu-chang (1986). 'The particle *le* in Chinese narrative discourse, PhD. dissertation, University of Florida.
Chao, Yuenren (1968). *A Grammar of Spoken Chinese*, Berkeley: University of California Press.
Chomsky, N. (1966). *Cartesian Linguistics: A Chapter in the History of Rationalist Thought*, New York: Harper & Row.
Chomsky, N. (1972). *Language and Mind*, New York: Harcourt, Brace, Jovanovich.
Chomsky, N. (1986). *Knowledge of Language*, New York: Praeger.
Clark, H.H. (1996). *Using Language*, Cambridge: Cambridge University Press.
Clark, H.H. and C.R. Marshall (1981). 'Definite reference and mutual knowledge', in A.K. Joshi, B.L. Webber and I.A. Sag (eds) *Elements of Discourse Understanding*, pp. 10–63, Cambridge: Cambridge University Press.
Comrie, Bernard (1976). *Aspect*, London: Cambridge University Press.
Cooper, R.L. (1969). 'How can we measure the roles which a bilingual's languages play in his everyday behavior?', in *The Description and Measurement of Bilingualism*, ed. L.G. Kelley, pp. 192–239, Toronto: Toronto University Press.
Craik, K.J.W. ([1943] 1967). *The Nature of Explanation*, Cambridge: Cambridge University Press.
Dik, Simon (1989). *The Theory of Functional Grammar*, Dordrecht: Foris Publications.
Dik, Simon (1997). *The Theory of Functional grammar. Part I: The Structure of the Clause; Part 2: Complex and Derived Constructions*, Amsterdam: John Benjamins.
Ding, Shengshu *et al.* (1961). *Xiandai Hanyu Yufa Jianghua* (Lectures on Modern Chinese Grammar), Beijing: Commercial Press.
Eggins, Suzanne and Diana Slade (1997). *Analysing Casual Conversation*, London: Cassell.
Fauconnier, Gilles (1994). *Mental Spaces*, Cambridge: Cambridge University Press.
Fauconnier, Gilles (1997). *Mappings in Thought and Language*, Cambridge: Cambridge University Press.
Fishman, Joshua (ed.) (1968). *Readings in the Sociology of Language*, The Hague: Mouton.
Fishman, Joshua A. (1972). *Sociolinguistics*, Rowley, Mass.: Newbury House Publishers.
Franckel, Jean-Jacques (1989). *Étude de quelques marqueurs aspectuels du français*, Genève: Librairie Droz S.A.
Frauman-Prickel, Maxine and Noriko Takahashi (1985). *Action English Pictures*, Englewood Cliffs, N.J.: Prentice-Hall Regents.
Geertz, C. (1983). *Local Knowledge*, New York: Basic Books.
Goffman, E. (1967). *Interaction Ritual: Essays on Face-to-face Behavior*, Garden City N.Y.: Anchor Books.
Goffman, E. (1974). *Frame Analysis. An Essay on the Organization of Experience*, New York: Harper & Row.
Grice. H. Paul (1975). 'Logic and conversation', in P. Cole and J.L. Morgan (eds) *Syntax and Semantics 3: Speech Acts*, pp. 41–58, New York: Academic Press.
Gu, Yueguo (1999). 'Towards a model of situated discourse analysis', in *The Semantics/Pragmatics Interface from Different Points of View*, ed. K. Turner, pp. 149–78, Amsterdam: Elsevier.

Gumperz, J.J. (1982). *Discourse Strategies*, Cambridge: Cambridge University Press.
Halliday, M.A.K. ([1985] 1994). *An Introduction to Functional Grammar*, 2nd edn, London: Edward Arnold.
Hinds, John (1979). 'Organizational patterns in discourse', in T. Givon (ed.) *Discourse and Syntax (Syntax and Semantics*, Vol. 12), pp. 135–56, New York: Academic Press.
Hopper, Paul J. (1979). 'Aspect and foregrounding in discourse., in T. Givon (ed.) *Discourse and Syntax (Syntax and Semantics*, Vol. 12), pp. 213–41, New York: Academic Press.
Hopper, Paul J. (ed.) (1982). *Tense and Aspect: Between Semantics and Pragmatics*, Amsterdam: John Benjamins.
Hopper, Paul J. (1988). 'Emergent grammar and the apriori postulate', in *Linguistics in Context: Connecting Observation and Understanding*, ed. B. Tannen, pp. 117–34, Norwood, N.J.: Ablex.
Huang, Lillian M. (1988). *Aspect: A General System and its Manifestation in Mandarin Chinese*, Taipei: Student Book.
Huang, Lillian M. and Philip W. Davis (1989). 'An aspectual system in Mandarin Chinese', *Journal of Chinese Linguistics*, 17/1: 128–65.
Huang, Yan (1994). *The Syntax and Pragmatics of Anaphora*, Cambridge: Cambridge University Press.
Hymes, Dell (1974). *Foundations in Sociolinguistics. An Ethnographic Approach*, Philadelphia: University of Pennsylvania Press.
Johnson-Laird, P.N. (1983). *Mental Models*, Cambridge: Cambridge University Press.
Johnson-Laird, P.N. (1993). *Human and Machine Thinking*, London: Lawrence Erlbaum.
Kamp, Hans and Ulre Reyle (1993). *From Discourse to Logic*, 2 vols, Dordrecht: Kluwer.
Kennedy, G.A. (1991). *On Rhetoric: A Theory of Civic Discourse by Aristotle*, New York: Oxford University Press.
Kim, Kwangjo (1998). 'On the usage of the linguistic signs LE, LAI, YE in the Ponyok Nogoltae', Paper presented at the IACL-7 and NACCL-10, Stanford University, California.
Kress, Gunther (1985). *Linguistic Processes in Sociocultural Practice*, Victoria, Australia: Deakin University Press.
Kress, Gunther (1988). *Communication and Culture*, Sydney: NSW University Press.
Lakoff, George (1987). *Women, Fire and Dangerous Things: What Categories Reveal About the Mind*, Chicago: University of Chicago Press.
Lambrecht, Knud (1994). *Information Structure and Sentence Form: Topic, Focus and the Mental Representations of Discourse Referents*, New York: Cambridge University Press.
Levinson, Stephen C. (1992). 'Activity types and language', in *Talk at Work*, eds Paul Drew and John Heritage, pp. 66–100, Cambridge: Cambridge University Press.
Lewis, D.K. (1969). *Convention: A Philosophical Study*, Cambridge, Mass.: Harvard University Press.
Li, Charles N. and Sandra A. Thompson (1981). *Mandarin Chinese: A Functional Reference Grammar*, Berkeley: University of California Press.
Li, Charles N., Sandra A. Thompson and R. McMillan Thompson (1982). 'The dis-

course motivation for the perfect aspect: the Mandarin particle LE', in Paul J. Hopper (ed.) *Tense and Aspect: Between Semantics and Pragmatics*, pp. 19–44, Amsterdam: John Benjamins.

Li, Ing Cherry (1999). *Utterance-final Particles in Taiwanese: A Discourse-pragmatic Analysis*, Taipei: Crane Publishing Co., Ltd.

Li, Ping (1990). 'Aspect and *aktionsart* in child Mandarin', Doctoral dissertation, Leiden University.

Li, Wei and Li, Yue (1996). ' "My stupid wife and ugly daughter" ': The use of pejorative references as politeness strategy by Chinese speakers, *Journal of Asian Pacific Communication* 7/3–4: 129–42.

Liao, Chao-chih (1994). *A Study on the Strategies, Maxims, and Development of Refusal in Mandarin Chinese*, Taipei: Crane.

Lin, Jian and Jiang Shaoyu (1995). *Jindai Hanyu yufa ziliao huibian: Yuandai Mingdai juan* [A Compilation of Reference Material for Early Mandarin Grammar: Yuan and Ming], Beijing: Commercial Press.

Liu, Jian, Jiang Lansheng, Bai Weiguo and Cao Guangshun (1992). *Jindai Hanyu xuci yanjiu* (A study of Early Mandarin particles), Beijing: Yuwen Press.

Liu, Xunning (1985). 'Xiandai Hanyu juwei LE de laiyuan' (The origin of the sentence-final *le* in modern Chinese), *Fangyan* 2: 128–33.

Liu, Xunning (1990). 'Xiandai Hanyu juwei LE de yufa yiyi ji qi yu ciwei LE de lianxi' (The grammatical meaning of modern Chinese particle *le* and its relation with verbal *-le*), *Shijie Hanyu Jiaoxue* (Chinese Teaching in the World), 12/2: 80–7.

Liu, Xunning (2001). 'Xiandai Hanyu juwei LE de yufa yiyi ji qi jieshuo' (Explaining the grammatical meaning of the sentence-final *le* in modern Chinese), Paper presented at the 10th International Conference of Chinese Linguistics, in conjunction with the 13th North American Conference on Chinese Linguistics, California, under the auspices of the Department of Linguistics, University of California on 22–24 June.

Longacre, Robert E. (1996). *The Grammar of Discourse* 2nd edn, New York: Plenum Press.

Lu, John H.-T. (1975). 'The grammatical item "le" in Mandarin', *Journal of the Chinese Language Teachers Association* 10/2: 53–62.

Lü, Shuxiang (1991). *Xiandai Hanyu babai ci* (Eight hundred words in Modern Chinese), Beijing: Commercial Press.

Mann, William C. and Sandra A. Thompson (1988). 'Rhetorical structure theory: a theory of text organization and its implications for clause combining', in *Discourse Structure*, ed. Livia Polanyi, Norwood, N.J.: Ablex.

Mei, Tsulin (1981). 'Mingdai Ningbohua de *lai* zi he xiandai Hanyu de *le* zi' (*Lai* in Ningbo dialect in Ming and *le* in modern Chinese), *Fangyan* 1: 66.

Mei, Tsulin (1994). 'Tangdai, Songdai gongtongyu de yufa he xiandai fangyan de yufa' (The grammar of the common language in Tang and Song and the grammar of modern dialects), *Zhongguo jinnei yuyan ji yuyanxue* (Languages and linguistics within China) 2: 61–97.

Ohta, Tatsuo (1958). *Chugokugo rekishi bumpo* (A historical grammar of modern Chinese), Tokyo: Konan shoin. (Chinese translation by Jiang Shaoyu and Xu Changhua. Beijing: Peking University Press [1987].)

Oliver, Robert T. (1971). *Communication and Culture in Ancient India and China*, Syracuse, N.Y.: Syracuse University Press.

Pan, Weigui and Yang, Tiange (1980). '"Dunhuang Bianwen" he "Jingde Chuandenglu" zhong LE zi de yongfa' (The uses of *LE* in Dunhuang Bianwen and Jingde Chuandenglu), *Yuyan lunji* 1: 22–8.
Pike, Kenneth L. (1954). *Language in Relation to a Unified Theory of the Structure of Human Behavior*, Glendale, Calif.: Summer Institute of Linguistics.
Plantin, Christian (1996). 'Le trilogue argumentatif', *Langue Française* 112: 9–30.
Rohsenow, John (1977). 'Perfect *le*: temporal specification in Mandarin Chinese', *Studies in the Linguistic Sciences* 7.2: 142–64.
Rohsenow, John (1978). 'Aspect in Chinese', University of Michigan doctoral dissertation.
Romijn, Elizabeth and Contee Seely ([1979] 1986). *Live Action English*, Hayward, Calif.: Alemany Press.
Ross, Claudia (1995). 'Temporal and aspectual reference in Mandarin Chinese', *Journal of Chinese Linguistics*, 23/1: 87–136.
Saussure, Ferdinand de ([1917] 1967). *Cours de Linguistique Générale*, Paris: Payot.
Schank, Roger C. and Robert P. Abelson (1977). *Scripts, Plans, Goals and Understanding*, Hillsdale, N.J.: Erlbaum.
Schegloff, Emanuel A. (1980). 'Preliminaries to preliminaries: "Can I ask you a question?"' *Social Inquiry* 50: 104–52.
Schelling, T.C. (1960). *The Strategy of Conflict*, Cambridge, Mass.: Harvard University Press.
Schiffrin, Deborah (1987). *Discourse Markers*, Cambridge: Cambridge University Press.
Searle, John (1969). *Speech Acts. An Essay in the Philosophy of Language*, London: Cambridge University Press.
Searle, John (1976). 'A classification of illocutionary acts', *Language in Society* 5/1: 1–24.
Searle, John (1995). *The Construction of Social Reality*, New York: Simon & Schuster.
Shi, Qisheng (1996). 'Shantou fangyan de LE ji qi yuyuan guanxi' (The uses of Shantou dialect *LE* and their origin), *Yuwen Yanjiu* 3: 43–7.
Shih, Yu-hui (1986). *Conversational Politeness and Foreign Language Teaching*, Taipei: Crane.
Shi, Z.Q. (1989). 'The grammaticalization of the particle LE in Mandarin Chinese', *Language Variation and Change* 1: 99–114.
Shi, Z.Q. (1990). 'Decomposition of perfectivity and inchoativity and the meaning of the particle LE in Mandarin Chinese', *Journal of Chinese Linguistics* 18/1: 95–123.
Spanos, George A. (1979). 'Contemporary Chinese use of le: A survey and a pragmatic proposal', *Journal of the Chinese Language Teachers Association* 14/1: 36–70; 14/2, 47–102.
Stalnaker, R.C. (1978). 'Assertion', in P. Cole (ed.) *Syntax and Semantics* 9: *Pragmatics*, pp. 315–32, New York: Academic Press.
Steuten, A.A.G. (1998). 'Structure and conference in business conversations', in Mike Hannay and A. Machtelt Bolkestein (eds) *Functional Grammar and Verbal Interaction*, pp. 59–75, Amsterdam: John Benjamins.
Sun, Chaofen (1996). *Word-Order Change and Grammaticalization in the History of Chinese*, Stanford: Stanford University Press.
Sybesma, Rint (1992). 'Causatives and accomplishments: the case of Chinese *ba*', Ph.D. dissertation, Leiden University, the Netherlands.

Sybesma, Rint (1999). *The Mandarin VP*, Dordrecht: Kluwer Academic Publishers.
Tai, James (1984). 'Verbs and times in Chinese: Vendler's four categories', in D. Testen *et al.* (eds) *Papers from the Parasession on Lexical Semantics*, Chicago: Chicago Linguistic Society, pp. 287–96.
Teng, Shou-hsin (1974). 'Double nominatives in Chinese', *Language* 50.3: 455–73.
Thomas, Jenny (1995). *Meaning in Interaction: An Introduction to Pragmatics*, London and New York: Longman.
Thompson, J. Charles (1968). 'Aspects of the Chinese verb', *Linguistics* 38: 70–6.
Tomasello, M. (2003). *Constructing a Language: A Usage-Based Theory of Language Acquisition*, Cambridge, Mass.: Harvard University Press.
Van den Berg, Marinus (1989). *Modern Standaard Chinees: Een Functionele Grammatica*, Muiderberg: Coutinho.
Van den Berg, Marinus (1998). 'An outline of a pragmatic functional grammar', in Mike Hannay and A. Machtelt Bolkestein (eds) *Functional Grammar and Verbal Interaction*, Amsterdam: John Benjamins.
Van den Berg, Marinus (2001). 'Making a move: the social construction of discourse', *First International Conference of Discourse Analysis*, May 20 to 22 (1998), Universidad Complutense de Madrid (CD ROM).
Van Dijk, T. (1977). *Text and Context: Explorations in the Semantics and Pragmatics of Discourse*, London: Longman.
Van Dijk, T. (ed.) (1997). *Discourse as Social Interaction*, Amsterdam: John Benjamins.
Vendler, Z. (1967). 'Causal relations', *Journal of Philosophy* 64: 691–703.
Wang, Li (1947). *Zhongguo yufa lilun* (Theories of Chinese grammar), Shanghai: Commercial Press.
Wang, Willian S.-Y. (1965). 'Two aspect markers in Mandarin', *Language* 41.3: 457–70.
Wardhaugh. R. (1985). *How Conversation Works*, Oxford and New York: B. Blackwell in association with André Deutsch.
Wu, Guo (1998). *Information Structure in Chinese*, Peking: Peking University Press.
Wu, Guo (2000). 'The origin of the Chinese discourse particle LE', *Journal of the Chinese Language Teachers Association* 35/1: 29–60.
Wu, Guo (2005). 'The discourse function of the Chinese particle NE in statements', *Journal of the Chinese Language Teachers Association* 40/1: 47–81.
Yang, Jun (2003). 'Back to the basic: the basic function of particle LE in modern Chinese', *Journal of the Chinese Language Teachers Association* 38/1: 77–96.
Yip, Po-ching (2001). 'The semantic and grammatical properties of the sentence particle le,' *Journal of the Chinese Language Teachers Association* 36/1: 1–14.
Yule, George (1996). *Pragmatics*, Oxford: Oxford University Press.
Zhao, Shikai and Shen, Jiaxuan (1984). 'Hanyu LE zi gen Yingyu xiangying de shuofa' (Equivalent English expressions of Chinese sentences with *le*), *Yuyan Yanjiu* (Language Studies), 6/1: 114–26.
Zhu, Dexi (1984). *Yufa jiangyi* (Lectures on grammar), Beijing: Commercial Press.

Index

a particle 11
accomplishment marking 112–13, 114
action, completed 18, 22
action ladder *81*
action theory 3
action-picture stories: contextual comparison 215–16; data 14, 100–8, 266n1; deviation 116–17, 118, 120–1, 122–3, 134, 136–7; discourse acts *102*; endings 131–2; institutional setting *107*; LE form 108–11; *le* particle 110–11, 115–36; *-le* verbal suffix 109–12; opening lines 103, 116–17; participatory roles 105–7; peak events 121–4, 131–2, 133, 134, 136–7; procedural discourse 100–3, 136–7; progress reports 103–5, 110, 114, 121–4, 132–4, 216; updatings 104–5, 127–8, 133, 224; verbal interactions 105–7, 224
action-response pair 191–2
actuality value 42–3, 254
address, direct 137
adjacency pairs 70–1
advertisement example 259–60
agenda, negotiating 179–80, 211, 230–1
alteration 70–1
Andreasen, Andrew John 23, 37–8, 254
announcements 11–12
anteriority marking 54–5, 157, 161–4
appending moves 172–3
appreciation 148
argument 180, 230–1
Aristotle 154, 268n8
asking for directions 194–5
assertion 75–6, 231–2; common ground 81; hotel setting 193, 231–7; moves 172; step by step 209–10; *ye* 98–9

assumptions 10, 32–3, 178
attending moves 172
attitudinal marking 11
autonomy 79

background knowledge 1–2, 3
backgrounding/foregrounding 28, 37–8, 163, 168, 170
Bal, Mieke 139
beginnings 235–6, 250–1
Berger, Peter L. 83–4
bi (completive) 87–8
Bianwen literature 89
Bie utterances 31
Bisang, W. 43–6, 254
boundary marking *48,* 54, 255
buying-and-selling 74–5, 158–9, 192
Bybee, Joan 56–7

Cao, Guang-shun 87
cause-effect 161
chains 71–2, 130–1
Chan, Marjorie K.M. 156–7
Chang, Jung-hsing 10, *48,* 98, 255
Chang, Vincent Wu-chang 3, 38–42, 254; common knowledge 258; contextual comparisons 7–8; event structure 55–6; *la* 262; *-le* verbal suffix 161–4; narrative use 7–8; realisation 156–7; two morphemes/two functions 23
change of state: Chao 58; common ground structure *250,* 263; contextual comparison 10; Huang and Davis 52–4; Li and Thompson 28–32, 41; state of affairs 50, 246; weather 245–6; *see also* situation change
Chao, Y.R.: benchmark data 212; change of state 58, *A Grammar of Spoken Chinese* 6–7, 17–18; Immediate

Index 279

Constituent analysis 18–19; isolated event 51; two morphemes/multifunction 253–4; uses of *le* particle 3–4, 55, 60, 238–9
children's stories 15, 85, 138–9; anteriority marking 162–3; anticipation 252; change of scene 165; characters 141–2; common ground 141, 194; data 14, 138–9; deviation 152–3, 165; dialogue 143–4, 217; goal attainment 162; information flow 223; *le* particle 144–54, 164–6, 216–18; -*le* verbal suffix 154–66; narrated monologues 143; peak events 146–7, 154–5, 157, 158; progress report 142; solutionhood 165; statistical comparisons 213–14; verbal interactions 143–4, 147–8, 151–2, 225–6; writing styles 140–4
Chuandenglu text 90
Chuanzhang Bobo (Uncle Captain) 149
Chunggan Nogoltae 95, 96, 98
Clark, H.H.: action ladder 81; adjacency pairs 70–1; chaining 71–2; common ground 3, 74, 262; imagining 139–40; joint projects 69–71; jokes 84; language use theory 60, 62, 66–72, 261; linguistics 61, 241; participatory actions 68; relevance 24
classical expressions 40
closing a statement 35–7
cognition 1, 2
cognition index 12
cognitive marking 17
cognitive organisation 1–2, 10, 13, 62
cohesion 161–2
common ground 72–6; appeal to 196–7; building up 166, 217; children's stories 141, 194; Clark 3, 74, 262; construals 185, 187–8, 211, 218–19; conversations 181–90; co-ordination 5, 11, 58, 86, 140, 167, 183, 213, 231–7; co-ordination device 5, 65; co-ordination points 217–18, 227; cultural 76, 210, 222, 237, 244, 258; equalising 184–6; initial 128; markers 131; narrative discourse 169; personal 73–5, 76, 99, 127, 181–3, 192–3; shared 34, 45–6, 64, 131, 187, 194, 241; updating 201–2
common ground structure 1, 243, 244–53; change 250, 263; conversations 170, 210–11, 226–31; narrative discourse 225–6; participant status 248–50; procedural discourse 223–4; solutionhood 192, 200
common sense approach 241
communication 1, 27, 83–4, 222–3
completives 87–8
compliance 70, 203–4
confirmation 221, 229–30, 237–8, 240, 252
confronting move 180, 220–1, 240
Confucian tradition 222
conjunction 161
consequent clause 18, 21
construals 80–2, 229; common ground 185, 187–8, 211, 218–19; conversations 178, 237, 252; deviation 240, 249; interpersonal relations 182; prolonging moves 189–90; *yiding le/la* 199
content co-ordination 68–9, 231–7
contextual comparison: action-picture stories 215–16; Chang 7–8; change of state 10; conversations 215, 218–22; interactive social 17; *le* particle 214–22; Li and Thompson 9–11, 24–8; narrative 215
continuing moves 173
contradicting function 13, 229
conversations 175–8, 259; asking for directions 194–5; autonomy 79; business 77–8, 174–80, 190–2, 210–11; business/personal 192–6; casual/pragmatic 82–3, 85; common ground 181–90; common ground structure 170, 210–11, 226–31; construals 178, 237, 252; contextual analysis 215, 218–22; co-ordination points 252; data 14, 15–16, 170–1; deviation 220, 234; feedback 196–200; genre 82–5; goal attainment 177, 200–7; information exchange 230; joint actions 258; joint projects 77–85, 228–9, 244, 251–2; *le* particle 85–6, *170, 171*; -*le* verbal suffix *170, 171*; minimal/extended joint projects 169; personal 77–8, 85, 174–80, 210–11, 226, 228; politeness 79, 207–9; restaurant settings 191–2, 194; restoration cycle 234–5; self-worth 79; solutionhood 234–5; statistical comparisons 213–14; topics 79–80; working environments 195–6
co-operative principle 47, 51

co-ordination device 5, 26, 65, 68, 85, 240, 241–4, 248, 262
co-ordination marker 264n3; *see also* common ground, co-ordination
co-ordination points: agenda-setting 211; assertion 231–2; common ground 217–18, 227; conversations 252; information 246; *le* particle 215–16, 240, 258; questions 238; realisation 243–4
countering opinions 43
Craik, K.J.W. 63
cue 68–9
cultural community 72–3, 119
Currently Relevant State 24–8, 35–7, 43, 44, 53, 58, 75, 245

Da Erduo (Big Ear) 146–7
Da Jiangjun (The Great General) 148
Da Pa Shan Jia (The Great Mountain Climber) 151–2
Da Sheyingjia (The Great Photographer) 149–50, 217, 225
Da Zhentan (The Great Detective) 144–5, 213
dangran le/la 197–8, 211
Davis, Philip W. 87; boundary marking 48, 255; change of state 52–4; domains of language use 243; focus marking 10, 56; interruption 75; upcoming events 118–21
declination 70, 71
deterioration 131, 155, 158, 216
developing moves 202–3
deviation: action-picture stories 116–17, 118, 120–1, 122–3, 134, 136–7; children's stories 152–3, 165; construals 240, 249; conversations 220, 234; goal attainment 123; hypothetical 209; involuntary effects 215; narrative discourse 251; physical 249; solutionhood 194, 214–15, 218, 240, 242, 246, 252; verbal interactions 126
dialogue 143–4, 217
Dik, Simon 42–3, 254
directional verbs 235–6
disagreement 180
discourse marking 12–13, 254
discourse structure 15–16, *102*
discourse-final particle 38, 41
dispositional differences 186–8
double marking 156
dui le/la 196–7, 200, 211

Eggins, Suzanne 16, 84, 171–2, 174, 268n4
elaboration 173
embedded models 63, 71, 72
emotion 11, 267n20
endpoint marking 235, 250–1
enhancement 173, 204
Ernü Yingxiong Zhuan 96
essays/conversations 80
evaluative remarks 131
event boundary marking 49–50, 52–3, 88, 124
event flow 215, 254
event line 240, 243
event state 246
event structure 255
event–reaction pairs 117, 128–9, 191
events: announcement 251; cognitive structure 260; co-ordination point 248; endpoints 235; event time 253; narrative time 253; and procedures 250–1; realisation 214; series 213, 255; status 236; structure 55–6
events, types: described 234; deviant 218, 234; everyday 213; institutional 118, 251; isolated in past 18, 21–2, 45–6, 51, 239; main 217, 235, 243; merged 217; natural 245, 246, 248, 249; new 216ff, 245–6, 248, 260; non-real-time 255; observed 217; preparatory 243; in progress 113–14; public 74–5, 234, 250–1; shopping 257; side 217, 234, 235–6, 242; spatial 248; technical 217; upcoming 118–22, 215; *see also* peak events
experts 174–5, 184
extension 173

factual statements 40–2
feedback 196–200
festivals 118, 120
finality marking 35–7
focus location 10, 56
foregrounding/backgrounding 28, 37–8, 163, 168, 170
functional analysis approach 1
Functional Grammar 42

goal attainment: children's stories 162; conversations 177, 200–7; deviation 123; joint activities 66–8; *-le* verbal suffix 112–13, 159; procedures 107–8; seasonal festivals 118; speaker 58

goal–reaction pairs *132*
grammar 1, 5; *see also* sentence grammar
gratitude 154
greetings 172, 173–4, 191
Grice, H. Paul 51, 255

haggling 192
Halliday, M.A.K. 16, 161
hao la/le 201–4
Hinds, John 157, 158
Hopper, Paul J. 37
hotel setting 193
Huang, Lillian M. 87; boundary marking *48*, 255; change of state 52–4; domains of language use 243; focus marking 10, 56; interruption 75; upcoming events 118–21

identifications/predicates 42–3
idiomatic expression 132, 137, 146, 147
imagining 139–40, 222
immediacy 68
Immediate Constituent analysis 18–19
inchoativity 4, 8–9, 18–19, 21, 156–7, 260
inference 27
information exchange 81–2, 188–90, 222–3, 230, 243, 246, 252
initiating moves 172, 185, 219, 243
institutional setting *107*, 118, 119–20, 215, 253
instructions 101–3, 109, 116, 124–6
instructor/apprentice roles 215, 223
interactions 82–3, 98–9; *see also* verbal interactions
interactive analysis 33, 46–7, 120
interpersonal relationships 182, 226, 259
interpretation 65
interruption 75
involuntary effects 117, 121–2, 128–9, 215
isolated past event 18, 21–2, 45–6, 51

jing (completive) 87–8
Jingcha Bobo (Uncle Policeman) 144–5
jiu (then) 31–2, 186, 190, 200
jiu keyi le 204–5
jiu shi le 204–6
jiu suanle 206–7
jiu xing le 204
Johnson-Laird, P.N. 1, 63–4
joint actions 68–9, 73–5, 80–2, 242, 258

joint activities 2, 3, 66–8
joint projects: Clark 69–71; conversations 244, 251–2; extended 71–2, 77; instructor/apprentice 100–1; minimal 103–5; proposing 176; supermarket buying 158–9
jokes 84

Kim Kwangjo 92–6
knowledge 205–6, 245
Korean textbook 92–6
Kuaile de Tanzhang (The Happy Inspector) 146

la particle 11, 210, 262, 264n3
Lakoff, George 241
language development 243
language processing 1–2
language use theory 1, 2–3, 241, 255–9; Clark 60, 62, 66–72, 261
language-as-action 61, 62
language-as-product 61–2
Laoshu Danzi (Mouse Timid) 155
LE form 14, 15, 17, *48*, 137; action-picture stories 108–11; direct address 137; one morpheme/one function 57–8; one morpheme/two functions 47–57; two morphemes/multifunction 17–23, 253–4; two morphemes/two functions 23–47, 254
le particle: action-picture stories 110–11, 115–36; Chao 3–4, 55, 60, 238–9; children's stories 144–54, 164–6, 216–18; common-ground co-ordination 140, *167*; completed action 18, 22; consequent clause 18, 21; contextual comparison 214–22; conversations 85–6, *170*, *171*; co-ordination device 240, 241–4, 248, 262; co-ordination points 215–16, 240, 258; co-ordination process 222–31; data analysis 14–15; event–reaction pairs *129*; functions 6–7; goal–reaction pairs *132*; historical development 87–92; inchoative 4, 8–9, 18–19, 21, 156–7, 260; instructions 124–6; involuntary effects *122*; isolated past event 18, 21–2; language use theory 2–3; -*le* verbal suffix 5, *213*, 260; narrative discourse 3, 12; new situation 4, 18–20, 46–7, 148; obviousness 18, 22–3; openings 121; origins 6–7, 16,

le particle *continued*
98–9, 263; Perfect Aspect marker 37–8; sentence-level analysis 8–9; statistical analysis 212–14; time 134–6; upcoming events *119*; verbal interactions *127*
-*le* verbal suffix 3–4; action-picture stories 109–12; analysis 112–15; Chang 161–4; children's stories 154–66; contrasting views 156–7; data analysis 14–15; goal attainment 112–13, 159; instructions 116, 125–6; *le* particle 5, *213,* 260; Liu 91–2; origins 6–7, 16; peak events 154–5; perfective 156–7; Perfective Aspect marker 37–8; progress report 214; realisation 159, 243; statistical analysis 213–14
LE-a (lexical verb) 96–7
LE-b (completive) 97
LE-c (verbal -*le*) 97
LE-d (particle le) 97
Lewis, D.K. 68
Li, Charles N.: change of state 41; contextual comparison 9–11; Currently Relevant State 43, 44, 53, 58, 75, 245; discourse marker 12–13; *jiu* 186; progress report 246–8; speech act 11–12; tense 47; two morphemes/two functions 23, 24–37, 254
Li, Ping 57–8
liao (to complete) 6–7, 87–8; discourse-final position 89–90, 91–2; lexical meanings 88–9; remarkableness 90–1; state of affairs 90; stative situations 89; *ye* particle 93–6
liaoye 91–2
linguistic analysis 261
linguistics 2, 3, 60, 61, 241; rational 255–6
Liu, Jian 87
Liu Xunning 23, 46–7, 87, 91–2, 254
Longacre, Robert E. 15, 101, 107, 139, 140, 157, 158
Luckmann, Thomas 83–4

Mann, William C. 124
Mao, Zedong 12
Mei, Tsulin 87
mental models theory 1, 63–5, 241, 257–9, 263; context 62; information flow 256
Ming period 95

monitoring moves 172–3
mood words 11
move typology 171–4, 263

na (connective) 39–40
narrated monologues 143, 217
narrative discourse 15, 84; Chang 7–8; common ground 169; common ground structure 225–6; contextual analysis 215; deviations 251; *le* particle 3, 12; notional structure 140; peak events 159–64; *see also* children's stories; storytelling
native speakers 38–9, 50–2
natural events 245–6, 248, 257
natural speech data analysis 14–15
negative sentences 31
negotiation 70, 179–80, 222, 230–1
notional structure 140

obligations 74
obviousness 18, 22–3
Ohta, Tatsuo 96
opening moves 171–2
openings 103, 116–17, 121

participant status 248–50, 258
participatory acts 3, 15–16, 66–8, *115,* 219, 232
participatory role 105–7, 191, 249–50
particles 8–13
peak events: action-picture stories 121–4, 131–2, 133, 134, 136–7; children's stories 146–7, 154–5, 157, 158; information 243; -*le* verbal suffix 154–5; narrative discourse 159–64
Perfective Aspect marker 37–8
perfectivity marking 18, 42, 54–5, 57, 156–7
permissibility 64–5, 256–7
politeness 79, 207–9, 222, 259
Ponyok Nogoltae textbook 87, 92–6, 98
possibility 64–5, 114, 222, 256–7
pre-constructed domain 4, 44–6, 58
predicates 42–3, 89
preparatory events 114–15, 119–20, 123–4
pre-sequences 71, 72
procedural discourse 15, 266–7n4; action-picture stories 100–3, 136–7; common ground structure 223–4; contextual analysis 214–15; deviations/solutions 169; non-occurrence of *le* particle 110–11;

schema 107–8; statistical comparisons 213–14
procedures 107–8, 250–1
progress reports 246–7; action-picture stories 103–5, 110, 114, 121–4, 132–4, 216; children's stories 142; -le verbal suffix 214; participatory acts 115; state of affairs 33–4
projection 65
prolonging moves 172–3, 189–90
public events 74–5, 250–1

qi (completive) 87–8
Qing period 96
qingjiao 208–9
questions 176–7, 189, 238, 261, 263

reacting moves 173, 179–80, 184, 219–21, 243
realisation: co-ordination points 243–4; *dui le* 229–30; -*le* verbal suffix 127, 137, 159, 243; markers 157, 158–9; new event 260; time 245
rejection 178, 229
rejoinders 172
relevance 24–8, 51–2; *see also* Currently Relevant State
remarkableness 43, 90–1, 254
replying 43, 196–200, 202–4
requests 145
restaurant settings 191–2, 194
restoration cycle 155, 158, 216, 234–5
resultative construction 234–6
Rohsenow, John 57
rule-breaking 190–1, 193–4

Saussure, F. de 60
Schegloff, Emanuel A. 72
Schelling, T.C. 68
semantic operators 64
semantics, updating 12, 65
sentence grammar 10, 61–2, 63, 241
sentence-based models 60, 61–2
sentence-level analysis 8–9, 49
Shantou dialect 96–8
Shen, Jiaxuan 47
Shi, Qisheng 98
Shi, Z.Q. 48, 54–5, 87, 255
situation change 4, 18–20, 46–7, 58, 148
Slade, Diana 16, 84, 171–2, 174, 268n4
social situations 117
solutionhood 123–4, 221–2; children's stories 165; common-ground structure 192, 200; completion 131; conversations 190, 234–5; deviation 118, 127, 134, 136–7, 194, 214–15, 218, 240, 242, 246, 252; stative verbs 233; verbal interactions 126–7
Sonaiya, R. 43–6, 254
Song period 92
Southern Min finality marker 264n3
Spanos, George A. 38, 48, 50–2, 255
spatial events 248, 257
speaker's intent 47
speech-act theory 8, 11–12, 68
Stalnaker, R.C. 50, 75–6
state of affairs 24, 29–35, 50, 57–8, 90, 246
statistical comparisons 212–14
stative verbs 233
Steuten, A.A.G. 175, 252
storytelling 84, 132–4, 139–44, 153–4, 166
sub-topical discourse units marker 39–40
success 222
supermarket buying 158–9
surroundings module 257
sustaining moves 171–2, 185–6
Sybesma, Rint 9, 58, 241
synchronisation 70, 120, 135, 137

tai (excessive) 47, 166, 260
tai hao la 201–4
tai keqi le 207–8
Taiwan 264n3
Tang Dynasty 88–9, 95
temporal particles 48–50
tenses 9, 46–7, 48–50
Thompson, J. Charles 48–50, 118–21, 255
Thompson, R. McMillan 12
Thompson, Sandra A.: change of state 28–32, 41; context comparisons 9–11, 24–8; Currently Relevant State 43, 44, 53, 58, 75, 245; discourse marker 12–13; event analysis 124; *jiu* 186; progress report 246–8; speech act 11–12; tense 47; two morphemes/two functions 23, 24–37, 254
ti (Yaruba) 43–4
time 31–2, 134–6, 233, 245, 253, 263
topics in conversations 79–80
tripod model 222, 237, 244, 256
truth 61, 222

upcoming events 118–22, 215
updating: action-picture stories 104–5, 127–8, 133, 224; common ground 201–2; co-ordination points 237; semantic theory 12, 65
utterance final particles 13
utterances 31, 65, 91–2; *see also* speech-act theory

van den Berg, Marinus 23, 42–3, 254
verbal interactions 64, 100–1; action-picture stories 105–7, 224; actions 174–5; children's stories 143–4, 147–8, 151–2, 225–6; deviation 126; joint actions 242; *le* particle *127*; pragmatic approach 241; solutionhood 126–7; *see also* conversations
verb–object constructions 232–3

Wang, Li 87
warnings 110, 129–31, 148, 267n21
weather changes 229, 245–6
withdrawal 70, 71
wo dong le 199–200

working environments 195–6
writing styles 140–4
written stories 85, 139–40; *see also* narrative discourse
Wu, Guo 75, 76, 93, 218, 256

Xiao Chuanfu (The Little Boatsman) 141–4, 150, 152–4
xiaoxin warnings *130*
Xixiangji (Romance of Western Chamber) 95

Yang, Jun *48,* 56–7, 255
ye particle 89–90, 93–6, 98–9
yi (completive) 87–8
yiding le/la 198–9
Yip, Po-ching 234–5, 260
Yonggan de Jingzhang (The Brave Sheriff) 148, 164
Youqi Shifu (The Master Painters) 149
Yuan period 95
yuqici (mood words) 11

Zhao, Shikai 47
Zhuzi Yulei conversations 92

eBooks – at www.eBookstore.tandf.co.uk

A library at your fingertips!

eBooks are electronic versions of printed books. You can store them on your PC/laptop or browse them online.

They have advantages for anyone needing rapid access to a wide variety of published, copyright information.

eBooks can help your research by enabling you to bookmark chapters, annotate text and use instant searches to find specific words or phrases. Several eBook files would fit on even a small laptop or PDA.

NEW: Save money by eSubscribing: cheap, online access to any eBook for as long as you need it.

Annual subscription packages

We now offer special low-cost bulk subscriptions to packages of eBooks in certain subject areas. These are available to libraries or to individuals.

For more information please contact webmaster.ebooks@tandf.co.uk

We're continually developing the eBook concept, so keep up to date by visiting the website.

www.eBookstore.tandf.co.uk

For Product Safety Concerns and Information please contact our EU representative GPSR@taylorandfrancis.com
Taylor & Francis Verlag GmbH, Kaufingerstraße 24, 80331 München, Germany

www.ingramcontent.com/pod-product-compliance
Lightning Source LLC
Chambersburg PA
CBHW052153300426
44115CB00011B/1656